Juggling Flaming Chain Saws

Academics in Educational Leadership Try to Balance Work and Family

A Volume in Work-Life Balance

Series Editors:
Joanne M. Marshall, *Iowa State University*
Jeffrey S. Brooks, *Iowa State University*
George Theoharis, *Syracuse University*
Latish C. Reed, *University of Wisconsin Milwaukee*
Bonnie Fusarelli, *North Carolina State University*
Catherine A. Lugg, *Rutgers University*

Work-Life Balance

Joanne M. Marshall, Jeffrey Brooks, George Theoharis,
Latish C. Reed, Bonnie Fusarelli, Catherine A. Lugg
Series Editors

Juggling Flaming Chain Saws:
Academics in Educational Leadership Try to Balance Work and Family (2012)
edited by Joanne M. Marshall, Jeffrey S. Brooks, Kathleen M. Brown,
Leslie Hazle Bussey, Bonnie C. Fusarelli, Mark A. Gooden,
Catherine A. Lugg, Latish Reed, and George Theoharis

Juggling Flaming Chain Saws

Academics in Educational Leadership Try to Balance Work and Family

Edited by

Joanne M. Marshall and Jeffrey S. Brooks
Iowa State University

Kathleen M. Brown
University of North Carolina, Chapel Hill

Leslie Hazle Bussey
Georgia Leadership Institute for School Improvement

Bonnie C. Fusarelli
North Carolina State University

Mark A. Gooden
The University of Texas-Austin

Catherine A. Lugg
Rutgers University

Latish Reed
University of Wisconsin-Milwaukee

and

George Theoharis
Syracuse University

Information Age Publishing, Inc.
Charlotte, North Carolina • www.infoagepub.com

Library of Congress Cataloging-in-Publication Data

Juggling flaming chain saws : academics in educational leadership try to
balance work and family / edited by Joanne M. Marshall ... [et al.].
     p. cm. — (Work-life balance)
   Includes bibliographical references.
     ISBN 978-1-61735-909-5 (paperback) — ISBN 978-1-61735-910-1 (hardcover) —
ISBN 978-1-61735-911-8 (ebook) 1. College teachers—Psychology. 2.
College teachers—Job satisfaction. 3. Work-life balance. I. Marshall,
Joanne M.
   LB2333.2.J84 2012
   378.1'25—dc23

                                                              2012020703

Printed in the United States of America

CONTENTS

PART II: MIDCAREER SCHOLARS

PART III: SENIOR SCHOLARS

FOREWORD

The See-Saw of Work Life Balance

Michelle D. Young

It seems that just about everywhere you look these days you see references to work-life balance. Universities are sponsoring seminars on bringing balance into your life. Workforce organizations are emphasizing balance as part of their wellness programs. Even the National Science Foundation has developed a set of strategies to support researchers' lives outside of the lab. Ten, even 5, years ago, this was not the case. It is an important change, and one that I hope is here to stay.

From my perspective, balancing ones work life and ones personal life is a bit like a see-saw. It is rarely perfectly balanced. At times personal life has significantly more heft, and at other times it is one's work-life that pulls heavily like an anchor. Granted, the back and forth can be a bit jarring, but it can also be energizing and enjoyable.

I have spent the last 12 years directing the University Council for Educational Administration, the last 15 years serving as a faculty member in educational leadership and policy, the last 16 years serving as a mother, and the last 22 years as a partner to my husband, Derek. These and other roles define me as a person and professional and include a variety of responsibilities, some more important and pressing than others.

When I wrote this foreword, I was in the midst of relocating the University Council for Educational Administration from the University of Texas to the University of Virginia. While the activities leading up to the reloca-

Juggling Flaming Chain Saws: Academics in Educational Leadership
Try to Balance Work and Family, pp. ix–xii
Copyright © 2012 by Information Age Publishing

tion involved planning and negotiation, the real-time and energy-consuming work occurred closer to the actual relocation and included packing, recycling, determining what to move and what to leave behind, shutting down accounts at one institution and opening them back up at the next, migrating databases, setting up and changing contact information, posting positions, hiring new staff, working with a new set of college and university staff to set up new accounts and process, setting up the actual office space, and so on—all while ensuring that the activities of the organization continued with little interruption. It is an understatement to describe the process as challenging.

Simultaneously, I moved my family from Austin, Texas, to Charlottesville, Virginia. Anyone who has moved a household knows that moving, whether across town or across the country, can be both exciting and exhausting. It becomes quite a bit more complicated when your move involves a partner and children, particularly school age children. Buying and selling a home, packing and unpacking, transferring school records, finding new doctors, dentists, and veterinarians barely begin to capture the vast array of activities that fill your days. Moves also have a significant emotional element. In our case, we left friends, colleagues, and family behind. This kind of transition is a test in work-life balance, but life presents challenges of varying shape and size just about every day.

For me the notion of balance does not mean that I keep my work life separate from my personal life; rather, both flow into one another. Some people are adamant about and really good at keeping their work and home life separate. I never have been. It is not that I never separate them. I think it is important to make time for reading with my children, movie nights, evening walks, and conversations with my family members. However, I spend a lot of time working, thinking about work, and interacting with colleagues, and I want that part of my life to be as accessible to my family as any other part of my life. I honestly cannot recall a time when I thought of my work and personal lives as completely separate. Our dining room table has been used as often for dinner and homework as it has for my work projects. Balance for me means that I feel like I am doing good work, fulfilling my responsibilities, contributing to my family and the public good, and finding joy and happiness with the people in my life and the work I engage in.

In my quest to balance the various aspects of my life, I have tried just about every organizational method, calendar device, and others, thinking that once I was organized things would seem less chaotic and more balanced, that I would have more time to think, and feel like I do better work. If you are reading this book, you may have had a similar experience. The strategies I use to keep my life balanced are far from unique, but I can tell a difference in how I feel when I am using them and when I am not, and in my current transition, they have played a critical role. I will mention four briefly: planning, prioritizing, delegating, and communicating.

I find it both important and calming to have things planned out. I approach many challenges, events, and projects in a similar way: identify the end goal and time frame, determine the key steps in between, decide if there is enough time and energy available to take on the task, and identify the resources needed. Once these determinations have been considered, I add prioritizing to the mix. Prioritizing one's various responsibilities is key, but it can be a rather personal activity. Many factors, including values, culture, and traditions come into play when determining what is most important and/or takes priority in the various facets of your life.

Setting priorities, though obviously an important step, does not provide the more practical framework for supporting balance. I pair it with planning. If something is a priority then I believe it should be integrated into a plan, recognizing, of course, that other issues or activities may emerge as priorities midstream and require some rethinking. Delegating is also essential in both one's work and home life. There is absolutely no way that I could ever accomplish all that I, the University Council for Educational Administration, and my family need to accomplish without delegating or sharing some tasks and responsibility with others. Finally, communication is perhaps one of the most important elements of life balance. From informal conversations and checking in with family, friends, coworkers, and students to scheduling planning meetings, communication is key to getting things done, to keeping things on track, and to leading a more balanced and less hectic life.

Although I would never claim a 100% success rate, I tend to be optimistic about my ability to support balance in my life. Of course, I realize that what I consider balance does not reflect how others define it—hence the value of a book like this. This book contains the stories, advice, and lessons learned from a variety of individuals with different life experiences and perspectives on work-life balance. Though no two individuals enjoy the same experiences or face the same work and personal life challenges and opportunities, there are enough similarities to make the sharing of experiences and strategies like those provided in this book quite helpful.

INTRODUCTION

Why Juggling Flaming Chain Saws in Educational Leadership?

Joanne M. Marshall

In the research literature, the tension between the demands of work and the demands of what I will call here "not-work" is usually referred to as "work-life balance." And while the metaphor of balance is helpful, bringing to mind a teetering see-saw, or perhaps an extended yoga position, it is not as evocative as Catherine Lugg's metaphor of juggling flaming chain saws, which comes from a description of her own faculty life. As academics we are not street performers showcasing our ability to keep several dangerous heavy objects in the air simultaneously, and the consequences of our "dropping" one of our tasks might not be as dire, but Lugg's metaphor gives a sense of the urgency and the stress that we feel. At the same time, the hyperbole provides comic relief. Our tasks are not *that* dangerous. They are serious, and important to us and our students and our families and even to society at large, but not life-threatening. As Lugg writes in her own chapter in this book, sometimes it is hard not to see "striving for a 'balanced life'" as "so much middle-class whining" (p. 318). We acknowledge the privilege it is to have jobs, outstanding educations, and choices. At the same time, we acknowledge the challenges inherent in this work, challenges which often stem from policies and practices that remain from the time when higher education was populated mostly by married White male faculty who were successful in their academic work because they depended upon the support of their wives to manage many of the not-work aspects of their lives. I imagine a tweedy White man, coming home from the university to greet his wife and children and eat the dinner she's prepared for him, and then disappearing into his study for the rest of the evening with his pipe to write and think great thoughts. If that professor ever existed, he is now emeritus.

Juggling Flaming Chain Saws is the first book in a new series with Information Age Publishing on these challenges of managing academic work and not-work. There has been a growing research base on work-life balance in higher education which ranges across such fields as economics, labor relations, sociology, law, women's studies, and higher education administration, some of which are cited below. Balancing work and life has also been the focus of blogs and regular columns like Mama PhD (http://www.insidehighered.com/blogs/mama-phd) in *Inside Higher Ed* and the "Balancing Act" column (http://chronicle.com/section/Advice-Columns/144/) in *The Chronicle of Higher Education.*

This book uses the methodology of autoethnography to introduce the work-life issues faced by scholars in educational leadership. Like the essays in books such as *Mama, PhD* (Evans & Grant, 2008), *Papa, PhD* (Marotte, Reynolds, & Savarese, 2011), and *Professor Mommy* (Connelly, 2011), *Juggling Flaming Chain Saws* provides insight into how people are managing both their academic careers and the rest of what they do. The writing is often emotionally powerful and poetic. However, unlike these other books, the essays here situate scholarly work lives within the context of a particular discipline—in this case, educational leadership. While the experiences of scholars in this volume are echoed across other fields in higher education, educational leadership is unique because of its emphasis on preparing people for leadership roles within higher education and for preK-12 schools.

The authors of this book are most often people who have been preK-12 teachers or school administrators and now are working at the higher education level, training educators to be school principals or superintendents. Thus, there are chapters not only about the pressures of publishing while caring for others or managing severe health issues, but also about comparing the faculty role with previous school administrative roles, as in Rosemary Papa's chapter; of working with future school leaders, as in Kathleen Brown's chapter; and of merging the personal and professional in areas of research, as Bill Black does in his chapter.

Our research and our teaching focus on ways that leadership and schools can be improved so that all children can learn. This idea of "all" is key. It has been emphasized in our discipline as what Sergiovanni has called a "moral imperative" (1992, p. 104) and as essential for ethical leadership (see, for example, standard eight from American Association of School Administrators, 1993; or standard five from the National Policy Board for Educational Administration, 2007). More recently, the idea of leading schools for the benefit of "all" students has been informed by the theory and practice of social justice leadership, which questions and critiques existing structures and policies and takes a stronger position of advocacy for the students who may not have been included previously in those structures and policies. For a helpful history of educational leadership's progress toward social justice leadership, see a 2009 article from Jean-Marie, Normore, and Brooks (all authors in this book). Social justice leadership values and strives for equity. It questions what is, and works toward what might be (see also Bogotch, 2002; Marshall, 2004; Marshall & Oliva, 2006; Theoharis, 2007).

Researching the topic of work and not-work in educational leadership complements the existing thread of social justice leadership. It explicitly questions and challenges the status quo; in this case not of preK-12 schooling, but of higher education. As Theoharis explains in his chapter on the methodology of this book, it is activist research. We can not change what we do not know. The chapters in this book give voice in a new way to the current experiences of scholars in our field, and brings them together in a collective.

These essays shed light on an area that we often hide. As professionals, we tend not to talk about our personal lives, unless there is a crisis that intrudes upon and keeps us from our professional responsibilities. However, that personal-professional divide is a false one. Parker Palmer has suggested that "who you are inwardly is what you teach outwardly" (1998, p. 2). That "inward" self is informed and created by personal relationships—by the families who raised us, by the families we have formed, by our friends and our colleagues and our communities. To extend Palmer's concept, our inward manifests itself in our outward: our research, our scholarship, our teaching, our service, and our outreach. They are inseparable. If you wish to test the connection, try this as an experiment: ask a scholar how or she became interested in his or her area of research. Chances are you will hear a personal story. He may research the achievement of migrant students, having had a first teaching job in a Texas border town. Or she became interested in educational policy because as a teacher she wondered how educational mandates were created at the state level.

Many chapters in this book are explicit about the ways work and not-work intersect for educational leadership scholars. For example, Tony Normore writes about how his values and his philosophy influence his teaching and research: "My work launches from a perspective that every interaction I have as a member of the education community must be consistent with my personal values system" p. 329). Linda Skrla writes of telling her students about her love of rock and roll, "as a way of illustrating the importance of not neglecting care of self while they pursue their doctoral degrees" (p. 347). Stacey Rutledge writes of researching accountability systems and then talking with her daughter's teacher about her daughter's test results. These essays and others give us snapshots of the ways in which academic lives of scholarship, teaching and service intertwine with the personal.

MENTORING THE NEXT GENERATION OF FACULTY

In higher education, graduate students and new faculty, in particular, benefit from mentoring as they are socialized into their discipline. In educational leadership, we also espouse the importance of mentoring people to be school leaders (see, for example, Crow & Matthews, 1998; Daresh, 2004; Gilmour & Kinsella, 2009; Peters, 2010). However, we are less good at modeling that mentoring ourselves within our own academic work environments, especially for females (Mansfield, Welton, Lee, & Young, 2010; Mullen, 2009; Sherman, Beaty, Crum, & Peters, 2010). While this book does not substitute for the personal relationship that mentoring offers, it does provide a much-needed introduction to academic life from a variety of points of view. In her chapter, Katherine Cumings Mansfield calls being a graduate student an "apprenticelike process," and cites her spouse as saying that its expectations need "to be communicated to people ahead of time" so that "a conversation with family and friends [can] take place concerning the expectations that will be placed on the student and their significant others" (p. 115). This book provides one mechanism for such proactive communication.

Much of our work in academic institutions is done alone, in front of our computers, in institutions with established norms and practices that predate us by decades. The essays in this book assure us that we are not alone in our experiences, and that those experiences are shared across a variety of institutions. Because of its multiple perspectives, this book can serve as a broad overview of the kinds of expectations that people do face, as well as the ways in which they meet them. It should be useful not only to the graduate students who are beginning the apprenticeship and the faculty who have recently finished it, but also to program coordinators, department chairs, deans, and other academic administrators who want a broader, deeper understanding of the ways in which people experience work and not-work.

THE RESEARCH BASE ON WORK AND NOT-WORK

This book contributes to and builds upon a strong research base across a several academic disciplines. Part of the rationale for work and not-work research in higher education has been seeking to understand why the professoriate is still dominated by White male faculty. In the fall of 2009, 60% of full professors were White males (U.S. Department of Education, 2010). If there are fewer female faculty and faculty of color at the full professor level, goes the argument, then perhaps there are structural inequities, which might be addressed by increasing faculty job satisfaction and changing policies. Thus, some universities conduct their own research, as Mary Ann Mason did in her role as graduate dean at Berkeley (2007), and some hire a research group such as the Collaborative on Academic Careers in Higher Education to survey their junior faculty on such topics as job satisfaction, role conflict, and campus climate. The Collaborative on Academic Careers in Higher Education surveys on job satisfaction have consistently identified the difficulty and importance of work-life balance as a theme (2006, 2008a, 2008b), a finding which has been echoed in other higher education literature.

Research on Work and Gender

The most frequent topic in the higher education research has been the relationship between faculty status and gender and raising children. There are explicit gender differences. The Collaborative on Academic Careers in Higher Education found, for example, that male faculty across every academic field are generally more satisfied with their work than their female colleagues (2010). But the difference between male and female faculty is not limited to job satisfaction, especially when motherhood is taken into consideration. Academic mothers are less likely to get on or stay on the academic track (Evans & Grant, 2008; Monroe, Ozyurt, Wrigley, & Alexander, 2008; Perna, 2005; Ward & Wolf-Wendel, 2004a; 2005; Williams, 2005; Wolf-Wendel & Ward, 2006; Wolfinger, Mason, & Goulden, 2009). Mary Ann Mason and Marc Goulden's cleverly titled "Do Babies Matter?" articles (2002, 2004) answer their own question with a resounding *yes*, babies do matter on the career track. Women who have babies within 5 years of their doctorate are 38% less likely to get tenure than their male counterparts at the same stage (2002). Only one in three women who enter the tenure track before having a child ever go ahead and have a child, with over a third of female faculty in one survey indicating that they had fewer children than they wanted (2004). Further, women are more likely to be single, and, if married when they begin their faculty career, are more likely to divorce or separate from their spouses than male faculty. Mason and Goulden conclude, "Women, it seems, cannot have it all—tenure and a family—while men can" (2004, p. 12).

However, academic fathers are also neglected, with few universities offering paid parental leave to faculty fathers, and, according to Mason (2009), none offering it to graduate student fathers, despite evidence that fathers are spending more hours in parenting and family work than any generation before them (Bianchi, Robinson, & Milkie, 2006), with a concomitant rise in men's reported level of work-life conflict (Galinsky, Aumann, & Bond, 2009). Those who write about masculinity and male roles note that our culture define men more by their work than it does women. Men are *expected* to be the breadwinner and to hold a good job. Men who choose to be more involved with their families are viewed in the workplace as good fathers. Drago and Colbeck call this phenomenon "Daddy privilege" (2003, p. 5). If a man leaves work to pick up children from school or take them to doctor's appointments, he is a good dad. But at some unidentified point of "too much" involvement with their children, fathers hit a "paternal wall" (Williams, 2004, p. 19) and are then viewed as less masculine (Coltrane, 1996; Doucet, 2006; Townsend, 2002; Williams, 2010). The title of Eric Houck's chapter, "Man, I Work Like A woman" illustrates this gendered expectation.

Life-Course Research

While there are definitely explicit gender differences related to work-life balance in academia, there are also issues of work and not-work common to other professions and informed by research related to what sociologists call "the life course." The timing of an academic career, like many other professional careers, is simply difficult, with different challenges at different generational stages. The prime career-building decades of a person's twenties and thirties overlap with prime child-bearing decades, leading to some of the gendered effects noted above. Research on Generation X workers, who were born 1964-1980 and are thus in their 30s and early 40s at the time of this publication, indicates that they are particularly interested in maintaining greater work-life balance (Families and Work Institute, 2002; Galinsky et al., 2009; Helms, 2010). In this book, Liz Hollingworth's chapter specifically addresses her identity as a Generation X faculty member. As the U.S. population ages, more people are caring for aging parents (Gatta & Roos, 2004; Varner & Drago, 2000), particularly people over the age of 40. A poll from *USA Today*/ABC News in 2007 on elder care revealed that 73% of surveyed adults had a living parent. Of those parents, 8% were living with the respondent, with another 8% living with a different relative. Eleven percent of the respondents were providing financial assistance, and 37% were providing ongoing personal care assistance such as regular visits or medical appointments. The effect of this caregiving took a toll: nearly half of the respondents who were providing assistance said that doing so created stress in their own lives.

Because being an academic requires a doctoral degree, which tends to delay the age at which people marry and the age at which people have children, academics may also be more likely to be members of the "sandwich generation" (Belden Russonello & Stewart & Research/Strategy/Management, 2001), meaning that they are caring for *both* children *and* their aging parents. In the United States, caregivers in the sandwich generation are reportedly more stressed, less happy, and, across all demographics, more likely to be female, regardless of whether or not the caregiver is employed (Cravey & Mitra, 2011). The sandwich generation may also be growing as young adults move back home. As of 2011, nearly 20% of young men and 10% of women ages 25-34 were living with their parents (Bernstein, 2011). All of this is to say that there is a lot of caregiving going on—for minor children and for elders in particular, with growing responsibilities for adult children as well.

Research on the Changing Family

In addition to the likelihood of caregiving responsibilities, the issue of work and not-work is salient because the structure of the American family has changed, but role expectations have lagged behind. Several historians, sociologists, and economists have explained that the traditional male-breadwinner and female-homemaker model of the 1900s changed first when men left their farms to work outside the home, then women entered the labor market, and again when the divorce rate increased. In *Gender and Families*, Coltrane and Adams (2008) report that in the 1940s and 1950s, traditional families (where a man works outside of the home and a woman works inside the home) outnumbered other types by two to one. In the 1970s, there were as many two-earner families as traditional families. And today the authors estimate there are twice as many two-earner families as traditional families, as well as more single parents. However, the expectation of traditional male-female gender roles has not kept apace, leaving working mothers with a "second shift" (Hochschild, 1990) of what economists call "unpaid work" or "invisible work" (Crary, 2008; Daniels, 1987) such as childcare, housework, and carpooling (Gornick & Meyers, 2003; Miller-Loessi & Henderson, 1997). While men are participating in more housework and childcare than they used to, women still do more. (Same-sex couples, on the other hand, are more egalitarian about sharing household work [see Miller & Skeen, 1997; Patterson, 2000; Peplau & Beals, 2004]). Public opinion also remains conflicted about working mothers. While only 19% of the American public, according to a Pew survey (Parker, 2009), agrees with the statement that women should return to their traditional, that is, nonworking, roles, 42% say that the ideal situation for a young child is a mother that does not work, and 40% say that an ideal situation is a mother who works part time. It is no wonder that working mothers feel judged by societal expectations, as described in chapters in this book by Leslie Hazle Bussey, Bonnie Fusarelli, and Kristina Hesbol, among others.

Not only has the traditional family changed because of labor market trends, but it has also changed to include other conceptions of family. There are more remarried and blended families. There are more single parents. There are more children living with grandparents. Overall, the marriage rate is decreasing, with more couples cohabiting (Coltrane & Adams, 2008; Smock & Manning, 2004). Nationally about 1% of couple households are same-sex couples, with 19% of those households reporting children living in the household (Lofquist, 2011). The number of single-person households has increased to 28% in 2011, up from 13% in 1960 (Bernstein, 2011). Only the number of households without children has remained relatively unchanged. As Barnett and Rivers pithily title a chapter in *She Works/He Works*, "Ozzie and Harriet are Dead" (1996, p. 1), while historian Stephanie Coontz (1992)has argued that they never existed, even in the 1950s when the show aired.

Changes in Academia: Research on the Ideal Worker and the Greedy Institution

These changes in the family are bound to collide with the expectations of academia. While family pressures are at their height, academic job expectations of research and time are greater than ever before. There are at least two phenomena at work: the "ideal worker" norm and the university as a "greedy institution." The ideal worker norm, writes Joan Williams in *Unbending Gender* (2000), is "the ideal of a worker who works full time and overtime and takes little or no time off for childbearing or child rearing" (p. 1). It thus excludes parents. I would extend Williams' definition of the ideal worker to include a worker who takes little or no time off for caregiving of *any* kind, whether care for one's self, one's partner, or one's elders, since in the United States work is valued and caregiving is not.

The second phenomenon pressuring the U.S. academic is the university as a greedy institution. Coser (1974) described greedy institutions as those which "seek exclusive and undivided loyalty and ... attempt to reduce the claims of competing roles and status positions on those they wish to encompass within their boundaries. Their demands on the person are omnivorous" (p. 4). Coser did not apply his definition to the academy, though he did apply it to homemakers, describing the family itself as a greedy institution. Others have applied his term to universities (Currie, Harris, & Thiele, 2000; Curtis, 2004; Shope, 2005), while Ward and Wolf-Wendel (2004a) have explored the potential conflict for academic women between the *two* greedy institutions of work and family. They concluded that trying to fill multiple roles between these institutions actually provided "unanticipated benefits" for the women in their study. They were able to "buffer" stress or failure in one arena by referring to success and satisfaction in the other, and they had a "broader frame of reference," which led them to, for example, transcend their fear of failure about tenure decisions. This positive spin on the tensions between work and family is one which surfaces occasionally in the literature, but seems a little like making lemonade out of lemons, since most of the literature, especially that from Joan Williams and Mary Ann Mason, instead focuses on the sacrifices that female academics make, such as not having children or of taking a part-time or adjunct position. Even if female academics choose to make those sacrifices, they and others argue, those choices are limited both by constraints of the academic job and of society's gendered expectations about work and family. While academics may embrace the language of "choice," those choices are contextual, and some of that context is beyond our control. All of us are subject to the expectations of our families and of our universities. Those expectations are rooted in and changed by our experiences with both family and work, which is another reason why the autoethnographies of this book can be helpful in understanding the context of each.

The potential clashes between family and work have consequences not only for current faculty job satisfaction and burnout (Watts & Robertson, 2011), but for the academic pipeline. A recent study of graduate students found that both men and women cited work-family balance as a top concern that weighed against them seeking a faculty position (Mason, Goulden, & Frasch, 2009). They found a faculty career incompatible with the idea of having children, even when many of them did not have children yet. This is not a good result. Academics who leave the academy at any point represent lost potential and lost knowledge. The fact that women are slightly more likely to make that choice is a gender equity issue. But one could also argue from a human capital standpoint that a broken pipeline represents lost resources, and that lost resources hurt the U.S's capacity to compete in a global economy.

To summarize the previous research on work and not-work: Managing work and not-work is an issue for all U.S. workers, not just those in higher education, and not just those in educational leadership.It is also an issue that is gendered, since both men and women face cultural expectations about their work and not-work roles, expectations that have not changed even as more women have entered the workforce and family structure has changed. However, academic work expectations are different from that of other workplaces, in that they combine the ideal worker norm with increasingly "greedy" expectations of productivity.

In addition to what we know about work and not-work from the research base, I would add two other characteristics that make academic work unique. First, we have a very flexible work schedule, with commitments that expand as much as we allow them. Teaching may require a limited number of hours of face time with a class, but it also involves potentially limitless hours reading and preparing and revising curriculum, and grading, advising and working with students. Research takes limitless time to read and be informed about our subject, to track references, collect data, analyze that data, write it up, submit it for publication, and revise it. The work of teaching and research will be as good and as prolific as the time that we devote to it, and the ongoing message from our institutions is that the work is never enough and finished. Second, academic work is about ideas and the life of the mind, which we literally carry around with us at all times. When we are showering or driving or cooking, we can be thinking about work. It takes a deliberate effort to stop that work, to be mindful instead of the moment and of the people in front of us. This second point has been exacerbated by technology, which gives us communication tools available around the clock to check information, to teach a course, and to call or e-mail students or colleagues. Third, like those in many other disciplines, those of us in educational leadership believe that our work matters. Whether we are researching school finance or federal educational policy or the inclusion of students with special needs or ways school leaders can be transformational leaders, we believe that *our workmatters* for educational leaders, and, by extension, for children in U.S. schools. Thus we may feel driven to, or justified in, making work the center of our lives. The end result of combining all of these characteristics is a group of scholars who feel triple pressures: of never producing enough, of never truly leaving their work behind, and of believing so strongly in the purpose of the work that sacrificing one's own health or happiness is immaterial. It is a work situation always tipping toward unbalance.

STRUCTURAL AND POLICY CHANGES

Some universities have moved to make structural changes to improve work-life balance, usually via flexibility in tenure policies. The American Council on Education (2009) has suggested several "promising practices," such as stopping the tenure clock and offering part-time positions or paid leave for life changes such as child-rearing or elder care. However, there is variability among institutions as to which policies they enact. For example, 86% of research universities offered tenure-clock extension according to a Center for the Education of Women survey (Smith & Waltman, 2006), but only 7% of associate-degree institutions did. About one third of research institutions offered a part-time track or modified duties, while other institutions were much less likely to do so. Even if such policies are offered, however, it is not clear how many people take advantage of them, simply because of their concerns about how such a move might be viewed by their colleagues (Ward & Wolf-Wendel, 2004b). And Thornton's work (2009) in the field of economics indicates a distinct lack of clarity about how clock-stopping policies, for example, are viewed by external review committees, with some reviewers raising their expectations of productivity when the clock is extended.

There has not been research on family-friendly policies in education as a discipline, but there has been research on job satisfaction. In the 2010 Collaborative on Academic Careers in Higher Education survey of job satisfaction among all faculty, education faculty ranked *ninth* out of eleven disciplines—far below physical sciences and humanities, and above only visual arts and (ironically) health (Truong, 2010). There is thus a lot of work to do at the institutional level in enacting policies, in creating a climate where academics feel safe to use them, and in researching how we are doing in both.

THE BOOK AS RESEARCH: AUTOETHNOGRAPHY

George Theoharis's chapter on autoethnography, which is the methodology of this book, provides a foundation for and explanation of the ways in which the book was put together. The genre of personal narrative and writing from experience that autoethnography requires is unfamiliar for most of us in educational leadership. As authors submitted their chapters, many of them wrote of how hard writing this chapter was for them, but how they found it ultimately to provoke reflection, or, as some said, to be "cathartic" or "therapeutic."

Theoharis has identified common themes about writing the book: fear about how the work would be perceived, questions about how to represent the other people in their lives, finding a purpose in this kind of scholarship, and feeling both liberation and discomfort with the process of writing. This was not easy work for people to complete, and the authors should be recognized for their courage.

I must also note, as the person to whom chapters were submitted, that countless people wrote me to ask for an extension of the submission deadline because the personal had temporarily overwhelmed the professional. People needed more time to deal with emergency surgeries, babies which arrived prematurely, new jobs and ensuing moves, new relationships, sick children, and hospitalizations. Some withdrew from the project altogether, acknowledging the irony with a phrase such as, "My work-life is too out of balance right now, ha ha." I have a new appreciation for the scholarship and teaching that people conduct, knowing that they often have had to overcome imperfect circumstances to do so. Academia is sometimes referred to dismissively as an ivory tower. If we accept that metaphor, then we should recognize that some people have to cross large moats of snapping crocodiles in order to get to it, while then scaling it slowly and painfully one crevice at a time, occasionally juggling a flaming chain saw.

HOW THIS BOOK CAME TO BE

The history of how this book and series came to be illustrates its wide appeal. It begins with my story and ends with the stories of others. My first academic conference in educational leadership was in the fall of 2004 at the University Council on Educational Administration in Kansas City. My first child had been born prematurely 5 months earlier, and there was no possibility of leaving him at home. He needed to eat, and I was his primary food source. Kansas City was within driving distance, so my spouse and I loaded up our car with the equipment we thought necessary to support us for the 3 days we would spend at the conference: bassinet, stroller, car seat, bouncy seat, blankets, diapers and wipes, toys, and clothes. Checking into the conference hotel 5 hours later (for what is normally a 3-hour trip), we looked as if we could provide supplies for at least three babies. Everyone else in the lobby was in smart business attire; we were harried and stained and had a baggage cart overflowing with colorful plastic. I presented papers, attended sessions, and tried to meet colleagues in between feedings and switching baby duty with my spouse, who was trying to work from the hotel room. For 3 days, none of us slept more than 3 consecutive hours. It was not the ideal conference experience.

A few years later, again at the annual meeting of the University Council on Educational Administration, having by then produced a second child, I had an epiphany while on the conference hotel escalator. There *had* to be other people at this conference who had young children. In fact, I knew a few of them did: Jeff Brooks. George Theoharis. Bonnie Fusarelli.

Michelle Young. How were they managing to attend this conference? What were they doing with their children? More importantly, how did they manage the rest of the year to make this job work for them and for their families? These academic heroes of mine were *here*—published, bright, and put together. I wanted to know their stories and strategies. *How were they doing it?* What could I learn from them?

In 2009, I contacted some of those academic heroes and asked them to join me in a conversation session at the University Council on Educational Administration about work-life balance. I asked for other names, hoping to diversify the session beyond straight, White married people, and we quickly had a panel of nine. That first session I asked people to send two slides: one photograph of their families and one strategy they used which has helped them with their work and lives. It was to be followed with sessionwide discussion about next steps we might take as a group of scholars.

The session was sparsely attended—the panel was larger than the number of people who attended—but after some initial awkwardness, conversation flowed. An emerging theme from that emotionally powerful session was that work-life balance is not an issue just for parents, or just for the partnered, or just for research-extensive university faculty. It is an issue for *everyone*, whatever the life situation, whatever the academic position. At a 2010 session, another group gathered to share their stories, using a format similar to the *This I Believe* radio series and building upon the theoretical framework of autoethnography, which "uses the self as a starting or vantage point from which to explore broader sociocultural elements, issues, or constructs" (Cole & Knowles, 2001, p. 16). The willingness of people in the room to share their narratives reminded us that *everyone has a story*. If they are willing to tell it and we are willing to hear it, then as Tierney suggests, we "gain multiple representative registers to analyze the topics with which we are involved" (1998, p. 66).

This book is a collection of those multiple registers about the general topic of work and not-work. It includes graduate students, untenured faculty, and senior scholars. It includes people at different places on their career and life course trajectory, people who are partnered and single, gay and straight, with children and without, caring for elders, and managing illness. It includes people who fit into more than one of those categories. The authors represent different geographic areas of the nation, different ethnic backgrounds, and different types of institutions. What all have in common is commitment to engaging with this topic, to reflecting deeply upon their own experience, and to sharing that experience with the rest of us. Come read and learn with us.

REFERENCES

American Association of School Administrators. (1993). *Professional standards for the superintendency.* Arlington, VA: Author.

American Council on Education. (2009). *An agenda for excellence: Creating flexibility in tenure-track faculty careers.* Washington, DC: Author.

Balancing Act. (n.d.) *Advice Columns.* Retrieved from The Chronicle of Higher Education website: http://chronicle.com/section/Advice-Columns/144/

Barnett, R. C., & Rivers, C. (1996). *She works/he works: How two-income families are happier, healthier, and better-off.* San Francisco, CA: Harper.

Belden Russonello & Stewart & Research/Strategy/Management. (2001). *In the middle: A report on multicultural boomers coping with family and aging issues.* Washington, DC: AARP.

Bernstein, R. (2011). *More young adults are living in their parents' home, Census Bureau reports.* Washington, DC: U.S. Census Bureau.

Bianchi, S. M., Robinson, J. P., & Milkie, M. A. (2006). *Changing rhythms of American family life.* New York, NY: Russell Sage Foundation.

Bogotch, I. E. (2002). Educational leadership and social justice: Practice into theory. *Journal of School Leadership, 12*(2), 18.

Cole, A. L., & Knowles, J. G. (2001). *Lives in context: The art of life history research.* Walnut Creek, CA: AltaMira Press.

Collaborative on Academic Careers in Higher Education. (2006). *COACHE survey highlights report.* Cambridge, MA: Collaborative on Academic Careers in Higher Education.

Collaborative on Academic Careers in Higher Education. (2008a). *Highlights report 2008: Selected results from the COACHE-tenure track faculty job satisfaction survey.* Cambridge, MA: Harvard Graduate School of Education.

Collaborative on Academic Careers in Higher Education. (2008b). *Perspectives on what pre-tenure faculty want and what six research universities provide.* Cambridge, MA: Harvard Graduate School of Education.

Collaborative on Academic Careers in Higher Education. (2010). *The experience of tenure-track faculty at research universities: Analysis of COACHE survey results by academic area and gender—Selected results from the COACHE Tenure-Track Faculty Job Satisfaction Survey.* Cambridge, MA: Harvard Graduate School of Education.

Coltrane, S. (1996). *Family man: Fatherhood, housework, and gender equity.* New York, NY: Oxford University Press.

Coltrane, S., & Adams, M. (2008). *Gender and families* (2nd ed.). Lanham, MD: Rowman & Littlefield.

Connelly, R. (2011). *Professor mommy: Finding work-family balance in academia.* Lanham, MD: Rowman & Littlefield.

Coontz, S. (1992). *The way we never were: American families and the nostalgia trap.* New York, NY: Harper Collins.

Coser, L. A. (1974). *Greedy institutions: Patterns of undivided commitment.* New York, NY: Free Press.

Crary, D. (2008, March 6). Report finds men pitching in more with chores. *USA Today*. Retrieved from http://www.usatoday.com/news/nation/2008-03-06-sharing-chores_N.htm

Cravey, T., & Mitra, A. (2011). Demographics of the sandwich generation by race and ethnicity in the United States. *Journal of Socio-Economics, 40*(3), 306-311.

Crow, G. M., & Matthews, L. J. (1998). *Finding one's way: How mentoring can lead to dynamic leadership*. Thousand Oaks, CA: Corwin.

Currie, J., Harris, P., & Thiele, B. (2000). Sacrifices in greedy universities: Are they gendered? *Gender & Education, 12*(3), 269-291.

Curtis, J. W. (2004). Balancing work and family for faculty: Why it's important. *Academe, 90*(6), 21-23.

Daniels, A. K. (1987). Invisible work. *Social Problems, 34*(5), 403-415.

Daresh, J. (2004). Mentoring school leaders: Professional promise or predictable problems? *Educational Administration Quarterly, 40*(4), 495-517. doi:10.1177/0013161x04267114

Doucet, A. (2006). *Do men mother? Fathering, care, and domestic responsibility*. Toronto, Ontario, Canada: Buffalo: University of Toronto Press.

Drago, R., & Colbeck, C. (2003). *The mapping project: Exploring the terrain of U.S. Colleges and universities for faculty and families: Final report for the Alfred P. Sloan Foundation*. University Park, PA: Pennsylvania State University.

Evans, E., & Grant, C. (2008). *Mama, PhD: Women write about motherhood and academic life*. New Brunswick, NJ: Rutgers University Press.

Families and Work Institute. (2002). Generation and gender in the workplace. *National Study of the Changing Workforce (NSCW)*. New York, NY: Author.

Galinsky, E., Aumann, K., & Bond, J. T. (2009). *Times are changing: Gender and generation at work and at home*. New York, NY: Families and Work Institute.

Gatta, M. L., & Roos, P. A. (2004). Balancing without a net in academia: Integrating family and work lives. *Equal Opportunities International, 23*(3-5), 124-142.

Gilmour, S. L., & Kinsella, M. P. (2009). *Succeeding as a female superintendent: How to get there and stay there*. Lanham, MD: Rowman & Littlefield Education and American Association of School Administrators.

Gornick, J. C., & Meyers, M. (2003). *Families that work: Policies for reconciling parenthood and employment*. New York, NY: Russell Sage Foundation.

Helms, R. M. (2010). *New challenges, new priorities: The experience of Generation X faculty*. Cambridge, MA: Collaborative on Academic Careers in Higher Education.

Hochschild, A. R. (1990). *The second shift*. New York, NY: Avon Books.

Jean-Marie, G., Normore, A. H., & Brooks, J. S. (2009). Leadership for social justice: Preparing 21st century school leaders for a new social order. *Journal of Research on Leadership Education, 4*(1).

Lofquist, D. (2011). Same-sex couple households. *American Community Survey Briefs*. Washington, DC: U.S. Census Bureau.

Mansfield, K. C., Welton, A., Lee, P. -L., & Young, M. D. (2010). The lived experiences of female educational leadership doctoral students. *Journal of Educational Administration, 48*(6), 727-740.

Marotte, M. R., Reynolds, P., & Savarese, R. J. (2011). *Papa, PhD: Essays on fatherhood by men in the academy*. New Brunswick, NJ: Rutgers University Press.

Marshall, C. (2004). Social justice challenges to educational administration: Introduction to a special issue. *Educational Administration Quarterly, 40*(1), 3-13.

Marshall, C., & Oliva, M. (2006). *Leadership for social justice: Making revolutions in education.* Boston, MA: Pearson/Allyn & Bacon.

Mason, M. A. (2009, February 24). Men and mothering. *Chronicle of Higher Education.*

Mason, M. A., & Ekman, E. M. (2007). *Mothers on the fast track: How a new generation can balance family and careers.* New York, NY: Oxford University Press.

Mason, M. A., & Goulden, M. (2002). Do babies matter? *Academe, 88*(6), 21.

Mason, M. A., & Goulden, M. (2004). Do babies matter (Part II)? *Academe, 90*(6), 10-15.

Mason, M. A., Goulden, M., & Frasch, K. (2009, January/February). Why graduate students reject the fast track. *Academe Online.* Retrieved from http://www.aaup.org/AAUP/pubsres/academe/2009/JF/Feat/maso.htm

Miller, D. C., & Skeen, A. (1997). Posslqs and pssslqs: Unmarried academic couples. In M. A. Ferber & J. W. Loeb (Eds.), *Academic couples: Problems and promises* (pp. 106-127). Urbana, IL: University of Illinois Press.

Miller-Loessi, K., & Henderson, D. (1997). Changes in American society: The context for academic couples. In M. A. Ferber & J. W. Loeb (Eds.), *Academic couples: Problems and promises* (pp. 25-43). Urbana: University of Illinois Press.

Monroe, K., Ozyurt, S., Wrigley, T., & Alexander, A. (2008). Gender equality in academia: Bad news from the trenches, and some possible solutions. *Perspectives on Politics, 6*(2), 215-233.

Mullen, C. A. (2009). Re-imagining the human dimension of mentoring: A framework for research administration and the academy. *Journal of Research Administration, 40*(1), 10-31.

National Policy Board for Educational Administration. (2007). *Educational leadership policy standards: ISLLC 2008.* Austin, TX: National Policy Board for Educational Administration.

Palmer, P. J. (1998). *The courage to teach: Exploring the inner landscape of a teacher's life.* San Francisco, CA: Jossey-Bass.

Parker, K. (2009). The harried life of the working mother. Washington, DC: Pew Research Center.

Patterson, C. J. (2000). Family relationships of lesbians and gay men. *Journal of Marriage and Family, 62*(4), 1052-1069.

Peplau, L. A., & Beals, K. P. (2004). The family lives of lesbians and gay men. In A. L. Vangelisti (Ed.), *Handbook of family communication* (pp. 233-248). Mahwah, NJ: Erlbaum.

Perna, L. (2005). The relationship between family and employment outcomes. *New Directions for Higher Education*(130), 5-23.

Peters, A. (2010). Elements of successful mentoring of a female school leader. *Leadership and Policy in Schools, 9*(1), 108-129.

Sergiovanni, T. J. (1992). *Moral leadership: Getting to the heart of school improvement.* San Francisco, ca: Jossey-Bass.

Sherman, W. H., Beaty, D. M., Crum, K. S., & Peters, A. (2010). Unwritten: Young women faculty in educational leadership. *Journal of Educational Administration, 48*(6), 741-754.

Shope, J. H. (2005). Reflections on the no-uterus rule: Pregnancy, academia, and feminist pedagogy. *Feminist Teacher, 16*(1), 53-60.

Smith, G. C., & Waltman, J. A. (2006). *Designing and implementing family-friendly policies in higher education.* Ann Arbor, MI: The Center for the Education of Women, University of Michigan.

Smock, P. J., & Manning, W. D. (2004). Living together unmarried in the United States: Demographic perspectives and implications for family policy. *Law & Policy, 26*(1), 87-117. doi:10.1111/j.0265-8240.2004.00164.x

Theoharis, G. T. (2007). Social justice educational leaders and resistance: Toward a theory of social justice leadership. *Educational Administration Quarterly, 43*(2), 221-258.

Thornton, S. R. (2008, December). *The implementation and utilization of stop the tenure clock policies in Canadian and U.S. Economics departments.* Paper presented at the annual meeting of the American Economic Association. Retrieved from http://www.insidehighereducation.com/news/2009/01/06/stc

Tierney, W. G. (1998). Life history's history: Subjects foretold. *Qualitative Inquiry, 4*(1), 40-70.

Townsend, N. (2002). *The package deal: Marriage, work, and fatherhood in men's lives.* Philadelphia, PA: Temple University Press.

Truong, K. (2010, July 12). Survey of job satisfaction finds physical sciences among happiest fields. *Chronicle of Higher Education.* Retrieved from http://chronicle.com/article/Survey-of-Job-Satisfaction/66255/

U.S. Department of Education. (2010). Table 260. In 2009 Integrated Postsecondary Education Data System (IPEDS). Washington, DC: National Center for Education Statistics.

USA Today/ABC news elderly care poll. (2007, June 24), Retrieved from http://www.usatoday.com/money/industries/health/2007-06-24-elderly-care-poll_N.htm?loc=interstitialskip

Varner, A., & Drago, R. (2000). *The changing face of care: The elderly.* University Park, PA: Penn State University Department of Labor Studies and Industrial Relations.

Ward, K., & Wolf-Wendel, L. (2004a). Academic motherhood: Managing complex roles in research universities. *Review of Higher Education, 27*(2), 233-257.

Ward, K., & Wolf-Wendel, L. (2004b). Fear factor. *Academe, 90*(6), 28-31.

Ward, K., & Wolf-Wendel, L. E. (2005). Work and family perspectives from research university faculty. *New Directions for Higher Education, 130,* 67-80.

Watts, J., & Robertson, N. (2011). Burnout in university teaching staff: A systematic literature review. *Educational Research, 53*(1), 33-50.

Williams, J. C. (2000). *Unbending gender: Why family and work conflict and what to do about it.* New York, NY: Oxford University Press.

Williams, J. C. (2004). Hitting the maternal wall. *Academe, 90*(6), 16-20.

Williams, J. C. (2005). The glass ceiling and the maternal wall in academia. *New Directions for Higher Education, 130,* 91-105.

Williams, J. C. (2010). *Reshaping the work-family debate: Why men and class matter.* Cambridge, MA: Harvard University Press.

Wolf-Wendel, L., & Ward, K. (2006). Academic life and motherhood: Variations by institutional type. *Higher Education, 52*(3), 487-521.

Wolfinger, N. H., Mason, M. A., & Goulden, M. (2009). Stay in the game: Gender, family formation and alternative trajectories in the academic life course. *Social Forces, 87*(3), 1591-1621.

A NOTE ON METHODOLOGY

Authethnography and Other Reflections

George Theoharis

This book is a the result of sessions Dr. Joanne Marshall organized at the University Council of Educational Administration (UCEA), annual meeting around the topic of work-life balance. The first of such sessions left many people in attendance personally moved, wanting more, and looking to engage in this personal topic again. It was suggested that given the personal nature of the first UCEA session, this topic seemed to "call for autoethnography," and since the group in attendance were all scholars, that we should "go with our strengths, and write about our own experiences" with work-life balance. The following year a panel of participants shared their autoethnographic statements, many of which became the springboard for chapters in this book.

This second UCEA session on work-life balance was filled with tears, laughter, applause, hugs, and thick emotion, as those presenting shared vulnerable moments, personal struggles, and instances of personal triumph. During that session many in the audience wanted to tell their own stories of work-life balance and struggle. It was clear that not only did people want to share their own stories, but that in this sharing and hearing other people's stories there was a sense of connection, a sense of solidarity, a sense that everyone is dealing with "stuff," and a sense that we are not alone in our work-life balance struggles. This personal and connecting experience is certainly not typical of academic conferences or the

Juggling Flaming Chain Saws: Academics in Educational Leadership
Try to Balance Work and Family, pp. xxxi–lii
Copyright © 2012 by Information Age Publishing
All rights of reproduction in any form reserved.

higher education rewards structure. Those sessions helped lead to this book.

AUTOETHNOGRAPHY

The essays in this book draw upon the tradition of autoethnography (Cole & Knowles, 2001). Coles and Knowles define autoethnography as a research design that "places the self within a sociocultural context ... autoethnography uses the self a starting point or vantage point from which to explore broader sociocultural elements, issues or constructs" (p. 16). Autoethnography or autobiography (Bullough & Pinnegar, 2001; Coles & Knowles, 2001; Ellis, 1997; Graham, 1991; Reed-Danahay, 2001; Theoharis, 2008; Tierney, 1998) and reflective practitioners research (Anderson, 1996; Anderson, Herr, & Nehlen, 1994; Anderson & Jones, 2000) are growing in their acceptance and use as modes of inquiry. Numerous scholars have used autoethnography as a methodological tool (Cole & Knowles, 2000; Dews & Law, 1995; Ellis, 2004; Jackson, 1995; Meneley & Young, 2005; Theoharis, 2007, 2008) in research ranging from studies on an anthropologist's experience in Africa to studies on school leaders.

We are higher education faculty committed broadly to issues of equity. We feel examining work/ life balance through the use of autoethnography enables us to make this work both more personal and more reflective. Tierney (1998) suggests that being personal and being reflective are essential elements to meaningful scholarship: "a necessary methodological device to move us toward newer understanding of reality, ourselves and truth" (p. 56). The principles of autoethnography and self-study in this book open our experiences to study in a critical, reflective manner. Further, this work aligns with what Ellis (1997) asserts, that engaging in serious autoethnography can "let the audience feel the emotion of the autoethnography. Bring life to research. Bring research to life" (p. 2).

Tierney (1998) also endorses autoethnography as a method of research as a form of countering dominant narratives and reclaiming voice, which directly relates to our commitment to equity. He states:

> Autoethnographic texts create the possibility for reclamation of voices that have been either absent from traditional social science texts or misrepresented as ways to understand whole schemas of cultures. By representing reality in our own ways and with our own categories, autoethnography confronts dominant forms of representation and power in an attempt to reclaim, through a self-reflex response, representational spaces that have marginalized those of us on the borders. (p. 66)

Given that higher education has a history of being a male-dominated profession and has positioned issues of family and life balance as secondary to the academy and scholarly pursuits, we see this methodological choice as, in Tierney's words, "a reclamation of voices." Navigating work-life balance is an essential part of the twenty-first century university, in particular with respect to faculty that are growing more diverse in terms of gender, culture, sexual orientation, and race. In this book the work-life balance and struggles are foregrounded, and are intentionally not positioned as "lesser" to our scholarly pursuits. In many cases work-life issues are the principal and central aspects of many of our lives. Thus, we combine the scholarly form of autoethnography as a way to honor, make space for, and be open about the realities facing faculty of twenty-first century higher education.

While each of the authors might not identify as an activist researcher, I see important connection between this book and the tradition of activist research. Fine (1994) explains that activist research captures at least one of four different strategies: "breaking the silence," "denaturalizing what appears so natural," "attaching what is to what could be," and "engaging in participatory activist research" (pp. 24-30). This book relies heavily upon the "breaking the silence" strategy, as doctoral programs, university expectations, and faculty conferences rarely acknowledge the difficulty of work-life balance as an integral part of the realities facing diverse higher education faculty. "Breaking the silence" is critical to this book in that we seek to create space for the creation and sharing of autoethnographic texts about the struggles and successes of navigating work-life balance in higher education. When the silence was broken during the UCEA session, it was a powerful, affirming, intellectual, and emotional space. We are seeking to create a similar space with this book.

Guidelines for Chapter Authors

In the interest of transparency of the process used to create this book, I share the editorial guidelines presented to the chapter authors. The guidelines are based on the personal narrative guidelines associated with the National Public Radio series, "This I Believe" (thisibelieve.org).

The book will be a collection of brief chapters written in an easy, conversational style. The purpose is to engage readers, encourage reflection and to share strategies (both successful and unsuccessful) for creating and maintaining work-life balance. Chapters will each be 10 pages in length, maximum. Suggestions for organizing your chapter include:

- *Two stories:*   Ground your chapter in the events of your life. Consider telling two different or contrasting moments—when moving through a work-life balance was easy and successful, or painful, or central to your actions, or required courage, or was an act of privilege/invisible.
- *Be positive:*   Please avoid preaching or editorializing. Tell us what you do or have done, not what you might do or haven't done. Speak in the first person.

If you have any lessons learned or tips that have worked for you, please share at least one toward the end of your chapter.

Reflections on This Experience of Writing/Creating This Book

As chapters were submitted to section editors, we noticed that they were often accompanied by a personal note. After most chapters had been submitted, the editors decided that it would be helpful to gather those reflections systematically. I sent each author a note asking for their reflections on the process of writing. Those reflections are summarized here.

In writing the chapters for this book a number of issues were on the forefront of the authors' minds, reflections, and struggles to engage in this autoethnographic work. Some common and salient ones authors shared were: feeling fear about how this work will be perceived, wrestling with how to balance the voices and experiences of other people in their lives, recognizing their own purpose for engaging in this kind of scholarship, experiencing a sense of liberation or freeing through this experience, and having discomfort with this style of academic writing. These issues are highlighted with quotes from authors' personal reflections on this project.

It is important to recognize that a number of authors felt fear or anxiety about how this work would be perceived. They wondered if this project would be taken seriously, if they would be seen as a lesser scholar for undertaking this kind of personal work. One author wrote,

> There was an evil spirit with a pitchfork on one shoulder whispering in my ear: "People are going think you are silly writing about being a middle-aged rock-and-roll fan. Why would you want to expose yourself like that? You've worked so hard to gain credibility among the stodgy, humorless educational administration professors ... you shouldn't be doing this.

Another author reflected,

> I was also a little scared of writing the chapter, let alone being part of the book, for fear that writing about being a mom (in particular) would get in

the way of people seeing me as a scholar. Would this work be viewed as "serious" or "scholarly" enough? Given how insular our field is and how much promotion and tenure depends upon external reviews from other people in the field, I feel as if I have to worry about what other people think.

What I'm scared of for my own piece is that I have enough distance from it to convey any lesson learned that someone else might benefit from. And I worry that a book is so dang permanent, and I will regret something I have written, or since I've written about my child he might hate it, and me, someday, or that I'll overshare and my essay will sound like a therapy session imposed on the reader, who is rolling his or her eyes and thinking, "Get over yourself."

This second reflection helps remind us that the fear of this kind of work comes from pressure from multiple locations. In this case it comes from a relatively small scholarly world of educational leadership—a world that historically has been conservative in accepting this kind of scholarship. But the pressure also comes from ourselves, and not wanting to disappoint or portray our experiences in ways that might hurt others in our lives.

A number of authors experienced this particular tension—walking the line between sharing one's own experience and recognizing that other people in our lives are impacted by our own work-life struggles. This project raises the question of how do we write about our own experiences without overstepping the privacy of those in our lives (families, partners, colleagues, etc.).

One author reflected,

[Writing this chapter was] a bit cathartic, but I am still considering some of the framing—it is still difficult to represent others' contributions and while I want to share the journey, I also am uncomfortable with a "heroic" narrative, even though it is important to share the narrative. You may know this as well-many people deal with some of these issues as "normal," albeit they are difficult. And, I am not sure whether Jessica's [author's wife] contribution is adequately represented—yet there are issues associated with representation written about as crises of representation that I find more difficult with those close to me.

In my own experience in trying (perhaps unsuccessfully) to respond to this tension of not overstepping in this work on those in my life, I chose to take my chapter out of this book—it is not published. The experiences I originally had written about were too painful for those close to me, and I was asked not to include my essay. In the end, I could not rectify the tension of including the essay about my experience while hurting someone else in the process—so I choose not to publish it. However, a number of the chapters in this book took different approaches to tackling this tension about writing about people in our lives. For example: two spouses (Jeff and Melanie Brooks), both in higher education, wrote their own chapters. There are chapters coauthored by parents and their children (from Gerardo Lopez, Matt Militello, and Lisa Kensler). One scholar described the power and tension in writing with family and children.

> The process of writing the chapter as a family unit was both exciting and stressful. We had never collaborated on a particular writing project that would lead toward publication. Therefore, the girls were excited and thrilled that they would be "published" authors just like their parents.... On the other hand, the three of us were also very nervous throughout the entire process, especially as the chapter unfolded.... For the most part, I was constantly fearful that my girls would air the family's dirty laundry in their respective sections. Part of me wanted to control the process, while another part of me struggled with just letting go and having the girls write their own truth.

Another wrote about the tension that might arise in her institution and issues with her partner,

> As a public document about my professional and personal struggles as a working mother, I wasn't comfortable completely "airing the dirty laundry" of my workplace. I still want to make "full professor." That desire, coupled with my husband also working at the same institution, required a thoughtful balancing of my desire to be transparent with my experience, my need to protect my career and at the need to forthright about my husband's very different lived experience.

The multiple ways that the authors dealt with these tensions of representing or speaking with/for others provide strategies to ameliorate the tension of writing about oneself without having an undue impact on those in our lives. In some cases, the way authors approached this tension came from why they chose to be a part of this book.

Authors had different purposes for engaging in this project. Some did it because they were a part of the UCEA sessions and found it to be an important experience, others saw this as a way to think through their own tensions and struggles with work-life, some had diverse personal or professional reasons, many thought it was an engaging idea, and still others hoped their experiences would be informative or instructive to others in the field or new emerging scholars. One of the authors reflected about her purpose:

> The goal of the chapter for me was to present some of the trials and tribulations I faced while navigating through the academy as a first-year professor to those individuals who are considering pursuing a career in academia. I

know how difficult it is as a junior faculty member trying to balance all of the responsibilities associated with being a new professor while at the same time still having an active personal/social life, and I am always open to listening to others' advice about maintaining a work-life balance. I think for new professors, in particular, to be able to have some suggestions from others who have recently gone through their "rookie" year in the profession as to how to approach the challenges and complexities of being a new professor is crucial and not often provided by even your closest colleagues.

While the purposes were varied, one experience shared by a variety of authors was a sense of catharsis or affirmation of having reflected, analyzed, and written about the personal nature or work-life balance.

One author shared,

The reflective writing also affirmed that making time for personal-self matters means "getting back" to work-life issues with a renewed/refreshed perspective and the energy needed to stay focused, engaged and productive when involved in family activities or work activities. Balance of work-life issues is not a description I would use to depict my daily lived experiences, rather focused and productive time spent performing all that needs to be done is what I strive for.

Another shared his sense of liberation.

Writing this chapter was both challenging and liberating.... The liberating part was for the first time being able to share the lessons I have learned and insights I have gained. For me, this was a reflective exercise allowing me to really evaluate why and how I do my job, support my family, and make a greater contribution. In the end, I realized that I am working everyday doing something I really enjoy (even with all of the pressures).

Another reflected on the sense of catharsis,

The experience of writing the chapter was actually cathartic. It helped me to see yet again that I remain out of balance a lot of time (even when I am supposed to be writing a chapter about balance).

And for another author, writing provided an important rejuvenating experience:

Writing this chapter ushered me back into the necessary hum of life, but with renewed purpose. This chapter was the first piece of writing I completed all summer and I was so proud of myself for completing it after not writing for 5 months. Most of all, thinking about my life and my work and then putting pen to paper, helped me to turn my soul back toward the things that matter. The chapter reminded me of the things I love, my commitments, my core beliefs.

Even though many of these scholars had a cathartic and personally important experience, it was still a struggle for many in that this is not the kind of writing they have done or the kind they had been trained to do. They also found tension in delving into these issues based on their own social identity. One author commented,

> I am not self-reflexive by nature. Therefore, writing this chapter was a difficult experience. I tried to structure this piece as I would structure an academic article. Upon comments by reviewers, I tried to add more personal anecdotes and stories. It was very difficult, however, to leave the basic academic framework that I have come to reply on for my academic work.

Another discussed the very different nature of this kind of writing,

> I know how to review an array of facts, identify relationships among those facts, and define an engaging narrative that guides the reader through a logical argument, supported by evidence. I know how to write a research study, identifying a problem and a research question, reviewing what is known about that problem, and laying out methods for investigating the problem. I know how to report results and know how—though I could stand to work on this part quite a bit more—to capture conclusions that can be drawn from those data. None of that knowledge or skill as a writer helped me in writing a chapter about myself and my struggles to become a mother and a person.

Another author found this work challenging as he felt a particular tension based on his identity and privilege.

> While I enjoyed this writerly experience, I found the authoring of my contribution to be particularly challenging for a number of reasons.... I will focus on what I found to be the most challenging aspect of this reflexive exercise. The writing of the work-life chapter forced me to revisit, and work through, a number of insecurities I have regarding my positionality as a critical scholar who also happens to be a White, heterosexual male. I found myself wrestling with whether or not I, as privilege incarnate, deserved to complain about the difficulties I associate with obtaining the illusive work-life balance. Consequently, when reflecting upon the unique plight of my peers, I felt unsure and uncomfortable when commenting upon the structural complexities I consider to be inherent to the PhD chase at highly competitive institutions

We hope this book resonates with others inside and outside of higher education who wrestle with work-life balance. We recognize that work-life struggles and balance are not only relevant to higher education. In fact, faculty in higher education have a great deal of privilege when looking at jobs and careers across the United States because of the flexibility, positionality, and potential security of the job. However, pretending that work-life balance is not a part of higher education or not making space for an open discussion of these issues does not serve a diverse faculty or community well. As such, one of the powerful aspects of this project for me has been a feeling of community.

> I wish a moment of pause for the readers of this book to reflect that we are not alone in struggles with regards to work-life balance.

I recognize that work-life balance is not fixed in time and the struggles we had 5 years ago may be entirely different to how we deal with the work-life balance in the future. Yet, the autoethnographic stories in this book provide space and voice to real and ongoing dilemmas of work-life balance. As discussed, writing this book has had a real impact on the authors. I close this piece on methodology with reflective notes from many of the authors who were comfortable sharing their reflections on this project. In the section above some of the quotes came from the reflection below, and some were from anonymous reflections across the entire group of authors. The notes that follow are in no particular order, but they provide an important glimpse into the power of an autoethnographic project in a competitive field that does not often embrace this kind of scholarship in how it rewards individual accomplishments. It seems fitting in a book of autoethnographic essays to close this note of methodology with the authors of the work reflecting on the experience themselves. Peace.

AUTHORS' REFLECTIONS

> I felt like turning this opportunity down at first, because autobiographies are very challenging processes, in which we need to confront and negotiate several layers of self as researcher–participants. For this book's topic: (a) I had to revisit my experiences and select points of tension related to work-life balance. I recognized that some of the tensions related to systemic gender/ethnicity problems in higher education; (b) I had to make my personal life vulnerable to my colleagues and the general public, recognizing to what extent these influenced my professional experiences; (c) I wanted to restory experiences that would add and promote the growth of others; and (d) I wanted to honor those who positively influenced my work. In addition, the trust and support I received from the colleagues in this book, some of which are long-time collaborators, and some of whom I developed admiration and strong working relationships throughout the years, were definitely influen-

tial in building trustworthy spaces for the candid nature of this work. The editors and scholars in this volume are the next generation of highly dedicated advocates and academics in the field of educational leadership, who encourage us to become strong scholars ourselves. Among them, I felt safe to develop this autobiographical work.

—Elizabeth (Betty) Murakami-Ramalho

Writing the work-life chapter was an enjoyable undertaking. It was a diversion from the usual academic process of writing, which was a nice change, and it allowed, actually required, me to take a breath and reflect on my work, my life, and the balance between the two. As I began to mentally prewrite, thinking off and on for days about how to approach the question I was to address in the chapter—How do you balance work and life?—I realized I couldn't answer this question. Rather, I had to reframe it. This reframing in a sense did, however, provide an answer to the original question. That is, the way I try to balance my work and life is to see both of these as one in the same—my life. The ways in which I attempt to balance my life is through balancing myself. If I can, indeed, stay balanced, neither clinging to or avoiding anything that arises, then work and life are also balanced. Thank you to the editors for inviting me to participate in this project and giving me a nice little vacation of reflection.

—Kathryn Bell McKenzie

I asked Dominic [my son] to respond to the question about the experience of writing this chapter along with me. [Dominic's response is next.]

—Matt Militello

I felt very excited, proud, and nervous to be asked to coauthor this chapter. There were two reasons I felt this way. First, the youth voice is almost always missing in talking about education and life. I think that it was a great way for my voice to be heard being a youth. I was very happy I was able to represent the youth voice. So was my school. They will put the chapter in the school showcase. Second, I always enjoy working with my father. And how many kids get to be with their dad at home and at work? This was a great experience.

—Dominic Militello

The process of writing the chapter as a family unit was both exciting and stressful. We had never collaborated on a particular writing project that would lead toward publication. Therefore, the girls were excited and thrilled that they would be "published" authors just like their parents. In many ways, this gave me a sense of deep satisfaction and fulfillment that they were following in my footsteps. On the other hand, the three of us were also very nervous throughout the entire process, especially as the chapter unfolded. Marina felt that she did not fully express herself in her narrative and that her responses were somewhat short and underdeveloped. Cora felt that she finished too quickly and worried that her responses were incorrect or off the mark (NOTE: Cora finished her section in about 2.5 hours, while Marina and I took close to a week). For the most part, I was constantly fearful that my girls would air the family's dirty laundry in their respective sections. Part of me wanted to control the process, while another part of me struggled with just letting go and having the girls write their own truth. In many ways, I really wrestled with how to balance the "researcher" hat with the "father" hat while learning to work with my children as coequals/coauthors.

—Gerardo R. Lopez

After some time thinking about what to write, I decided to approach the project by describing what I call the three self's: work-self, family-self, and personal-self. Writing the chapter for the work-life book contribution was both a reflection and examination of the tension I had/have about how to create more quality time to devote to my family, work, and personal-self. The writing process unearthed and confirmed my growing feelings of wanting to spend more time with my energetic and curious toddler, yet I know and understand the demands of academic work—and the work does not distinguish between those who have a child and those who do not. I also reflected that both work and family matters have been monopolizing the majority of my time since having a child and that my personal-self was often put aside so time, attention and energy can be devoted to doing academic work and taking care of and being involved with my child. It's funny that I use the word "energy" in the previous sentence … since often I have little energy for myself left after most days and especially after demanding days that tug at me for attention to work/family matters. The reflective writing process affirmed that making time for personal-self matters is critically important in order to regroup and recharge my energy level and enthusiasm to do things. The reflective writing also affirmed that making time for personal-self matters means "getting back" to work-life issues with a renewed/refreshed perspective and the energy needed to stay focused, engaged and productive when involved in family activities or work activities. Balance of work-life issues is not a description I would use to depict my daily lived experiences, rather focused and productive time spent performing all that needs to be done is what I strive for.

—Kathrine Gutierrez

Writing this chapter was both challenging and liberating. The challenge came from trying to articulate, in a concrete way, the struggle of being a professor and having some kind of personal life. This profession is rife with paradoxes: we have a lot of time, until it runs out; we are supposed to equally value scholarship, teaching, and service, but it depends on what kind of institution you end up working; and just when you think that you are doing a good job, there is continuous pressure to do more. The other challenge was critiquing the process of tenure and promotion, which we all must go through, whether we like it or not. We end up being pawns in a larger game that we may not condone, but nevertheless, still support. The liberating part was for the first time being able to share the lessons I have learned and insights I have gained. For me, this was a reflective exercise allowing me to really evaluate why and how I do my job, support my family, and make a greater contribution. In the end, I realized that I am working everyday doing something I really enjoy (even with all of the pressures). As I stated in my writing, work-life balance is a process and it is one that requires ongoing attention and engagement.

—**Floyd D. Beachum**

While this chapter did not inflict existential angst upon my psyche, it did raise a fair number of quite uncomfortable questions. In particular, I am still in the process of sorting out the issue of "when does helping become enabling at work." That said, for me, it's been a very helpful exercise. I'm becoming better at protecting my "down time." I am also far more assertive in what I need to do my job and keep my back pain level to a tolerable level. Since I don't think work-life balance is achievable (and this notion actually offends my blue collar soul), I'm happily opting for less crazy in my life. Writing this chapter gave me the time and space to think things through.

—**Catherine Lugg**

Writing has been an integral part of my professional identity for all of my adult life. I know how to review an array of facts, identify relationships among those facts, and define an engaging narrative that guides the reader through a logical argument, supported by evidence. I know how to write a research study, identifying a problem and a research question, reviewing what is known about that problem, and laying out methods for investigating the problem. I know how to report results and know how—though I could stand to work on this part quite a bit more—to capture conclusions that can be drawn from those data. None of that knowledge or skill as a writer helped me in writing a chapter about myself and my struggles to become a mother and a person.

The process of writing the chapter impacted me at two levels: the first was simply the superficial and immediate impact of writing. The level of emotional introspection that was necessary to clarify my ideas left me drained at the end of the 2 days it took me to write a brief 2,000 word essay. This was followed by a paralyzing fear of sharing what I'd written. Would I be ashamed or regretful if my family were to read this? Would I regret having published this if my children were to read it? I sent it to two dear trusted friends for feedback, and their responses were wonderfully supportive. This buoyed me tremendously until the day that I was expected to read this aloud at a UCEA session. Looking around at the group of other contributors, I was overwhelmed with insecurity as a scholar, writer, and person. My stomach was a knot of anxiety and worry. I deferred my turn reading until last because I was so panicked. I hoped that there would not be enough time for me to share mine. But there was enough time. And the sense of relief, camaraderie, and support I felt from and for the other contributors and session attendees after I read my piece was a high that lasted for several days.

It lasted until I sat back down to revise the draft and, with my writing editorial hat on, felt that what worked well in a narrative read-aloud form was still not in the ballpark of what I would usually consider solid, tight writing. Through three or four revisions, I still have not arrived at a point where I feel the piece meets criteria that I would normally use to prepare "good" writing. But I have had to let it go and did so by telling myself that while I know about standards for good writing in my professional practice, I do not know anything about standards for what is "good" writing in conveying something as personal as the struggles and transformation I have undertaken as a mother. On some days I reread the piece and find it acceptable. Other days I read it and am nearly nauseated at the thought that it will be published with my name on it. The latter are days when I need to have a glass of wine.

The second impact was more profound and lasting. When I got home from writing the first draft, I called my partner and read it to him over the phone. It immediately provided us with a platform for discussing one of the most difficult stages of our marriage in terms that were more clear than I had ever been able to communicate before. I have come to understand myself—and my children—more deeply and with less judgment. That is, rather than spending so much emotional energy trying to squelch my core desires and inclinations, I am learning to listen to myself (and my children) more carefully. I am working hard on helping my daughters develop the habits of introspection that allow them to know, with conviction, who they are and what they want. In many ways, this has helped me become a more empathetic mother since I am also just now learning these habits. We are learning this together, each at our own developmental level. Honestly, I like myself better after writing this piece. I am more honest, more authentic. I respect myself more. And I have a greater insight professionally about how I can use my personal struggle—a microversion of the macrostruggles that community and school leaders face in navigating external social expectations—to coach and support the leaders who come to GLISI for help in leading school and district improvement.

—**Leslie Hazle Bussey**

[Writing this chapter was] a bit cathartic, but I am still considering some of the framing—it is still difficult to represent others' contributions and while I want to share the journey, I also am uncomfortable with a "heroic" narrative, even though it is important to share the narrative. You may know this as well—many people deal with some of these issues as "normal", albeit they are difficult. And, I am not sure whether Jessica's [my wife's] contribution is adequately represented—yet there are issues associated with representation written about as crises of representation that I find more difficult with those close to me. Thanks for the opportunity to share and reflect."

There is a tension that I also think is epistemological—as even with the quite varied and open training I have, I still am most comfortable navigating a postpositivist, or perhaps constructivist "object" of study. This calls for what might be a more radical subjectivist position in which traditional notions of truth and the criteria used to judge it is suspended. In my case, I felt that the object of the reflection was a journey, which is fragmented through subjectively selected events that I had an odd lack of parameters to represent—as liberating as it is, it is unfamiliar. And, in my case, I don't particularly find the autoethnographic approaches of Carolyn Ellis particularly engaging or illuminating—at times even overly narcissistic. And if I don't just talk about myself, then it is tricky to represent others, most particularly those that are closest to you that I want to protect.

—Bill Black

My experience writing the chapter was pretty much like what I write about in the chapter—a real struggle for balance. Like standing up in a hammock, as my mother would say. There was an evil spirit with a pitchfork on one shoulder whispering in my ear: "People are going think you are silly writing about being a middle-aged rock and roll fan. Why would you want to expose yourself like that? You've worked so hard to gain credibility among the stodgy, humorless educational administration professors … you shouldn't be doing this." Meanwhile, a good spirit with a halo is bouncing up and down on the other shoulder and whispering (excitedly), "YAY! It's about time you used the platform you've struggled to build, board-by-board, to stand on and say something important about being a person and not just a machine that cranks out grants, books, articles, and doctoral students. Have some fun! Journey ON, sister!"

—Linda Skrla

I am not self-reflexive by nature. Therefore, writing this chapter was a difficult experience. I tried to structure this piece as I would structure an academic article. Upon comments by reviewers, I tried to add more personal anecdotes and stories. It was very difficult, however, to leave the basic academic framework that I have come to reply on for my academic work. I tried to add more anecdotal information in via the use of footnotes, a la David Foster Wallace's legendary essays in Harper's back in the 1990s. Not being as smart as DFW (who is?), I question even now how well I pulled this off. Upon reflection, the structure of the final piece reflects some critical tensions within my own life; specifically, the preference I have for compartmentalization and the difficulty I face in integrating the two dimensions in question.

—Eric A. Houck

Working on writing my chapter for *Juggling Flaming Chain Saws* was at first an honor and a welcome opportunity. Once I began to actually write it, however, it became a double-edged sword: an important platform from which to be deeply introspective, while serving as a nagging source of disequilibration. As I attempted to describe my work-life balance, it became crystal clear to me that it paralleled my journey to the professoriate. At first, I took a detached reporter approach. Despite my attempts to describe the progression objectively, feelings of embarrassment, frustration and sadness began to emerge, and blocked my writing process. This is, in fact, a story of a 30+ year odyssey, paralleling dramatic changes not only in my life but more importantly, in my foundational and paradigmatic worldview. Wrestling with confessions of social and cultural ignorance from the mental models of a person whose experience was more a result of being sheltered by a controlling spouse than of privilege, I recognized that so many of the proverbial stepping stones along the way were placed there in order for me to evolve into who I continue to become today. I made a conscious decision as I wrote to blow my own cover in the name of informing the reader about my authentic experience. It would also quickly become apparent to readers who know me how old I am, a fact about which I have never been ashamed. It juxtaposes the social upheaval of the 60s with my embarrassing willingness to do what someone else wanted me to do, resulting in shelving my desire for an academic career for 3 decades.

This writing process was deeply personal; I decided that to exclude several passages that show my exhusband in an unfavorable light would be disingenuous. I allowed incidents to happen, and thereby froze my intellectual, social and cultural development for more than 2 decades. I debated about how my grown sons would respond to my writing—sharing deeply personal glimpses about a woman who is more complex than the woman who always smiled and acted like everything in life was wonderful. That coping strategy contributed, however, to some of my contemporary work-life coping mechanism, so my option for candor was appropriate. As I increasingly recoiled against compliance, so did my resonance with issues of social justice.

—Kristina A. Hesbol

Since becoming a full-time professor almost 10 years ago, seeking balance in my professional and personal life has been an ongoing pursuit. So in writing this chapter, it propelled me to reflect more deeply on the final year of my doctoral program because it was the most stressful period of my life (i.e., attending graduate school and working full-time as an administrator in higher education). Thinking about that period was therapeutic because it was filled with memories of lost happiness and achievements. While some of these memories have been tucked away, I am grateful for the opportunity through this writing to unearth them as I approach new milestones.

—Gaetane Jean-Marie

The experience of writing the chapter was actually cathartic. It helped me to see yet again that I remain out of balance a lot of time (even when I am supposed to be writing a chapter about balance). In the past I have included people in my life in my work and this was no different for me except I find myself more protective of my personal life than I used to be. I find that keep some things for me and creating some kind of barrier helps to create a greater sense of balance of work and personal life. Lastly, I shared the chapter and the process of writing the chapter with my students who found it "a relief" to hear that a professor struggles with writing and with maintain balance. I think we often forget that writing is a solitary and excruciating process—the fun part is only when you see your work published' and that lasts about 5 minutes—then it is back to sculpting another manuscript.

—Autumn K. Tooms

When I wrote the chapter, I was ending the second year in a position that was not a good fit for me. I was unhappy with the work that I was doing, and I believe it shows. I have since moved to a new university and am now in a tenure-track assistant professor position. My son attends a great childcare and my girls are happy in their new schools. My husband is delighted because I am content. I find that working outside the home is better for my spirit. Before, I sat for hours at the kitchen table or on the couch teaching online. Now, I leave the house early and have a full day doing the work I enjoy: teaching online, conducting research, and participating in service. I feel valued in my new position, and although I will continue to teach online, I now have the freedom and ability to conduct research, meet with students and faculty, and participate fully in committees. Interestingly, the balance between work and family is easier now because although I am away from home more, I am much more joyful. What I take away from this experience is the lesson that when one section of my life is out of balance, then my whole life is out of balance. Now that I've found a better fit, things are returning to a good equilibrium, which is good for everyone.

—Melanie C. Brooks

Two things occurred to me as I wrote my chapter. First, that I made assumptions about the audience that is inconsistent with getting the most out of this kind of writing. I wrote my chapter in Teacher Mode, meaning that I was dispensing advice rather than reflecting as deeply as I might. I have written other narrative research where I did much more soul-baring, but here I was imagining speaking to someone who was struggling and needed a positive pep-talk rather than exploring the tensions in my own life like I might have. Second, I was one of the people who recruited authors for this book, and it really struck me that every one of them (a) told me that they found the experiencing very rewarding, and (b) wondered if I read their chapter and asked me what I thought. This suggests a kind of isolation we routinely avoid discussing in academe—on some level most of us have self-doubt, are dealing with very complicated personal and professional lives, and work in places that extoll the value of collaboration while simultaneously creating barriers that prevent people from working together. Moreover, if we raise concerns about this status quo the culture of academe is much that we can quickly become branded a dreamer, a complainer, out-of-touch, or worse ... writing this book has not been a liberating experience for me, exactly, but it has raised my awareness that being a professor is as much about dealing with isolation when we need to interact to do our best work, managing relationships in places that demand a lot of our time, and creating something from nothing, due to the ambiguity of the promotion and tenure guidelines and processes in which we operate.

—Jeffrey S. Brooks

I will say that my chapter gave me the opportunity to write about something that I've been reflecting on since my children entered elementary school, namely, navigating my role as parent with my role as researcher, specifically in the area of high stakes accountability. Because I only had 10 pages, there were elements that I didn't include that I might have with more space (I would have included more dimensions on the tension). Based on the reviewer comments, I decided to be more focused on one particular tension. I will say that it did feel strange to be sharing something with the world that I tend to talk about with friends, family and a few colleagues. We'll see how I feel once it is in press! I did enjoy writing it; it was a welcome departure from academic writing.

—Stacey Routedge

It was somewhat difficult for me to write the chapter because I needed to relive some of the struggles I faced as a closeted school leader and an out scholar who identifies as queer. Sometimes colleagues assume because I am "queer," which is only a part of my identity, that I must "do queer work." I approached this chapter by sharing my experiences with colleagues who became my close friends, especially in Texas when I accepted a position as a tenured track assistant professor due to the personnel policy, however, realizing that I was told I would be fired for "being gay" … and my line of inquiry was "insignificant because no one cares about those issues" (the lived experiences of marginalized populations). My close friends/colleagues talked me through the process of finding work-life balance, my present struggles/tensions, and how my lived experiences influence my capacity and courage to live what I write.

—Christa Boske

Even though I'm a qualitative researcher who is used to discussing issues of "reflexivity" and "researcher identity" in my research (that is, I try to be transparent in my work in describing how my personal experiences and perceptions shape my writing), this chapter was particularly challenging for me to write. We were encouraged to write about our experiences in the first person and to share stories that illuminated our work-life balance challenges—but I kept asking, "Why would anyone care about my experiences?!" I'm not used to being the subject and I'm still left wondering whether my chapter is at all in concert with what other folks think about when it comes to this subject. My preference—and comfort zone—is writing (and reading) about others.

—Peter M. Miller

Writing this chapter provided a unique opportunity to reflect on the people, issues and tasks that are most important in my life. Any type of writing opens the author up to a certain level of vulnerability; this is compounded when the task at hand is to share elements of your personal life. The ability to embrace this vulnerability makes us better researchers and writers. I'm currently teaching a seminar for first-year doctoral students. I refer to this particular chapter throughout this course, as the act of writing this chapter has reinforced my belief in the need to talk with new and emerging scholars about the importance of taking time to nurture their physical, emotional and spiritual selves. I wish someone had talked to me about this need for balance while I was completing my doctoral studies.

—**Susan C. Faircloth**

I was surprised by how long I had to think about what to focus on for the chapter. As a public document about my professional and personal struggles as a working mother, I wasn't comfortable completely "airing the dirty laundry" of my workplace. I still want to make "full professor." That desire, coupled with my husband also working at the same institution, required a thoughtful balancing of my desire to be transparent with my experience, my need to protect my career and at the need to forthright about my husband's very different lived experience. Therefore, I chose to focus more on my personal (home life) experience and not as heavily on the institutional response to my struggles. There are volumes written on the horrors of academic life. Even so, I still believe that it is a privilege be an academic. Even with the complicated context of the nature of the work, I have enormous freedom in my career. I can choose the line of research I want to pursue. I don't have to punch in on a time clock, document restroom and lunch breaks, or submit paperwork to take personal leave to go to a doctor's appointment. In the chapter, I didn't want to come across as whining when I know that I have it better (different—but definitely more flexible) than most working women. The exciting aspect of writing the chapter for this volume is that it builds on the hope that as a result of such sharing, things may even get better! Universities should set the agenda and tone of a national conversation on work-life balance issues. We have the "academic freedom" and protection of tenure that allow us to air issues that other less protected employees would expose at a potentially much higher personal and professional cost. I appreciate being a part of the dialog and the journey.

—**Bonnie Fusarelli**

As I wrote and the more I wrote, the insights to me were surprising in writing this chapter. Living life and reflecting on my life lived brings an awareness of the developing characteristics of my leadership that have become sewn into my professional life. To gain this deeper appreciation was very rewarding to me as I acknowledged the bumps in the road as just that. These bumps, gave me courage and strength to continue when I was worried I would fail at all the roles I was juggling: mommy, daughter, sister, wife and educational administration professor. I often tell my daughters and my graduate students, to be brave and take the chances that will help them to soar. I am now more aware of my soaring!

—**Rosemary Papa**

It took me considerable time reflecting about possible approaches to take in developing my chapter before I actually began writing it. During an early morning walk—one of my commitments to creating and sustaining work-life balance—I recalled what stimulated my goal to become a professor. That recollection served as the catalyst I needed: Drafting the chapter became an easy task, one that I accomplished in a few hours. I set aside the chapter draft for few days and then made a few revisions before sending it to a book editor. After receiving feedback from a peer reviewer (i.e., another chapter contributor to this book), I made suggested revisions and again ignored my chapter for several days. I conducted a final critical review before sending it back to the book editor. My chapter has become a self-created talisman, a contract I made with myself to sustain a work-life balance. Thus far, my chapter has served me well—once published, I know I must stay faithful to my contract lest someone asks me about my balanced life.

—Tricia Browne-Ferrigno

Spending time reflecting on work-life balance felt odd. I wondered why I was dedicating time to this, and not to work … or life. In a sense, the time was like taking a retreat. The act of taking a retreat is paradoxical: one departs the everyday world in hope of gaining some strength or perspective that helps in engaging this everyday world. In something of a similar manner, the very act of reflecting on my work-life balance took time away from both, thus upsetting further whatever tenuous balance might exist. Yet I hoped that the reflecting would help me in this ongoing quest for balance. I approached writing this chapter with this hope, and found that talking it over with my wife and life partner was, in fact, beneficial. I write this reflective paragraph at 4:31 A.M., up in the middle of the night due to insomnia that I know can be attributed in no small measure to work-life imbalance. Clearly I have a long ways to go! Writing the chapter forced me to collect my thoughts on how the balance is so essential, yet so elusive.

—Martin Scanlan

My response to the invitation to contribute a chapter about work-life balance was immediately positive, as this has been a topic of interest of mine for my entire adult life. My interest has not been one of scholarship, but more of a personal nature—trying hard to "get it right" and most often feeling that I did not. I began my reflection process with some reading of other popular articles and considering what balance has meant to me over the years. I found that I felt very much at a loss regarding what I would write. I had said yes so quickly and then the reality was that I really did not know how or what to write about. I lived uneasily with the questions and self-doubts I was having and then one day it occurred to me that I might bring a method to my reflection and inquiry. I have training in appreciative inquiry (AI) and felt that a positive approach to this project may be more productive than the unsettling examination of all the ways I had failed to find balance over the years! Loosely following AI, I asked myself, "When in my life had I feel most balanced?" I wrote some reflections on this question with little clarity and then found myself deeply curious about how my family members would answer. I designed a set of three questions that I included in my chapter:

(1) In our family, was there a time when you felt like we got the balance between our lives and work right? When was that? I really want to hear whatever details come to you.... Was there a time that popped to mind as soon as you heard the question? I want to hear that and any others that come to mind.

(2) As you think about work-life balance in your life, what is most important to you?

(3) What conditions might best support a healthy work-life balance?

I first discussed the idea of interviewing and writing about the interviews with my family members (husband, and two daughters, 23 and 19 years old). I assured them that they could choose not to participate. Everyone agreed that it sounded like an interesting project. I interviewed each family member separately, without conversation about others' responses. I then reflected on the interviews and wrote the chapter. Each family member read the chapter, contributed their feedback, and approved the final version. The process turned out to be fascinating for me and has led to further conversations within my family.

—Lisa Kensler

Writing this chapter was extremely beneficial to me. I had the opportunity of engaging in an assignment that required serious reflection. This work-life balance chapter allowed me to reexamine whether there was indeed a sense of balance and what modifications are needed to achieve equilibrium between my work and personal life. Throughout the writing process, I discovered that there was a cognitive dissonance in what my perceived thoughts were concerning my work-life balance and what existed in reality. As a professor of educational leadership, I often talk to my students about the idea of understanding their leadership platform. I tell my students to be aware of any cognitive dissonance that might exist in what they profess as a leadership platform and the reality. Thus, as I was writing my work-life balance chapter, I soon realized that maybe I didn't have the type work-life balance as I might have professed to myself. Ergo, this assignment has truly led me to reexamine my work-life balance and to begin to truly interrogate its meaning to me.

—Carlos R. McCray

Writing this chapter happened during the summer of my discontent. I had a nice drive in an ambulance, got four bags of blood, and had emergency surgery. For 3 months I wasn't too happy with my life and certainly didn't care about work. I had to rely on people physically and emotionally. I was on so much medicine that I couldn't watch TV, pay attention to my smartphone, or log on to my computer. My energy level was so low that I literally had to take a nap every 2-3 hours. In spite of all of that, completing this chapter was cathartic. Writing this chapter ushered me back into the necessary hum of life, but with renewed purpose. This chapter was the first piece of writing I completed all summer and I was so proud of myself for completing it after not writing for 5 months. Most of all, thinking about my life and my work and then putting pen to paper, helped me to turn my soul back toward the things that matter. The chapter reminded me of the things I love, my commitments, my core beliefs. My circumstances this summer caused me to spend many hours wondering about the purpose of things. I found myself (and others) giving me speeches about forgetting work and dealing with life. The funny part is that I actually missed work! I missed the new ideas, feeling productive, and working alongside colleagues who I realized were friends. After feeling so fragmented this summer, writing this chapter helped me define work-life, the intersection of my life and my work. Recognizing this has been a good things. I stopped the imaginary tug of war between work and life, and happily embraced both in my whole self. And the whole of my self is good.

—Noelle Witherspoon Arnold

There is a definite tension even now while I reflect on my chapter. It is an honest portrayal of a cutaway ... a scene ... a glimpse into my journey as a doctoral student/father/husband converging at the moment of reflection when prompted to do so. I sometimes feel like the chapter places too much emphasis on the "group enterprise," where maybe I should have dug a little deeper into other parts of my experience that I struggle with. Is this really about my family, or is it really only about me? Do I lack the fire in the belly to push on? Do I truly believe I have the talent, the persistence, and the resilience to do it? My knowledge of narrative inquiry interferes with my reflectivity, because I know there is not one thread one can pull out of his/her narrative that resembles the whole. In the end, I know my chapter represents one part of many plots that coexist in my experiences as a professional, as a student, as a parent, as a husband, and son.

—Doug Wieczorek

The best part of this experience was reading other people's chapters as part of the editing process. It's liberating and refreshing to read the frank accounts of work-life balance from colleagues around the country.

—Liz Hollingsworth

REFERENCES

Anderson, G. L. (1996). What does practitioner research look like? *Teaching and Change, 3*(2), 173-206.

Anderson, G. L., Herr, K., & Nehlen, A. S. (1994). *Studying your own school: An educator's guide to qualitative practitioner research.* Thousand Oaks, CA: Corwin.

Anderson G. L., & Jones F. (2000). Knowledge generation in educational adminis-tration from the inside out: The promise and perils of site-based research. *Educational Administration Quarterly, 36*(3), 428-464.

Bullough, R. V., & Pinnegar, S. (2001). Guidelines for quality in autobiographical forms of self-study research. *Educational Researcher, 30*(3), 13-21.

Cole, A. L., & Knowles, J. G. (2000). *Researching teaching: Exploring teacher develop-ment through reflective inquiry.* New York, NY: Allyn & Bacon.

Cole, A. L., & Knowles, J. G. (2001). *Lives in context: The art of life history research.* Walnut Creek, CA: Alta Mira Press.

Dews, C. L., & Law, C. L. (Eds.). (1995). *This fine place so far from home: Voices of aca-demics from the working class.* Philadelphia, PA: Temple University Press.

Ellis, C. (1997, November). *What counts at scholarship in communication? An autoeth-nographic response.* Paper presented at the annual meeting of the National Communication Association. Chicago, IL.

Ellis, C. (2004). *The ethnographic I: A methodological novel about autoethnography.* Lanham, MD: Alta Mira Press.

Fine, M. (1994). Dis-stance and other stances: Negotiations of power inside femi-nist research. In A. Gitlin (Ed.), *Power and method: Political activism and educa-tional Research* (pp. 13-35). London, England: Routledge.

Graham, R. J. (1991). *Reading and writing the self: Autobiography in education and the curriculum.* New York, NY: Teachers College Press.

Jackson, M. (1995). *At home in the world.* Durham, NC: Duke University.

Meneley, Y. & Young, D. (Eds.) (2005). *Autoethnographies: The anthropology of aca-demic practices.* Toronto, Ontario, Canada: Broadview Press.

Reed-Danahay, D. (2001). Autobiography, intimacy and ethnography. In P. Atkin-son, A. Coffey, S. Delamont, J. Lofland, & L. Lofland (Eds.), *Handbook of eth-nography* (pp. 407-425). London, England: Sage Publications.

Theoharis, G. (2007). Social justice educational leaders and resistance: Toward a theory of social justice leadership.*Educational Administration Quarterly, 43*(2), 221-258.

Theoharis, G. (2008). "At every turn:" The resistance public school principals face in their pursuit of equity and justice. *Journal of School Leadership, 18*(3), 303-343.

Tierney, W. G. (1998). Life history's history: Subjects foretold. *Qualitative Inquiry, 4*(1), 40-70.

PART I

EARLY CAREER SCHOLARS

CHAPTER 1

WORKING THE SPIRIT

Narrating Work and Life

Noelle Witherspoon Arnold

I have to admit, when I was first invited to write this chapter, the task seemed really daunting. I had just moved to a new city and university, began my fourth year as a professor, was serving as a convention cochair for a conference, planning a wedding, and transitioning as the major breadwinner while my partner finishes his dissertation. All of this was occurring while I was heading into my sixth year of biweekly flights across the country as a consultant for a major educational company. I also was recovering from a bad case of say-yes-to-everything-you're-asked-to-do-itis caused by a hyperfocus on obtaining tenure. Underneath this façade of grace and graciousness, I became painfully aware that I needed an intervention and I needed it quick.

I have been a journalist since I was very young. No, I don't mean the "working for the *New York Times*" kind of journalist. But I have journals that I write in to chronicle all the "stuff of life." In this age of Facebook and Twitter and instant "thought messaging," I still prefer holistic and sometimes fragmented nature of the narrative, the life story. Putting words to paper is my alternative instead of the "sound bite" culture that is so prevalent today. For me, pen and paper is the best way to be present in my life. What seems "old fashioned" and the stuff of grandmothers, has

Juggling Flaming Chain Saws: Academics in Educational Leadership
Try to Balance Work and Family, pp. 3–10
Copyright © 2012 by Information Age Publishing
All rights of reproduction in any form reserved.

served as a way to connect me to the world and most importantly to myself. I don't know if it is for my good or to my detriment, but I write *everything* down. I have a box that contains journals all the way from freshmen year in high school to the present. (My best friend has been ordered to immediately burn these should anything ever happen to me.). I have smaller boxes containing note cards with poignant thoughts or prayers written on them. All over my house, I have notes written on the backs of bills, on napkins, and scrap pieces of paper. I have even been known to carry a small notebook or note cards in my purse to write down things I read, or hear or even say, that I want to remember.

Writing this chapter risks this reading as a 12-step list of things everyone "should" do, but it is not intended that way. Each person has to find their own ways of practicing presence and mindfulness. However, I do know that sometimes reading what others say about their experiences often forces us to reflect on our own. Both my work and my life focus on the saliency of narratives in understanding both work and life separately and all their intersections. Literary theorist Barbara Hardy (1968) once asserted that narrative ought not be regarded as merely "an aestheticinvention used to control, manipulate, and order experience, but as a primary act of mind transferred from life" (p. 12).

Narrative can be regarded as locally illuminating, a central way we organize and understand experience (Mishler, 1986; Van Manen, 1990). It is also a primary way we construct our multiple identities as human beings for whom race, gender, class, culture, ethnicity, language, ability, sexual orientation, role, and position make a profound difference in the nature and interpretation of experience (Tatum, 1997; Thompson & Tyagi, 1996). In my own research, I do not begin in the scholarly tradition of framing an educational problem by connecting it to current policy and practice and/ or to the relevant literature. Rather I start with narratives of professional and personal practice that bring these things into sharp relief. Narrative, my research approach, is not only "illuminating but also that it has the capacity to contain and entertain within it contradictions, nuances, tensions, and complexities that traditional academic discourse with an expository stance and more distanced impersonal voice cannot" (Cochran-Smith, 2004, p. 83). In fact, I pursue stories in my work due to my belief that "the language of theory is rarely the language of things" (Pagano, 1991, p. 194).

Reading others people's lives can become one's own act in gaining perspective or improvement. Oftentimes in the academy, I am aware there are people on the extreme sides of work and life: there are those who view work and life too extremely, that is, work *is* life, or those who view work and life too rigidly, i.e. work and life are separate. My own *alternate narrative* views my work and my life along a single continuum. For this reason, I choose to think of work and life as *work/life* (without the notion of balancing) as vitally connected to one another in the whole of life story. By exploring "stories of experience" (Merriam, 2002, p. 286), I can unpack interchangeable nature of what I like to think of as work/life *negotiation*. I have been told that there is a line between work and life, when in fact, for me, this line is illusory. As in the research I have chosen pursue, I realize that imaginary dichotomies (such as work-life balance) tend to silence certain alternate work-life narratives instead of what these narratives could teach us. Work is part of my life story. "The good news is that at best we live as authentic human beings in our work. We write our history—though not all of it, to be sure—in our work (Starratt, 1996, p. 19). Unlike how academics are often told to order our work with abstract dimensions, variables, factors, narrative works the other way by pulling seemingly disparate things (such as work and life) together (Roof, 1993, p. 4).

In the next view pages, I offer my own narrative that highlights what I believe are intersections and negotiations between work and life. Rather than focus on individual acts of work-life balance, I narrate from the overarching themes that inform my WHOLE self in work and in life. The term narrative has a variety of uses and meanings. Narrative can be seen as a story or interview data as told to a researcher (Atkinson, 1992), the societal structures and discourses in which the story is situated (Tierney, 1993); the way in which the story is told (Munro, 1998), or the "end product" of the text itself (Clandinin & Connelly, 2000). The narrative told below is not neat or linear in occurrence or time. In this same way, I resist the urge to structure myself to align with ordinary notions of work and life.

WORK/LIFE

Take time to share your story, share your story, share your story. (Hambrick, p. 81)

About-Tos, Mindfulness, and Spirituality

When I was growing up, the elders in my family gave instruction with phrases that signaled the meaning or importance of what they were saying. "Mind your" were always the two words in front of some action or thing that you were expected to do. "Mind your manners. Mind your words. Mind your thoughts. Mind your business." These two words represented something you were supposed to remember to do. Little did I know at the time but these words were more than a command. These words were meant to focus, to pay attention to, and to be present in. If I was "minding" my manners, I was present in whatever moment, space and place, but keeping my mind centered on an overall purpose. In this case, that meant being polite and exercising deliberate care over my behavior.

It seems that the rest of the world has caught on to an important lesson contained in my elders' wisdom: practicing mindfulness. I used to think mindfulness was some exotic ritual, some new-age thing that did not seem compatible with my notions of spirituality. I was wrong. In essence, all it really means is to train our minds and souls to focus on what matters, be present in the moment, and to resist distractions. There may be no mental skill more essential in this age of constant distraction.

I have always considered myself as spiritually sensitive. I can sense the "air" around me change when something is not right. I can walk into a room and literally feel the energy in a room. I absorb others' pain or happiness and I have great abilities for compassion. I know when to grant grace to others. I read somewhere that these are "about-to moments." The about-to moments are these spiritually sensitive moments, but also the split-second moments before I speak or act. Practicing presence involves paying attention to certain physical sensations and the about-tos, and embracing the opportunity to pause before acting and be present in what I am about to do or say. There is an opportunity to prepare myself for giving kindness and grace. It is also an opportunity to ask, "How does it make me feel? How do I feel in certain situations, or while pursuing certain activities, or when I am around certain people or in certain spaces and places? Will what I'm about to do or say lead me and those I love to, or further away from peace?" So often I find myself doing things I really do not want to do. Sure, sometimes we all do some things we don't want to. I am not talking about those times. I am talking about the times when I go against my spiritual and mindful convictions and take on things that I *know* I should not. I am thankful for this mindful, and indeed spiritual, sensitivity that allows me to return to it and *ground* myself in it in all my dealings in work/life. I am learning to be mindful and "listen" to the "voice" that tells me what research and life projects to take and pursue and to only take those things that are edifying for me and those around me. There is a *sacredness* in the art of listening to oneself and others.

Grace and Paying it Forward

Philip Yancey (1997) in his book, *What's So Amazing about Grace*, defined grace as freely given, unmerited favor and love of God. Wow. I want to be grace-*full* but this seems so hard. It seems almost sentimental and maybe I feel that way because the world around us so often seems devoid of it. I see it every time I watch the news, in politics, and even in the places I live and work. This state of ungrace often manifests itself in self-righteousness, pride, meanness, and judgment among a host of other things. After reading that book, I know what I want my life to contain narratives of grace due to giving and receiving of grace by me and those around me. Rather than become discouraged by *ungrace*, I press on in the pursuit of this state of being because I realize that being graceful is not just about *doing* but also *being* in work/life. I am still rough around the edges sometimes, but I am learning. I am learning to read the world around me and myself as I work and live in it. And to tell you the truth, I have found that am happiest when I practice being grace-full to myself and to others. When I practice grace, I look at the work I do with different eyes and see that work as an extension of the things I value, my selfhood, and my commitments. When I don't practice grace to myself, to others, or toward my work, I complain and experience fear.

Grace for me is another way to pay it forward. It doesn't wait for someone else to jump in or, be the mentor, or give an assist. I consider it an honor to take the kindness and compassion that I have been given and bestow them on others. Being grace-full doesn't cost me anything. I don't grace others because they deserve it or don't deserve it, but because of the *value* of every human being. Besides, I read somewhere that practicing grace and compassion can help you live longer. I wanna live a long time!

Practicing Pleasure and Restorative Treatment

Anyone who knows me well also knows that I take a trip to a salon every 2 weeks to get my hair washed and conditioned and to get a pedicure. Those who know me well also know that I get massages at least once or twice a month. And they also know that I go to Pilates three times a week. (Okay, so I started Pilates to lose weight for my wedding, but hey, I love it now and I am quite strong). And most of all, they know that I know appreciate a daily nap. What seem like acts of decadence and vanity are actually mindful acts of restoration. These are appointments are times of meditation and purposeful, conscious effort to do things I normally would not make time for. I read books that have nothing to do with my job. Or sometimes I watch guilty pleasure TV. Other times, I close my eyes and focus on happy thoughts or engage in silent prayer. These standing appointments force me to slow down, take care of myself, and do things that actually give me pleasure. When I do, I am better in my work/life.

INVESTMENT, LIVING OTHERS LIVES, AND AVODAH

I use a phrase all the time regarding how I view my work/life, "It ain't *that* deep." I don't mean that our engagement with individuals and communities is unimportant. I don't mean that obtaining tenure is unimportant. I don't mean that how we serve in work/life is trivial. And I certainly don't mean to imply that teaching, research, and advocacy are meaningless. The meaning of that phrase has everything to do with *investment*. Actions are in your control and outcomes are frequently out of our control. Sometimes we achieve goals, but sometimes we get the exact opposite of what the goal was. I've learned that I don't need to solely invest in the outcome. I have found that when I invest in the process and practice mindfulness in my relationships and my actions in work/life, the desired outcomes mostly come. For me, what all of this *does* mean is that I think people too often myopically place more importance on a few things in their lives, rather than place "all our things" within the totality of their life story.

I am not one to often listen to people who have over a billion dollars. I mean, sometimes I think corporations and wealthy people's narratives offer poor lessons for *ordinary* folks. However, I find myself meditating a quote by Apple founder, Steve Jobs. He said, "Your time is limited, so don't waste it living someone else's life. Don't let the noise of others' opinions drown out your own inner voice. And most importantly, have the courage to follow your heart and intuition. They somehow already know who you truly want to become. Everything else is secondary" ("You've Got to Find," 2005). This mirrors for me a thought by life coach Srikumar Rao. He said, "if you do not wake up with your blood singing at the thought of being who you are and doing what you do, you are wasting your life (and life is too short for that!)" (Rao, 2010).

MY BALANCE: WORKING THE SPIRIT IN WORK AND LIFE

I hope you, the reader, will not be disappointed to hear me say there doesn't seem to be a work and life *balance*. I have constantly fought against both sides at one time or another—my work is drowning out my life and my life is interfering with my work. And both sides have beaten the other on various occasions and seemed to suck the life-spirit right out of me. Both work and life have seemed to drain my soul at some point and time. I realized that a part of this life-spirit drain was due to the internal war pitting life against work and vice versa. It left me unhappy, tired, ungrateful, and ungrace-full.

Rather than keep up the war, I chose to practice mindfulness and work the Spirit. I decided to consciously create a dialogic relationship between work and life and embrace what I find in each. I also reaffirmed my need to practice trust in the One who takes care of my work and my life. I want the whole of my life to be life breathing to others and to myself. For sure, my life is present in and gives *life* to my work, and my professional pursuits give *life* and a certain energy hum to my life.

I love the Hebrew word *avodah*, which literally means "work as worship." *Avodah* indicates little separation among spirituality and work/life. Just be-ing who we are is a spiritually mindful act. When I choose to focus on that belief, I am more content with my work/life. Neither work nor life is elevated above the other. They are simply extensions of *avodah* for me in my work and my life. By themselves, neither is all there is to the story. And if I don't meet every goal in my work/life, it's not the end of the story. When I am wounded, stressed, burned-out, or discouraged, I am mindful that these moments don't define my story in work or in life. Once I do that, I find harmony between work and life and they can make beautiful music.

REFERENCES

Atkinson, P. (1992). *Understanding ethnographic texts*. Newbury Park, CA: Sage Publications.

Clandinin, D. J., & Connelly, F. M. (2000). *Narrative inquiry: experience and story in qualitative research*. San Francisco, CA: Jossey-Bass

Cochran-Smith, M. (2004). *Walking the road: Race, diversity, and social justice in teacher education*. New York, NY: Teachers College Press.

Hambrick, A. (1997). You haven't seen anything until you make a Black woman mad. In K. M. Vaz (Ed.), *Oral narrative research with Black women* (pp. 81-90). Thousand Oaks, CA: Sage Publications.

Hardy, B. (1968). Towards a poetics of fiction: An approach through narrative. *Novel, 2*, 5-14.

Merriam, S. B. (2002). *Qualitative research in practice: Examples for discussion and analysis*. San Francisco, CA: Jossey-Bass.

Mischler, E. G. (1986). *Research interviewing: Context and narrative*. Cambridge, MA: Harvard University Press.

Munro, P. (1998). *Subject to fiction: women teachers' life history narratives and the cultural politics of resistance*. Philadelphia, PA: Open University Press.

Pagano, J. (1991). Moral fiction: The dilemma of theory and practice. In C. Witherella & N. Noddings (Eds.), *Stories lives tell: Narrative and dialogue in education*. New York, NY: Teachers College Press.

Merriam, S. B. (2002). *Qualitative research in practice: Examples for discussion and analysis*. San Francisco, CA: Jossey-Bass.

Rao, S. (2010, May 14). Moving from a 'me' to an 'other-centered' universe. *Huffington Post*. Retrieved from http://www.huffingtonpost.com/srikumar-s-rao/how-to-be-happy-moving-fr_b_570730.html

Roof, W. C. (1993). Religion and narrative. *Review of Religious Research, 34*(4), 1-13.

Staratt, R. J. (1996). *Transforming educational leadership: meaning, community and excellence*. New York, NY: McGraw Hill.

Tatum, B. (1997). *Why are all the Black kids sitting together in the cafeteria?: A psychologist explains the development of racial identity*. New York, NY: Basic Books.

Thompson, B. W., & Tyagi, S. (1996). *Names we call home: Autobiography of racial identity*. New York, NY: Routledge.

Tierney, W. G. (1993). Self and identity in a postmodern world: A life story. In D. McLaughlin & W. G. Tierney (Eds.), *Naming silenced lives: Personal narratives and the process of educational change* (pp. 119-134). New York, NY: Routledge

Van Manen, M. (1990). *Researching lived experience: Human science for an action lived sensitive pedagogy*. Albany, NY: SUNY Press.

Yancey, P. (1997). *What's so amazing about grace?* Grand Rapids, MI: Zondervan.

"You've got to find what you love," Jobs says. (2005, June 14). *Stanford News*. Retrieved from http://news.stanford.edu/news/2005/june15/jobs-061505.html

CHAPTER 2

THE JOURNEY TO FULFILLMENT

Varied Paths, Same Destination

Lisa Bass

INTRODUCTION AND DISCLAIMER

As a single woman, I feel left out of most of the discussions on balancing work and life. However, when I briefly explained my thoughts regarding this omission to series editor, Joanne Marshall; she welcomed my perspective as a single woman to the discussion. I accepted the invitation, and I am grateful for the opportunity to discuss what the journey has been like for me, as a single woman, on the proverbial tenure track. Before continuing, I should qualify that this chapter is based upon my personal experiences as a single woman, and may not represent the feelings and experiences of other single faculty members. Though other women have shared that they identify with my experiences, I do not claim that my personal trek is generalizable to the greater single population.

NEGOTIATING SINGLENESS AS AN ACADEMIC: FOOTLOOSE AND FANCY FREE?

When interacting with married colleagues, friends, and family members, I feel that the perception that accompanies singleness is that single people, particularly those without children, have endless time and financial

Juggling Flaming Chain Saws: Academics in Educational Leadership
Try to Balance Work and Family, pp. 11–19
Copyright © 2012 by Information Age Publishing
All rights of reproduction in any form reserved.

resources. The perception is that we have no encumbrances or obstacles to prevent us from completing our work since we do not have to be concerned with children or a partner competing for our time. This perception is usually not openly stated; however it seems to be implied and understood. I have heard it spoken both overtly and more covertly between the lines, as married friends or colleagues, especially those with children, offer tales of the woes they encounter as they attempt to negotiate and balance their responsibilities. In doing so, they assume that my life is free and easy since I do not have the responsibilities they believe hold them back from being more productive. Their internalized, unspoken perceptions emerge when responsibilities are distributed, or as they are sharing their plans for the evening or weekend. I do not take their misdirected looks and expressions personally, because I know their challenges are real; just as my challenges are real. Their looks of inquisitiveness or even pity, sometimes follow telling notions or assumptions that I am either living the life of Riley; that I should be more grateful for all the time I have to myself; or the 'don't worry, one day your prince will come' comment. Perhaps they are nostalgic of how they think their lives used to be before family, or maybe it is the grass is greener on the other side syndrome kicking in; but I reason that there must have been something that attracted them to the family life or they too would still be single. When times are good, they share stories of their adventures with their families and it is during these times that I doubt that they would trade their joyful (and sometimes challenging) experiences with family to be alone.

Although my feelings are my reality, I would argue that the experiences as a single person on the tenure track vary greatly per geographic location, institution, gender, and the intrinsic needs and personality of the single person. As a single person on the tenure track, I have made tremendous personal sacrifices that perhaps have kept me from being one who has the opportunity to balance work and family life—yes, I said it opportunity! These sacrifices include living in geographic regions that made it less likely for me to enjoy a social life, date, or to enjoy the vibrancy of a major city. Further, the economic opportunity cost of leaving a career to become an academic has kept me from my passion of frequent travel, both nationally and internationally.

NEGOTIATING OPPORTUNITY COSTS, CONSIDERING THE INVESTMENT

I enjoy the nature of my academic work, but it has come at a high cost. I attended universities away from my family in geographic areas where I was less likely to have the opportunity to begin a family of my own. I chose to attend or work at these universities because of my desire to attend universities of high acclaim, or because they offered me compensation to attend. The university where I received my doctorate was located in remote State College Pennsylvania. Yes, Penn State is a large burgeoning research university, but the surrounding area and social life beyond the university gate is not; particularly for older-than- (undergraduate) college-age African American women. Along this academic journey called the tenure track, I have paid the price of being isolated, and often lonely. The geographic locations where I have lived have had very small African American populations, and few men who were open to dating outside their own race. Additionally, there were few women with whom I could call "friend" as well as colleague. This was difficult for me because I enjoyed such rewarding friendships and the opportunity to build relationships during college, as well as during my first professional position after undergrad. Over the years, I have had wonderful professors and colleagues; but this did not take the place of dating or establishing personal relationships.

Following the completion of my coursework at Penn State, I accepted a fellowship at the University of Vermont. I accepted this position because it included a year of predoctoral opportunity, followed by a year of postdoctoral work. I believed that this position would better position me for the job market since I would gain valuable teaching and faculty experience while still a graduate student; combined with an additional year of experience after graduation. Although I loved the landscape and bridges of Vermont, beautiful warm summers, the presence of both lakes and mountains, and the beauty of the changing leaves in the fall; this opportunity again, came at a social cost. I was once again socially isolated. Once more, I found myself in a space where the dating pool and social opportunities for African American women was very limited. Although I am open to those of other backgrounds, the men of the Vermont area did not demonstrate a preference for Black women—not even the few Black men.

I started my academic journey at Penn State in graduate school in 2004, and have now been an assistant professor since 2008. Since then, I have been in position after position where *I find myself by myself*, and this has presented challenges that I constantly have to fight through in order to be productive. I struggle with my ideals of family not yet being realized in my own life. I struggle to negotiate and navigate an alternative path; a compromise that will allow me to somehow find fulfillment. And I struggle with the perceptions, thoughtlessness, and even the pity of married friends and colleagues who have no idea of what it is like to live the single life when this is not one's desire.

CAN WE TALK? THE NEGOTIATION BETWEEN
THE IDEAL AND THE REALITY

Being raised in the context of a loving, functional, two-parent household, I grew to value children and the ideal of family. I was taught to appreciate family meals, lively discussions, the rumble of "family noise," and the sharing of good times and bad, times of prosperity, as well as leaner financial times. I viewed summers as the time for family vacations. While growing up, I was never presented with a model of how to live and function alone. I thought being grown up met being married and having children. That being said, it is difficult for me to negotiate the world as a single academic. In fact, the concept works against my philosophy of life and my internalized paradigm of how life should be. I assumed that I would be part of my own traditional family: have a husband, children, and maybe a pet or two. I saw myself reading to my children at night, and being part of the Parent Teacher Association. I saw myself in a loving supportive home, where I would be super mom, holding it all down, while keeping it all together.

THE QUEST FOR FULFILLMENT

Being a single academic; or a professional in any field that requires large amounts of concentrated time alone to produce work has been a challenge for me. I value people, conversations, relationships, and interpersonal connectedness. To this end, I would like to enjoy meaningful conversations and some type of human interaction at least a few times a week. A meaningful conversation could be related to work; or something personal. An interaction might simply be enjoying a movie or activity with another person. The nature of the conversation or interaction does not matter as much as the fact that I am connecting genuinely and meaningfully to another person. These conversations are not only necessary for my well-being, but also for my productivity. I get some of my best ideas for papers or research from meaningful conversations with colleagues. Unfortunately, I do not always get to have these conversations or interactions in the academic setting. Our work is so busy, deadline driven, and often so intense, that much of the office conversation is based on small talk or conversations about the weather, as colleagues scurry about the office working to beat deadlines. I have invited colleagues to indulge in more substantive and even lengthy conversations at times; but these are few and small between. I sometimes sense I am impeding upon their need to complete their work if I indulge for too long. I understand their need for quiet time alone, because neither our job description, nor our work responsibilities include lengthy conversation with colleagues in the office, and so I do not expect such. Basically, we get no credit for "talking" in our profession unless we are behind a podium, so I temper my conversations because of the professional respect I have for the work space of my colleagues.

When I get home, there is generally silence. The silence, at times, is deafening and makes it difficult for me to be my personal best or to perform to my full potential. The silence at home, as well as the lack of interaction served to put me in a state of *understimulation*, discussed below. Don't get me wrong, I love my dog Buddy who is always there to greet me at the door; but he is a little short on conversation—despite the fact I feel he is gifted and talented, and has above average intelligence for a Shih-Tzu!

FULFILLMENT FROM "SOMETHING NEW": FROM EUPHORIA TO ENHANCED PRODUCTIVITY

I realize that colleagues who face their challenges in finding enough time to balance work and family may be scratching their heads regarding my circumstances, and thinking that they would gladly trade problems; however, I am not convinced that more time is what is needed for greater creativity and productivity; I believe it is contentment in life, balance of time and responsibility, and focus, or the ability to render 100% to the present moment. Rendering 100% to the present moment, or acting *mindfully*, means completely focusing on the task is at hand. This means that when you are working, that you are *working*—not spending hours on the Internet, Facebook, or responding to e-mails. If we are counseling students, we are 100% with the student; and when we are doing service, 100% of our effort is designated to whatever service we are attending to; when we are at our leisure, 100% of our energy is concentrated to that leisure activity. Focus and concentration not only allows us to perform at higher levels, but gives way for more excellent work. When we spend focused, concentrated energy on work, we are much more efficient. Excellence and efficiency will allow us to complete higher volume, higher quality work. Also, those whom we give 100% of ourselves (students, friends, family members), will likely be happier with the quality of the resulting communication, interactions, and the relationships.

I have asked several colleagues who recently transitioned from being single to married; or from being married without children to married with children, about their balance of work and family. I ask because I am curious to see how life's transitions impact work productivity, because I believe that I too will someday transition. Remarkably, they all reported that they are actually more productive with the additional responsibility than before. The report that they are more focused on completing tasks because they are more settled and content, and because they have something to look forward to at home. They know that they must complete a certain amount of work, in addition to spending time with their families in order to survive at home and at work. The colleagues I inquired of, mostly women of color; have reported that they are actually more organized because they are forced to set boundaries around their time. As such, they are no longer free to procrastinate or to get off schedule, or to fall asleep, either mentally or physically, from understimulation.

I believe my colleagues in their descriptions of their renewed energy and focus as a result of their new found fulfillment and joy. I too have experienced greater productivity during times when I have something new to look forward to, or even the hope of something new. If I have an event to look forward to, something fun planned on my agenda, or even if I am awarded a long awaited publication; I am energized, and live off of the joy of my anticipation or accomplishment. Therefore I am also realistic, about my perception of my colleagues. Most of the people I inquired of have recent life changes. Their energy and focus might be due to the euphoria and joy of their situations because they are new; not because they are necessarily easier. Therefore, I believe that the amount of time they will benefit from their changes (by way of greater focus and productivity), is based upon the nature and quality of their life changes or new relationships; their level of maturity; how long they waited for the change; and how much they genuinely enjoy their change.

UNDERSTIMULATION

One might argue that the life of an academic is stimulating in and of itself. I agree, in that the work and the resulting discoveries are exciting and interesting. In fact, I cannot think of any other profession that I would enjoy as much as the work that I do in and around high poverty schools. The understimulation I refer to is due to having fewer meaningful interactions than necessary to be at one's best, academically and psychologically. Not that the nature of the work is not stimulating.

Understimulation, perhaps only truly understood by those who experience it, or have experienced it, can be characterized by the state of lethargy, or mental dullness brought on by extended periods of boredom and/or the lack of mental or physical stimulation or personal fulfillment. The occurrence of understimulation and what it takes to experience it varies from person to person. It is also dependent upon the person's need to interact with others; as not everyone needs this interaction to be productive. Understimulation is physically and mentally exhausting because those suffering from it must fight to maintain their interest and energy level. Understimulation does not happen overnight, but is a silent, often undiagnosed condition that creeps up on its sufferers slowly and over a period of time. This state or condition is painful on several levels. First, the sufferer does not understand that the way they feel is not her fault—at least not directly. They feel guilty because they know that they should be doing more, but are unable to do so during times of understimulation. Understimulation is a condition that is often mistaken for disinterest or aloofness—and is similar to the common childhood disorders labeled ADD or excessive daydreaming. If it goes on too long, understimulation might also bring with it a sense of hopelessness or despair. This condition is serious and must be dealt with, because it can even lead to depression.

FROM UNDERSTIMULATION TO MOTIVATION

I can speak to the condition of understimulation first hand, not only through my observation of serious cases in others; but because I have experienced it myself. Yes—I had my work, but that was not enough. Thankfully, I came to understand the feelings associated with chronic onset understimulation and how to counteract its effects before I drifted too far down that dangerous and destructive path. This understanding came from self-reflection, and through comparing experiences with colleagues. When interacting with more fulfilled colleagues, I could feel their energy and realized that something was awry in my own life. Their energy reminded me of how I felt when things were better. I knew how my work flowed when I was on my game, and realized that I had drifted from this ideal space. I knew that if I wanted to return to my best self, my happiest and most fulfilled self, and to and to be successful, that I would have to find ways of motivating myself and making the effort to maintain areas of interest.

One of the things that has kept me motivated was memories of people who I knew who had flatlined into their jobs. They did not seem disparaging or depressed; but they lack a spark, passion, or joy. They kept teaching and doing their work, but it was obvious that they were missing something. However, after years of investing primarily in their work, work was all they had. Rather than forging relationships, they invested all of their younger years into their work in hopes of a return, and now, they have little else to their credit. Thankfully, the investment paid off in terms of promotion and tenure and even full professor in some cases; however, there was no one at home to celebrate with. Witnessing episodes like this caused me to examine my own station in life. *Was I also understimulated and working mindlessly toward tenure in a solitary academic bubble? Would I too wake up one day, still alone, but tenured and yet unfulfilled?* When I considered my life, I promised myself that I would make changes to improve my status and to be sure that I didn't regret my decisions later in life. As such, I purposed as my goal to *"hold hands and not books"* on my death bed. I want to live in such a way that I am surrounded by loving supporters in my latter years. What I essentially mean, is that I value my work and will continue to work hard; however, I choose to prioritize investing in building meaningful relationships with caring friends, colleagues, and family. If this is not accomplished, the books, articles, and publications will mean little.

PROVEN COPING STRATEGIES FOR OVERCOMING THE SILENCE AND UNDERSTIMULATION

When I examined my life, I found that it consisted of five parts: eating, going to work (the office), working at home, going to the gym, and going to church. As such, I was a prime candidate for becoming a casualty of understimulation. There were few social outlets. My coping mechanisms have improved since I took inventory of my life and saw where it might be headed if I didn't intervene and change course. I have still decided to use much of my spare time to work out in the gym, to help in the community by volunteering in mentoring programs and helping students achieve goals they have with their school, and to spend time on my personal and spiritual development, for example, reading books, discussing spirituality with friends, and attending a mindfulness retreat. However, I have also learned to entertain myself by traveling and being open to opportunities that come my way. I have reached out to establish friendships both locally, nationally, internationally, and in the research community. I attend conferences regularly, and spend my summers away. In the past couple of summers, I have sought professional development opportunities, such as the month-long Inter-University Consortium for Political and Social Research summer program for quantitative research at the University of Michigan, as well as returned to Vermont to teach summer classes. I also spend time with my family when I can afford to go home. The most refreshing thing I did as of late was to spend a semester away at another university. I had the opportunity to spend the semester at Emory University and to work on a pilot program, Teaching in the Urban South.

My home university graciously provides junior faculty with a one semester teaching leave to work on research prior to tenure. Spending time in a large, bustling, metropolitan area has been the single best decision I have made in my short career; and my most enjoyable semester to date. Seeking out an opportunity to spend a teaching leave or sabbatical in a city that has more activity and opportunities for social engagement is a bit scary; but is an excellent way to experience a change of scenery, to expose oneself to another faculty, as well as to explore another social scene. Not all faculty members can do this, even if they are single. The problem of gaining justification and permission to leave your own university may present a challenge, so applying for a postdoc or Ford Fellowship that will allow you to complete a project at another university is also an option. It is important to note that the object is not necessarily to run away; but to keep yourself meaningfully engaged in productive activity while growing your scholarship.

Growing as a scholar and as an individual is imperative for continued personal growth, either as a single person, or a married person. However, I have learned through my own private reflections, as well as in my conversations with others, that there is not one formula for balancing work, family, and life; and that this effort is no easy feat for anyone, regardless of status—though the attempt is necessary in order for us to learn what we need to reach our personal best and what we need to achieve contentment. For me, balancing work, family, and life has come to meaning learning what is necessary for me to be truly happy and pursuing that; to seek to be productive in all that I do; and to make meaningful contributions to my family (regardless of status), to my students, my work, and to the community in which I reside.

CHAPTER 3

FINDING BALANCE IN A TILTED WORLD

Karen Stansberry Beard

THE TILTING OF OUR WORLD

The Earth sits on its axis at a slant. The axis is tilted in the same direction in relation to the stars and yet the earth is in constant motion, revolving around the Sun. Our seasons and climates are shaped and vary because of the tilting of the earth, and the amount of energy derived from the sun. Were the Earth not on a tilt, there would be no seasonal change. Earth and each area of Earth would remain relatively constant, with the same climate daylight throughout the year. Earth would have little complexity or differentiation. It would be a place ripe for boredom. Csikszentmihalyi identified boredom as a negative emotion that produces "psychic entropy." Csikszentmihalyi (1997) described psychic entropy as a "state in which we cannot use attention effectively to deal with external tasks, because we need it to restore an inner subjective order" (p. 22). While physical entropy traditionally is defined as a measure of disorder, entropy in this context refers to chaos of the mind. Csikszentmihalyi (1990) described a person's ability to organize consciousness as a battle, "against the entropy that brings disorder to consciousness" (p. 40) and therefore, the struggle for control over attention and disciplined concentration is a battle for the self. He also understood that complexity was essential to the development of self:

Juggling Flaming Chain Saws: Academics in Educational Leadership
Try to Balance Work and Family, pp. 21–28
Copyright © 2012 by Information Age Publishing
All rights of reproduction in any form reserved.

It is by becoming increasingly complex that the self might be said to grow. Complexity is the result of two broad psychological processes: differentiation and integration. Differentiation implies a movement toward uniqueness. Integration refers to its opposite: a union with other people, with ideas and entities beyond the self. A complex self is one that succeeds in combing these opposite tendencies. (p. 41)

Without differentiation and integration within the same context, there would be no need to direct intentionality toward equilibrium, no need for the collective sharing of perspective, or the tendency to enact individual thought to problem solve. Hoy and Miskel (2008) stated, "the recognition of a difficulty or disharmony in the system is the first step in the decision-making process" (p. 329). They referred to decision making as the "sine qua non of educational administration" (p. 325). Prolonged experiences of disorganization and ineffectiveness cause us to loose the desire to invest attention and pursue goals. The necessity for balance in work and life is critical to our interest, desire, and our motivation to invest attention and produce good work. In educational leadership, the balance is particularly necessary in order to make good decisions.

WORK, LIFE, AND BALANCE

I draw from the illustration of the titling earth because it parallels the way we go about living our lives, seeing things from the slant of our individual perspectives and world view. Looking back over the landscape of 50 years of living and working, I've come to the conclusion there has not been a time I've known absolute work-life balance. I'm not sure there really is such a thing. We live and work in a tilted world both literally and figuratively. When balance is attained, it isn't long before disequilibrium interrupts. As our conscious receives new information, we determine its usefulness as it confirms, alters, or threatens our world-view. Whenever information disrupts consciousness by threatening its goals, we have a condition of inner disorder, or psychic entropy, "a disorganization of the self that impairs its effectiveness" (Csikszentmihalyi, 1990, p. 37) in work and in life.

While I cannot say I know a great deal about balance. As I consider my years of living and working, I don't recall any time of absolute balance, at least not long periods of time. What I know more about is seeking peace as I've strived to balance work and life. I know about the search for balance when the tilt in my world had noticeably increased. When events occur or new information enters into our consciousness, we individually interpret the information in the context of our own interests, values and goals. Work and life balance then is intricately bound and dependent on our own differentiated perception, the seasons of our life, and the ways in which we make individual meaning in complex situations.

I have known a great deal of *work* as an educator and principal in which I have found interest, frustration, creativity, stress, personal expression, productivity, accomplishment and identity. I have also known an abundance of *life* and living through both wonderful and challenging experiences. I've known love, friendships, marriage, births, and the special tender moments that come in raising children. I've known disappointment, betrayal, loneliness, fear, death, and a multitude of experiences in between. I have laughed until I cried, and I've cried myself to peaceful sleep, only to wake refreshed and ready for another day of life and work. I have enjoyed optimal experiences and have been able to organize my consciousness and attention so even the most mundane, routine work became purposeful and enjoyable. Therein, may be the balance. *Balance* may be a result of all of the seasons of our living in full.

We each have a unique purpose (work) for our appointed season. Our varied circumstances require reliance on our strengths and skills as we examine, prioritize and commit to the core values that help us cope, sustain us, and allow us to flourish in context. Through each season and change I find myself initially, vulnerable, asking the same question, "Lord, what would you have me to do here?" Almost immediately followed by, "do I have what I need to make thing better, to turn this around and move toward balance?" Making myself available to divinity helps realign my thoughts toward my bend, my belief system, and my values, which are at the core of all decision making. Similar to the Earth's constant tilt, our bend remains consistent with our values. When I lean into my values and faith, I find myself in favor, my steps are ordered and the direction of my work is clear to me. While anxiety, fear and other negative emotions occasionally surface, I am much more sure of my direction and am able to make decisions that yield a better balance.

Controlling disorder and creating order from mental chaos requires more than the absence of negative emotions. It requires the presence of positive emotions such as: hope, engagement, meaning, (positive) relationships, and accomplishment. It is through positive emotions we are able to turn adversity into opportunity. The work of a school administrator is to identify problems and turn them into opportunities for finding solutions. The ability to recontextualize problems into opportunities has been key in how I've defined my work and made meaning of my life in each season. It is how I've learned to persist with confidence throughout the most challenging and complex situations. Our intentions help focus our attention and energy in the short term, and goals focus the direction of our work for long-term achievement. The decisions we make to create balance vary with respect to our season in life. For example as a young woman, the motivator in making a career decision, was to choose something that I would enjoy doing every day. Within a few years, the motivation for my next opportunity was centered on decision making that would allow me both to sustain or improve my living while still affording me time to continue to learn and explore new challenges. Both of those motivators were differential and seasonal. When I become the parent of three children all under the age of 6, my focus changed as dramatically as had my circumstances and season. No longer in pursuit of my personal enjoyment, I found myself preoccupied with the pursuit of those things I believed would be in the best interest of the needs of our children, both short and long term. When our life style as two professionals working long hours tilted too far out of balance, we had to reconsider our priorities, readjust and make hard, sacrificing decisions for the better of all rather, than our individual selves. With values and goals clearly established and in focus, whatever the season, I've been able to enjoy it as much, if not more than any previous one.

VALUES IN LIFE AND WORK

There are times we find ourselves pushing through to the next thing that must get done. In these times, when I slip out of my best balance, or when confusion enters or negative, unproductive responses surface, writing down my priorities, goals, and thoughts pertaining to my values, has been a useful exercise. In doing so, I consciously and subconsciously realign myself, renew my energy and rechart my direction. Clear goals direct focus, give opportunity for clear feedback, and create room for positive psychic energy. Once values are rooted, behaviors and decision making almost effortlessly move us toward a more desirable outcome: an outcome in harmony with our values and beliefs.

I am often asked why I entered into this work at such a late stage in my life. The answer is that this work helped me create balance and make meaning out of my own life-work experiences. Prior to entering academia, I worked as a school administrator. I was a principal in pursuit of superintendency and had served in an urban setting for over 15 years. I elected to finish my doctoral degree after receiving my superintendent certification. At the close of the first year of my doctoral studies, our son was denied involvement in the AP curriculum at his private school. I was keenly aware that the opportunity being denied him was significant to his future academic opportunities. At that moment in time, all of my work (teacher, administrator, researcher) and my most precious relationship (parent) converged and collided. A tilt.

I decided to use my informed roles to fight the school, and fight we did. As conversations with the headmaster "grew increasingly more formal, we became keenly aware of the intentionality of the administrator's actions" (Beard, 2011, p. xxvii), we were offered a settlement in exchange for our silence in this matter. Instead, we elected to take the course detailed by our values. We "withdrew all of our children, and walked away with our dignity and our story" (Beard, 2011, p. xxvii). When faced with a decision and opportunity to realign with our values, that old enemy (racism) had divinely and in prophetic order become my stepping-stone.

Through that experience, I learned of my resilience and tenacity to my beliefs. I'd been taught that the "highest level of courage is to dare to be you in the face of adversity. Choosing right over wrong, ethics over convenience, and truth over popularity." These indeed, are the choices that have measured my life. I revealed all to our children and then promised them, I would do all I could (my work) in the hope and optimism that other children, would not have to go through the same fight for equitable educational opportunity that we went through. I needed a bigger platform than superintendency. I needed to publish. I used my skill, experiences, and the perspective of positive psychology to begin to meet the challenge of working for other children in a different way. I imagined and worked in my writing, teaching and service to help produce the best opportunity for an equitable educational opportunity for our children and for those who were not my own. The direction of my work was redefined, as I sought peace, meaning and the need to create better balance in this season.

TIME, TRAVEL, AND ATTENTION: A BALANCING ACT

In the first year as an assistant professor, I found myself driving 2 hours from home to spend 3 days away, only to return to manage our home in the same way I did when I was there daily. My circumstances had changed, but my mindset, and the expectations I had for myself hadn't, needless to say, things tilted. Not too far, but far enough I knew I needed to write about the areas that were slipping out of balance. Writing both commits and releases me. On one hand, it reveals my authenticity as it helps clarify and order my thoughts. It also releases me from the need to mull over complications and disappointment so I have more room for creativity and new information of interest and intrigue. Often the process of writing yields affirmation statements like:

1. I will nurture my spirit and my well-being by eating delicious, nutritious food and exercising daily (even if only to stretch).

2. I will define myself by choosing to free myself from the yoke of projected definitions of me. I will author my own destiny. It is mine, so I am therefore, the author.

3. I will appreciate and give thanks for my blessings: my family, children, friendships, work, and a sound mind.

4. I will handle my money and not allow it be the other way around. I will carefully order it (right side up, by denomination) and keep it in order in my accounts.

5. I will forgive by choice, and resist offense.

Every week, I spent between 7 and 10 hours in travel. In addition to the cost of gasoline, the cost in time away from reading, writing, relationships, and leisure was tremendous. I had to learn to maximize the use of driving time in the creation of balance. Writing of course, not being possible, I kept a voice recorder nearby in case I had an idea. I would immediately note these ideas upon my arrival where I typically started my day writing for an hour. I decided to allow myself to be read to while in route. I listened to books on tape, including Gladwell's *Blink* and *Outliers*, Pink's, *A Whole New Mind*, Covey's the *Seven Habits of Successful People*, and Obama's *Dreams of My Father*. I longed for textbooks on tape to help me better prepare for teaching. When I wasn't listening to books on tape, I listened to a variety of SiriusXM music radio stations for enjoyment and relaxation.

I also committed to walking, began exploring yoga, and scheduled full body massages twice a month, thus, forcing me to stop, spend time being nurtured, and to consider other appointments and practices to tend to my own health care needs. These remedies helped me feel more in balance and in conversations with colleagues, learned I was keeping pace with their reading. The writing necessary to continue this work, I worked on in short time blocks during the day and longer set aside times (writing boot camps). I created pretty good systems to try to attend to many facets of the work, while keeping balance, with the exception of relationships.

RELATIONSHIPS: LAUGHING AND LOVING IN A NEW SEASON

One area that can very easily fall out of balance is that of relationship. When work becomes the greatest consumer of time, it can also complicate, if not become, the primary relationship in your life, creating an imbalance, a tilt. Our need for love, understanding, and acceptance is as Maslow (1970) interpreted in his hierarchy, necessary for development and motivation. Hoy and Miskel (2008) believed that belonging, love, and social needs are extremely important in modern society (p. 138). Steers and Porter (1991) referred to needs as internal states of disequilibrium that cause us to pursue certain courses of action in order to regain an internal equilibrium. When there is disequilibrium, we strive to regain internal peace. When maintaining a healthy relationship becomes work, too strenuous, confusing or consuming an extraordinary amount of time, energy and creativity, it too can create an imbalance. Relationships can dominate our thoughts and limit our ability to work productively.

Our marriage of 21 years yielded many experiences in relation to work and life. I have come to learn marriage also has seasons. The duration of a marriage is as unpredictable as the evolutionary direction of the individuals involved. What appears to be strong and unbending in any given season—changes. One way we have coped with the complications that make up our union is through common goals of interest, prayer and humor. I have found this to be true, not just in relation with my husband, but also in relation with my children.

When my daughter turned 15, she asked for a Facebook account. Untrusting of cyberspace, I responded with a resounding "no." Her older brother overheard the discussion and privately informed me that I could watch her from within if I also opened an account. That was my entry and introduction to the world of social media. The positive aspect was a welcome surprise. It helped me see and communicate with my children in the context of their world-view. I learned more about their friends, and was able to share more openly with my teenagers. Our communication strengthened over time as I understood more of what was relevant to them and as they began to see me as more than just their mom. Facets of my life were revealed in pictures and positive relationships I'd enjoyed over the course of my lifetime. My children saw me to be more than their mother in single dimension. It was also very useful in communicating with my children, especially as I traveled and as they matured and were doing the same. Not properly managed, however, social media can create an imbalance. The pursuit of balance came here in helping them understanding that while the medium of communication has changed, the pull for their attention had not. I cautioned them to guard the avenues of their mind jealously and carefully. Csikszentmihalyi (2003) said "we shape our lives by deciding what to pay attention to, and by how long and how intensely to do so because attention is what makes things happen in consciousness" (p. 177).

CONCLUSION

The balance between work and life is what we individually internally strive for, a place of peace and state of equilibrium. In the sum of work-life seasonal experiences, balance for me equated to having had just enough challenge to stay engaged, just enough skill to take on the challenge, just enough disappointment to stay humble and appreciative, and just enough courage to call on values deep from within. The process for finding balance is critical as it employs our individuality in complex situations. The quality of our life and abundance in living exists in the balance of our thoughts. Csikszentmihalyi (1997) noted, "the point is to be happy while doing things that stretch our skills, that help us grow and fulfill our potential" (p. 122). As we mature through our seasons we settle into a peaceful acceptance of experience. Our experiences then inform our work. When our work also informs our experiences, we find ourselves in a beautiful place of better balance, momentarily. This is the kind of complexity that yields good work and a good life. "A person who is fully differentiated and integrated becomes a complex individual—one who has the best chance at leading a happy, vital, and meaningful life" (Csikszentmihalyi, 2003, p. 29). In educational leadership it is imperative that those who are doing the work consistently battle for self and seek peace in balance. Our work, our living, our world-view, and our tilts, affect the lives, work and balance of others.

REFERENCES

Beard, K. S. (2011). Working with Wayne K. Hoy: A student's perspective. *Leading Research in Educational Administration: A Festschrift for Wayne K. Hoy, 10,* xxv–xxxi.

Csikszentmihalyi, M. (1990). *Flow: The psychology of optimal experience.* New York, NY: Harper & Row.

Csikszentmihalyi, M. (1997). *Finding flow: The psychology of engagement with everyday life.* New York, NY: Basic Books.

Csikszentmihalyi, M. (2003). *Good business: Leadership, flow and the making of meaning.* New York, NY: Penguin Books.

Hoy, W. K., & Miskel, C. G. (2008). *Educational administration: Theory, research, and practice* (8thed.). New York, NY: McGraw-Hill.

Maslow, A. H. (1970). *Motivation and personality* (2nd ed.). New York, NY: Harper & Row.

Steers, R. M., & Porter, L. W. (Eds.). (1991). *Motivation and work behavior* (5th ed.). New York, NY: McGraw-Hill.

CHAPTER 4

REFLECTIONS FROM THE BRINK OF TENURE APPLICATION

Working Through Various Pathways

William R. Black

In this essay, I frame my reflections on my particular struggles to balance work and life around three stories that begin with my first months as a professor and end with my application for tenure. In reference to the book title, in the first story, I felt like a chain saw brutally severed a large branch and as a consequence, my family and I continuously find ways to grow differently. The second story relates to our decision to move from Indianapolis to Tampa in an attempt to "juggle the chain saws" and find support and balance. The third story describes my landing in a situation in which many outlying limbs were being cut and how the trimming stopped and the growing season continued. I finish with a reflection on imperfect notions of balance.

"I HAVE A SNEAKING SUSPICION YOUR CHILD IS NOT NORMAL"

Jessica and I had moved to Indiana from Austin with our 3-month-old son, Gabriel, to start my first semester as a professor in January of 2005. A

Juggling Flaming Chain Saws: Academics in Educational Leadership
Try to Balance Work and Family, pp. 29–36
Copyright © 2012 by Information Age Publishing
All rights of reproduction in any form reserved.

month later, waiting in the crowded waiting room, the pediatrician stated to a shocked and later angered mom, "I have a sneaking suspicion your child is not normal." We spent March 11, our fourth wedding anniversary, in an all-day genetics and developmental pediatrician counseling session. The geneticist had 40 years of experience and had only seen a handful of children with 18 chromosome abnormalities. He told us that there is only one other reported case of the genetic combination particular to Gabriel in the literature: that child did not come to term. We went to dinner at a Turkish restaurant on the edge of downtown Indianapolis that cold evening with a light snow falling and tried to tread above the waves pathologized scripts for Gabriel's life that we received that day. Below is excerpt from the genetics counseling report dated March 22, 2005:

> Dear Dr. Black and Ms. Montalvo,
>
> As we discussed, chromosomes are packages of genetic material; in each of our cells we should have 46 chromosomes which are arranged into 23 pairs. The first 22 pairs are numbered 1-22, and the final pair is the sex chromosomes. On each chromosome there is a constricted area called the centromere; the shorter "arm" on one side of the centromere is called the "p" arm, and the longer arm on the other side is called the "q" arm. Gabriel's chromosome result was 46,XY,del(18)(p11.1)[28]/46,xy,i(18)(q10[3]. As we discussed, his chromosome analysis revealed mosaicism, or the presence of two cell lines. In the first cell line the small arm of one copy of chromosome 18 is deleted or missing; this is called monosomy 18p or 18p-. In the second cell line, there is an isochromosome 18q, in which there are two copies of the long arm and no copy of the short arm present; this results in trisomy 18q or 18q+ … at this time, his physical features are more reminiscent of monosomy 18p than trisomy 18q. Monosomy 18p is typically associated with growth deficiency, developmental delay, and mental retardation, various physical changes and potential medical complications. IQ reported ranges between 25 and 75, and speech may be significantly delayed. Facial features may include hypertelorism; a wide, downturned mouth; large, prominent ears; broad nose and ptosis. Low muscle tone is common, and 50% of affected individuals have microcephaly (small head circumference).

Since he turned 3, Gabriel has lost expressive language and had been diagnosed with autism as well. He can be described as nonverbal—the son of an anthropologist and educational leadership professor who make their living and have tied parts of their identity to their ability to use and understand words and their meanings.

Gabriel, like other children, is who he is. He will make decisions partially as a result of the opportunities we provide. We have found alternative frames of strength and resiliency for ourselves. Gabriel was blue when he was born (a Duke blue, we would later say in reference to our alma mater) after many hours in labor—he wanted to come to us when the vast percentage of pregnancies with 18 chromosome "abnormalities" don't come to term. He was strong enough to come to us. He moves through bumps and bruises, does not complain excessively when sick or when he goes to one of the eight or nine different doctors or five therapists he regularly sees. So, we choose the subject position of strength and resiliency as a counternarrative to scripts of pathology and abnormality that surround him. We also attempt to stay current on the small amount of research on chromosome 18.[1]

Gabriel has the ability to make people like him and to make people happy. He laughs joyfully, dances to music, and rides horses. He tricks us with incredibly quick hands and leads us into new and interesting activities. He hugs tightly and is now a very proud big brother. He also helps me to appreciate a lot of what I don't know.

Yet wedded to resilience, his personal gifts, and his right to be who is on his own terms, are my fears of susceptibility, and an almost constant anxiety about his future. Many in the world don't know how to relate to individuals with significant disability and the institutions we see don't often set up opportunities to interact. I see a horizon of [dis]ability which includes the increased chance that he will get seizures, the growing gaps in measured academic abilities between Gabriel and his peers as he gets older, the increased vulnerability to sexual abuse, and what he will do when we are no longer able to care for him. There are significant monetary costs—for autism upwards to $40,000 a year for therapies, and we struggle to pay for therapies even with support from relatives and some coverage from insurance. There are significant time commitments—some have estimated that parents or relatives of individuals with significant disabilities spend up to 20 hours a week on care beyond what is often required of typically developing individuals. Gabriel has his own therapy schedule which we manage with calendars and Jessica and I spend hours in tasks such as insurance claim forms and insurance denials, meeting with attorneys to set up trusts, and preparing for IEP meetings. In terms of schooling, as Gabriel finishes first grade, I have come to know that some have documented a growing resegregation of schooling for students with significant disabilities. I recently saw that only 10% of students with two diagnoses (roughly similar to Gabriel) are included in classes with typically developing peers for 80% of the day.

How to introduce Gabriel in this essay is complicated issue. Who does it serve to write about Gabriel? By writing about the exceptional journey we take, do I participate in constructing the type of heroic tales and exceptionalism that can serve to continue to marginalize people signified as (dis)abled? Yet there seems to me to be a responsibility to figure out ways to share about him in this forum and in others as a means of shaping the world around him.

FAMILY, WORK, AND A SEARCH FOR BALANCE: DECIDING TO MOVE TO TAMPA

I found that my colleagues in Indiana went out of the way to support us— "take the time that you need"; "we all go around the track, it just is in different ways and at different speeds"; and "know that we will be there for you" were what I heard. There were no publications submitted those first months and since then I have come to understand that there are ebbs and flows in the writing and publication cycles—sometimes are more productive as your energy (rather than time) can be directed to research and writing. As well projects evolve and they take time. I was able to get several pieces out by the end of the year, all of which got published.

Yet, we struggled with finding ways to balance the demands of work with creating the kinds of supports that Gabriel needed. As happens in many families with children with exceptional needs, one partner had to devote considerable time to managing his therapies and doctor appointment (Gaby has had his own calendar for years). With my job demands and Gabriel's needs, Jessica had less time to devote to her dissertation and up to now, full time jobs have been difficult to imagine as a possibility, even as we could use the income. It can be stressful on a relationship if as possibilities become limited by a combination of choice, time, and responsibility. I saw that many of my senior colleagues at my institution and in other institutions had left long-term relationships and we had the added issues of wanting to provide the greatest amount of early intervention that we could. Jessica has made stronger sacrifices than I have.

We both had no history or family members in Indiana and during my first year as a professor my father passed away and my mother lived in Tampa. We have family members in Miami and had said that if there were an opportunity to move to a couple of cities for family issues, then we should to consider it. Even though I had support from my colleagues, good services for Gabriel through the early start program and the university hospital, after 2 years in Indiana I applied to one job only and was hired as an assistant professor at the University of South Florida in Tampa. Jessica grew up in Florida and I had spent lots of time in the state, so this was closer to notions of home.

I was also attracted by the promise of a young and aspiring university setting in major and diverse metropolitan setting. The greater Tampa Bay area that the university serves has approximately as many people as the entire state of Indiana. We are the ninth largest college of education in the country and serve a diverse student body. Florida provides an interesting venue for research on accountability policy and immigrant students, which was the focus of my dissertation research, as well as interesting policy initiatives that play out across a diverse landscape of education. I was and am excited to work here.

CHURNING AND TURNING THROUGH FOUR DEPARTMENT CHAIRS, TWO INVESTIGATIONS, ONE SUBPOENA, AND AN APPLICATION FOR TENURE

This chapter is written at a particular point in time. As I write this, I am sending off my packet for external review, and by the time the piece is published, I may know whether I will earn tenure. Even through Gabriel's diagnosis and the stress of moving and trying to sell a house at the bottom of the real estate market, my arrival at this juncture has been more tumultuous than I expected. While I knew that there had been some tension in the department before I arrived, I did not realize the extent to which that lingered in the department and would come to be exacerbated through several events. When I arrived, an interim chair had started her third year in the position. As I participated in the recruitment of a new chair in the fall of 2007, I came to realize that three faculty members had been removed from committees and departmental deliberations, yet they taught in the department. This was unsettling as I tried to piece together notions of where I was. Then we got a new chair in the spring and that person was removed from the chair position in a little over a year. An associate dean came in and functioned as an interim chair for another year, and again I participated in a new chair search. We then hired the fourth chair I had in a little over 3 years of my tenure earning time period. This chair has stating publically that the number one priority is getting tenure for the assistant professors and I have moved forward with my work over the last year. However, during my second year I was called into two equal opportunity investigations that dealt with conflict in the department. The same year, a doctoral cohort of students wrote a letter to administration about lapses in the program. Last year I was subpoenaed as a third party witness to a case involving the department chair and a faculty member on another campus. Churning through this, one colleague stated that there was no difference between associate and assistant professors when it comes to service and teaching responsibilities, which was very different from my previous experience and personal perspective.

I have always enjoyed working for a community and in relationship with others. Yet, there have been times when I have taken on self-interested stances of removal—"the put your head down and do your work" school of thought. This is a stressful and sometimes anxious position for me and a few times I did notice that I become upset or angry more quickly than I usually do. A colleague described me as tense. I had work hard to slow down and concentrate on things I could do. I did find that networks and colleagues extend beyond the department level—national service becomes a great way to create friends and colleagues in the field. Finding colleagues in special education, foundations, and anthropology at the University of South Florida has been rewarding and they helped me to create more healthy and productive spaces during those times. Nevertheless, in 2009, I had no publications and I had a less than stellar annual review after strong reviews in previous years, as well as in 2010. Yet, this does mean that the anxiety of gaining tenure has felt fairly constant.

REFLECTIONS ON NOTIONS OF BALANCE

I am not convinced that balance is an appropriate term—there are swings and times in which there will be less balance for a short period of time. This fall I submit my tenure packet. David recently joined our family, as Gabriel became a big brother on April 8 and life seems busy. I feel that now as I push toward tenure and I am not as relaxed as I have been in other times in my life. I am not sure that will necessarily change, but that is not a bad thing either. Some tension can be productive, just as too much over time can be destructive.

What I have found is that I am more beholden to a schedule than before in my life. I do not do as well doing work at home—there is always a household task, a therapy schedule, an activity I could and should be doing with Gabriel and David. I limit my work related activities at home and do work in the office or in another space. I struggle with this, but I find it more useful to attempt to manage my energy on work tasks, rather than time (although a schedule is important). I can always do more at home. I can always do more at work. I have concluded that this will not change, so I do try to shorten and limit the scope of my work horizon, defining what I can today, this week, this month, this year and giving myself a break if I do not finish it all. In my calmer times, I know I just have to do the work I can for the day and have a sense of faith that things will get finished.

One strategy that I have come to embrace relates to strategically engaging the personal with the professional. Drawing from critical and poststructural perspectives I also engage the narrative that I construct of Gabriel's life in my teaching and research, as I begin from difference and contest marginalizing uses of the term "normal" (like "at risk") and try to point out that notions of disability are often invoked in order to invisibly construct the "able" (or the non-"at risk"). Although not trained in the area, I have begun to coalesce my "homework" with my professional work by making one of my areas of research focus disability, ethics, leadership, and the politics of special education. I am serving on special education doctoral students' dissertation committees and this provides a way for me to learn and to make connections in the Tampa Bay area. Nevertheless, I feel conflicted in that I know that I participated in practices that were poor as a teacher and administrator, and I may not know what I don't know, but I also know that disability policy and practice can be much better and that my work for Gabriel cannot be for his benefit alone.

When we were speaking of doctors that we might want to change, Jessica noted the other day: "they are practitioners, once a practice becomes common, then they will adopt it." I reflected on my own teaching and research. In our field we talk of common standards and students often want to be taught how to do things that are common in particular situations. Yet, most of the doctors we see have an appropriate checklist of procedures. Yes, I want competence in common practices, but I often think about how to help reach the uncommon with an orientation toward inquiry in my students—the same kind of curiosity and inquiry-centered practice I would like to see with Gabriel's doctors.

I also struggle with how to integrate my professional dispositions into personal practice. As we believe in inclusive practices, but we live in a district that I read as decidedly not committed to full inclusion for students with significant disabilities, the juggling chain saw metaphor seems appropriate. If Gabriel were to be "included" in a classroom with little schoolwide commitment to inclusion and set of integrated supports, he could become an isolated island in the mainstream of activities. Yet, continued complete segregation in the name of clustered skill-building supports is not only problematic in consequentialist terms, it is morally unacceptable in a human rights frame. I make compromises and I worry as I am convinced that inclusive supports were more robust in Indiana better in Indiana and certainly better in the other states. So, it is a source of tension, particularly as I get frustrated as not only a parent, but as someone who is supposed to prepare future leaders to have an impact on equitable and inclusive practices. And I know that when I argue as a parent I can be dismissed as emotional and as a professor, as theoretical. Yet to be fair, even if I were invited to do so, I do not have the time to fully commit to doing action research and taking on a supportive role in a school—particularly as this has not been the area of my training. This is a balance I will have to figure out and it will inevitably involve compromise.

What I often state to students is that those of us in education have the privilege doing meaningful and important work—something most people struggle to realize during their lives. My work-life and life-work can converge at powerful intersections. There are various and distinct pathways I expect to navigate in the future. As professors we can change the parameters of our jobs as we inquire into new phenomena that come to interest us. Gabriel has led me to a new dimension of inquiry to my professional life, as well as added purpose to my life as a professor and parent.

NOTE

1.   Readers can visit http://www.positiveexposure.org/ for counternarratives to texts of pathologized disability. More information on 18th chromosome issues may be found at www.chromosome18.org. In addition, http://www.disabilityisnatural.com/ is an excellent resource for teaching about people first stances and language.

CHAPTER 5

IN AND OUT

Finding Work-Life Balance as a Queer Scholar

Christa Boske

Three years ago at the age of 40, I found myself in the best work-life balance. For the first time, I did not fear being "out" at work. I received all of the same benefits and respect for my work and family as every other person employed at Kent State University. Sexual orientation was a protected marginalized group, domestic partnership benefits were offered, and equal rights signs were posted on faculty doorways in the School of Education. However, for most of my adult life as a teacher, school social worker, school leader, and assistant professor, I spent enormous amounts of energy experiencing an imbalance between work and life. For 20 years, I carefully considered my pronouns, responded to questions with more questions, and cleverly avoided sharing personal information. As a closeted, suburban, Midwest, White mother of an adopted Latina child and life partner of 15 years, being identified as a member of the underrepresented lesbian/gay/bisexual/transgender/queer/intersex/ally (LGBTQIA) presented its own particular challenges in leading schools and working in higher education. This chapter briefly focuses on two life-altering periods of my life. The first section of this chapter offers the reader insight to the repercussions of remaining a closeted queer school leader, and the second section illustrates steps I took to rebalance my work-life.

Juggling Flaming Chain Saws: Academics in Educational Leadership
Try to Balance Work and Family, pp. 37–44
Copyright © 2012 by Information Age Publishing

LIVING IN FEAR AS A CLOSETED QUEER

Throughout my entire university schooling, words such as "gay" or "lesbian" were not discussed in class by professors, peers, or within course readings. Universities I attended as well as public schools I served promoted a culture in which not all of its members demonstrated the inclusion of LGBTQIA populations. Words such as fag, dyke, and other derogatory terms were used not only to describe a group of people for which I identified; these terms were also used by my peers and colleagues. They used these words to discredit, isolate, and humiliate LGBTQIA adults and children.

During my doctoral work and first position as a school leader, my partner and I wanted to raise a child. However, I realized school district and state board policies did not support me as a queer school leader or being a pregnant "single" mother. Living and working in a Midwest state was difficult as a queer educator. "Out" queer leaders were fired for identifying as gay or lesbian, and queer parents were not allowed to foster or adopt children as a couple.

Throughout the 3-year process toward parenthood, doctoral studies, and leading schools, I did not feel safe sharing the most significant event of my life—becoming a mother—with peers, professors, or public school colleagues. I spent long hours preparing for our daughter's arrival. I realized as a closeted queer leader, I could not afford having a colleague discover my "other" life, so I remained private. I only discussed issues at work. This often resulted in me feeling lonely. I recognized the risks of becoming close friends with peers and colleagues. Sharing personal information might lead to sharing my "queer" life.

So what did that mean for me and finding work-life balance? I was definitely unbalanced. Not only did I not form close friendships with colleagues, I also immersed myself in work and school. I worked from 7:00-5:00 at school, taught from 6:00-10:00 at a community college, and attended doctoral classes on Friday evenings and Saturday from 8:00-5:00. I did not want to leave any room for someone to question what I did as a "single" woman with my time.

During the adoption process, one of the requirements was to ask my supervisor to write a letter of recommendation regarding my work ethic, ability to parent, and interactions with adults and children. This conversation was quite difficult for me. First, because I was mandated to ask Aeisha, my principal, to write a letter about me as a person, a potential parent, even though she knew nothing about my personal life. And second, I witnessed Aiesha use words such as faggot and dyke to discuss rumors about employees, to describe student behaviors (i.e., acting like a faggot), and making jokes about LGBTQIA populations. Therefore, I made a concerted effort to be a private person. I could not afford for Aiesha to associate me with being queer.

Aiesha was impressed with my strong work ethic; however, she worried about me. She thought I spent too much time at work versus life outside of school. Aeisha's concern translated into attempts to set me up on blind dates, because she, as well as others with whom I worked, did not want me to be "lonely." When she attempted to fix me up, I made up excuses about prior commitments. I appreciated Aiesha's efforts, but I was also conscious of the possibility of losing my job, because I was queer.

As the adoption process continued, Aeisha grew more concerned about my work-life balance. She realized my commitment to children, families, and the community at large played a significant role in my life. Aeisha wondered how I would "juggle" my doctoral work, school leadership position, adjunct position, and being a "single mother." I shared with her the decision I made to save my sick days over several years in order to take family medical Leave (FML). I knew I had to make choices about my time and priorities, which centered on my daughter, but at the same time, I also realized I could not stop working. Aeisha was impressed with my ability to "juggle" my new responsibilities as a single mother, my commitment to the school, and the sick leave/personal days I saved along the way to prepare for parenthood.

Before I left for my FML, the faculty and staff surprised me with a baby shower. They were extremely supportive of me wanting to be a "single" mother of an adopted child, and offered to help me in any way they could. This extra support included babysitting, advice, and a listening ear. When I returned after 3 months of FML, I was offered a position as a principal at another inner-city school. Although the driving involved 2½ hours one way, which meant I left for work at 4:30 A.M. and returned by 8:30 P.M., I was under the impression the move to this district would afford me an opportunity to be "out." Both district and county policies stated employees could not be discriminated against due to sexual orientation. However, although policies protected employees who identified as gay or lesbian, several central office school leaders in this district made derogatory comments during private and public meetings about LGBTQIA populations. These derogatory comments included accusing gays and lesbians of being pedophiles, perverts, and involving themselves in the child sex slave trade. Some adults even made comments about threatening the safety of LGBTQIA people, because they were considered social deviants, and "didn't deserve to live."

When faculty, support staff, families, and children asked whether or not I was a parent, I chose to share being a mother of an adopted 1-year old Latina child. I was careful not to mention my life partner. I feared losing my job due to hostile comments made about LGBTQIA people. I worked long hours, drove 5 hours each day to and from work, came to school on the weekends, and committed myself to improving student learning. I was spending 80 hours a week at work versus taking time for my daughter, family, and personal health. Being closeted added to my stress on the job. I did not feel comfortable responding to queer jokes or derogatory remarks about gays and lesbians. I feared for my professional livelihood and safety.

Over time, one person made the decision to use my choice to remain private as an opportunity to interrogate my personal life. The threat came as a response to a person's increasing discomfort with her work ethic. Janice, a central office leader, felt uneasy when she was confronted by her superiors about her attendance and required service to multiple schools. She was responsible for reporting to schools several times per week for full school days; yet, it may have been weeks before anyone saw Janice on their campus. As she received more and more pressure as to why she was not attending to her responsibilities on our campus, she seemed to search for ways to divert attention away from her attendance issues.

Janice requested a mandatory meeting with me after everyone had left the building. She closed the office doors even though no one was in the building. She made it clear that the purpose of the meeting was to uncover what was "wrong" with me. Janice said I was too private about my personal life. She shared her suspicions of me hiding something. And finally, she accused me of being a pedophile. Janice pointed her finger at me. She said she would find out exactly what was "wrong" with me.

I remember driving home late that night. My head was pounding. I could feel my headache in my eyes, jaw, and neck. I was nauseated. And later, I experienced chest pains. My heart would race and I would start to sweat. I was under enormous stress, and the experience significantly disrupted my work-life balance as a closeted queer leader and new mother of an adopted child. I decided to share the incident with central office. During the discussion, the people with whom I spoke were in disbelief. They called Janice into the office to discuss the situation. She admitted to making the accusations. One of the central office members asked her, "So you said this to Christa? You accused of being a pedophile?" Janice replied, "Yes." The person asking the question shook his head in disbelief. The other person asked, "Why would you say something like this to her?" Janice replied, "Because I know there is something wrong with her. She is just too private."

After explaining how I understood the reason why Janice may have lashed out in a hostile manner, one of the central office members informed me Janice did not mean anything by the comments made. He explained it was now my responsibility to apologize to Janice for the miscommunication. I reiterated the significance of making false accusations toward employees, and the implications of making derogatory comments regarding pedophilia; however, I was informed again, no harm was done, and it was my responsibility to "clear the air" with Janice.

I decided to take a leap of faith and share this experience with Janice with Hannah, an administrator in my doctoral program. She identified herself as an "out" lesbian. After sharing the accusations made toward me, Hannah grew concerned about my welfare. She took me under her wing and introduced me to "out" professors on campus, invited me to LGBTQIA functions, and offered support throughout my school leadership experiences. I was encouraged by Hannah, who knew I was queer, as well as other professors, who did not know I was queer, to enter higher education due to my experiences, passion, and efforts to build bridges between underrepresented and mainstream populations in schools.

I accepted a position at a southern university specifically because the university's personnel policy did not discriminate against employees due to their sexual orientation. I assumed I could be "out" and be safe, but I was wrong. I traveled with my parents across the country in a U-Haul leaving my daughter and life-partner behind, because we had not sold our home. I lived in an apartment by myself over a thousand miles away for several months from my family and LGBTQIA community. I requested a meeting with my mentor Daniel in order to deepen my understanding of what was expected of me as a new faculty member teaching three new courses. My mentor made comments about my physical appearance by informing me of my beautiful blue eyes, looking me up and down, and saying "mmm … mmm … mmm." Daniel continually asked me why I wore a ring on my left hand, what it symbolized, and who I was dating. After attempting to focus on the development of courses versus his inappropriate questions and remarks, I responded, "Her name is Rebecca." I felt confident in my response due to the university's personnel policy; however, Daniel immediately excused himself from the table. He returned and informed me I would be fired for being queer. I went back into the closet for 2 more years.

OUTING MYSELF AS A QUEER FACULTY MEMBER

No matter how much I prepared to come out at work, I was reminded time and time again of the courage necessary to come to terms with what it means to be "out." Finding work-life balance finally happened for me when I attended Gay Straight Alliance (GSA) meetings at a national leadership conference. Through my involvement with the GSA, I met faculty across the country who were "out" at their universities. Listening to scholars who identified as queer, scholars who were allies of queers, and faculty whose research focused on the lived experiences of queers opened my eyes to discovering work-life balance. I learned how living in the closet robbed me of living a full life, of being at peace with myself, and the liberation of outing oneself in safe spaces.

I met Autumn K. Tooms at the GSA session. She invited me to apply for the assistant professor position at Kent State University. During my interview, I did not share my personal life, but I took notice of the Equal Rights signs posted on doors throughout the School of Education. I also remember faculty using words such as queer, gay, and lesbian in positive ways. These terms were associated with research agendas, university student organizations, and populations to address in course work. I remember being offered the position before I left for the airport. I felt relieved, because for the first time in my educational career, being "out" and being "safe" was a *real* possibility. I saw it on campus. I heard it during conversations. I felt it when I interacted with potential colleagues.

Through this journey, the freedom of being out shifted from an abstraction of work-life balance to a lived reality. One week later, after accepting the position, I received a phone call from my future dean. He wanted to share some "exciting news" with me. Kent State University decided to offer domestic partnership benefits. The dean wanted me to know that if I had someone "special" in my life, then this person would receive the same benefits afforded to people who were legally married. He asked me if the university could fly me back to Kent, Ohio, to look for housing. For the first time, I felt safe acknowledging the existence of my family. I asked the dean if he would allow my life partner Rebecca and 4-year old daughter to search for housing with me. Not only did he offer to pay for their plane tickets, he told me about organizations on and off campus that might be of interest to me and my family. Again, he said, "Me and my family." The potency of self-affirmation as an "out" queer assistant professor provided me with a fresh start—a new beginning for me in my search for work-life balance.

The more I came out during casual conversations at work, displayed photos of my family including my brother and his husband, and addressing LGBTQIA topics throughout my courses, the more dramatically the process improved my work-life balance. I know no longer felt the need to hide, which translated into feeling like a second-class citizen. I was out to my neighbors, my daughter's teachers, and colleagues. I did not feel the need to pour myself into my work in order to avoid conversations or close friendships.

I became more confident in my ability to come out to people at work and within the community at large. Autumn played a significant role in affording me spaces to feel comfortable coming out at Kent State University. I looked to her as a mentor and trusted friend. Autumn asked me to write about my journey for a chapter in our upcoming coedited book. The book focused on the lived experiences of faculty who faced issues of social justice and equity. Autumn thought this was an excellent for conducting a self-study. Engaging in this work was the most uncomfortable and difficult process for me as a junior faculty member. I recognized why this study was stressful. I had to "come out" in writing. I realized readers would have access to *knowing me* in personal, private ways. However, despite my increased anxiety, again, it improved my work-life balance. I no longer perceived coming out as something to be held against me.

I felt more comfortable in coming to terms with my sexual identity. The process of outing myself as a queer scholar, parent, and neighbor was a gradual process. I became more conscious of what I chose not to say rather than what I said to people. For example, I was invited to be a representative for the LGBTQ studies at Kent State University. In the past, I would have panicked as to why someone might ask me to participate in such an organization and would have declined the offer in fear of being associated with queers. But now, I felt comfortable being a representative, an ally, a member, and an advocate for LGBTQIA studies. Not only did I volunteer to be on the committee, I also noted my membership on my vita for my annual review.

During one of the LGBTQ study meetings, the organization's chair announced the need for volunteers for a panel discussion titled "The Modern Family." Undergraduate students of the university's Gay Straight Alliance were working in coordination with other university student organizations to stimulate dialogue about problematizing what it meant to be a member of a modern family. The chair announced the need for an LGBTQIA family to speak at the evening event.

I went home and asked Rebecca and our 7-year old daughter if they would be interested in volunteering for the panel presentation. We discussed the significance of deepening understanding and knowledge about people who may differ from them, especially in the area of sexual diversity. As the presentation grew closer and closer, my family grew more excited about the opportunity. They were preparing themselves to discuss the positives of being a queer family, lived realities we faced, and ways we worked together to address challenges along the way.

We arrived 15 minutes early. All of the chairs were empty. We wondered if the event would be cancelled; however, at the top of the hour approximately 150 people arrived. Rebecca, our daughter and I shared our lived experiences and responded to questions from the hosts of the event. After the panel discussion, my family spent additional time being interviewed by a journalist, and the interview as well as a photo of us as a member of the new modern gay family was published by the university.

I shared the opportunity with my brother Glenn, who is also queer and legally married. I have only witnessed my brother cry a few times—my grandparents' funerals, coming out, and his wedding day. His emotional response surprised me. Glenn shared how proud he was of me and my family for having the courage to speak openly about being queer. He believed this significant experience would improve my work-life experience as a scholar, a parent, and a partner. These experiences impacted my daughter's life in significant ways. She feels confident speaking openly with her teachers, neighbors, friends, and strangers about having two mommies. My daughter identified herself at the age of 5 as a "social justice leader" and "wants to be a professor like Mommy because she teaches people to be kind and accepting of one another … because we are all brothers and sisters." My daughter's sense of hope is inspiring, and encourages me to continue to strive for inner peace as well as the courage to bring people together for a common purpose.

I realize the process of outing myself is gradual process. I am committed to improving my work-life balance as a mother, partner, and scholar. As I reflect on the impact of external and internal factors briefly discussed in this chapter that span over 22 years, I recognize the courage necessary to establish and reestablish work-life balance. Maintaining balance between my personal and professional life is complex and often challenging. Taking care of myself and coming to terms with my sexual identity occurred because of love and support from family and friends, as well as my willingness, ability, and commitment to doing the necessary work. Although I have much more to learn, I am still actively engaged in the process of finding work-life balance. I continuously reflect on these experiences—how they influence who I am, who I have become, and who I strive to be.

CHAPTER 6

myworklifebalance.edu

Melanie C. Brooks

My office is the kitchen table. I often find myself sitting among cereal crumbs and coffee working to catch-up with the conversation that occurred overnight. I teach online classes which, love it or hate it, are here to stay. I've taught education and library science classes online for 2 years, and when I entered the professorate I did not think that I would be teaching online as much as I have, but online learning is rapidly expanding in higher education. It is profitable for the institution and offers flexibility for nontraditional students. My class sizes are large and I often work with a teaching assistant, however, I struggle with finding a good balance between the demands of 130 students a semester, meeting the needs of my four young children, and finding time for my husband and myself. I have yet to find a good way to balance these conflicting needs, but some days are better balanced than others.

When I see students interested in a topic and engaged in conversations, the amount of time I spend "discussing" can easily get away from me and 1 hour at the kitchen table turns into 4. I use quotes around the word "discussing" because it really is an asynchronous, typed conversation that may or may not receive a response to a question posed, an idea challenged, or an insight made. Although not all lines of inquiry will be discussed, my best days are filled with students excitedly posting responses to each other, pushing their classmates' to see topics in different ways or with new meanings. My worst days are filled with feelings of isolation from my

Juggling Flaming Chain Saws: Academics in Educational Leadership
Try to Balance Work and Family, pp. 45–50
Copyright © 2012 by Information Age Publishing
All rights of reproduction in any form reserved.

coworkers and students with no office neighbor to bounce an idea off of, grab a coffee with, or discuss the opinion that was strongly stated. What follows are my experiences teaching online, its benefits (yes, there are some) and detriments (yes, we can probably all name a few). Of course my experiences are unique and mine alone; however, I hope that you will find a little of yourself in my quest for balance at a time when online teaching has become a 24/7 occupation.

balancingworkwithbaby.net

I was in labor, bouncing on a birthing ball, and teaching two online courses. I chose not to take time off because there was a month left in the semester and this was my fourth child. I did not tell my students that I was expecting and that my due date was in late March. Being an experienced mom, I could do it all, couldn't I? I did let my teaching assistant know that I was having a baby and would probably not be online as much that week. His response was positive and said that he would work to facilitate conversations on the discussion board. I went into labor on a Tuesday night and I wanted to comment on the discussion board to advance the week's discussion, even if it was only to spark a conversation. In between contractions I read posts and typed responses. Eddie wrote, "Intellectual freedom for all people is essential to a functioning democracy." I responded, "How do you feel about districtwide filtering software? What role do schools have in 'protecting' children from 'dangerous' informa- tion?" On to the next post. Susan commented that as a teacher and a Christian, she would not choose or allow her students to read materials that supported a homosexual lifestyle, giving the example of the book *And Tango Makes Three* by Justin Richardson and Peter Parnell. I responded, "What if you have a student in your class with two moms? Will this change the way you interact with this child? How would you explain this to a child who might ask you why Joe has two moms?" Okay, needed to breathe. Another contraction.

I then clicked through several links to view the progress of discussion in my second class. Two people posted thus far. As I tried to think of a com- ment, a nurse interrupted for a blood pressure reading. Everything was fine, as I expected. I refocused and breathed through a contraction. I read Jane's post, "the American system of education is often imposed on devel- oping countries without care for local customs, local economies, and local needs." Steven responded, "Yes, but globalization makes it necessary that kids in developing countries have an education that gives them the opportunities to be employable and earn a good living." Another contrac- tion. Okay. I thought about what to say. I commented, "Let's consider our individual beliefs as to the purpose of education. Is the purpose to develop skills for the workplace? To understand Shakespeare? To be able to work well with others? What should schooling include and who decides?" And with that, I closed my laptop to concentrate on the task at hand.

The next day Jürgen slept peacefully swaddled on the bed and I was back online. Checking. Commenting. It was a difficult delivery. The baby didn't breathe. He had a tube coming out of a vein in his head. I was tired. But I continued to type. In my experience, graduate students in online classes expect immediate responses to their questions and comments. My evaluations are largely dependent on how students experience me as a teacher, and that means my active participation in the classes. Consequently, I feel pressured to be "on call" when classes are in session, even if that means working while I am in labor. When my phone signals an e-mail, I check it, even if I am in the middle of dinner with my family. When I have a minute to spare, I check the discussion board on my laptop. I want students to have a positive learning experience, but the question I can't seem to answer: What personal cost must I bear to be a successful online instructor?

multitaskingisamust.com

One of the benefits of teaching online is my ability to work from home and be the primary caretaker of my young son. To do this effectively, I am an expert at multitasking. Finding the necessary time to work amongst diaper changes, laundry loads, vacuuming, grocery shopping, baby feedings, and dog walking is often challenging—and to be honest, at times rather boring. I find myself working when the baby is sleeping, forcing myself to ignore the mess made by the six little hands that hurried to eat breakfast before catching the school bus. I dislike a messy house, but I've learned to ignore the chaos because the time available to work uninterrupted is too fleeting. It just takes a small cry to lose my train of thought. I will find it again later, often late at night after bath time and bedtime stories.

I can't complain though. I have the opportunity to hold Jürgen when he wakes from a nap, watch him run around the house, and listen to his babbling. I greet my three daughters when they arrive home from school. But, I have to ask myself, even though I am home, am I really present? So often I have my head in my computer working. Frequently (I am ashamed to admit) I find my daughter trying to talk with me about an event from school and I do not hear her because I am focused on responding to an e-mail or reading a post. When I catch myself doing this, I stop, look up, and ask her to repeat what she said, which she obliges. In the afternoons, Jürgen plays in his playroom and the girls go downstairs to watch television. Mom is home, but the teacher is at work. In our society, multitasking is a good skill to have. But, am I really multitasking or just misappropriating my tasks? How do I balance the demands of online teaching with the face-to-face needs of my children? Do I have the luxury to stop, put down the computer, and yet not shortchange anyone? I really don't know, but I would hazard a guess that someone will get the short end of the stick. Could that be me?

imaginaryequilibrium.org

Even though I seek to find balance, it is common that I become irritable and frustrated when faced with recurrent student questions and problems. I answer their concerns supportively, directing them to where the information is in the syllabus or explained in the assignments, but underneath the nice e-mail I am frequently aggravated. I wonder if students read the syllabus, my comments, the announcements, the discussion boards, and the requirements for successfully completing the course. Miscommunication is an exasperating aspect of online teaching because so much emphasis is placed on comprehending the written word. To give a small example, at the beginning of each class I ask the students to sign their e-mails with their full name and identify the class in which they are enrolled. I cannot know all the students' usernames and so when hhb329 or bcj219 e-mails me without identifying who they are, my feathers become ruffled and I think, didn't they read the announcement and the syllabus where e-mail guidelines are clearly addressed? Little annoyances like this consume a lot of valuable time. To respond to hhb329 or bcj219, I spend 5 minutes clicking through multiple secure pages and passwords to match the username to the student.

Other time consuming online aggravations that upset my imaginary equilibrium include: students not closely reading posts and misinterpreting a classmate's or my intent; not answering questions asked or writing answers to questions not asked; misspelling words (principal versus principle); and providing excuses as to lack of participation (illnesses, computers crashing, work demands, travel, honeymoons). I spend a lot of time juggling responsibilities and find that I have little patience with student excuses and questions that are answered in course documents. Responding takes time to think through. It also takes time away from teaching and reinforcing concepts, explaining theories, and discussing experiences. It diminishes my joy of teaching and overall happiness, a state of mind that has a tendency to seep into every corner of the house. I do not want the tensions of my work life to influence my home life, but when home is also the office, leaving the stresses of work at work is simply not possible.

teachinginpajamas.biz

One of the simple benefits of online instruction is the ability to teach in pajamas. What a privilege to do so, not to mention the money saved on gas and a professional wardrobe! Although this sounds pleasant, there is another side worth mentioning: professional isolation. Wearing casual clothing everyday makes me feel unprofessional and unworthy of a professional position. Not getting up and out the door in the mornings easily develops into slow-moving days with the only "meetings" to attend are online conversations. Yes, I do have the benefit of staying home with my toddler and many mothers would love the opportunity. However, it is a trade-off that I wrestle with on a daily basis. Being out of the loop exacerbates feelings of isolation. Coworkers do not take interest in what or how I teach. This lack of concern or care is coupled with the glaring absence of professional support and instructor development. In my experience, I am wholly alone. I am responsible for every aspect of the class. Whether anyone is aware of my instructional choices and teaching abilities remains a question unanswered.

youtubeandbeyond.co.uk

In order to make online education engaging for both my students and myself, I take advantage of the vast resources available on the Internet. Several of my classes benefited from my teaching assistants' online participation while they lived in other countries or studied abroad. First hand accounts from India, Egypt, and Korea provided students unique opportunities to ask questions and receive answers from "people in the field." When I do not have students reporting from the field, I look to online resources to help explain concepts. I incorporate videos, websites, and other Internet resources into the questions I pose and in the comments I provide. I spend hours searching for the right website or video to explain a leadership theory. Often I find informative interviews of researchers and practitioners. Including this type of e-content takes time, and as a consequence, I find that hours pass quickly. I am frustrated when this happens, but I do take my role of instructor seriously. The time invested in creating and sustaining an engaging course is more than most people understand (or may want to invest).

This past semester I traveled to the United Kingdom for 2 weeks to arrange a faculty-led study abroad program. The main reason behind the development of the program was to give distance students the opportunity to meet their classmates and build community. It would also give my coworker and me the opportunity personally meet the program's students and establish new international contacts. With only a 6-hour time difference between the two countries, I was able to participate seamlessly in the two online classes while I traveled on trains, lounged on hotel beds, met with British faculty, and visited a friend's cottage in Bognor Regis. The students knew I was traveling and my ability to continue teaching was significant because it allowed me to frame our discussions in a global context. The ability to teach from anywhere at any time is an extraordinary opportunity available to online instructors. Yet, students still want the face-to-face learning opportunities. I hope that creating an abroad program for distance students will break down feelings of isolation, not just for them but also for me.

sowhatnow.edu

After all this, so what? What does my experience show about online instruction and achieving a balance in my professional and personal life? Well, my answer in four words or less: "get used to it." Online learning is changing the face of higher education because it provides educational and career advancement opportunities through an accessible, flexible, and 24/7 format. Additionally, online programs generate new revenue sources for universities at a time when financial support is lessening and costs are increasing. More universities, colleges, departments, schools, and programs are developing online programs to expand their reach, with many offering programs in countries around the world. What does this mean for an online instructor? How can I find satisfaction in both my personal and professional lives when the demands of teaching are so high? Will it be worthwhile to create an abroad program for distance students? Honestly, I don't know and I do worry that the demands placed on me will keep increasing as more and more students enroll. But, for now, I continue working to find a balance that meets the needs of both my family and my students. I don't have the answer yet, but I do believe that it is worthwhile to strive for a work-life balance that will provide my family with a mom that they (and I) can live with.

CHAPTER 7

THE "GOOD MOTHER"

One Woman's Battle
With the Hegemony of Work-Life Balance

Leslie Hazle Bussey

I am a working wife and mother and I have a story to tell. This is not a story for women who have waited all their lives to have babies. This is not a story for women whose "clocks are ticking." I am in my late 30s and my clock has never ticked. This is a declaration that is difficult for me to make because virtually every social message about "what I should be," direct or indirect, has told me that if I am both female and alive, by this point I would have been overwrought with a biological impulse to procreate.

One might wonder how such a person came to be. All the usual factors pointed to a person whose clock would be ticking so loud, you could hear it right now as you read this. I am the daughter of a commander in the U.S. Navy. A self-described depression baby, my father grew up in a modest home in Ohio, served his country, and spent his vital years working to provide for his family. My mother grew up in Manila during World War II. She told me that from the time she was a little girl, she dreamed of marrying an American serviceman and coming to America to raise a family. She did just that and within a short time, had two little boys—my older brothers, 5 and 6 years older than me. My mother's dream was nearly com-

Juggling Flaming Chain Saws: Academics in Educational Leadership
Try to Balance Work and Family, pp. 51–55

plete. Except that her sister was a dressmaker for prominent socialites in Manila, and my mom spent her youth in Manila's high society modeling my Tita's beautiful dresses accessorized with impossibly high-heeled and breathtakingly beautiful shoes. My mother had a biological need to dress a child in pink ruffles and bows, and my brothers weren't meeting that need. When they found out she was pregnant with me (this was in pre-ultrasound days), my parents painted the nursery pink and put a canopy over the crib. If the wishes of their hearts were to come true, I would be the girliest girl in the history of the world.

My mom sprinkled my childhood with remarks like, "You need to learn how to cook because someday you will need to cook for your husband and children." My dad would say, "The divorce rate is 50% so chances are good someday you will be responsible for taking care of your children by yourself." It was a done deal for him that I would have children, but he was modern enough to consider that I wouldn't need a man. All the while, my mom faithfully stayed home and modeled the pinnacle of all I could hope to be as a woman by spending the bulk of her days planning, preparing and cleaning up dinner for her family. (And she can make some mean lumpia and pancit).

The sum of my life experience to that point created a psychology of "should" that differed profoundly from the reality of me. I mainly blamed my parents' expectations for this discrepancy, and wrote them off as old-fashioned and culturally inaccessible. Little did I know then that this battle of "should" versus me would become the central conflict in my quest for work-life balance.

Eventually I found a partner who understood me, and shared my expectations for who I wanted to be rather than comparing me against a vision of who I should be. We had a marvelous 9 months of marriage before the night I learned that I was pregnant. (It's been a spectacular 12 years of marriage since then, to be sure, but it changed dramatically that night). I had such reservations about becoming a mother that I essentially denied the whole thing right through my daughter's first birthday.

But when she was a year old, we moved from Boston—and my full-time job and network of friends—to the suburbs of St. Louis, where the low cost of living meant that I could "live the dream" of staying home with my toddler. I hunkered down and threw myself into being mommy: I made homemade play dough; I transformed meal planning into an elaborate system of menus and calendars; Gymboree class was on Monday, Mommy & Me swim class was Wednesday, and Kindermusik was on Friday. Everywhere I turned, I heard messages that told me I should be happier than I'd ever been: *Having a stay-at-home mom is the best thing for children. Women who can afford to stay home with their children are lucky. Staying at home with children is the most important work a woman can do.*

Of course, with all my heart and mind I wanted to provide an affirming and loving home to my daughter. But I also felt myself dying. And I worried most of all that by starving my own needs, I would be unable to be the mother my daughter needed and deserved. I spiraled into unhappiness and depression feeling condemned to a life of failure. If I rejected this "opportunity" to stay home, it would be a tacit rejection of my daughter and a personal failure to step up to my responsibilities. If I stayed at home where I was "supposed" to, I would fail as a person, incarcerating my intellectual identity in Elmo's World.

Reason did not play a very prominent role during this dark time. Everything was about either/or. My warped senses framed everything as an epic choice between good (everyone else) and evil (me). Ideas about what "should" be were deep-seated and pervasive, and were much louder and clearer than my own aspirations and beliefs.

It was on a trip by myself to California visiting my brother that some rational thinking was reintroduced. My brother made an off-hand remark that my child was having such a different experience with me as her mother than any of us had in our home. It was a basic statement of fact, but it blew me away. I could be a mother, and not be *my* mother. I felt that the heavens opened up and poured out celestial knowledge. I *was* a mother! I had been for 15 months. And I was *still* Leslie. I could be both a mother *and* Leslie. I didn't have to choose. It was not a choice at all. It was not *either/or*. It was *and/also*.

Armed with a new understanding that I had to forge my own path, I returned home with many questions. I needed to break down these external expectations that I had accepted as barriers to my happiness. What did *I* want, and what expectations was I allowing some unnamed "they" to impose on me? Who were these people with these expectations I was so afraid to defy? My parents? They lived 2,500 miles away. And I was approaching 30 years old. My neighbors in suburban St. Louis? They scrapbooked, played bunco, and wore Christmas sweaters. I was nothing like them. I couldn't identify anyone who had any power over my life that would be disappointed if I got happy. It didn't take very long for me to realize that I was the Trojan horse of my own demise.

All of the messages that I was loaded up with while growing up through some combination of social forces and unique conditions of my experience came to attack me from within, and I passively allowed it. Was it true *for me and my child* that staying home was best? What measures would satisfy *my standards* of being a "good mother"? I realized I could log thousands of hours making homemade play dough and not begin to approach my vision of influence on my child. It required an explicit articulation and intentional embrace of my values and vision of my role in my child's life for me to overcome the crippling externally imposed, but fully internalized, picture of what I "should" be as a mother.

My journey to listen to and privilege my own voice over others' expectations of me continues, but along the way I have learned the discipline of blocking out messages from outside my family and looking no further than myself or my children to tell me whether I am doing "enough" for us. While my relationship with work-life balance—characterized by a joyful sense of emancipation every time I kiss my children good bye as I head off to work—is different from the common struggles I hear from my friends who yearn for more time with their children, I do suspect that the underlying pathology is the same: there is an externally defined notion of how much time is "enough" time to spend with children, and working parents never have enough time. Who is defining "enough"? How do you know it's not enough? Not enough for whom? (And for the record, I feel just as joyful when I walk back through the door each evening and we hug and kiss each other like I've been away at war rather than working for 7 hours down the road while they are at school).

If I wanted to get all feminist and critical theorist, I would say we need to ask who benefits from creating this sense of dissatisfaction in working parents that we are not doing well enough for our children? Do these commonly accepted norms disproportionately impact women? What values are perpetuated by the very notion of "work-life balance"? Is the quest for work-life balance a marker of privilege? What assumptions about our children—their capacity and their dependency on us—are implicit in our work-life struggle? What impact does our anxiety over work-life balance have on our children?

Indeed, what lessons can I learn from this coming-of-age experience that are useful in the context of my work, which is concerned with preparing school and district leaders to enact leadership that in many ways defies societal expectations for what "should" be? The very same constraints of external or presumed expectations shackle schools and districts. Small communities especially are tightly bound to the way they have always done things. *"African American students have never enrolled in AP courses, so they shouldn't start doing so now." "Students from economically disadvantaged families are always going to drop out, so it's just a moot point to try to identify early warning indicators and develop interventions to keep them on track."* Enacting leadership that defies those expectations is an act of extraordinary courage and conviction, and like my defiance of expectations that I would be the happiest and most successful stay-at-home mommy that ever lived, it comes with a good share of censure from people whose disapproval is hurtful. But in both cases, the short-term hurt pales in comparison to the long-term pain, whether it be a community of children systematically raised to conform to a desolate image of what students of color from low-income families "should" be, or a single person, a mother, who systematically subverts her true self to serve a false image of who others think she "should" be.

CODA

Today I am the mother of two school-aged children and am working full time with an intermediary organization that builds leadership capacity in districts across Georgia. I am tired at the end of the day and feel pretty good if I manage to cook a proper meal twice a week. I don't make it to every single school function. But my daughters understand that I choose to work, that my work helps leaders and teachers to be the best they can be for the kids they serve, that I love what I do, and that no matter where I am, I love them with an unstoppable, immeasurable, unimaginable love.

You are certainly welcome to nominate me for the Mommy Dearest Hall of Fame and think to yourself that my children are destined for the FBI's Most Wanted. You may be right.

I'm afraid what you think no longer matters to me.

CHAPTER 8

FANTASIES AND STRATEGIES

A Graduate Student's Critical Examination of Work-Life Balance

Bradley W. Carpenter

Commissioned by the nonprofit organization Grad Resources, sociologist Dr. Robert Woodberry recently conducted a study surveying over 675 graduate students to examine the patterns of stress that exist for persons pursuing advanced degrees (Repak, 2010). Woodberry's findings revealed the majority of today's graduate students suffer from "emotional fatigue" while struggling to secure the "elusive balanced life" (para. 9). Over the course of the past several years, the efforts of graduate students to achieve such a balance have been complicated by the ascension of neoliberal ideology within the field of higher education, as individual and social agency have been primarily defined through "market-driven notions of individualism, competition, and consumption" (Giroux, 2002, p. 426).

Thus, while the values of democracy and equity upon which public universities were originally founded have not been completely displaced, they are often overshadowed by policies informed by the discourses of efficiency and accountability (Rivzi & Lingard, 2010). Consequently, while policymakers at the state level continue to defund public universities, administrators, professors and graduate students are finding it increas-

Juggling Flaming Chain Saws: Academics in Educational Leadership Try to Balance Work and Family, pp. 57–64

ingly difficult to maintain a healthy work-life balance. Graduate students in today's universities are negatively effected by the stress imposed on supervising professors who are asked to simultaneously defend and increase their research efforts, while being audited through productivity analyses used to quantify an institution's return on investment. As a 2011 PhD graduate of a Tier I university I can personally attest to the substantial pressures currently being placed on professors and graduate students within institutions of higher education. Additionally, as a husband and father of three children under the age of 9, I can verify that such pressures are not conducive to an individual's struggle to secure a healthy work-life balance.

The premise of this chapter is that the ability of today's graduate student to obtain the proper work-life balance is significantly influenced by the discourses of neoliberal ideology and the shallow enactment of democracy, what Dean (2009) refers to as *communicative capitalism*. To support this argument I call upon two resources: (a) Dean's (2009) critique of communicative capitalism, and (b) a narrative examination of the lessons learned during my attempts as a PhD graduate student to secure what I considered to be a reasonable work-life balance.

The purposes of this chapter are to expand the conversation regarding graduate work-life balance by recognizing the ways in which communicative capitalism has altered the contextual constructs of higher education. Additionally, this chapter is meant to offer insight to both professors and graduate students that operate within this context by describing the specific strategies developed when attempting to balance my scholarly responsibilities with issues pertaining to marriage, fatherhood and personal well-being.

To accomplish these purposes the remainder of the chapter is divided into two sections. Within the first section I provide a brief explanation of Dean's (2009) concept of communicative capitalism, thus outlining what I consider to be the contextual circumstances that influenced my experiences as a graduate student. In the second section I briefly describe the animated consequences of communicative capitalism, discuss my understanding of how such consequences effect today's graduate students, review a selection of coping strategies developed throughout my PhD career, and provide a brief synopsis of lessons learned.

COMMUNICATIVE CAPITALISM
AND ITS EFFECT ON HIGHER EDUCATION

Dean (2009) suggests critics opposed to the neoliberal assault on higher education have failed as a result of "communicative capitalism," which she frames as a "democracy that talks without responding" (p. 22). It is within this shallow enactment of democracy where the *mediated dimension* of politics—a democratic arena where varied interests struggle to gain recognition through television, radio, websites, blogs, et cetera—is seemingly disconnected to the *institutional dimension* of politics—a democratic arena where decision making is determined primarily amongst bureaucrats, lawmakers, judges and other representatives of the state (Dean, 2009).

Therefore, the political capital of interests advocating against the neoliberal reconfiguration of higher education has been weakened by the "multiplication of resistances and assertions" (p. 22), and have been unable to build and sustain the successful political counter movement necessary to alter the current trajectory of higher education policy. Consequently, the contextual constructs of higher education are increasingly shaped by the market-based assumptions underlying neoliberal ideology, as institutions of higher learning continue to outsource job responsibilities to temporary faculty and private providers; dispense of disciplines and subjects not directly related to science, technology, engineering and mathematics; increase student count numbers and tuition costs; and publicly question the value of academic freedom and tenure (Giroux, 2011).

In the following sections I highlight Dean's (2009) understanding of how communicative capitalism is animated, share my interpretations of how these animations influence the experiences of today's graduate student, outline the strategies developed in an effort to work toward what I believed was an appropriate work-life balance, and summarize the lessons learned during my tenure as graduate student within a highly competitive PhD program.

SEEKING PATHS OF VICTORY IN AN ERA OF COMMUNICATIVE CAPITALISM: STRATEGIES OF A HUSBAND/FATHER/GRADUATE

When I began my PhD journey in 2006 I was 31 years old, had two children under the age of 3, and had just left my position as a public school principal. Five years and one child later, I am working through my first full year as an assistant professor. During my tenure as a graduate student I learned as much about my values and myself as I learned about the ways in which education policy should be crafted for the future generations of children in the United States. My experience as a graduate student was always challenging, often rewarding, and sometimes overwhelming. It is my hope that by describing a number of my experiences as a graduate student this chapter may provide a glimmer of hope and/or insight, both for professors who are tasked with guiding graduate students, and for those students who are just beginning their journey as a PhD scholar.

THE FANTASY OF ABUNDANCE: QUANTITY VERSUS QUALITY

Within her critique of communicative capitalism, Dean (2009) highlights three "fantasies" which are animated through this particular enactment of democracy: abundance, participation, and wholeness. While the fantasy of wholeness is an important concept in Dean's work, I chose to focus on the fantasies of abundance and participation, as it is my interpretation that these two fantasies most directly determine whether or not today's graduate student is able to establish a reasonable work-life balance. The first fantasy, that of *abundance*, is characterized by the belief that "enhanced communications access facilitates democracy" (p. 25). Dean believes this fantasy shields democratic participants from understanding, as the abundant production of work/opinions are diluted within the "larger flow of data" (p. 26). It has been my experience that the relentless pursuit of *abundance* directly influences the ability of graduate students to secure an appropriate work-life balance.

Graduate Implications

"Publish or perish" is a mantra that haunts those seeking tenured positions within higher education. This refrain directly relates to the fantasy of abundance, as the values guiding decision making within higher education are increasingly influenced by the precepts of today's "audit culture."[1] Consequently, it is assumed that professors and graduate scholars should be judged on their ability to publish numerous articles within peer-reviewed journals. Yet, as most persons have been taught since primary school, the difference between quality and quantity are often vast. While professors and graduate students author quality publications, the pressure to push for quantity contributes to issuance of work that, while relevant, fails to provide a unique contribution to the broader field of educational research. Thus, the many critics of higher education target such substandard research, calling attention to the wasteful and inefficient use of publicly funded resources.

With the reduction of fellowships, student aid and funded research opportunities, I have repeatedly witnessed graduate students emphasize quantity over quality, as they felt as if they were forced to compete for a continuously dwindling pool of financial resources. It has been my observation that this competitive environment not only promotes the development of poor research habits, it also contributes to graduate students who dismiss mental and physical well-being and fail to fulfill their responsibilities to family and friends.

As a PhD student within a highly competitive institution I repeatedly encountered the pressure to produce. Though I certainly had professors who acknowledged my many responsibilities (work, marriage, parenthood, etc.), I experienced a great amount of anxiety during the first year of my program, as I witnessed a number of my peers reap the benefits of spending their time and energies working on professorial projects initiated outside our regular coursework. Initially, it was this select group of students who were the ones most often rewarded with the publication opportunities a graduate student needs to build a competitive vita. Though the correlation between time spent working with a professor and academic opportunity makes logical sense, those of us who were fathers and mothers and those of us who had full-time jobs often felt as if we were being left behind.

Strategies for Success: Mentorship and Collaboration

As a beginning PhD student I quickly recognized that I would never be able to commit the same amount of time that many of my peers could afford; however, I also discovered a number of professors and senior scholars that were empathetic to the unique plight of married students who had children and full-time jobs. Subsequently, during the second semester of my studies I established a close relationship with a trusted professor and two of the more senior students in my program. By establishing a quality relationship with willing mentors, I was able to discuss the many challenges I faced regarding the amount of time I could commit to sustained projects. In addition, I began to build professional relationships that provided me with an "insider's" understanding of how to navigate the journey that is the PhD. Furthermore, the mentors I selected not only shared their knowledge and lessons learned, they began including me in their research endeavors with the understanding that my contributions would at times be limited by professional and family-oriented obligations. The establishment of mentor relationships built upon mutual trust allowed me to reorganize my life and helped me to develop the work-life balance I needed to successfully complete my studies.

Lesson(s) Learned

Seek trusted mentors (professors and senior scholars) as quickly as possible upon entering a graduate program. The earlier a graduate student is able to build collaborative mentor relationships based upon mutual trust, the sooner they can begin balancing the multitude of responsibilities they will most certainly encounter during their tenure as a PhD student.

THE FANTASY OF PARTICIPATION: CONTRIBUTING TO THE FIELD

Dean believes the second animated enactment of communicative capitalism is the fantasy of *participation*. Characterized by the belief that "one's contribution matters, that it means something within a context broader than oneself" (p. 31), the fantasy of participation contributes to a subjective detachment from "actual impact or efficacy," as participants develop an "interpassivity" that precludes actual action from happening (p. 31).

Graduate Implications

As discussed in the prior section, the current emphasis on abundant production in institutions of higher learning implicitly privileges quantity rather than quality. In regards to the fantasy of participation, I have often witnessed professors and graduate students dismiss researched activities after submitting the written product to a respected journal. Reflecting back on my experiences as a graduate student, I realize now that the increasing pressure to *publish or perish* made scholars feel as if they needed to move on to the next publication rather than invest the necessary time and effort to promote completed studies. Thus, many studies were never presented at academic conferences, and more importantly for the field of educational administration, at practitioner-specific venues.

It has been my observation that professionals in higher education can be seduced by the false notion that when one's work is released to the masses it will aide the field based upon its own merit as a publication. It is my opinion that the implications of this seduction damage the reputation of higher education. Throughout my time as a graduate student I have repeatedly listened to critics of higher education as they complain about the persistence of "aloof" researchers who prefer talking to each other through the publication of articles within academic journals rather than work with and for the practitioners in the field.

Strategies for Success: Engaging Communities

It is my belief that scholars can gain considerably when choosing to actively engage communities in the findings of their researched publications. Sadly, I have witnessed professors and graduate students who operate under the illusion that if they attend too many conferences, or if they spend too much time engaging practitioners they will be unable to obtain the desired work-life balance and will place themselves at a disadvantage in the race toward tenure. Yet, throughout my experience as a graduate student, the scholars who chose to attend conferences and interact with practitioners were often presented with opportunities that actually helped them obtain a more desirable work-life balance while also bolstering their professional portfolio. Engaging practitioners in the field of educational administration frequently provides opportunities for publication, creates opportunities for working relationships with other experts in the field, and establishes the trust necessary to initiate collaborative research efforts.

Lesson(s) Learned

Attend academic conferences and engage participants in researched activities. Additionally, professors and graduate students should find avenues to work with, and for, practitioners outside of academia. While graduate students may feel such efforts are detrimental in their attempts to balance work and life, my experiences have shown that there are many personal and professional rewards that may only be realized through such efforts.

LIKE A ROLLING STONE: THOUGHTS ON ADVOCACY

Political activists that embrace music and poetry have always inspired me, often serving as the catalyst for me to *act* on my beliefs and reminding me that, in the words of musician Ben Harper, "I can change the world with my own two hands." In Bob Dylan's 1965 song *Like a Rolling Stone,* he poetically explores the intense feelings of loneliness. In the five years I spent as a PhD student Dylan's words resonated too often for myself and many of my peers, as we often felt alone when attempting to earn an advanced degree while balancing the daily responsibilities inherent to our adult lives. Fortunately, many of us found ways to cope by crafting strategies that would allow us to grow as scholars while maintaining a relative amount of well-being.

I strongly believe that today's graduate professors should, for themselves and for the graduate students they are called to serve, resuscitate the conversation regarding the importance of attaining a work-life balance. As higher education continues to endure attacks from its critics, and as the shallow enactment of democracy continues to influence the working conditions within our nation's universities, it is critical that we all realize our responsibility as advocates for institutions of higher learning as well as for careers that are both productive *and* healthy.

NOTE

1.   Term employed by Henry Giroux in his 2011 article, "Militarized Conservatism and the End(s) of Higher Education."

REFERENCES

Dean, J. (2009). *Democracy and other neoliberal fantasies: Communicative capitalism & left politics*. Durham, NC: Duke University Press.

Dylan, B. (1965). Like a rolling stone. On *Highway 61 revisited*. [Record album]. New York, NY: Columbia.

Giroux, H. A. (2002). The corporate war against higher education. Retrieved from http://louisville.edu/journal/workplace/issue5p1/5p1.html

Giroux, H. A. (2011, April 5). Militarized conservatism and the end(s) of higher education. Retrieved from http://www.truthout.org/militarized-conservatism-and-ends-higher-education

Harper, B. (2002). With my own two hands. *On diamonds on the inside* [Compact disc]. New York, NY: Virgin Records.

Repak, N. (2010). *Emotional fatigue: Coping with academic pressure*. Retrieved M from http://www.gradresources.org/articles/emotional_fatigue.shtml

Rivzi, F., & Lingard, B. (2010). *Globalizing education policy*. New York, NY: Routledge.

CHAPTER 9

RUNNING AGAINST THE CLOCK

Staying Present on the Road to Tenure

Sarah Diem

Finding and maintaining balance in life is a constant struggle for most people. While it is possible to live fulfilling professional and personal lives, if we are unable to strike a balance between the two we can find ourselves in unwanted and unhealthy situations. This is particularly true in universities as the lines between work and life are often blurred. On the surface, the organizational culture of academic institutions provides higher levels of autonomy and freedom as compared to other sectors of the workforce, making it seem like the ideal profession for work-life balance to exist (Bailyn, 2003 as cited in Gatta & Roos, 2004). However, the flexibility present within academic institutions, coupled with the demands of promotions and tenure, can actually make establishing and maintaining work-life balance more difficult (Gatta & Roos, 2004). Thus, as scholars who wish to find a work-life balance, we must be able to wrestle with and identify what we value in life and align ourselves professionally to what we personally believe to be of importance. We need to reframe the work-life balance conversation into one that views both work and life positively, transcending the current discourse on work-life balance to include

Juggling Flaming Chain Saws: Academics in Educational Leadership
Try to Balance Work and Family, pp. 65–72
Copyright © 2012 by Information Age Publishing
All rights of reproduction in any form reserved.

a new language that allows each of us individually the ability to privilege our own values and participate in our own lives accordingly (Caproni, 2004).

In this chapter, I describe my own efforts in trying to find work-life balance. The perspective I bring is guided by my experiences as a first-year tenure-track assistant professor at a major research institution. In the following sections, I illustrate the ways in which I have tried to seek a work-life balance and offer tips to help better prepare other new faculty as they begin their own journeys within the academy. It is my hope that by sharing my experiences as a first-year professor and acknowledging my continual evolution both in and outside of the university, I can help others begin to think differently about their professional careers, which can eventually lead to and bring about more fulfilling lives.

THE LIFE OF A FIRST-YEAR PROFESSOR

Finding a great deal of satisfaction in both my career and personal life, I am one of those people who finds herself engaged in a constant battle between wanting to succeed professionally and being able to enjoy my personal life. I feel fortunate enough to be in a profession where my values as a person coincide with and are reflected in my daily work. My research is meaningful to me on a personal level and expands far beyond the walls of the academy. I study the politics of education, student assignment policies, equity issues in preK-12 schools, and how issues of race and racism are being engaged in university classrooms. Through my research, I seek to discover the ways in which school districts are providing equitable educational opportunities through their student assignment policies, how the perpetuation of school segregation continues to impact metropolitan communities, and how universities are preparing school leaders to address issues of race and racism in the schools they will eventually lead.

While I have a great deal of passion for my work and enjoy being a scholar, it has become increasingly challenging for me to be able to completely shut off work at the end of the day and focus my mind on matters outside of the academy that are equally, if not more important in my life. The feeling of knowing there is always something I can be working on at any given time makes it difficult for me to find a sense of balance and thus allow myself to take part in personal activities that I value and enjoy. I often question my use of time and feel a sense of guilt whenever I choose to put work aside and participate in activities with family and friends. Moreover, I feel that there must be a better way to be more productive while also having a fruitful social life; I just simply cannot figure out how to make this happen.

Ironically, I have always thought of myself as someone who has been able to maintain a sense of balance in my life. I possess a relatively calm demeanor and am able to effectively multitask without feeling too overwhelmed. My colleague recently remarked that one of the reasons she thinks we work so well together is because I possess a zenlike disposition when it comes to managing the research process while she considers herself to be a bit more frantic.

When I am at work, I try to use my time in a way so that at the end of the day, I am able to feel good about what I have accomplished and still have time to take part in other things that bring happiness to my life, such as exercising, reading, seeing live music, going out to dinner with friends, and spending quality time with family. I live by the mantra that work is a part of our lives, not our entire lives. Recognizing that work does not define my entire existence has helped me to lead rewarding professional and personal lives. However, when I began my career as a professor, the ability for me to maintain a sense of balance was tested more so than ever before, as I struggled to stay grounded. I found myself in a very unfamiliar territory. To say that I was feeling a bit overwhelmed would be putting it mildly. The stress of being a new professor was paralyzing. I began questioning my abilities: Could I handle this new position? Was I in over my head? It was at this point that I decided I needed to change the way I approach work and life. Instead of fighting against all of the changes happening around me, I embraced them, knowing that I would need to test out new methods that may assist me in becoming more productive professionally, which in turn would positively impact my personal life as well.

In the following sections I describe the three main components of this change process as realized during my first year as an assistant professor, which include joining a writing group, protecting my time, and establishing a routine. I illustrate how seeking work-life balance often includes stepping out of a space of comfort and into a new, unfamiliar setting that may provide additional advantages and opportunities.

Joining a Writing Group

During the first semester of my new role as an assistant professor seeking to establish a work-life balance, I decided to join a writing group with fellow colleagues from my department. The purpose of the writing group was to meet on a weekly basis to share ideas on the writing process while at the same time offering feedback to a different individual each week on a particular writing piece in a whole group setting. We ended our weekly sessions by sharing with the group our individual short- and long-term goals. By stating our goals "out loud" to each other we established a sense of accountability to ourselves and to the group, which would serve as an internal motivational mechanism when attempting to carry out our own work.

While the group incorporated what was believed to be the necessary methods to create a setting that would not only serve as a place to connect with other faculty, but also one that would help keep each other motivated and prolific with our writing throughout the course of the semester, after just 2 months the writing group disbanded. As group members felt expectations were not being met, too much time was being put into the group and not enough rewards were gained, and the time/day when the group chose to meet became an issue, we decided to stop meeting. This is not to say that participating in the writing group did not provide positive moments. Personally, I valued the constructive criticism offered by my fellow peers and incorporated the feedback given into the manuscript I was working on during the time our writing group was meeting. However, when a group established to help you succeed in your professional endeavors becomes somewhat of a burden and even causes unnecessary distress, it is probably best to rethink the way in which the group should operate.

Looking back at this experience, I think the main reason the group was unsuccessful was that it was entirely too big. There were a total of eight people in the writing group. Having never been a part of a formalized writing group before, I believed a larger group membership would be advantageous to everyone involved: more feedback would be provided, more time would be available to work on our writing as we would not be asked to share our work with the group too often, and we would feel less stressed trying to produce something to share with the group every week. This turned out to not be the case. There were members who provided more feedback than others, some members expressed that too much feedback was creating added pressure and thus adding anxiety to their already full plates, and some members felt that having too much time in between presentation dates actually resulted in less productivity. All of these factors were a part of my experience with the writing group at one point or another. Depending on the week, I was able to provide more or less feedback to the group. The one time I did present my work to the group, I felt extremely nervous prior to the meeting and feared that my colleagues would think my work to be subpar. I admire and respect all of the people who participated in the group and wanted them to recognize my ability as a writer. Additionally, I sought acceptance from my peers, which in turn pushed me to be more critical of myself than is necessary. Looking back at my experience with the writing group, my productivity level actually dropped when I actively participated with the group. I focused all of my energy trying to write a Pulitzer Prize worthy paper for far too long and let a number of other projects fall by the wayside.

Fortunately, outside of the writing group I had formed two additional working groups with colleagues both inside and outside of my department that I continue to work with presently. These groups look much different than the larger writing group; they are informal, and we meet once or twice a week for a few hours over coffee and/or breakfast/lunch and work on our individual projects. These casual working groups serve as a means to check in and get together with one another without the added pressure of having to produce something every time we meet. No judgment is made if someone is unable to complete what he/she wished to accomplish for the day, rather we talk about what measures need to be put in place the next time that can help to reach the goals set forth. This type of collaborative reflection serves as a powerful tool in seeking work-life balance. It allows you to closely look at the time you allocate to specific tasks and helps you decipher if the ways in which you are working are helping or hindering your ability to meet your end goal.

Protecting Time

Along with participating in working groups that help me gain more work-life balance, I have also attempted to protect specific amounts of time during the week to focus solely on my research and writing. I have found that if I block off chunks of time on my calendar and not schedule anything during those times, I can be extremely productive. However, this method of protecting my time only works if I force myself not to get sidetracked by e-mails, phone calls, people coming in and out of the office, and so on. Therefore, what I have been doing more recently is working outside of the office, either in a coffee shop or at home, and turning my phone and e-mail off, so that I can avoid any distractions that may present themselves and interrupt my time to focus on my research and writing. I have also tried to embrace some of the interruptions that will undoubtedly come up from time to time, rather than beating myself up and getting upset with not being able to work the exact amount of time I may have allocated for myself. I know the work will eventually get done; it always does. I just need to maybe rethink how I negotiate my schedule, adding some cushion time, which will account for the unexpected.

Establishing a Routine

My experience as a first-year assistant professor has taught me that in order to take advantage of the flexibility provided in academia, be productive, and possess work-life balance, establishing a routine is essential.

When I began my first semester as a professor, I remember thinking to myself I must be the luckiest person in the world to be in a profession where I can pretty much establish my own schedule and work whenever I want. I realized that no one would be looking over my shoulder making sure I was in the office at exactly 8 A.M., I would not get reprimanded if I took too long of a lunch, I would have plenty of time to exercise on a daily basis, and I would even have time to go out in the evenings. Unfortunately, I would soon realize that this type of freedom meant that there would be no one present to make sure I was making the right decisions in regards to allocating my time to work and play and meeting the demands that would help me to achieve the ultimate goal of tenure.

While a year has gone by and I am still attempting to develop an ideal routine, I feel more at ease with the way I am choosing to spend my time in and outside of the university. I also feel confident that I will eventually craft a routine that will allow me to shut off work and will give me time to stay active, get outside, and find additional enjoyment in my life. When you are a first-year professor, you are experiencing everything for the first time; you are advising students, preparing for courses, serving on dissertation committees, spending time on external committees, and so forth. Although I felt prepared going into the position from the training and mentorship I received in graduate school, there were still a number of things I needed to experience myself, as a professor, in order to fully comprehend the expectations placed upon me. Now that my "rookie" year is officially over, I now know how the academy functions and feel better equipped and more poised beginning my second year.

STRIVING FOR MORE THAN JUST BALANCE

While the research shows that more people are seeking a work-life balance, we are still very much a society that places a high priority on our professional lives. Americans are particularly interested in how and to what scale each other contribute professionally to the greater good. It is as though if you work harder, you are considered to be more productive. However, what is often missing from this equation is how we as a people can learn to work smarter so that more time is available to enjoy the many other important and enjoyable aspects of life.

Although finding work-life balance is very personal and specific to each person, through my experiences as a new professor, I have identified a few key tips I believe can assist others in achieving better balance in their lives. In no particular order, these pieces of advice have helped me become smarter about my professional obligations and have provided me with more time to enjoy things outside of the university that bring joy and fulfillment to my life.

Take Time to Self-Reflect

One of the first steps in finding a work-life balance is determining how we spend our time and asking ourselves if this time is aligned with our values. Developing a process of self-reflection helps us make decisions that affect our balance. Self-reflection has helped me learn more about how I operate as an individual and a professional. For example, since I started being more reflective in life and being more aware of how I spend my time, I am now intimately familiar with the times of the day when I am most productive and therefore set aside that specific time to complete important and timely projects. I am also more aware of what personal activities satisfy me the most and allocate more time doing what I enjoy.

Learn to Say No

One of the biggest lessons I have learned during my first year as an assistant professor is that it is okay, and even necessary, to not be involved in every opportunity that may come across my desk. "Learning to say no" is something I struggle with every day as a new assistant professor working toward tenure. What if I say no to an opportunity that may lead to additional opportunities down the road? What if saying no now means that I won't be asked again to participate in a similar activity? At some point you have to tell yourself that it is not physically, mentally, or emotionally possible to participate in everything that is asked of you. Moreover, doing things because you feel guilty or obligated to do so can lead to an additional layer of stress and feeling of being overwhelmed to what is more than likely an already full workload. It may be hard at first, and I can vividly remember the first time I chose not to attend a meeting that I technically should have gone to but had no desire in the subject matter discussed. However, once you say no to things that you feel as if you are unable to handle, do not value, or are not interested in doing, you will feel a sense of liberation knowing that you have the choice of doing what matters to you and will bring about more balance in your life.

Be Flexible

Every week, my yoga instructor ends our practice by placing a small sheet of paper next to our mats while we are in shavasana (the last pose performed that concludes a yoga practice). On these sheets of paper are what my instructor has coined as "yogi thoughts of the day." The thoughts are offered as a means to inspire and encourage each of us, the students, to develop a sense of well-being; something that can be carried over and maybe even implemented in each of our individual lives. A quote that particularly stood out and had meaning to me in my journey to seek a work-life balance is by the Buddhist Zen master, Thich Nhat Hanh. Hanh states,

> No matter how much structure we create in our lives, no matter how many good habits we build, there will always be things that we cannot control—and if we let them, these things can be a huge source of anger, frustration and stress. The simple solution: learn to go with the flow.

Through his words, Hanh recognizes that unpredictability and lack of control are normal parts of living and trying to fight against them can cause more harm than good. Establishing a work-life balance is an organic, constantly evolving process. If we choose to define what work-life balance means for us individually, we can allow ourselves to be in a state where the unexpected may be more welcomed and less thought of in a negative light. We can remain present in our mind and handle the bumps and hiccups that will inevitably cross our paths and throw our equilibrium off. Moreover, we can stop feeling guilty for not working 24/7 and manage a healthy lifestyle.

REFERENCES

Bailyn, L. (2003) Academic careers and gender equity: Lessons learned from MIT. *Gender, work, and organizations, 10*(2), 137-153.

Caproni, P. J. (2004). Work/life balance: You can't get there from here. *The Journal of Applied Behavioral Science, 40*(2), 208-218.

Gatta, M. L., & Roos, P. A. (2004). Balancing without a net in academia: Integrating family and work lives. *Equal Opportunities International, 23*(3/4/5), 124-142.

CHAPTER 10

NAVIGATING THE TERRAIN OF THE THREE SELFS

Work-Self, Family-Self, Personal-Self

Kathrine J. Gutierrez

I choose to use and embrace the word "navigating" over the term "balancing" when it comes to describing what I call the three selfs: work-self, family-self, and personal-self. I liken the phase "navigating the terrain" to that of "surveying the landscape." In my view, one has to know what the terrain looks like in order to navigate how to move or maneuver through life and plan contingencies to obstacles. I believe one also should create back up plans to best accomplish the tasks demanding attention from the three selfs. Hence, I manage my daily life activities by navigating the terrain of the three selfs considering my work-family role as a "Mama Academician." Each of the three selfs are first briefly discussed and then interwoven into the narrative as all three selfs play out in my daily life—*however* ... not all three are in harmony on any single day or on any day for that matter, often times one of the "selfs" consume most of my waking hours, and by waking hours sometimes this would mean no sleep for 2 exhausting days!

Juggling Flaming Chain Saws: Academics in Educational Leadership
Try to Balance Work and Family, pp. 73–81
Copyright © 2012 by Information Age Publishing
All rights of reproduction in any form reserved.

Work-Self

At the time I decided to pursue a PhD, I was certain that after I received the degree that I would be steadfast on the blazing trail to becoming a tenured faculty member. I did not think about how I would accomplish getting tenure with a young child to care for and a husband who would be on the same tenure track process—more of that discussion to come! I have always had a high work ethic and strong commitment to performing well at any task that I set my mind on doing. I had a robust and productive doctoral education which prepared me for the demanding work of an assistant professor. I take my role as an assistant professor seriously and I strive to do good work in all areas of my research, teaching and service. Given the time demands and variability of each responsibility, research, teaching and service, there is literally no clear demarcation of a daily time clock in which one would start and end the work day. I'm typically working 7 days a week to keep up with all tasks and hoping to make a "dent" in the so-called inbox of activities. I feel academic life consumes you and you can always be working on something ... this I believe is especially more so during the work intensive and time-consuming pretenure years.

Family-Self

I am a mother to a young, energetic and curious toddler, and my husband coincidently is also an assistant professor. My husband and I have a unique family-work life situation. We both are employed in the same university, same college, same department, and we were earlier following the same tenure-track time line. In essence, we are a dual academic household. I know of few faculty members where both spouses are faculty members. I believe, there is much more complexity, tension, and stressors when both parents are faculty members—even though there is flexibility with academic work, the work is ALWAYS there 24/7 and grows! And one should be mindful about ensuring family time is tended to as well, especially when one has a child.

The care of our young child is primarily shared between my husband and me since we do not have any family living in the area. Outside the home, childcare centers are limited for our child given his age, our time preferences, and the adequacy of what we perceive as both quality and affordable childcare centers. As an untenured faculty member and mother of a fast-growing and developing toddler, I wonder what my child would say to me about my work and our home/family life if he could articulate more thoughts. Actually, ever so often when I am working from home, he does say to me "no work mommy!" and comes over to close my laptop! A faculty member, pretenured with young children, said to me one day, "The days are long but the years are short"—this in regards to our conversation about trying to find "writing time" and also to find/make "quality-time" to engage in activities with our children. We shared a smile and exclamation at the coincidence of us needing to work around our children's sleeping time to able to get any writing done at home. For me, writing at home during typical daytime hours was doable when my child was much younger. Now that my child is more energetic, playful and can articulate his feelings and dispositions more, working from what my child and I call the "home office" is only productive for me if I work during the early morning hours while my child sleeps. Also, as my child grows I am seeing the need to be more engaged with him and he also wants that engagement from both of his parents. This fact signals to me that I need to strategize even more how to do "well" work/home-life responsibilities and to strategize time dimensions for everything to happen during the day/week/month/year. In our dual academic household, we rely on synchronizing our home/work-life calendars so there is no overlap in the days we teach, making sure we set aside research/writing time, meeting time and so on, and ensuring we have quality time with our child independently and as an entire family.

Personal-Self

I married my husband in 2005 in what was leading to the last year of my doctoral studies. Up to that time, I was used to working long days for most of the days. I did not see it any other way in terms of doing what I needed to do to accomplish tasks and to stay ahead of the work demands. Marriage changes your daily work-life routine and having a child *quickly* changes your routine even more! I had little to no time for personal-self activities during the early months of raising a young child, but to maintain a positive and healthy self—I quickly have come to realize the importance of making time for myself whether it be sleeping early (a rare occasion!), meeting up with a friend for lunch, window shopping, reading a magazine, or getting that haircut that I've been putting off ... and so on. However, I *do* delight in being a mom to my young child and being with my family. But a little disconnect every now and then helps me to regroup from the responsibilities of work-family life. With all the juggling of responsibilities, I have come to realize that if I am not feeling well or begin to feel overwhelmed by all that needs to be done, it is a signal to slow down the pace; a time for me to enjoy the day as it unfolds, delight in the big smile and happy face of my child, and know that this too shall pass and whatever is pressing/urgent will get done ... eventually, even if that means giving up my personal structure of wishing to do it all in the pre-set, often self-imposed, time frame.

THE BEGINNING OF MY FACULTY WORK-FAMILY LIFE STORY

My husband and I started working at The University of Oklahoma in August 2006. At that time we were not thinking about having a child/ren but hit the ground running to perform the tasks of research, teaching, and service. Shortly after our first academic year and taking our first year work experience as assistant professors "all in," we began to chat about if we would have a child. "Could we do it all?" Was it possible for us to work long hours and care for a young child? I talked to a faculty friend at another institution who has children while she was still untenured to see what her life is all about. I was set on asking what I thought was the most important question of "when is the right time to have a child, pretenure time or after tenure?" For her, she unequivocally stated that having her children early on in her tenure progress was good because she was "in the throes" of research projects and could not imagine doing them and start-ing a family. Her advice to me was to have a child/ren earlier rather than later. In hindsight, I should have asked her several other *important* ques-tions: "How difficult is it to be a mom and simultaneously a faculty mem-ber?" "How do you and your husband manage to both work and care for your children?" "What advice or tidbits would you give me to navigate family-work life responsibilities?"

Other friends I talked to who had yet to start a family and were also early into their faculty/research career were also struggling with a similar question, "how difficult will it be to perform full-time faculty/research work and be a mom to a young child?" My husband was supportive with whatever decision we made in terms of having a child—having a child early into our career, or having a child after we received tenure. The deci-sion was ours to make and it was a life-changing important and weighty decision that I took a long time to ponder and decide.

I had a child in April 2009 and I was completing my third academic year as an assistant professor at my institution. While I was pregnant, a friend and colleague loaned me her book to read entitled, *Mama, PhD* (Evans & Grant, 2008)—an edited work that includes a collection of sto-ries from women writing about being a mother and academic life. I recall reading some of the stories and vaguely remember thinking to myself, "Gosh, is that situation going to be me?", and "my situation is different." I guess I was just too exhausted at that time to think about the whole "Mama Academician" role that I was soon to be in and the reality that for the first few years after the birth of my child both family-self and work-self would overtake my personal-self. This thought of course became a moot point months after my child was born and until I got a handle to be able to let go, pass up, and share some of the responsibilities of work-family life tasks.

Since my child was not expected to be born until April 2009, I figured I could fast track teaching my two graduate courses in a condensed format that spring semester and have at least 3 weeks to prep before the *baby* arrived. Also prior to the arrival of my child, I tried to stay ahead in terms of my research, writing, and scholarly activities. A coauthored paper I submitted for review in the fall of 2008 was accepted with revisions needing to be made and was selected for inclusion in the March 2009 edition, which meant I was working on it up through the day before I had my baby! Of course, the research publication process takes a variable amount of time, but who would have guessed that it would be wanted around the time of my expected due date! Coincidentally, I was back to the manuscript approximately 2½ to 3 weeks after the birth of my child to make the final edits to meet the publication deadline! I remember being still sleep derived from trying to figure out life with a new born baby and working around the 2-hour window spurts of when the baby was asleep to get the writing done. Funny ... as I am finishing up this chapter, I am doing so while my child is taking an afternoon nap but the circumstances are a whole lot different now given the less around-the-clock care that is needed now as opposed to when my child was a newborn and just a few weeks old.

To draw upon the cliché "life changes once you have a child" ... yes, that is certainly true in my case, especially since both my husband and I are full-time academic employees. It is great that we have flexibility in terms of teaching on different nights, trying to arrange meetings, graduate exams and advising on different times. But, the rest of the work does not end even if I am not physically at the university office. For the *work-self*, research progress needs to be maintained and followed through, committee work continues, students need advising, class work and preparation need to be attended to ... and so on. All the responsibilities of research, teaching, and service are expected to be fulfilled to the highest involvement as possible and with great attention to quality production of research and scholarly activities. For the *family-self*, housework needs to be tended to, grocery runs are needed, meals need preparing, care time and playtime and involvement time with my child needs to happen on a daily basis. For the *personal-self*, time is needed to decompress and do activities that are relaxing and enjoyable to me such as cooking homemade meals, celebrating holidays and special occasions, traveling, and having conversations with friends and family. However best I try to "map out" my activities to the expectations and demands of each of the three selfs something is bound to come up that throws a well planned and strategized weekly calendar out of whack! Despite the hurdles of life surprises, I truly rely on my electronic calendar to highlight my daily, weekly, and monthly activities and responsibilities as far in advanced as possible. The electronic calendar has become a most used assistive tool for me as I coordinate what I need to do and most importantly what is essential to do.

THE COMPLEXITY OF TRYING TO HARMONIZE
THE ROLES OF EACH OF THE THREE SELFS

Since the birth of my child, I have slowly gotten better at orchestrating the various responsibilities and tasks that need attention in order to be effective in my roles as work-self, family-self, and personal-self. From the reflection of the *work-self*, when I was pregnant with my child I had a chat with my department chairperson to figure out my options for work time. I wanted to know if an extension of tenure was available for such incidents as the birth of a child, and, if so, when I should initiate such a request. It turned out that I did not need to make a request in haste of actually needing to take an extension to my tenure time line. So I forged ahead without requesting for an extension *at that time* in consideration of my flexible work schedule and advanced talk with my husband about coordinating his work schedule with mine. We anticipated that we *could manage* to "pull it off"—meaning we could have a full-time career and also be full-time parents with no other caregivers to watch our child for the first few months of our child's life. That's exactly what transpired up to the point of when my child was about 18 months old. My husband and I decided that our child could benefit from socializing with children his age and that we really needed more time to focus on doing work. At that point, I was all for it.

We searched for and visited several child care centers in our area searching for a program that would meet our needs and desires for a quality and caring program available for the specific times we needed to have someone engage with our child. It was not easy finding what we perceived as the "right" program for us. We decided on a place where our child would attend 2 days a week for a few hours each morning. Again, despite this bit of what I term "focused" work time, the demands of each role of the three selfs were still there and building up for both the work-self and family-self.

I am fortunate to work in a department in which members of the faculty are sensitive and encouraging to the growth and development of untenured faculty and supportive of my work needs given my role as a mother to a young toddler. However, all the support and encouragement given still does not negate the fact that the work needs to be performed by me and that my attention and time was being tugged at primarily between the work-self and family-self, and my personal-self was being worn down and I was getting more and more exhausted ... something had to give. I initiated the conversation about requesting for an extension to my tenure time line in fall 2010. However, the pivotal point in my realization that I *really needed* an extension to my tenure time came when I was supposedly on "winter break" visiting my family in December 2010. It was the end of the fall 2010 semester and my travel plans were set in advance, of course, for a time when I thought all work responsibilities would be completed. I faintly recall being haggard by the rush of the end of the semester to-dos and getting ill and then having to pack and plan for the family trip. I still had a few days to get in the final grades for the courses and thought "no worries!" ... I can finish up grading a few papers on the long plane ride and electronically post the grades when we reached our destination. On top of that, I also had a manuscript to review for a journal due at the similar time.

As luck would have it ... my child got ill and was miserable the entire trip we took to visit my family. During our layover, I did manage to complete the journal review and grade a few papers, but I was still not done. When we reached our destination, not only was I exhausted from the long trip, but also worried and concerned for my child's health. To top that off, the stress level kicked in when I realized that I had fewer than 24 hours to grade the remaining papers and post grades ... yikes! Once my child drifted off to sleep, I fueled up on caffeine and started to get to work. I remember thinking ... "I am so exhausted!" but I stayed up and posted the grades before the deadline. Needless to say, I officially submitted my request for an extension to my tenure time line in fall 2011 through the necessary administrative channels. I was granted an extension! This is nice breathing room for me. Although the demands of work and family are still there, I am thankful I have some wiggle time to tend to research and scholarly activities ... and oh yes, perhaps to be able to get in a few more hours of sleep when I can!

KNOWING WHEN TO ASK FOR A BREAK AND NEXT STEPS

As I mentioned, the work still does not end despite having an extension to my tenure time line. It means that I am able to take additional time to do what is still required of me to do in order to receive tenure. I contractually work 9 months out of the year and have the summer "off" if I decide not to teach summer courses or engage in advisement for students wishing to complete their doctoral research and sit in at student degree related exams. Since hearing word about my approval of my extension request, I planned for the summer 2011 to engage in more research and scholarly activities, but as the saying goes … "things happen"! While faced with an upcoming manuscript deadline in May of 2011, my child was ill and was up through the night on several nights, which meant I was also up through the night. I thought … "I can make the deadline, I have 3 more days to get it in." Oh no … I was working on limited sleep already and the final night I stayed up to get it done. Well … I felt it still needed to be reviewed and edited and did not feel it was ready to submit. I decided I had to throw in the towel and ask for some extra time to complete the manuscript, which meant that the project would be carried on into the summer. It is circumstances like these when I know that I can't do it all and at optimum proficiency and that it is "okay" for me to cut back and to be at peace with that decision.

As far as next steps, I continue to rely on my electronic calendar to "navigate the terrain" of the roles demanded for each of the three selfs. I also continue to give attention to whatever task or situation is in need of my full attention at the time. I plan for more family-time given the needs and curiosity of a growing toddler. And I know when it is time to leave work at work whether I'm at the university office or my home office. My thoughts and focus need to be at the place where I am at. In my case, this implies to keep my mind where my feet are. When I am "working," I need to focus on when I am "working," I need to focus on getting the work done within the time frame I allotted myself to do the task. When I am with my child/family, I try to keep my focus on the activities and engagement with my child/family and not wander off to my laptop to check e-mails or to do work. My time is shared between the three selfs: work-self, family-self, and personal-self. Sharing is a term I use loosely because for me, daily balance between the three selfs is not how I would describe my circumstance and not what I strive to achieve. Focused and productive time spent performing all that needs to be done is what I strive for. Of course, it does not hurt if I can "pencil in" more time to sleep and relax through my work-family life journey …

As to lessons learned and thoughts for pretenured faculty members on the verge of starting a family, I would say you can never truly predict a "set" schedule to do your productive "in the zone" writing time, but you make plans for every new development stage as you progress through parenthood and according to the changes/needs of your child(ren) as they grow. But as a saying goes "plans are just plans—things happen, change happens." Even though I rely heavily on my calendar, there are days when I am not able to get it all done and that is OKAY now, because life continues and the work will still be there.

REFERENCE

Evans, E., & Grant, C. (Eds.). (2008). *Mama, PhD: Women write about motherhood and academic life.* New Brunswick, NJ: Rutgers University Press.

CHAPTER 11

WORKING WITHOUT A NET

One Professor's Reflections on Work-Life Balance

Kristina A. Hesbol

I never intended to become an academic—to say nothing of becoming engaged in compelling, methodologically complex research that actually has potential to impact leadership that improves teaching and learning for every student. I was raised in the 1950s—the era of *Leave It to Beaver* and *Father Knows Best*. My role models from that era didn't break gender molds or command space shuttles. I taught for less than 4 years when I gave birth to our first son, and then was delighted to stay at home for what I imagined to be an indefinite period. I describe these seemingly scripted scenarios to review the concept of work-life balance. From my early days as a young wife and stay-at-home mother, the sole purpose for my days was focused on my family—from having my husband's shirts ironed to planning and preparing healthy meals. During this time in my life, my sons and I enjoyed days filled with excursions to explore libraries and museums. We played outside, explored the woods, collected rocks, made projects on inclement weather days, and we read—and then read some more. It was understood in our family, as well as across a large sector of American families of that era, that I was, as a wife and mother, respon-

Juggling Flaming Chain Saws: Academics in Educational Leadership
Try to Balance Work and Family, pp. 83–93
Copyright © 2012 by Information Age Publishing

sible for everything related to caring for our home and raising our sons. I've been asked repeatedly why I worked so hard to create this facade of the "perfect family." I don't ever remember a day that I felt tired or sick; every day, I'd prove that I was a "good wife" and "good mother," but it's unclear to whom I was proving anything. In retrospect, my energies could have been used in other productive ventures. The "perfect life" was not, in fact, so perfect after all, either personally or professionally. Work-life balance? My work WAS my life, and vice versa. Once I gave birth to my first son, I stayed at home for 12 years; I never even considered the possibility of working outside of the home before my youngest son was in school full time. I didn't know any working moms, and wasn't aware that there were even such resources as quality child care alternatives within a short distance of our home.

As a committed PTA volunteer, I was astounded when several mothers approached our board and asked us to support the establishment of a before and after school child care program in one of the district schools. What a ridiculous idea, I thought; if those parents really cared about their children, then they'd stay home, like I did. During the months that followed, a contentious debate developed among my acquaintances. On one hand, the school seemed like a perfect place to provide quality care for students, before and after school. On the other hand, I knew few working moms in the community (even though my own mother had worked since I was 8), knew all of our sons' friends and their families, and assumed that all of the neighborhood families could afford to have mom stay at home with the children. I reflectively recognize now that I was trying to defend the *status quo*, viewing the situation from a very narrow, constrained vantage point, without trying to understand other perspectives. My chain saws were not only flaming—they were engulfing me in flames with my blinders on, but I wasn't paying attention.

For the first 8 years, I never considered the possibility of working outside the home. Then I began to substitute teach in our neighborhood district, but only on the days that my sons went to school. The social expectations were still dominant. The role that I assumed was that of keeping the proverbial plates spinning, and to do whatever was necessary to make sure that none dropped. I needed to have nutritious meals prepared as usual, get the boys to piano lessons and sports team practices, dental appointments, help them with their homework, and keep the house clean. If I had acknowledged that parenting practices which were different from my own had advantages to both the child and the parent, then I'd also open the possibility to subconsciously allow myself to consider that the denial of my own calling need not take a backseat to the societal norms to which I was unquestioningly conforming.

In retrospect, the imbalance I experienced for decades established a normative basis for the work-life balance challenges I've encountered since becoming an academic. It always irritates me to hear people talk about the life of a professor as some kind of perpetual vacation. At least 1-night weekly, I sit up writing well into the night. Sometimes it's about being in what Csikszentmihalyi (1990) refers to as "flow." At other times, it seems to be a challenge to choose between seemingly endless interests and opportunities, each competing to combine into a potential research study, annual meeting presentation and/or journal article. In any case, it's never okay to regularly lose a night's sleep; such a pattern is, instead, a strong indicator of a lack of work-life balance.

Early career professors with whom I have the privilege of serving as faculty colleagues (as well as my own grown children) have a dramatically different world view, in which no specific tasks are based on gender. It must be very difficult for twenty-first century partners to comprehend the notion of one parent kicking back and reading the paper, waiting for dinner to be served, while the other parent ensures that everything is done to meet the needs of the entire family. Some moms have always worked—and over the past few decades. I have come to understand that they are "good moms" and that their children are well adjusted, contrary to my naïve and poorly informed earlier judgment.

Most of my adult life has been spent in a preK-12 educational context. I have served as a teacher in elementary and middle schools and a school principal in several diverse communities, have held several director and coordinator positions, and spent 4 years as the assistant superintendent for human resources at a large unit school district. Most school cultures reward compliance, and focus a great deal of energy protecting tradition and resisting change. As I began to discern inequity within each of the systems, I took great pride in collaborating with teacher leaders and others to develop processes and procedures that worked to eliminate the inequitable treatment of children. At one point in my career trajectory, I was recruited to serve as a principal in a high-profile Midwest suburban school district. While there were more than a dozen elementary schools in this district, ours was one of only two which non-native English speaking students attended. Imagine my stunned surprise when I accepted the position and arrived to find that despite very small class sizes, each teacher had a full-time assistant, who worked at a folding table outside the classroom—with "those" children. The Parent Teacher Association president told me that she was delighted that her children attended this school, where they could participate in fund raisers for poor children who also attended the school. She told me that the instructional assistants at the tables outside the classrooms were hired to keep the neighborhood children "on track," to ensure that "those children won't slow down children from neighborhood families." She suggested that she'd heard how uncomfortable I was making many teachers feel, questioning practices that had been long-standing at "the little school with the big heart." An hour after I referred to these entrenched and discriminatory practices at a faculty meeting, I got a call from the superintendent. He wanted me to know that I was upsetting the teachers, and warned me that I needed to spend more time "being a principal and less time asking questions." In January of my first year, I tendered my resignation, effective at the end of the school year. I vowed that I would find a professional home where I could train school and district leaders to challenge and replace the *status quo* with equitable, high-quality instructional best practices that provide access to rigor and high levels of both expectation and support for every student. After I left, those same inappropriate practices returned—and were reinforced by the new principal, a district veteran principal who was transferred from another building to "smooth things over"—which translates to a return to socially unjust practices which exacerbate achievement and opportunity gaps for minority students.

Two years later, at age 52, I accepted my first academic appointment as a tenure-track professor at a selective Research I university, in the educational leadership department, where I prepared principals and superintendent candidates. Work-life balance? What would that look like for me as a university professor? Would I be able to build on my experiential base to construct meaning in this new context?

REINVENTING MYSELF

In a study of more than 16,000 professors, the tenure track was identified as the primary impediment to female faculty professors (Parker, 2003). In my first academic appointment, I was introduced to the college of education faculty by the chair of my search committee as a "staff developer." As the only female preK-12 faculty member in the educational leadership department, I was asked to get coffee for my colleagues, but never was mentored about the expectations for junior faculty at this institution. Due to a revolving administrative turntable, I had no formal performance reviews during the first 3 years, no mentor, and few publications. And in spite of this rocky beginning, I chose to continue to carve out a niche as an assistant professor at another university, and find deep satisfaction from what I do. What's not to love about long stretches of time to think, plan and write, and an opportunity to teach and develop research around issues about which you are deeply committed and passionate?

TEACHING

Although I entered the academy with decades of leadership and teaching experience, I was expected to attend "how to teach" seminars, designed to support new faculty. The feedback document provided by the department's appointment, salary, promotion, and tenure committee at my current institution at the end of my first year suggested that I should seek support from colleagues, since some student feedback on course evaluations indicated that I didn't know how to teach, since I raised issues that made students feel uncomfortable. Many of our graduate students resist ambiguity; they want to know exactly what *the* one univocal right answer is. Some actually remind me of my own naïveté, back in the days that I took a stand opposing the development of child care at our local school. My school and district leadership experience tells me that being able to tolerate ambiguity is an essential skill for resilient leaders. So I consistently design experiences with which they are likely unfamiliar, in order to provide opportunities to surface and challenge their mental models. I scaffold opportunities for them to be successful with assignments, while gradually reducing the clarity and specificity of the directions, so that they experience a glimpse of the relentless ambiguity and change that is de rigeur in the daily demands of a school/district leader. While such *praxis* still is unfamiliar for most students, I'm learning to address it proactively, in order to help them understand why it's important to experience situations that seem unfamiliar and therefore uncomfortable to them. Over the course of the past 25 years, I have hired, coached, and evaluated hundreds of teachers, principals and central office administrators. Now as I approach the compilation of my tenure dossier, I worry about demonstrating evidence of competency as a professor who teaches these skills, based on the adverse student reactions to experiencing such disquieting practice. Course evaluations have significant impact on the tenure process at my Carnegie teaching-intensive university. It's sometimes hard to believe that evaluations come from students who took the same class. "She changes the syllabus during the course, showing her disorganization" comes from a student in the same class as this comment from another student: "She pushed me beyond my comfort zone—and in the process, helped me see the possibilities of my own leadership, instead of leaning on what I've always been told and expected to do." I continue to learn, even as I teach.

Several colleagues have experienced scenarios in which they posed a controversial scenario, or introduced a world view inconsistent with that of a handful of students, and then have received very low ratings on their course evaluation. Becoming a school or district leader is not about being safe or staying within a comfort zone. It is, rather, a process whose bottom line demands courageous leadership, as well as thorough understanding of a deep and broad spectrum of evidence-based, best instructional strategies to support continuous learning and improvement for *every* student preK-12.

Prior to the start of each semester, I send an online survey to incoming students, to gather information about their experiences, coursework they've taken, etc. As a result of this data, I make adjustments to the syllabus throughout the semester to meet their needs. The courses I teach include human resource courses, having served as the lead negotiator for the board of education on six union collective bargaining agreements in 4 years as an assistant superintendent for human resources—but students become disequilibrated if I make changes to a syllabus. When students have told me about schedule conflicts that impact more than several students, I have changed the due dates of major projects. In these course evaluations, I am consistently criticized for making changes to the syllabus. Trying to balance conflicting paradigms tends to throw work-life balance into chaos. Increasingly, the prevailing motivation behind my decisions relative to such changes involves sorting out course expectations for students that are most important—what students need to be able to demonstrate as a principal or superintendent. As long as I can accurately describe the reasoning behind such negative student course feedback in a written narrative, I will continue to make choices about how best to shift paradigms for our students—even (and especially) if it means that they have to leave their comfort zone behind. Their newly discovered confidence and self-efficacy may support them to continuously improve teaching and learning for every student, and to courageously reculture inclusive communities of practice.

SERVICE

After reviewing my résumé for a grant proposal, an administrator from our college told me, "If you're doing all that service for your appointment, salary, promotion, and tenure report, that's enough now." As a relational leader, I find meaning in the service side of the triumvirate at the national, university, college and departmental levels. But, as in most good things, I tend to overindulge in service, and end up working at the keyboard at 4:30 A.M., because the little balance I have tends to be distributed first to those for whom my service makes a difference. As my sons grew up, two of them became Eagle Scouts, and developed solid networking skills, and identifying key community resources to support valued initiatives. They continue to be engaged in service to their communities, a testament to the impact that service has on many lives. My sons' service and my own are correlated, and while we each derive great satisfaction from it, we make contributions to our respective fields in the process.

Whether chairing or serving as a committee member for a doctoral examination or a dissertation proposal hearing, a great deal of time and focus goes into such local service. Researching and writing the doctoral exam is a collaborative initiative, centering on the student's research interests and developing the question's components so that they broadly examine the appropriate literature. Being available to students is another important responsibility for academics. Today's ubiquitous technology applications blur previous boundaries, making it possible to be available online for a majority of hours in any given day. Texting responses to grad students in the states while on vacation 6,000 miles away last year is evidence of how teaching and service tend to intertwine—and how they impact work-life balance. All academics face comparable opportunities to engage in nearly continuous access by students. Setting flexible boundaries in the name of a reasonable work-life balance makes sense.

I am grateful for these opportunities, which continue to socialize me into the academy. The average age of women expecting to be awarded a PhD is 34 (Mason, 2009). Considering the 6 to 7 years until they're eligible for tenure, most women are about 40 when they're awarded tenure. Men are more likely to achieve tenure than women, according to a report from the University of California (Davis) (Parker, 2003). When I submit my tenure dossier next year, I'll be 62. Many of my friends have recently retired, while I'm staying up into the wee hours, analyzing data and writing research proposals. Because of a myriad of influences, including today's economic realities, an increasing number of older women are electing comparable experiences. While many of us were able to stay at home to raise young children, we don't have enough years invested into teachers' retirement systems to fully benefit, as our male counterparts do. We also learn from our younger colleagues and daughters, and are enjoying previously unavailable options, outside of the field for which we originally were trained as undergraduates. Our experiences in the field bring a rich experiential tapestry to our work in the classroom, as well as a first-hand understanding of much of the evolving research literature. That said, the escalating pressures of attaining promotion and tenure seem daunting, and unattainable if we haven't been mentored to begin publishing early in our careers in top tier, peer-reviewed journals.

Work-life balance doesn't come naturally. My husband of 16 years is a prince—not a monarch. He has encouraged and supported me to make the leap from preK-12 district leadership into the academy. Ours is a twenty-first century relationship; there are neither demands nor expectations about particular roles ascribed to/by either of us. I travel at least 3 days weekly, and since our home is 100 miles from campus, my work schedule continue to be unbalanced, and significantly dissimilar from those of several colleagues, who come into the office to work daily. Does the commute automatically contribute to a tilting work-life balance? Not specifically, because the tradeoff is being able to live "at home." A study done by the University of Chicago found that 15% of female professors live in a different community than their spouse, while only 8% of male professors do (Terrien, 2008, p. 14). For my first year of a new faculty appointment, I rented an apartment, in order to become familiar with the departmental culture. Since all of our students are graduate students who work during the day, I learned that I could effectively commute from our home to/from campus to teach and participate actively in a variety of meetings on campus, in an effort to develop some "normalcy," focusing on an improved work-life balance.

I'm coming to accept the contradictions in my life, and recognize them as lessons waiting to be learned. I can see how narrow my worldview used to be, and work constantly to expand and broaden it now. While I spent a great deal of my life unquestioningly accepting assignments and roles, I now insist on and champion opportunities to work interdependently. Most women my age in preK-12 who became superintendents either chose not to have children or were among the early pioneers who established high-quality child care—a diametrically different experience from my own. Having watched countless friends and family wrestle with balance, it's becoming increasingly apparent that, as a professor, I have opportunities to use my time in a way that few others have. My goals now take more midcourse corrections, rather than arriving empty-handed at a dead end. Midcourse does not refer to changing assignments in the middle of a semester; instead, it refers to the opportunity to examine my own actions and choices from what Senge calls a 20,000 foot view (Senge, 1994). The corrections are occurring more intuitively now; rather than waiting to arrive at what seems like a dead end, I can see what capacity a system needs to have built into it—or decide that the challenges are beyond my control and take myself out of harm's way. And now when I do occasionally hit the proverbial wall, I'm learning to understand that there is meaning in even those humiliating experiences from which my choices moving forward can be informed. When a board of education election changes the political tone, I am learning to understand that while their efforts to dismantle systemic work that supports disenfranchised families and focuses on eliminating a persisting achievement gap may quickly take place, that resisting at the local level tends to be less productive than to lobby at the policy level, to examine levers at the state and national level that make such very real and destructive practices more difficult. Jones (2011) suggests that *expecting* a good work-life balance is a study in futility and frustration. He suggests that setting clear boundaries for ourselves, as well as on expectations that others have about our time, opens the door to a healthier and more productive sense of balance. Instead of clear delineations of work-life balance, I'm learning to understand the intermittent and unpredictable the blurring of the lines. I recognize now that even when I stay up all night writing, there are lessons to learn. Like most people, I tend to invest more time and energy into things that are important to me, with lessons that are applicable across the work-family "line."

UNDERSTANDING HOW TO BALANCE

Survey respondents consistently report the highest job satisfaction in those employment con- texts which provide the greatest opportunity for work-life balance (Greenhaus, Collins, & Shaw, 2003). As a result of my own reflective inquiry, there are lessons that are becoming clear to me about my own work-life balance (or lack of it). Much like an airplane, which is on course only twice during any given flight (at takeoff and on landing), we never exactly achieve balance. We identify what it would look like, work toward it and make midcourse corrections as needed. So after spending hours grading a particularly complex assignment, I reflect on what makes my work meaningful. When I see students become willing to shift their paradigms about courageously leading change, I can temper such setbacks as a negative course evaluation by a student with optimism about the development of change leadership strategies that build capacity and sustainability.

Balance emerges from an overall sense of purpose. Instead of endlessly making do-to lists (which never get completed), I am learning to specify more focused goals. A research colleague and I conducted a research study on learning organizations and principal self-efficacy. Our findings indicated that balance may be strongly related to and influenced by self-efficacy, a belief that one has a personal sense of control over one's life, and can influence other outcomes. The stresses of today's workload may set academics up to deny the possibility of a balanced work-life. Instead of looking at the scarcity of time, I'm choosing to see the abundance of opportunities available every day of every semester. Last summer, I developed an elaborate writing calendar on which I scheduled the completion of numerous pending projects. By the end of the second week, I was no longer using it. I have subsequently discovered the website www.750words.com, a site which e-mails subscribers daily to encourage 750 words to be written every single day. It has been a useful tool because it helps me keep focused on specific goals rather than the minutiae.

My work and life are so interconnected that I learn from each and apply lessons to inform the other. The academy has traditionally separated faculty work and lives within the academic culture, wherein professors have been expected to check our personal life at the door. I've begun to understand how deeply complex a professor's work is, and have become increasingly clear on setting priorities such as time for exercise or gardening, in the midst of large-scale research goals. When I recognized that I was working 18+ hours daily, 7 days each week, I knew that I had to rethink my balance. Sometimes the momentum is fleeting, so that's when I'm learning to recalibrate the goals. I understand that I have multiple roles, and that each is inexorably linked to the others.

My friends who are female superintendents, close to my age, seem to fall into one of two categories: Either they opted not to have children, or they pioneered the concept of finding good child care. In either case, none has a 12-year gap in her resume, during which she wasn't serving in some fledgling instructional leadership capacity, building the journey to her current role as an experienced school district superintendent or executive director of state and/or federal agencies. In truth, despite the seemingly endless string of sleepless nights, I wouldn't trade it, as it continues to offer so many options—and lessons. It has all been part of a plan, apparently—and I'm becoming more certain that the events of my life happen, in part, just to surprise me. One of my favorite perfumes, a gift from my husband, is called "Miracle." I spritz it generously on days that I'm going to present a research paper at a national conference, for example. It's days like this that I hope that no one in the audience figures out that the presenter is really a woman who grew up exploring in the woods, whose academic career didn't formally begin until recently, rather than an academic who has spent decades researching the topic of the presentation.

Every once in a while, I refocus my lens and imagine the dreams that I've spent much of my life dreaming about—somewhere between letting go of one trapeze and catching the next. Some days in that space, that's a stunning reminder that I'm aging chronologically faster than I'd ever imagined, with so many contributions to make to the field in a relatively limited time frame. The distance between ages 35 and 45 seemed inconsequential; the space between 60 and 70, however, seems significantly more defining. Should I have become an academic early in my career? Was it the right decision to stay at home to raise my sons while they were little boys? Why didn't I give serious consideration to the professoriate earlier? So I take yet another balcony view (Heifetz, Linsky, & Grashow, 2009) of my work-life imbalance, and recognize that since I'm trying to squeeze several lifetimes into this one, it's no wonder there's always so much to do with so little time. I need to appreciate the gift I've been given—the chance to stake my claim, and reinvent myself.

The more I learn, the more I'm willing to take risks. It's not about safety—quite the contrary—but about balancing the risk and reward of working—and leading—without a net.

REFERENCES

Csikszentmihalyi, M. (1990). *Flow: The psychology of optimal experience.* New York, NY: Harper Row.

Greenhaus, J. H., Collins, K. M., & Shaw, J. D. (2003). The relation between work-family balance and quality of life. *Journal of Vocational Behavior, 63,* 510-531.

Heifetz, R. A., Linsky, M., & Grashow, A. (2009). *The practice of adaptive leadership: Tools and tactics for changing your organization and your world.* Cambridge, MA: Harvard Business Press.

Jones, J. B. (2011, May 27). Expecting balance. *The Chronicle of Higher Education, 57*(37). Retrieved from http://chronicle.com/blogs/profhacker/expecting-balance/33675

Mason, M. (2009). Balancing act: Is tenure a trap for women? *The Chronicle of Higher Education, 54*(15). Retrieved from http://www.law.berkeley.edu/files/Is_Tenure_a_Trap_for_Women.pdf

Parker, C. B. (2003, December 12). Faculty stats on work-life balance eyed. *UC Davis Dateline News and Information for Faculty and Staff.* Retrieved from http://dateline.ucdavis.edu/dl_detail.lasso?id=7164

Senge. P. M., Kleiner, A., Roberts, C., Ross, R., & Smith, B. (1994). *The fifth discipline fieldbook: Strategies and tools for building a learning organization.* New York, NY: Crown.

750words.com/about. (2011). Buster Benson, 2011.

Terrien, E. J. (2008). Review of faculty work-family conflict at research universities: Current state & best practices for achieving work-life balance. Retrieved from http://home.uchicago.edu/~eej75/terrienuofcprovostcasewriteup.htm

CHAPTER 12

"WHERE AM I AT RIGHT NOW, ANYWAY?!"

Blurred Boundaries of Home and Work Life

Muhammad A. Khalifa

I have come to believe that finding a sustainable work/home schedule is not only challenging, but also necessary for my long-term professorial career. "One of the biggest things to remember, is to always have clear boundaries between your home life and school life," one of my senior mentors warned me. "In the academy, there is always something *more* to do; so while you remain productive, you must set limits," he continued. But after 3 years since the start of my career, I still wonder if such a sustainable balance actually exists. And if it does, I certainly have not witnessed it in any of the persons who have given me such advice. The purpose of this chapter is to reflect and outline my own attempts—and in general, my persistent failures—at finding a "perfect" balance that responds to the needs of my family, my work, and other life commitments. The journey has been one imbued with fears, divergence, disappointment, despondence, and self-doubts. Indeed, in the end, it has been my commitments to the issues and people that I serve that have inspired my continued persistence.

Juggling Flaming Chain Saws: Academics in Educational Leadership
Try to Balance Work and Family, pp. 95–104
Copyright © 2012 by Information Age Publishing

AN ELUSIVE BALANCE

My inability to find a schedule that successfully accommodates my work and home lives dates back to the start of my career. One could surmise that I am concentrating most of my time and energy on either my family or my work. But ironically, I am most often left feeling that neither my work nor my home lives have been well accommodated. That there are no formulaic schedules that colleagues or mentors could impart has been both helpful and confusing. On the one hand, I have thrived with near autonomous scheduling and the freedom to "work" in my office, while in transit, or at midnight when most people are asleep. One the other hand, while this flexibility had been immensely useful, it has been precisely my challenge—maintaining a schedule that is healthy and sustainable. More than I would have liked, my work schedule has spilled over into my family time. I have neither defined nor maintained a consistent schedule. But I believe a greater challenge has been to craft clear work boundaries. In the coming section, I speak of the perils of my undefined schedule in terms of my research, teaching, and service; and I use examples to explain how my professional commitments have impinged on my personal life.

"CARRYING MY WEIGHT"

Part of the struggle with my work-life balance has been my difficulty in discerning an acceptable level of productivity in my research, teaching, and writing. Among my junior colleagues and I, it is widely perceived that departmental standards in many educational leadership departments do not offer clear research expectations for promotion and tenure. My difficulty with this therefore has been that my research "work" never feels acceptable or complete; there is always something else to do. Thus I am constantly working, yet never comfortable that I have published enough. My junior colleagues describe a similar difficulty in the balancing of their life and work schedules.

While my teaching and service have been more manageable, there are still challenges there as well. One difficulty has been in determining exactly when, and how much, I should deal with students. Again, there is no script or prescribed method for doing this. I can remember meeting students to speak about their research during weekends or evenings that I typically have reserved for my family. And almost annually, I spend a great part of August preparing syllabi for the fall semester; it has always been awkward and inexplicable to family when I've had to spend days from our vacation in front of my computer. Indeed, as one might surmise, this has led to a great deal of tension in both my home and work lives.

RESEARCH

The most consistent advice I have gotten has been to "write every day." I did actually try to conform to this oft-repeated advice, largely because the advice came from well-respected and prolific scholars and friends in the field. Despite my greatest effort, I have not been able to adjust to writing in that manner. I gravitate toward days blocked out in which I devote all of my time to a manuscript to get it finished. This project-based approach has been effective for me because I have been able to focus on a manuscript, one at a time, and give each its due. But it has truly been catastrophic for my family. I often report to the office on Saturdays and Sundays, silence the ringer on my phone, and say to my family, "ok, I'm off and I'll be back this afternoon; call me at the office in case of emergencies because my cell phone ringer will be off." Outsiders might find this routine strange, but in my "balance," it has become normal.

I keep telling myself: "After tenure, it will get better." But as I look at some of my senior colleagues, I cannot see that it has. While some have virtually stopped writing—something that I definitely hope to avoid—I see others who still send work-related e-mails during the middle of the night. I recall getting an e-mail at 3:30 A.M. that contained a draft of a conference proposal that my colleague and I were working on together. The e-mail requested that I finish a part of the proposal within a few hours of the e-mail, and to get changes back to him. Sadly, I was also up around that time! And I got the revisions back on time.

TEACHING

For teaching, one common piece of advice has been, "Always be accessible to your students." In fact, of the many factors on which our students evaluate us, accessibility to students is the most important. It is true that no colleague will argue that we must *always* make ourselves available. But there is always pressure to be accessible and quick in response. During one recent semester, I got a student remark on my evaluations that stated "the professor was not always accessible." I was quite surprised to receive the remark because I had no memory of any student that requested to see me. I went through all of my e-mails and phone messages from that semester; I thought back about any messages I might have received on the white dry-erase board outside of my office; and I reflected on my behavior in class. Of course, I remembered myself being affable and available. I could not understand what led the student to make such a remark about me. I reasoned that it must have been because I left the class when it ended. So when the next semester started, I would be ready. Despite the fact that my class ended at 8:15 P.M., I told myself that I would stick around after each class to chat with students, and to ask students if they had any questions about the course lectures or content. For the most part they did not. But one student, a retired military, self-described "empty nester," was very grateful for the time I spent. He kept me there after class every class period for at least an hour after the class ended. With the previous semester's comment embedded in the back of my mind, I listened to the student lament from one topic to the next and gave everything I had to accommodate his undying need to converse. After the first month of class, frustrated and tired after my 12-hour teaching days, I interrupted him after we spoke for an hour after class: "Hey Barry (pseudonym), man, I hate to interrupt you, but it is after 9 again; I've gotta get home to my family." "Absolutely!" he responded, "I totally understand; I'll catch you next week." Though he seemed to support my need to see my sons off to sleep, I could not help but think how this might lead to lower marks on my student evaluations that semester.

SERVICE

Like my teaching commitments, my service engagements have been rewarding, but at times frustrating and at other times hard to manage. While in teaching, it has been hard to define "accessibility," in service, I have not been clear about how I define my duties at all, This was perhaps best exemplified when one of my junior colleagues came up to me in a frantic rush about a recent annual review of junior colleagues: "Dude, I know that they are gonna talk trash about my service; I've gotta get on more committees so they don't think I'm not pulling my weight, you know?" And yes, I did know. I knew exactly what he was referring to, and like him, was quite stressed about our being asked to engage in so much service work. In some ways, we were being asked to participate even as much as our senior colleagues despite the higher research productivity expectation that junior faculty had. Moreover, it was as though we were doing service so that we could receive a positive vote for tenure, and not because we necessarily believed in the service work in which we were engaged. This ever-present need to engage in varied and multileveled service engagements has led to greater work-life imbalances for me. I believe that I often take on more than what an untenured professor should. I think "normal" service engagements would include: faculty meetings, department and college level meetings, national scholarly reviewing, and dissertation committee work. But then there are engagements that we—because of our convictions and attempts to make our work meaningful and relevant—decide to commit. For me, this has been my scholarship with racial disparities in school suspensions. This work entails developing and maintaining a variety of connections to school district personnel. But even more time consuming are the constant school bureaucracies that must be engaged and negotiated to access the data.

The advice from senior colleagues has always been "to ensure that your service work can lead to research and publications." Yet I rarely see the connection to research in many of the service opportunities. In fact, when trying to balance this advice with my hope to remain "coherent" in my research agenda, I have consciously decided not to engage in every opportunity that presents itself. So recently when I was invited to join a search committee to hire a new faculty member for our department, I refused while carrying deep feelings of guilt. Yet, I knew that it was a very laborious commitment, that it could not be connected to research, and that it would be insightful in my understanding of our unique departmental needs. Moreover, I knew that my senior colleagues were overwhelmed with commitments, and that it was to my benefit to participate since many of them were over 50 years of age and within years of retirement.

FAMILY TIME

Their Question: "When is *Family Time* this semester?"

My Answer: "Okay, *Family Time* is from 6:00 to 8:00 P.M., and half-day Saturday, and Sunday evening"

This dialogue between my family and I at the outset of my first of university teaching was similar to conversations that we have had throughout my professorial career. So much of what I do is not understood by my wife and two sons. In fact, my sons still describe my responsibilities in terms of meetings or teaching: "Wow, you only have to work 2 days per week?" they would inquire. Then I would go on to explain the responsibilities of research and service. Typically, the flexibility of being a tenure-track professor has been both challenging and beneficial. I have been able to get away when it counts: concerts, plays, family vacations, picnics, or even just a weekday of work-from-home have all been possible. But the challenge has been for me to explain my time away to my sons. In the last 18 months, I have presented research at eight international conferences, four of which were outside of the United States. My youngest son asked, "Dad, why do you have to take so many trips?" I didn't have a good answer for him, aside from saying that "It is something I have to do for my job." It was clear that my sons more clearly understood my role as a teacher. I left home before they got up and I came home every day around the same time that they arrived home from school; when I was home they had my full attention. In my current role, I am typically home when they leave for school and when they get home. But several times a month, I tell my boys that they cannot interrupt dad because I am working on a project. Earlier this year, my oldest son walked by me—as I was on the couch working—and saw me using my laptop in what he thought to be, "surfing the net." I explained to him that I was looking for a few articles on a topic, and that although I was lounging on the couch looking at the Internet, I was still working.

READING AND OTHER PERSONAL INTERESTS

In my reflection on my work/life balancing act, I realize that leisurely, news, or hobby-based readings have been the biggest causalities in my search for a work balance. My decision to focus on my writing and producing scholarship has also severely my limited my travel. My father and I have visited four continents in our travels together—Africa, Asia, Latin America, and Europe. A father can only spend so much time away, and when choosing between leisure travel or scholarly conference travel and research, the latter takes precedence. Part of the problem is that I constantly feel like I have to be working and that where one project ends, another begins. In fact, this manuscript serves as one of the first opportunities for me to deeply reflect on an issue of such paramount importance to my career. I was speaking to a colleague recently and discovered that she is spending 2 summer months in the Colorado Rocky Mountains. She said that she was doing some reading and writing, but mainly walking and deep reflecting. I look forward to the days I can return to focusing on my own interests. I suspect that I will feel comfortable doing so after I am awarded tenure.

I miss reading more than most other activities. I took an inventory of the books that I have recently read; with the exception of a couple of travel books about Somaliland and Kenya, places I recently traveled, most were books that would somehow support my scholarship. I have not had the pleasure to read much at all that would enlighten my financial health, improve my marksmen point averages, or broaden my spiritual outlook. My outdoorsmen activities and leisure travel have also come to a grinding halt. But I somehow have managed to find a way at becoming a better culinary artist.

One solution for me has been to combine my personal interests with my family time. With the constricted time, it has worked like a charm. This strategy has not worked so well with my dad, who lives in California. But my sons and I, even though we've had to combine interests, are able to spend time and not give up hobbies. The most recent example of this has been travel and our visits to a local archery range. Regarding travel, I would often take rugged, "roughing-it" trips by myself, but we would take the boys to the more family-friendly theme parks like Sea World, Disneyland, Cedar Point, or Great America. But they are now old enough to venture down into places like the Grand Canyon, as they did for the first time last summer. Thus, that is time we can spend together while still maintaining our personal interests. Our mutual interest in archery has been just as enriching. I have not only been able to improve my own aim as I released the arrows, but spend quality time with my sons as they became involved in one of Dad's hobbies. Recently, my wife has said that she would like to join us as well.

IS IT REALLY WORTH IT?

One of the questions that I rarely hear from others but that I often ask myself is: is the stress and personal distress that I and other assistant professors experience really worth it? Every time, I answer "yes." I, like many of my colleagues in Educational Leadership, left lucrative careers to join the ranks in academe. And like them, I am frequently invited back to industry, in some cases, with the lure of twice the salary and less time-consuming "work." Perhaps uniquely, I am sometimes invited to work in Asia, Africa, and the Middle East, all places that I have once called home, and to some of which I would love to one day return. Yet here, as an American professor of educational administration, I feel uniquely placed to positively contribute to the lives of the voiceless. In my case, I see myself as an advocate for issues in urban American contexts with marginalized peoples. My writings, along with the writings of some of my colleagues, are contributing to critical dialogues that look at these issues in unique and innovative ways. I am in regular conversations with school leaders in Detroit about how they might address their suspension gap, for example. More than the scholarship, conversations like this make it all "worth it" to be in the position that I am. Ultimately, it is my hope that we are reaching audiences and making a difference in ways that other professionals might not have the opportunities to do.

IDEOLOGICALLY "BALANCE" TENSIONS IN WORK AND LIFE

For the most part, I have written here about time management, a formidable challenge which I have accepted that I will likely never conquer. But what has been equally frustrating about addressing my work/life balance has been ideological in nature. It has been the problem of juggling the hegemonic tendencies and positionalities of academic liberalism and consumerism with my own personal orientations and understandings. I find that even some of my most "critical" colleagues are still confined to what the cultures in the academy say are acceptable, and when I (or others like me) step outside of this box, we can be described as "unorthodox." For example, many of my self-proclaimed "liberal" colleagues do not offer nonconventional solutions to the problems in their local communities. In a place like Michigan, with some of the most disparaging "rates"—dropout, homelessness, homicide, joblessness, health disparities, and many more alarming trends from which to choose—many of the scholarly dialogues to which I am privy seem to be removed from any of the social challenges that our local communities face.

Accepting a dominant academic discourse has been challenging for me because the urban contexts from which I come have been immune to the typical liberalistic solutions that come to them from academe, and consumerism has completely ravished the soul of many urban communities. For example, in discussions about improving the lives of young urban students, discussions among many colleagues somehow always drift to standardized testing. But in the Detroit schools that I have seen in which test scores are above average, I have not seen improved life circumstances for the children or their families. I believe the decision to focus on neoliberal tendencies is strongly linked to a focus on production and products in the broader society. For example, while 50 years ago, there was a semblance of community solidarity in many urban cities such as Philly, NYC, Chicago, or Detroit, now, the impulse toward individuality that is so ingrained in consumerist culture has removed any of the mobilizing efforts that were once commonplace in large urban areas. Courageous conversations around personal responsibility and community norms are virtually extinct.

One example that undergirds the tensions between dominant discourses in academe and the unique—and often contrary—needs of specific communities can be found when one looks at the sexual behaviors of young people. Despite the teenage pregnancy rate and the elevated STD rates (including, not the least of which is HIV/AIDS) in urban minority communities, many professors, whom I know speak about school and neighborhood reform, are virtually silent on sexual behaviors of young people. Their research and conversations on sexual "freedoms" are void of this issue, and so many others issues that impact urban America. Yet recently, in a television interview on given about Black American progress and challenges, one of the most highly regarded African American pubic intellectuals summed up the biggest challenges facing the Black community as "homophobia" and the "mistreatment of women."

Grave as these two issues are, I could not help but wonder about HIV/ AIDS, homicide, school failure, joblessness, or even structural racism. I often wonder if these two issues took precedence because they are more aligned with dominant academic discourses. I wondered how my collegiality might be viewed if I highlighted complexities around such issues. This serves as a tension between my work and life because this moves out of merely an academic discussion and into a personalized family and neighborhood discussion. I have family members that have been victims of violence and AIDS, and a great many that have become unwed teenage mothers. Yet, despite catastrophic impacts in my family and in local Black communities, I have primarily heard scholarly voices that conform to liberal academic discourse that have not been helpful to these issues. For example, at a recent University Council of Educational Administration conference, I was speaking with a group of scholars and mentioned that young urban Detroit schoolchildren might benefit from having a hip-hop based public school that celebrates their unique urban cultures. To my surprise, I was challenged on the "misogyny" that might be represented in the music. Yet, what bothered me was neither that there are a great number of affirmative and "conscious" hip-hop artists that are actually quite positive, nor even that there are greater challenges, such as violence and drugs, within the genre of music. Actually, I was most bothered because the *dominant discourse* has been most critical about representations of women and thus the professors seemed to follow suit. Indeed, I am a strong critic and opponent of misogyny. But even though misogyny is a grave problem that must be challenged, when compared to the over 80% dropout rate for male students in Detroit Pubic Schools, and with daily life in the murder capital of the world, it becomes clear that the popular academic discourses are somewhat off base. There are countless other issues that could be exemplified. So though I find much agreement between myself and discourses in academic cultures, my bigger challenge in the future will be to find ways that I might reconcile my own *differing* positionalities with those of the academy. For now, this reconciling is done by guarding my own voice. But I suspect that as I move deeper into the community and closer to tenure, it will become more necessary for me to speak and act in ways that are most beneficial to the communities I serve, despite the orientations of dominant academic discourses.

CONCLUDING REFLECTIONS

I have come to accept the absence of a prescribed work/life balance. For me, it has been whatever works on any given week; I suspect it will stay that way. Depending on research demands, changing family dynamics, or a host of other reasons, this balance is always one phone call away from a major readjustment. I have also come to accept a level of tension between my ideological self and the ideological trajectories of academe. And thus as I constantly search for a better balance in my work and life realities, I am coming to terms with the fact that I may already be here. It may not get any better than it already is.

CHAPTER 13

ONE FAMILY, DIFFERENT PERSPECTIVES ON WORK-LIFE BALANCE

Lisa A. W. Kensler

MORE QUESTIONS THAN ANSWERS

I had to laugh when I was invited to write a chapter about work-life balance. Whenever I mentioned the article to others, they laughed too. I am not even sure what it means for our work and lives to be in balance. I frequently feel as though I do a horrible job of keeping work and life in balance; I work on weekends more often than not, I bring work home in the evenings, and I am writing this chapter in the car on our way to spend a long weekend with family. I could write story after story about times when I felt out of balance. I have been a full-time mom at home, lived apart from my family for a full year, and struggled with everything in between. When I asked myself when I felt like my work-life balance was just right, my mind went blank. I really did not have a clear answer. As I further considered how to approach this project, I felt a deep curiosity about how my family would respond to questions about work-life balance. I decided to interview my husband and two daughters, reflect on their responses, and see what I might learn. I interviewed each family member during the spring of 2011 using these questions:

*Juggling Flaming Chain Saws: Academics in Educational Leadership
Try to Balance Work and Family*, pp. 105–112
Copyright © 2012 by Information Age Publishing
All rights of reproduction in any form reserved.

- In our family, was there a time when you felt like we got the balance between our lives and work right? When was that? I really want to hear whatever details come to you. Was there a time that popped to mind as soon as you heard the question? I want to hear that and any others that come to mind.
- As you think about work-life balance in your life, what is most important to you?
- What conditions might best support a healthy work-life balance?

I will share their individual responses to the first question and then discuss their answers to the other two questions in a more integrated fashion. Each family member read, suggested minor edits and approved the final version of this chapter. In order to provide a context for their responses, I will first provide a brief description of our family, paying particular attention to our work-life balance history.

WORK-LIFE TIME LINE

Mike and I have been married for nearly 26 years. Our daughter Emily is 23 years old and just finished her first year of life after college. Shelley turned 20 in August of 2011 and is a sophomore in college. When Emily was 8 months old I chose to decline acceptance to graduate school in favor of being a full-time mom. For 2 years, Mike pursued his MS degree full-time. I cared for up to four additional children in our home to help pay our bills. I also did some consulting work part-time—data entry and analysis on our home computer. I worked full-time outside our home while Mike was a full-time dad during the summer break in his master's program. During the next 4 years, I continued as a full-time mom.

I started graduate school when Emily was 7 and Shelley was 3. My schedule allowed me to pick them up immediately after school. Although I was on the PhD track, I saw the all consuming work life of my professors and seriously doubted that I would be able to do it all. I had fallen in love with teaching introductory biology labs to nonmajors and decided that teaching high school biology might be just as rewarding and more manageable than pursuing a career as a biology professor. I settled for my MS and quickly earned a teaching certificate in secondary science. I was a teacher, for a year in Norfolk, Virginia and then for 1 year in Annapolis, Maryland; we moved because Mike was promoted to a new job within his organization. When Emily was 10 and Shelley 6, we moved to St. Louis, Missouri where we lived and worked in a residential private school. Mike was dean of boys and I was a high school biology teacher. We lived in an apartment attached to the boys' dorm. Emily and Shelley attended the same school. After 7 years, I moved to Pennsylvania 1 year ahead of my family so that I could begin a doctoral program in educational leadership. The following year, Mike and Shelley joined me and Emily stayed in St. Louis to finish her senior year of high school. After 4 years, Mike and I both began new jobs at Auburn University. I am finishing my third year in a tenure track position here in the Educational Foundations, Leadership, and Technology department.

In my mind, I could not pick a perfect work-life balance phase of our lives. I recalled the struggles I felt as a full-time mom, wondering if I was giving up any hope of a meaningful career. Maybe if I knew then how things would work out I would have felt less worry about my future during what I know now was a very special time. As a new teacher, I had three first-years of teaching in a row. Each of those 3 years I taught in a new school and a new curriculum. I poured myself into teaching and loved it, but also felt perpetually torn between work and family. I felt sure that I was not doing either as well as I should. Although I found my rhythm as a teacher in St. Louis, living and working in the same very small community had significant challenges. I left those challenges behind in order to earn my doctorate and found a whole new set of challenges! Work has never been as all-consuming as doctoral study and the professoriate.

DISCOVERING DIFFERENT PERSPECTIVES

As I thought about interviewing Mike and the girls, I recalled the advice: "Don't ask a question, if you don't want to know the answer." Did I want to hear their answers? Would their answers confirm my fears that we never got it quite right? Would Mike wish that our life together was different? What would Emily and Shelley, as young women, remember about their childhoods? What would they have learned about work-life balance from our family life? I interviewed each of them separately. Emily lives in Phila-delphia, so we talked by phone. Mike and I talked in the car on our way to a Montgomery Biscuits baseball game (one of our favorite things to do in our work-free time). Shelley was sitting in an airport in Eugene, Oregon, on her way to a National Outdoor Leadership School course in Alaska, while we talked on the phone. I recorded notes during each interview. I did not formally analyze these notes, but I did reread and reflect on them many times.

They each had different responses to the first question about when we got our work-like balance most right. Emily knew immediately that it was when she was in elementary school and I was in graduate school for my Master's degree in biology/ecology. She recalled coming to school with me, going birding, owling late at night (I was taking a course in ornithology and had to log birding hours), collecting data in the wetlands, and other "exciting things." She described very vivid and positive memories of our family spending time together and said, "That time did not leave a stressful impression on me." She mentioned a "distinct separation between work and our home lives" and she said, "I don't feel like anything was lacking." My conversation with Emily reminded me of how much I enjoyed graduate school and living in Norfolk, Virginia. It did feel relatively easy to include the girls in much of my field work and we did spend our weekends as a family. However, financially, this was not an easy time for Mike and me. My staying home full-time and then entering graduate school left very little money in the bank at the end of each month.

Mike responded as quickly as Emily to the first question, but with a different time in our lives. He described the year we spent in Annapolis, Maryland (immediately following our time in Norfolk, Virginia) as the time we had our work-life balance most right. We lived in a great neighborhood with neighbors who were fun to hang out with. Kids ruled the neighborhood and the parents genuinely enjoyed each other's company. He enjoyed his job and for the first time we were able to save a bit of money each month. He acknowledged that it "was probably a more stressful time for you. You were learning a new job teaching middle school." He was right. That was a stressful year for me. Emily and Shelley went to after-school care, I came home every night with grading and planning to do for the next day, and middle school students were very different from high school students! By the end of the year, I decided to leave classroom teaching and work in an environmental education center where my hours would be more contained within an 8-hour work day. I hoped that would make our daily lives less stressful. Emily and Shelley had a babysitter all day, every day that summer. Unfortunately, I was not feeling any more peaceful about our work-life balance. I worried about how much TV they were watching and wondered if I could really trust their 18-year-old babysitter's judgment. When we were unexpectedly invited to move to St. Louis for Mike to assume the role of dean of boys, I enthusiastically supported the idea.

Emily and Mike both mentioned that the times they had just described were in stark contrast to our life in St. Louis, where our life was our work and our work was our life. Mike's work was constant and demanding, as the lead administrator for 80 to 100 high school boys and their six house parents. Emily described our years in St. Louis:

> It felt like one big and long transition between Annapolis and where we lived next [Pennsylvania]. I never felt like I was really from St. Louis. It never felt like my home. I feel like you guys worked there and I went to school there, but we didn't really live there.... Living where we worked made

it all blur together. It made me feel very strongly about having distinct boundaries between work and private time. At [school]—we had no work-life balance—there were always weekend responsibilities. Family time was never fully our time. Work mode was 100%. There was rarely a time when work responsibilities were not lurking in the background. I haven't put the two together before. But that is definitely why [I feel strongly about distinct work-life boundaries]—I did not like that blurring of work and family. Looking back at the two times—before [the school] and after [the school]—it was like having two families. The entire time we were at [the school] it was very stressful. Nothing about [the school] was stress free or fully peaceful, other than the summers. But those were small windows of time. They were nice and part of the yearly cycle. It was really fun doing our family trips. Those memories feel more like Norfolk, but they don't dominate in my mind from [that time].

Shelley's response to the first question surprised me the most. She said,

"I don't really know. I never felt like you guys did not care. You may have been working more, but I also had a busy schedule with practice, games, and riding. So, your guys' work life did not impact me that much. If anything, it was me not balancing family time ... I think you guys have worked pretty hard to keep a good balance."

I asked her specifically about our time in St. Louis. She simply said, "Dad worked a lot in the dorm, but he still spent time with us."

Their responses to my first question helped me see that work-life balance may very well reside in the eye of the beholder. All of my fears that we never got it right were not exactly realized. Emily's sense of clarity about work-life balance comes from her happy memories of our family time and feeling included in my learning and work. One of the years that I found most stressful, Mike found most balanced. His work was rewarding and fulfilling; our neighborhood culture was engaging and fun; and our monthly paychecks allowed us to save. Shelley seemed to associate a proper work-life balance with feeling cared for and she was sure we always cared.

DISCOVERING CONVERGING PERSPECTIVES

In response to questions two and three about what is most important to you and what conditions might best support a healthy work-life balance, their responses reflected more similarity than difference. Not feeling stressed was most important to Emily. Mike and Shelley expressed a similar desire for low stress. They all mentioned how important it is to enjoy one's work; meaningful work that you are proud of and where you like your colleagues and feel appreciated all contribute to making work enjoyable. Of course, earning a livable wage in a reasonable number of hours per week is also important. When one's work is rewarding, both emotionally and financially, it allows you to have the energy to come home and engage with family and friends. Mike was most clear about this when he said, "Balance is not work and recuperating from work. There has to be enough buoyancy and energy to engage with life outside of work." Mike also noted that our work life is improved by "leaving work behind, stepping back and gaining perspective." Shelley commented that she does not want to be burned out by work. She defined burned out as, "Mentally tired of what I am doing—a state of mental and physical exhaustion." She continued, "The key to balance is being able to do something long term without feeling like you need a significant break from it."

I hope to be a professor in educational leadership long into my retirement years. I don't expect to retire at 65. In fact, I have said many times that this job—work that I find engaging, meaningful, and important—is my retirement plan. Shelley's wisdom is sticking with me. Emily's clarity about the importance of keeping work time distinct from nonwork time challenges me. Mike's desire for us to have enough energy left over for enjoying our leisure time with friends and family reminds me that I am often exhausted in the evenings and still working on the weekends. I don't know if I can successfully meet the expectations of this job without blurring the lines by bringing work home. However, I do not want to burn out and I want to nurture my relationships with family and friends. I also agree with Mike and know that new insights related to teaching and research are more likely to occur when we fully step away and return refreshed. To me, fully stepping away means being wholly present in what one is doing—engaging whole-heartedly in that work-free time.

Near the end of each interview, I asked if there was anything else to add. Shelley said,

Communication is important. There are times now that I get frustrated because you are always working, but I understand it. I give you a harder time than you deserve because when I really need time with you, it is there. It is important to communicate and stay sensitive to what others need and making time for each other. Plan to make time for each other, if you are not naturally on the same schedule. Nobody wants to feel like they come second or are less important than work because jobs are replaceable and people are not. It is important to keep in mind your goals for each part of your life and regularly checking in on those goals to see if they conflict and be strategic in how you act upon them. It is really important for families to work together, communicating about and supporting each other's goals. We have always put family first—it has been give and take at times, but our long term goal has always been family first and overall it has been very positive.

TAKE HOME LESSONS

As I reflect on my family's response to my questions about work-life balance and on my first 3 years as an assistant professor in educational leadership, I am struck by the dichotomy we establish in our minds between work and life. I wonder if this dichotomy links to more mechanical images of balance. Many mechanical systems exist in a steady state. Well designed machines effectively and predictably operate as designed. I see a balance or scale with "work" on one side and my "life" on the other. Is the perfect balance when the two sides of the scale cease moving? Might we believe that we should be able to design a perfect schedule where we and our family members feel a peaceful sense of perfect balance? Too often, I have thought that if I could just find and stick to a perfect schedule, then life would feel easier. Maybe this fundamentally flawed assumption and related expectations have left me feeling perpetually inadequate at mastering the work-life balance challenge.

As an ecologist, I am reminded that living systems do not exist in a steady state unless they are dead and even then, decomposition does not leave them in that state for long. Living systems, from cells to organisms and populations, are constantly responding to external and internal conditions through continuous feedback. Equilibrium, then, is not a steady state; it is a constant adjustment between intolerable extremes. Individual cells within our bodies have to use energy to maintain their equilibrium. As an individual, maintaining a sense of equanimity through the inevitably changing contexts of work and family requires responsive, adaptive work. This work requires energy, attention, and commitment. I hear advice for this work in my interviews with Mike, Emily, and Shelley.

I would like to stop carrying the burden of finding the perfect work-life balance. I have one life and of necessity and choice, work fills much of my life's time. Mike shifted the work-life balance question for me by asking, "How much of your life does work consume?" I am asking myself, "How much of my life am I willing to let work consume?" I am going to need to live with this question for some time. Emily commented that, "Now that we are grown up and can fend for ourselves we hardly see you." Shelley commented, "Nobody wants to feel like they come second or are less important than work because jobs are replaceable and people are not." It really is all about relationships and communication. As our needs and the needs of the people in our lives change, we need to be listening well enough to discern the needs and respond with authentic care and love.

There are times when our work demands more of our full attention than we prefer to give and other times when people important to us need us to set work aside. Maybe the best indicator of a healthy work-life balance is the degree to which important people in our lives feel nurtured and loved.

We also need to listen to and nurture ourselves. Valuing time and thus, setting time aside, for gaining perspective, recharging our creative batteries and engaging in life's work-free adventures is something that I have done much better than I generally do now, as a new assistant professor. The challenge of learning a new job and the full list of associated responsibilities and never-ending series of deadlines has legitimately felt all consuming. In academe where our work is literally never finished, it might be too easy for me to mindlessly fall into a perpetual pattern of prioritizing work time over nonwork time. I could spend every waking hour and many of my should-be-sleeping hours working and still not accomplish everything I believe my job demands.

I dug into the writing of this chapter in the car on the way to spend a weekend with family and I am finishing it after that weekend. Prior to heading off for that trip, I voiced feeling stressed about taking the time and although I may not have said I did not want to go, I did think it more than once. What a mistake I would have made if I had, yet again, claimed I did not have time. Once with family, I fully engaged in all of the fun activities and found myself not even thinking about work responsibilities until I climbed back in the car for the 12-hour drive home. The time with my family was refreshing and energizing. I got to know two of my nephews for the first time. At 8 and 4, they now know their Aunt Lisa. I want to continue nurturing meaningful connections with them and other friends and family. When it comes to our work-life equilibrium, we have the power to choose the intolerable extremes within which we continuously adjust. After writing this chapter I am more conscious of that choice and less interested in finding a perfect balance.

CHAPTER 14

FLYING BY THE SEAT OF MY PANTS

Katherine Cumings Mansfield

"WELCOME ABOARD!"

I must admit that I was worried about sharing my story with you. How could I possibly give you anything that would be helpful? Sometimes I feel as if I have barely made it through this ongoing journey in one piece. After agreeing to do so, I immediately went to my husband and asked him, "Hon, did I do anything right? Or was I a total disaster?" When he looked at me puzzled I added, "You know, this whole becoming an academic thing. Is there anything we did during the past 5 years that could possibly be offered as helpful advice?" My husband reassured me that I was not a total disaster, but in fact, did many things "right" (God bless this man!). This chapter is an attempt to share my thoughts on balancing my life as: a wife; a mother of two adolescents; the daughter of an ailing mother, and; a friend and employee during the sometimes difficult and often adventurous 5-year journey as a full-time doctoral student. Sometimes it seemed more like "flying by the seat of my pants" rather than "work-life balance" so I turn to the words of wisdom shared by my flight attendant friend for assistance.[1]

Juggling Flaming Chain Saws: Academics in Educational Leadership
Try to Balance Work and Family, pp. 113–121

BEFORE EMBARKING

"As we prepare for takeoff, please be sure your seatback and tray tables are up, all electronic devices are off, and carry-on luggage is under a seat"

For most voyages, grand and not so grand, it is especially helpful to plan ahead. But, I am not sure whether anyone can adequately prepare for a journey that entails a plethora of transitions, including the transformation from student to academic. Shortly after takeoff, within the first semester of my program, I was nearly blown off course. I was not adequately prepared for the mental, emotional, and financial demands that doctoral studies required—and neither was my family. I remember sitting at the kitchen table just bawling my eyes out. I was crying. My husband was crying. Both our children were crying. All of us were so overwhelmed and none of us had the words to adequately describe what we were feeling or what was happening to us. And, quite frankly, I am still unsure how to adequately describe it. I just know that we were in a really bad place; I was devastated. It had been my dream to pursue the PhD for almost 20 years, but my family was more important to me than anything. All I could manage sobbing to them was, "I'll quit. I'll just quit. I won't put you guys through this anymore." And I remember my son, Ian (10 years old at the time) saying, "Mom, you can't give up your dreams! You can't quit now!"

What we were experiencing around the kitchen table that night was a type of culture shock; the realization that the voyage to the PhD was far different from just going back to night school. It was poles apart from getting the master's degree when I was out of the house a night or two per week and had some reading to do instead of watching TV in the evenings. I was—we were—being inducted into a different way of life that quite frankly, we just were not prepared for. We really thought it would be similar to grad school—just longer. No one mentioned the acculturation process that takes place during doctoral studies: Sitting on university and/or department committees; serving on peer-review panels for research conferences; the eventual mentoring of newer doc students; conducting research; teaching classes. You know, practicing all those things that actual professors do and becoming a colleague to these professors we admire so much. You are more than a student. In fact, you aren't really a student at all. It is more akin to being an apprentice. My first clue to this switch in roles was how most of my professors treated me. I was definitely treated more as a fellow life traveler rather than the typical teacher-student relationship that I was used to. That was the cool part. The not-so-cool part was collapsing at the kitchen table in a puddle of tears and seeing my beloved children and life partner falling apart before my eyes. Keeping up with the traditional student activities such as a heavy reading list and writing solid papers, in addition to taking on additional academic roles was surprising and overwhelming.

My husband, David is convinced that this apprentice-like process needs to be communicated to people ahead of time before embarking on this journey and that a conversation with family and friends needs to take place concerning the expectations that will be placed on the student and their significant others. While it may be true that no one can truly be prepared for the transformation that takes place, David believes that if some of the lifestyle changes had been mentioned in the recruitment literature for example, our conversations might have been different leading up to my eventual acceptance into a program. (However, we doubt that doctoral programs will be as open up front as perhaps they should be. After all, their goal is to enlist, not scare you away.) So, our first words of wisdom for those embarking on this life journey are to try to understand as fully as you can up front what this "going back to school" means and the full-bodied commitment it will take for the transformation to take place. Then, speak with family and friends about some of the financial and temporal costs that will be placed upon you, such as traveling at least 2 weeks out of the year to research conferences. Knowing this up front may help less experienced travelers prepare, if not financially and relationally, at least mentally. Not to mention that if green yet eager explorers know expectations in advance, some may decide this journey is not for them. As the flight attendant says when you need to get off the plane in a hurry, "Keep in mind: the closest exit may be behind you ..."

ANTICIPATING ROUGH TIMES

"We recommend you keep your seatbelt fastened at all times, as turbulence can occur unexpectedly"

Rough times occur in our lives unexpectedly and come in the form of minor illnesses (self or loved ones), financial setbacks (a flooded washing machine comes to mind), and so on. Just as a seatbelt grounds you in case of a turbulent flight, there are tools in our lives that can serve a similar purpose. For me, this meant staying fastened to my relationships and my aspirations. Despite the initial culture shock, my family and I decided to continue on this path we had started. I was blessed with an immediate family who supported my dreams, but since none of us had been on this trip to this place before, I committed to finding out coping skills with those who had. In the short time I had been a doc student, I had begun to establish some relationships with fellow students and professors, but had not been as honest as I perhaps should have been about the struggles my family and I were having in adjusting to this new lifestyle. My first order of business was to change that.

I admitted to a third-year student the doubts I was having about my abilities to get through the program. I remember admitting to him, "I just don't think I can do this." He listened to my angst and then said simply, "You *can* do this. You *are* doing this." This married father of two then said, "I'm assuming you've seen *Finding Nemo*, right? Well, this is going to sound so simple—and I promise I'm not trying to be demeaning— because the message in it may be simple but it is so important and so true. Just remember what Dori said: 'Just keep swimming.' Because if you don't, you'll die. Don't stop now. Just keep going. Even when you're too tired, too exhausted, too overwhelmed. Don't stop." He was right. It did sound so very simple, but it became my mantra for the next 4½ years.

That was just the beginning of my honest sharing with fellow travelers who were living what I was living and could understand what I was going through. This took courage and humility as I had to admit that I felt weak and inept. And ironically, when I was brave enough to share my vulnerabilities, fellow travelers were in a position to show me my strengths and encourage me and strengthen me during this time of significant growth and change. Two women in particular became my confidants and encouragers. It was interesting to us how it seemed we took turns being the "strong one" or the "weak one" over the next several years. One of us would listen as another would "vent" or one woman would give the pep talks and draw the other two along the path toward our goals. We were lucky that it was rare that all three of us were feeling completely defeated at any one time. We could play champion for each other as the situation called for. Again, this took a measure of humility and courage for all parties concerned. Not only does it take courage and humility to admit one's weaknesses to peers, but it takes guts to listen to classmates' struggles and an unassuming nature to sift through the chaff and the grain; offering support and encouragement with a nonjudgmental spirit. I honestly do not know what I would have done without the support of colleagues who came alongside me in this adventure. So, that is my second bit of advice: Find a few people you can trust whole-heartedly and be not afraid to bare your souls to them. Similar to the basic, sensible nature of the conventional seatbelt, good, old-fashioned, close friendships have the capacity to keep you grounded during turbulent times.

UNEXPECTED CRISES

"Always put your own mask on first and then help children or others near you"

In addition to turbulence, more serious crises can occur in our lives. Being the big sister from a large family, it seems there was always someone who needed something. I would characterize those moments as unpredictable turbulence that could be settled with a financial gift or a late-night conversation on the cell phone. But sometimes serious crises occur that test our mental and physical capacities more critically. Early on in my doctoral program, my mother went missing, was eventually found, and then diagnosed with early-onset Alzheimer's disease. Talk about unexpected drop in pressure and loss of oxygen! And the panic seeing those little yellow masks thrusting out of nowhere! And yet, regular life went on. My children and husband still needed fresh laundry and groceries and love and attention. I know I'm supposed to put on my mask first before helping others, but how do I do that? Thankfully, I had fellow colleagues who were helping me through the changes that were taking place in my world of academe. But how on earth was I going to cope with what was happening in the rest of my world? What do you do when the super hero gets sick and you're just not ready to be one yourself?

My mother's illness could have been a huge setback on my journey to academe. But, again, I had to rely on others in addition to being proactive on my end. First of all, I admitted to a few trusted professors what was happening. One woman at my institution was very sympathetic and promised she would be praying for me. She shared her story of losing her daughter a few years back and the difficulties she experienced during that time. Knowing this amazing woman's story and that she would be praying for me strengthened me greatly. Second, my dear husband and I took an honest look at our finances and found a way we could help my stepfather with medical expenses despite the fact that we were up to our eyeballs in debt due to student loans. We were still able to contribute to my mother's care and that was a great relief to my conscience as well as material relief to my first family. Third, I shared our situation with another trusted professor who lives in the same town as my stepfather. She immediately offered her home to me if I ever needed a place to stay during this time of economic and emotional upheaval. Indeed, I needed to accept her offer not long after she made it.

My mother's condition deteriorated rapidly. She was committed to a nursing home about a year after diagnosis. My stepfather felt in his bones that I needed to get out there as soon as possible. So, I made airline reservations for my daughter and me right away. And I called my generous professor friend and shared my travel plans. Without hesitation, she opened her home to us so we could love my mother up close and personal mere weeks before she passed away in her sleep.

Did I really put on my oxygen mask before helping others? Probably not. When it came to my mother's illness and death it felt more as if others saw my gasping for oxygen and lovingly forced the mask on my face so I could indeed help "children and others." It is very humbling to realize that any strength I have is actually derived from the generosity and love of others. I may be a singular soul on this journey called life, but I cannot claim to have achieved anything at all single-handedly. It wasn't until another medical emergency came unexpectedly that I finally learned how to put the mask on myself first.

In November 2010 my doctor broke the news: "Your cholesterol is out of control. You're going to die of a stroke or heart attack any minute if you don't do something now!" I was in shock. I knew I had gained a significant amount of weight during doctoral studies, but my weight had fluctuated in the past and I always had low cholesterol. Well, not anymore. The only good news he had was that my "good" cholesterol was great. He said, "It's very obvious that you cook with olive oil and eat a lot of fish." But the "bad" cholesterol required the latest, most expensive drug in addition to increasing the time I spent exercising. My family genes and my neglect of the care of the self had caught up with me, and I literally had to do something for myself first or I would not be on this side of the ground anymore.

I immediately went on medication, requiring further budgetary adjustments as a full-time student earning a very low salary with only minimal benefits. I spoke with my dissertation supervisor about the importance of compressing our schedule for defending the dissertation. The faster I got done, the more time I would have to care for myself. The more I cared for myself, the better position I would be to be an excellent teaching assistant for him my final semester. And I could better navigate the academic job search process. Thankfully, he supported my plan. I turned in my dissertation on December 10, 2010, and immediately started my new diet and exercise regime. On February 23, 2011, I interviewed at Virginia Commonwealth University and on February 25, 2011, successfully defended my dissertation. The months of March through May were spent tending my family, mentoring newer students, teaching classes, and continuing to care for this imperfect but precious vessel that carries my spirit on my life's journey. It is unfortunate that it took a big scare to wake me up to the realities of the damage I was doing to my body. But, I am so thankful that my doctor was so frank with me. He knew I needed to hear the unvarnished truth. I hope to never again neglect to place the mask on myself first before helping children and others.

LAST CALL BEFORE SIGNING OFF

"Thank you for your attention and once again, welcome aboard!"

You know, those flight attendants sure are smart. They know they have to thank us for our attention to their advice because their simple words seem undemanding on the surface. They tell us to keep our seatbelt fastened at all times, but how many of us do it? I mean, don't most of us just rip those things off as soon as the captain turns that little light on? I know I am guilty of that. "What do they know? Everything seems fine to me. The flight is smooth and easy. I don't see any clouds on the horizon." But, honestly, flight attendants know a lot. They've clocked many more hours in flight than we have. They know that turbulence can occur at any time. They've experienced it. They know how scary it is to see inexperienced travelers encounter unexpected storms. They've literally seen objects and people flying by the seat of their pants in their cabin midflight. So, I guess that's my final kernel of wisdom to offer for consideration: Listen to others. Be your amazing, intelligent, strong, and confident self, but also be humble and fearless when it comes to revealing your struggles and reaching out to others. Allow others a chance to be strong and brave for you. Present fellow travelers a chance to carry you when you're just too weak to go on. Provide your attention to those who know more about this life journey into academe. And in turn, some day, allow yourself to be the one that other weary travelers can lean on from time to time without judgment. Finally, I offer a list of ten things to consider before deciding to pursue a PhD. If you are already a doctoral student, my hope is that this list will help you successfully navigate the journey. "Thank you for your attention and once again, welcome aboard!"

TEN THINGS YOU SHOULD KNOW
BEFORE DECIDING TO PURSUE A PHD

1. **Everything takes longer than you think it will.** If your program publicizes their "rigor" believe them. If your program claims you can finish 78 hours of coursework and 12 dissertation hours (that's 90 hours, not counting the masters) in 3½ years, do not believe them. Sit down with the significant others in your life and determine how you will negotiate finances and relationships over the next 5 years. Discuss what you will do if medical or other emergencies arise during that time.

2. **It's sink or swim folks.** And it is up to you to find out what it takes to "just keep swimming." If you are not an independent, self-starter kind of person, steer clear.

3. **It's all about the three Rs (but especially two of those Rs).** If you aren't especially fond of reading and writing, don't even think about starting a doctoral program. You need to know that you will

read at least 2 hours every day for each course you take. Yes, that's about 6 hours a day pretty much every day of the week. Plan accordingly.

4. **Everything is magnified when you are a doc student.** Everything that bugs you BDS (before doctoral studies) will bug you more DDS (during doctoral studies). Everything that delights you BDS will delight you more DDS. (You'll understand what I mean when we proceed through the list together!)

5. **Mean people suck.** You know that old bumper sticker, right? Well, mean people suck even more when you're pursuing an advanced degree. There are mean people everywhere, and for the most part, we are able to work around that. But, during doctoral studies, when financial stresses abound and you miss your family and friends, dealing with sociopaths is even more difficult because you are short on time, energy, and strength. Only deal with mean people if you absolutely must and if possible, only after you have had enough rest, eaten a healthy meal, and prayed/meditated.

6. **Lazy people suck, too.** And by suck, I mean they pretty much suck the living, breathing daylights out of you. And unfortunately, lazy people have a keen eye for spotting the hard workers and will invite themselves to your small group project or tell you how "fun" it would be to "collaborate on a presentation or publication sometime." Learn quickly who these people are and do not make eye contact with them under any circumstances. Only speak with them if you must. Find out who has a strong work ethic and ally yourself with them every chance you can.

7. **Immature people will drive you to the edge of sanity.** Immaturity can take many forms and you will need to be prepared to sometimes, literally bite your tongue (if you must). In the field of educational leadership, it may be the student or professor who has never taught in a K-12 setting in their lives but they claim to know how to improve "teacher quality" or "parent involvement." Or, it might be the unattached student from a privileged background who just doesn't get why some in their cohort don't go out drinking at research conferences. (They just haven't noticed that you are working three part-time jobs to provide healthcare for your children and/or elderly parents.) Or, they will openly roll their eyes at you when you speak of "Karma" or "The Golden Rule" in your leadership ethics class. These people are generally pretty easy to dismiss at this point in your life, but the problem is: They will be fellow professors some day! This is a very depressing

thought and I'm sorry, it will not go away and I do not have any advice for you. Sorry.

8. **Kind-hearted, hardworking, and mature people are a godsend.** It won't take long before you wonder how you ever lived without them. Actively protect and cultivate these relationships. You may be able to survive without them but why try to?

9. **Take personal inventory once in a while.** (I have to do this often!) At times of frustration and exhaustion, you might become snippy or jaded. Take stock of yourself and apologize when you need to. If it has been awhile since you said, "Thank you" or "I love you" to those who deserve to hear it, please change that as soon as possible. Resist the urge to let the mean, lazy, immature people you encounter daily wear you down to the point that you surrender who you are and what you are meant to be and do.

10. **Find balance.** Banish naiveté and cultivate discernment. Be cautious but not devious; strong, yet tender. Be humble, but do not give away your self-confidence. Be careful but not crafty; focused and determined without being obstinate and unmoving. Someone cleverer than I said: "Be then as wise as snakes, and as gentle as doves." (Matthew 10:16).

NOTE

1. I wish to thank Tina Taucher, lifelong Delta Zeta sister (ΔΣ chapter) and flight attendant extraordinaire, for sharing her flight safety script for use in this project.

CHAPTER 15

SINGING ALONG
WITH "THE LONE RANGER"

Joanne M. Marshall

For me, work-life balance was not ever an issue until I had children. When I was teaching high school English, when I was a graduate student, and through my first year as an assistant professor it was mostly work, most of the time, and I was happy with that. My first child's arrival whomped me upside the head with the need for balance.

DELUSIONS OF THE WORKER BEE

I got pregnant the first year I took a job as an assistant professor at Iowa State University (ISU). The baby was due in mid-August. I was assigned a new course to teach that summer and I scheduled it in June, which I determined would finish up in time to leave me the whole month of July and part of August to finish work projects and manuscripts, get the nursery ready, and take it easy for the last few weeks of my pregnancy.

At my regular obstetrics checkup one Friday in mid-June, I was dismayed to find that I had gained 10 pounds in 1 week. Ten pounds! And my protein levels were high. These are symptoms of preeclampsia, which is high blood pressure in pregnancy, and about which I knew nothing.[1] If untreated, it can be fatal to mother and baby. (Fans of the TV show *ER*

Juggling Flaming Chain Saws: Academics in Educational Leadership
Try to Balance Work and Family, pp. 123–130
Copyright © 2012 by Information Age Publishing
All rights of reproduction in any form reserved.

might remember a harrowing episode from 1995, when a pregnant woman was misdiagnosed with a bladder infection instead of preeclampsia, and therefore died.) My doctor asked me to come back the following Monday to recheck the protein levels. They were even higher. She told me to rest and lie on my left side. I told her I was teaching summer school 9-5 every day and I needed to finish it. She said fine, rest as much as possible and come in for more testing tomorrow. The next day I taught summer school while sitting down instead of walking about, explaining to my class that I was supposed to rest, and collected urine discreetly in Tupperware containers, as directed, so I could take it in to be tested. (All together now: "Yuck!")

At the end of the day, I took my Tupperware containers to the hospital. It was after clinic hours, so my doctor wasn't there, but a helpful nurse took my containers to test. She took my blood pressure. Then she helped me into a hospital gown (ding ding ding—this should have been my first clue that something was seriously wrong). I felt fine—well, a little tired, but who doesn't? I had my work bag with me, and lay on my left side waiting for test results while reading and using my laptop to prepare for class the next day.

The next medical personage to arrive was the on-call obstetrician, who told me that my protein levels and blood pressure were ridiculously high, that my doctor should never have let me out of her office, and that he was sending me to Des Moines by ambulance because Des Moines was able to handle premature births and the baby might need to be delivered 7 weeks early. I said, "But I have to teach tomorrow." And the doctor glared at me, and said, "You *can't.*"

My spouse rushed home to gather what I thought I might need to take with me for a hospital visit of unknown duration, and then followed the ambulance down I-35 to the hospital, calling family along the way to put them on alert. I sent an e-mail to my class to cancel our session the next day. During the rest of that week, I vacillated between worry about the baby, whose heartbeat I could hear fluctuating on a monitor next to my bed, and worry about my class, which I prepared every day while my spouse and colleagues and department chair pitched in to teach it in my absence.

I didn't really understand how serious this illness was. Again, I felt fine, if a little winded. But the baby's heartbeat got much slower throughout the week. I silently cheered him on ("Come on, baby!"), but at the end of the week, at about 6 A.M. on a Sunday morning, he stopped responding to external stimuli. I watched him on an ultrasound move very, very slowly, while the technician pointed out the constriction of his umbilical cord, which was shutting off his blood supply. I seriously worried for the first time that he might die. We got test results from my blood showing that my own liver levels were dangerously close to failure, which meant I might die. The only solution was an emergency Caesarean section.

Peter was born weighing 3 pounds, 4 ounces, and for the next 5½ weeks I sat by his clear plastic box in the neonatal intensive care unit and cried and prayed and held and fed him. There was nothing seriously wrong with him, he was just early and little, known in neonatal parlance as a "grower and feeder." He's now healthy and happy and smart and even cute, and you'd never know that he started life looking like a miniature version of *E.T.*, the Extra Terrestrial.

Peter's arrival, and the reality of his tininess and of his dependence on me, made me realize how out of balance my life had been. No one knows what causes preeclampsia, but I felt responsible for it. And guilty. And stupid. And angry. I was angry at myself, at my class, and at my job. I got the worst teaching evaluations of my life, with student comments like, "I know it wasn't her fault, but ..." I had expected my students, these future educational leaders, to recognize how hard I'd worked on their behalf through desperate circumstances. Of course they did not, and it seems ridiculous now to have expected them to understand. Their reaction, coupled with the caring for Peter, made me realize that finishing my summer class had not been worth jeopardizing my health and the health of the baby. It also made me realize one very hard lesson: I had thought I could do it all. I couldn't.

My circumstances taught me more about work-life balance. I learned that academic deadlines wait for no one. The registrar wanted my course grades. American Educational Research Association conference proposals were due. E-mail poured in. It didn't matter that Peter was still in the neonatal intensive care unit, and that I was nursing or pumping milk every 3 hours around the clock, and that I was recovering from a C-section. So I did what I had to do. I graded papers and wrote a conference proposal in a blur and answered e-mail as I could. Not my best work, but good enough.

Ultimately, I learned that the only person who was going to look out for my ability to work and maintain Peter's care and feeding was me. A lesson I've extrapolated since with another child and to work-life generally. This seems like an obvious lesson for a grown-up, but it was hard for me. I have always been a good little worker bee, happy to do extra, wanting to achieve perfection and to get people's approval. I have let that go. I'm letting a lot go. I actually sing a reminder to myself, to the tune of *The Lone Ranger* theme song by Rossini: Let it go, let it go, let it go-go-go. Let it go, let it go, let it go-go-go. If you're ever nearby and hear me humming it, sing along with me.

It is not possible to do everything and it is not possible to do anything perfectly. I have to make choices. So if I need to skip a committee meeting, so be it. If a draft is not perfection in my eyes but it's due, in it goes. If an advisee wants me to do something by Friday, maybe I can and maybe I can't. If I have not been to the store and it's going to be pizza for supper tonight, okay. If somebody's mother has carved and hand-frosted five dozen reindeer out of Milano cookies for the Christmas preschool party, I will be awed but not cowed by her creativity. Okay, maybe a little cowed. But I am letting it go. And I think my balance is getting better.

THERE IS HOPE FOR THE WORKER BEE

While I was writing this chapter, Peter had another medical emergency, with what looked like a ruptured appendix but turned out to be something rarer and scarier called a Meckel's diverticulum.[2] Again we rushed to a Des Moines hospital, and again I sat by his bed around the clock praying and holding his hand while his body fought off peritonitis and septic shock and then while he healed from having the infected diverticulum removed and his small intestine spliced back together.

Care in the children's hospital presumes that there will be a parent or other adult advocate in the room 24 hours a day: someone to summon a nurse if the child is in pain, or needs to be disconnected from tubes to use the bathroom, or if the antibiotic pump line gets kinked and begins to beep. Someone has to be there to ask questions and to take notes and to remind the staff of what happened on the last shift, to encourage the child through painful and uncomfortable tests, and—sometimes—to tell people to leave him alone.

For nearly all of Peter's 2 weeks in the hospital, I was able to be his advocate. My parents drove over to take care of our household and younger son, while my mother-in-law flew in from Texas to sit with me beside Peter. And work was manageable. I have never been so grateful for my flexible schedule, the flexibility afforded by technology, and my fabulous colleagues. My class had finished meeting for the semester, and I was due to give feedback on their assignments online, so I e-mailed them to extend their final paper deadline when I took longer to give that feedback (despite having my laptop with me, one day I remained on the same page of the same student paper the entire day). I set up an "I am away with a family emergency" message on my e-mail account to let people know that I would take longer to respond to them. And I called our departmental administrator, Judy Weiland, to let her know that I might not be able to attend the full day of master's student oral exams I was chairing later in the week. Oral exams are sacred in the schedule at my institution, requiring much advanced preparation and paperwork and certain presence. Judy told me not to worry about a thing, changed paperwork and notified the Graduate College of the change, and then my colleagues in educational administration (Mike Book, Tyson Marsh, and John Nash) covered my place in the exams. All students passed.

This episode in our family history was far different from Peter's birth. While more agonizing from a medical and emotional perspective—I know him better now, and we came closer to losing him—it was less difficult from a work-life perspective. I've asked myself why, and though I'm still reflecting, I believe there are at least two contributing factors. One is a supportive work environment, about which I'll say more in the next section. The other is that I am simply more familiar with the balancing act required. Last time I was new to both parenting and the professoriate. I have a better sense of priorities now—of what can wait and what can not. Peter's illness occurred in the weeks immediately before the annual American Educational Association conference. I had to let some things go-go-go. I was ready to let go my ability to attend the conference entirely. But 2 days before my scheduled flight, Peter was released from the hospital, so I was able to attend and also do some other things like prepare a handout for my paper, attend a Special Interest Group meeting for which I'm an officer, and meet with friends and colleagues. I let go attending a couple of sessions and receptions and was not able to send my paper to the session chair ahead of time. I was not able to do all that I initially planned or wanted, but I could do some things. These choices are tough for good little worker bees. But they are the essence of balance: making decisions about what is most necessary, and letting the rest go

BALANCING WITH SUPPORT

It would be remiss and arrogant of me to pretend that I am able to achieve any balance whatsoever without a lot of help. For the first years of my children's lives, I had a babysitter who was a gift from heaven. I have a spouse who is not only a prince among humankind, but also a fellow academic, a techie engineer who helps administer the Virtual Reality Applications Center at ISU. Unlike our field of educational leadership, federal agencies and private companies call him and offer to fund his research on their virtual reality projects. The challenging side of his non-tenure-track position is that it is entirely grant-funded, so he has to travel extensively, have several grant proposals or grant projects under way at once, and manage a team of graduate students to be ready at a moment's notice to demonstrate their latest and hottest technology for a visiting luminary. These obligations bumped up against my own as an untenured professor, with the ever-present publication scythe hanging over my head. So despite my resolution to let it go, let it go, let it go-go-go shortly after

Peter's birth, our household model after two children was not working. My spouse and I were both exhausted and our calendars were full. My cholesterol was too high, our floor was crunchy, and we snapped too frequently at each other and our beloved offspring. I would wake up at 4 a.m., panicked that I had not written enough, and feeling as if I was not doing anything—not one thing—well.

However, we work at an institution which holds as one of its 5-year strategic plan goals to "foster a university culture and work environment that … supports a balance between work and life." In an effort to recruit and retain faculty, particularly in a part of the country that has beautifully big sky but not tourist-worthy oceans or mountains, Iowa State strives to be family-friendly. For nontenured faculty, there is a policy allowing parents to stop the tenure clock, 1 year per adopted or birthed child, up to two children in 5 years (though one wonders why only two, in sympathy with those whose children may not come evenly spaced or who want more than two). Most innovatively, in 2005 the faculty senate at ISU adopted a part-time policy[3] allowing faculty at any career stage to reduce their appointment up to 50% for personal reasons such as caregiving or family health issues. Tenured faculty also can reduce their appointment for professional reasons such as entrepreneurship. The Position Responsibility Statement, which outlines one's duties, is renegotiated. A typical faculty Position Responsibility Statement, which would allocate 40% of time to research, 40% to teaching, and 20% to service, would become 20-20-10, thereby reducing each semester's course load by half (in my case, from two to one each semester). With a 50% appointment, the tenure clock also is extended, so that 2 years at a 50% appointment would equal 1 year on the clock. While health care benefits remain the same, salary is reduced by the percentage of the appointment.

After the policy was passed at the state level by the governing board of regents, I considered it. My main concern was that people inside and outside the university would think I was not serious about my job, a possible career-killer in a profession that relies heavily on departmental votes and external reviews for promotion and tenure. I quietly sought the advice of mentors across the field and at ISU. I met and talked with the only woman on campus that anyone knew of who had negotiated a part-time policy. At home we ran budget analyses to see how a half-time salary might affect our household. The most important question—was it worth it?—was something we decided was ultimately unanswerable without trying it. So in the fall of 2007, with some trepidation, I asked my department chair to reduce my appointment to 50% for the calendar year of 2008. It was an experiment.

It's still an experiment after 4-plus years. People often ask me what it's like to work part-time, especially fellow faculty who understand that the requirements of publishing and seeking funding and the demands of teaching do not stop at the end of each day or during weekends. My answer has been to ask in return, "What's 'part-time' of 'It's-Never-Enough?'" And we laugh and shrug. When I come up for tenure review, we will see what my internal and external reviewers make of my situation, and whether what I've done has been "enough." While a recent survey of ISU's faculty (Pontius & Gahn, 2009) found that only 14% of faculty agreed with the statement that extra time on the tenure clock gave an unfair advantage, the two groups who were statistically significantly more likely to agree with that statement were (a) full professors and (b) men. Considering that both full professors and men are more likely to review my tenure dossier than any other group, I am fighting uphill. There is still work to do to change my own family-friendly institutional culture, let alone the culture of other higher education institutions across the rest of the country. One of our senior faculty members stopped me shortly after I'd started the part-time appointment and asked, "What are you doing with all your free time now?" I bit back several responses, including the observation that he'd achieved tenure 30-some years ago, under less rigorous standards, with a full-time partner taking care of him and his children, and things are different now. Instead I laughed and asked, "What free time?"

When faced with the occasional thoughtless remark like this—and they really have been only occasional—it helps to remember words of a warm and kind friend, who chose to remain nameless here. I complained to her one day about a thoughtless remark from a colleague, and she patted my arm and said, "Oh, Joanne. He is old and he will die soon." And then we both laughed like madwomen, shocked at the thought, knowing that neither of us would wish speedy death—or even retirement—on anyone. My thoughtless former colleague is a good guy. He meant well. However, my friend's statement is helpful because it reminds me of the way time marches on. The authors of this book—and you as readers—are the ones who will establish the current and future culture of higher education. It is up to us to figure out how to manage both work and family and to advocate for more flexible career policies, different from the traditional ones that presumed a full-time male professor supported at home by a full-time wife.

I am grateful for the flexibility of my own institution, and feel more loyalty to it as a result. The pressure is lighter because I feel as if I have more time. I am still not Super Woman, able to do it all, but our family eats better and is healthier, the floor is less crunchy some of the time, and I can chaperone a school trip or take a child to the doctor in the middle of the day without feeling work guilt. I still write as much as possible, prepare the best possible class, advise a ridiculously high number of graduate students, and serve on university and national association committees. The work has not really changed; I just have a longer timespan in which to do it. And that has been extremely worth it.

NOTE

1. For nontechnical articles about preeclampsia, which occurs in 5 to 10% of pregnancies, see: Gropman (2006) and Mayo Clinic (2011).
2. For more detail about symptoms and treatment, see Cincinnati Children's Hospital (2010).
3. For the policy, see http://www.provost.iastate.edu/faculty/handbook/current/section3.html#section-3.3.1

REFERENCES

Cincinnati Children's Hospital. (2010, August). Meckel's diverticulum. Retrieved from http://www.cincinnatichildrens.org/health/info/abdomen/diagnose/meckels-diverticulum.htm

Gropman, J. (2006, July 24). The preeclampsia puzzle. *The New Yorker*.

Mayo Clinic. (2011, April 21). Preeclampsia. Retrieved from http://www.mayoclinic.com/health/preeclampsia/DS00583/METHOD=print&DSECTION=all

Pettus, A. (2006, September-October). Prenatal competition? *Harvard Magazine*, 18-20.

CHAPTER 16

FROM CONDESCENDING CABBIES TO CARING COACHES

Basketball, Fatherhood, and the Shaping of Professional Feedback

Peter Miller

I was a member of my university's men's basketball team during my 4 years as an undergraduate student. It was a great experience that allowed me to play a game I love, to forge enduring relationships with teammates and coaches, and to travel all around the country. My most vivid memories of college, in fact, are almost all associated with my experiences as a basketball player. I remember running sprints, lifting weights, and perfecting my jump shot for countless hours. I recall the sights, sounds, and smells of the arena where my team practiced. I remember daily locker room joking and laughter. Without a doubt, my greatest learning and development during those years occurred not in any classroom or library, but as a member of the basketball team. This included an abundance of basketball learning—how to shoot the ball better, play better defense, and so on—but, more fundamentally, broader life lessons. Our coach was a font of such knowledge. He continually urged us to work hard, to sacrifice for each other, and to believe in ourselves in the face adversity.

Juggling Flaming Chain Saws: Academics in Educational Leadership Try to Balance Work and Family, pp. 131–135
Copyright © 2012 by Information Age Publishing

While I picked up pretty quickly on lessons relating to hard work and sacrifice—I eagerly immersed myself, for example, in the physical training regiments that the game demanded—I struggled in the area of self-belief. Unlike many of my teammates and competitors, I was not exceptionally tall or fast and I was not a highly touted recruit coming out of high school. I never admitted it to anyone, but I'm quite sure that I questioned on a daily basis if I was good enough to compete with everyone else. These self-doubts came to a head when I was a freshman and our team—which was struggling to get many victories that season—traveled to Durham, North Carolina, to play Duke, one of the very best teams in the country. I was overwhelmed by their loud crowd, famous coach, and exceptional players and, as I sat on the bench during the first few minutes of the game I was more nervous than I'd ever been. After a while, my coach looked down to me and said, "Pete, get in there and guard #33!" Putting on my bravest face, I trotted onto the court and located the Duke player with jersey #33—it was Grant Hill, the best player in the country. Grant Hill was 6'8", fast as a gazelle, and in just about every way, the perfect embodiment of a star basketball player. He was way out of my league and I knew it. Although I didn't make any major mistakes, #33 eventually enjoyed a couple easy slam dunks before I retreated to my more comfortable spot on the bench.

We ended up losing that game by a mere two points and, although I was disappointed about the loss and my individual effort, what I remember most about that night was the way that our coach critiqued us after the game. He was not satisfied with almost winning. "You guys can be so much better! We almost beat the best team in the country on their home court! Keep working hard and believing ..." He went on to delineate the specific areas that we needed to improve upon in order to get over the hump to become successful both as individuals and as a team. Coach's critique of our performance was well-founded, and it increased my personal confidence that we could become a really good team and that I could play an important role in helping us win some games.

We played well for the next several games, but, unfortunately, soon reverted back to our losing ways. One night, after experiencing a particularly difficult loss, and wanting to escape all thoughts of basketball, I asked my friend Mike, who lived down the hall in my dorm, if he wanted to head to a movie downtown. Neither of us had cars and, since the bus wasn't going to be coming for a while, we hopped in a cab for the short ride to the theater. The driver was an especially talkative guy who, shortly into our ride asked, "Did you guys see that basketball game today? Those guys sure do stink, eh?!"

"Yeah, they sure do!" Mike laughed in reply.

The cabbie continued, "I mean, they were really bad today. It got so bad at one point that they put Pete Miller in the game!"

As I slumped back into my seat, Mike happily inquired, "Oh, really? Who's that?"

"He's a freshman on the team. Seems like a pretty nice kid, but he's just not talented enough to play Division I basketball."

Mike gleefully interrogated the driver about my deficiencies (not fast enough, too skinny, etc.) for the last 5 minutes of the ride. Once we got to the theater, I slinked out of the cab without identifying myself. While Mike forced me to acknowledge a degree of humor of the situation, it was indeed one of the most humiliating car rides I've had!

As my skills developed and I gained more experience over the course of the next 3 years, I gradually developed more confidence. I never became anything close to the basketball player that Grant Hill was, but, benefiting immeasurably from my coach's sage guidance, I contributed considerably to my team's ultimate success.

My days as a basketball player are long past, but as I've moved through other phases of life—attending graduate school, working in a homeless shelter, teaching and coaching high school students—I've continually thought about how the many lessons I learned during those 4 years on (and off) the court have correlated with my broader life experiences. In recent years I have considered these lessons especially as they relate to my current roles as father and assistant professor.

My wife Lindsey and I have four children under the age of 8. Our days start early and are filled with changing diapers, making meals, cleaning the house, playing games, attending school events, and all the other things that tend to fill young families' lives. I have experienced father-hood as a real work in progress. I feel like I am a pretty accomplished dad in some areas—my ongoing bedtime story series about "Jerry the Boy Detective," for instance, is a smash hit with my sons—but know that I have much room for improvement in others. One of my favorite parts of being a dad is the constant formative assessment that I receive from Lindsey and our kids. What I mean here is that I even though I make lots of mistakes, I tend to get pretty rapid feedback about how I can get better at what I am doing. While the kids' feedback tends to be pretty direct and disproportionately geared toward the receipt of larger dessert portions, the conversations that Lindsey and I have about parenting have fundamentally supported my growth as a father. Like my old basketball coach, she rarely focuses upon our failures and shortcomings as indicators of inadequacy. Instead, Lindsey views our "parenting data" in its entirety (she's a highly skilled school psychologist!) and guides us toward the interventions that make most sense. Our constructive daily dialogue—

which is challenged by the balancing of our work schedules—has made fatherhood a most fulfilling, belief-filled journey.

My role as an assistant professor is also significantly affected by feedback—most notably in this instance from anonymous reviewers of my writing. One of my ongoing struggles is to receive this feedback as constructive guidance rather than summative judgment. When manuscripts or grant applications are rejected, for example, I tend to focus upon the "not good enough" aspects of the feedback rather than the "this is how you can be better" aspects. What is the difference between this feedback and that which I receive from my kids and wife? I think part of the answer can be found in my basketball stories. Specifically, my team accepted the ongoing critique and feedback from our coach in a formative manner because it was delivered in the context of time-established, respectful relationships. He understood our personalities, our assets, and our shortcomings and we understood his. He was aware that very few of us were "Grant Hills," but held us accountable for maximizing our individual and collective potentials. We knew that Coach wanted what was best for us. We understood ourselves as works in progress. This is quite similar to the dynamic I share with my family. Our formative conversations and critiques unfold upon solid foundations of awareness, love, respect, and understanding.

On the other hand, my tendency to receive both positive and negative professional feedback in a summative manner—that is, as an indicator that my work is statically "good" or "not good"—is more akin to my cab ride story. I gained nothing from the driver's blanket assessment of my weaknesses (aside from a mildly funny story to share) because I did not perceive that he really knew me or cared about my development. His words came across as distant—and even a bit dispiriting. The same can often be said of my reactions to anonymous reviewers' feedback on my academic work.

While my roles as dad and professor can in some ways be viewed as conflicting ones—that is, when I'm immersed in one of the roles I often feel like I should be spending more time in the other—I think that my "feedback experiences" as a dad have actually helped me become a better researcher and writer. Realizing that the generally positive nature of feedback in our family setting is rooted in the loving and respectful relationships we share with one another, I have made purposeful attempts to situate comments upon my work within the broader relational context in which I operate. When I receive feedback on a manuscript these days, I talk about it with trusted colleagues rather than just letting it simmer within.

Recently, for example, I received a manuscript disposition that commented upon the "serious weaknesses" of a paper that I had spent many months preparing. The highly critical disposition was seven pages long and quite discouraging for me to read. I shared the feedback with two professors in my department—both of whom know my work quite well. They quickly diffused my discouragement by noting that not only were the reviewers accurate, they were remarkably generous with their time and insightful with their remarks. One of my colleagues' e-mail responses, in fact began: "Wow!!!!!! This is unbelievable feedback! You should address every single one of their ideas ..." By bringing what I previously would have interpreted to be distant, biting critique of my work into the confines of trusted, established relationships, I was able to realize the formative potential of the feedback and ultimately develop a much stronger paper that was accepted for publication. I do not think I would have come to this place in my professional life if not for my "dad-based" and "basketball-based" relationships and experiences.

Being a dad has led me to understand that, while I need to be smart and attentive, my greatest efficiencies might be found not by yearning to become Grant Hill (which, in academia might translate to a sort of research and writing genius), but by finding professional correlates to Lindsey and our four kids. In concert with them, critical responders to my work can be engaged as caring coaches rather than condescending cabbies.

CHAPTER 17

WORK-LIFE BALANCE FOR LATINA FACULTY IN A HISPANIC-SERVING INSTITUTION

Elizabeth T. Murakami

When I was hired as an assistant professor in educational leadership, I knew very little about the expectations of professors in higher education institutions. Much like a large number of educators who migrate from K-12 schools to join the academy, I knew very little about the system of higher education. I did work at the university while in graduate school, but I did not have the opportunity to have a postdoctoral position to learn about the intricacies of serving as a faculty member, and learn more about higher education organizational structures.

Luckily when I began my position as a professor, I had several mentors in the department of educational leadership and policy studies who helped me transition from being a central office coordinator in a K-12 school, to beginning my new career. Moving from schools to academia was a dream job since I was interested in developing research related to leadership for social justice. However, I had also heard about the difficulties being a female, of color, and new to academia. As I moved into a new city and university with my two college age sons, I explored questions I had in

Juggling Flaming Chain Saws: Academics in Educational Leadership Try to Balance Work and Family, pp. 137–143
Copyright © 2012 by Information Age Publishing

relation to this new career, such as: "What does it mean to serve as a faculty member in higher education, and more specifically in a department of educational leadership?" and, "What are the tensions specific to Latinas in academia?" I found that among tensions related to Latinas laid the life-work balance dilemma.

WHAT DOES IT MEAN TO BE A LATINA FACULTY MEMBER IN EDUCATIONAL LEADERSHIP?

The aforementioned question relates to expectations, identity, ethnicity, and gender for Latinas as applied in a Hispanic-Serving Institution[1] (HSI). HSIs receive this designation when at least 25% of its student body is Latino/a. The department did not have structured mentoring systems for new professors, so I sought two professors to mentor me that first year: A Caucasian third-year male assistant professor who was familiar with the Midwest, where I lived for 5 years until I graduated; and a Latino, renowned male professor, who was the interim chair when I was hired. They, I hoped, would be able to clarify what were the expectations of a faculty member in that institution. I felt that both were interested in preparing me for the professorship, and were genuinely interested in my growth as a professor and scholar. Choosing males as mentors was not a coincidence. Among the full-time professors in K-12 educational leadership in that department, there was only one female. She was a Latina, with 1 year experience as an assistant professor in that institution. Another female in the department had been promoted to dean. The other six professors were males.

With the help of mentors, I learned about the 40-40-20% expectation of research, teaching, and service. Even though this is a teaching university. I learned about the pressing need to publish publish publish; student expectations; and the important search for grants. Other newly hired colleagues I were also discussing different institutions' expectations, which seemed to differ from place to place. In addition, the Latino mentor provided me with the context for an HSI. I learned that universities serving 25% or more Latinos are considered HSIs. Surprisingly, I also learned that graduation rates needed to improve for Latinos in our university.

WHAT ARE THE TENSIONS FOR LATINAS IN ACADEMIA?

Latina faculty members are not well represented in academia. According to the *Chronicle of Higher Education* (2010), in the 2007-2008 academic year, only 4%, or 1 in 25 tenured or tenure-track faculty positions held by women—were Latinas. At the same time, White women represented 78% of all female faculty, with Black women, and Asian women constituting 7% and 6%, respectively. As the tenured rank increases, the representation of Latinas decreases (Murakami, Nuñez, & Cuero, 2010). At the institution I was hired, only 5 out of 70, or about 7% of the female professors in the school of education, were female, Latina, tenured professors. So, even though the percentage of Latinas hired in this HSI were a bit higher than the national average, these professors were not being tenured. This fact could be related to Turner's (Turner, 2002; Turner, González, & Wood, 2008) studies which demonstrated that Latinas in the professorship still face exclusion, lack of mentoring, tokenism, uneven promotion, and inequitable salaries when entering the academy.

I am a Latina, who is born in Brazil. I am also third-generation Japanese. I look Japanese, but I speak, think, and act like a Latina. My family immigrated to Brazil about one hundred years ago. I wondered in what subgroup I was to be placed to represent the percentage ranks. Like many other Latinas, I was raised with strong family values, a Catholic influence, and in a culture that perceives women as instrumental in building families (Murakami et al., 2010). In fact, when focusing on the effects of religion, Padilla (2000) for example, discussed that a sense of predestination plays out among Latinas. He recognized that "Latinas' cultural background is characterized by its reverence of family" (p. 977). Therefore, work-life balance for me was divided between my sons' education and the professorship.

My two sons were entering college when I was hired as a professor. Even though there was no financial support for faculty children to enroll at the university, having them join the same HSI was a great opportunity. Forty-four percent of undergraduates at the university are presently Latinos (The University of Texas System, 2010). Nevertheless, the absence of financial support for my children, combined with the slim percentage of tenured and promoted Latina faculty in the College of Education, did not add up to a guaranteed formula for success—neither for me as a professor, nor for my children, as Latinos in a HSI.

Even though I was working at the university, my sons' college life was not necessarily easy in terms of navigating the structural requirements. College environments are exciting, especially to those who come from educated families. Families can model how to get the best out of college life. College students need advocates to help in understanding the intricate differences between high school and college. However, for first-time and nontraditional students, college can be complex, uninviting, and even intimidating.

For example, my son had difficulties finding offices, parking as a guest, and setting up classes. Even though they were successful academically, there were occasions in which I had to reach out to "someone I knew," in order to help them navigate the requirements for matriculation and graduation. These were important insights into learning more about how to serve many of the first generation students. Persistence, mentoring, and family presence seemed to be important issues for undergraduates completing their degrees. Not all students in an HSI are afforded all of these supports. Through my students, I find that some of these issues also affected graduate students.

WORK-LIFE REWARDING LESSONS

Due to my own children's experience in college, my teaching pedagogy became grounded in two important considerations in preparing students in educational leadership and policy studies: (a) addressing the needs of part-time students, who compose the majority of students in our programs; and (b) the retention and graduation of nontraditional and underrepresented student populations. Even though my research is focused on educational leaders, I see my teaching role as organic, and responsive to the student body at a local level. For example, with graduate students preparing to become school administrators, I toured the university campus, and we reflected on services that link P-12 and university access. This was especially important, because educational administrators are the ones promoting students to college. In addition, since the university carries a HSI designation, my Latina background and Spanish speaking skills plays a positive role in preparing educational administrators and to improve the conditions of students in underserved areas (Murakami-Ramalho, 2009). I include culturally relevant pedagogy (Rendon, 1994; Yosso, 2005) in my courses, and also invite emerging leaders to develop culturally relevant practices, and an awareness of social justice issues.

As a female, mixed-heritage, Latin-American-born junior scholar in my first tenure-track position in the field of educational administration, I have focused on increasing admissions, retention, and the success of students of color. With another colleague who is also of mixed Latino heritage, we concluded that we are often not perceived as Latina, by Latinas/os or non-Latinas/os. We feel that our phenotypes obscure our racial/ethnic identities and have conditioned our acceptance as Latina professors, in institutional and other professional settings (Nuñez & Murakami-Ramalho, in press).

Recognizably, there is a correlation between the low retention of Latino/a students, and low Latino/a faculty promotion. Is it possible that this correlation relates to Valencia's (2002) assertion about the "endogenous theory of school failure, [which] 'blames the victim' rather than examining how schools and the political economy are structured to prevent students from learning optimally?" (p. 83). Is it also possible that the same assumption applies to Latinas in academia? Thomas and Ely (1996) for example, remind us that even though organizations demonstrate a concern for discrimination and fairness by complying with outside pressures to increase diversity in universities, tenured faculty are the ones recommending their colleagues' promotions. If the organizational culture of the organization is not culturally sensitive (i.e., not familiar with existing struggles for people of color), there is a possibility that the organizational culture is preventing access and legitimacy to both students and faculty of color. Hatch and Cunliffe (2006) in fact assert that very few organizations attain a stage where "the organization learns to take full advantage of the benefits diversity brings" (p. 318), or actively learns about the function and role of cultural diversity and representation in a university.

After learning about the very small representation of tenured Latina professors in the college, several of us tenure-track Latinas in different departments created a collaborative to build our scholarly careers and support each other as new faculty (Alanís, Cuero, & Rodriguez, 2009; Murakami &Nuñez, in press; Nuñez, Murakami, &Ramalho, 2010; Oliva, Rodriguez, Alanís, & Quijada-Cerecer, 2011). The Research for the Education and Advancement of Latina/os collaborative was founded in 2005 to counter the isolation and competition in academia (Ek, Quijada-Cerecer, Alanís, & Rodriguez, 2010; Quijada-Cerecer, Ek, Alanís, & Murakami Ramalho, 2010). In regular meetings we created a community that conducted joint research projects, reviewed each other's work, generated relevant literature and lists of publication venues, and presented in conferences together. Our presentations have brought tears to the eyes of other Latina professors across the country who identified with issues of isolation and tokenism. In addition, we informally shared with one another experiences about navigating the academy, and developed strategies to manage work-life challenges such as balancing raising small children and academia. This process of peer mentoring also addressed the requirements and expectations for promotion and tenure (Nuñez& Murakami-Ramalho, in press).

CONCLUSION

In this chapter I provided an example of significant issues that bring work and life into correlated circles. This year, five Research for the Education and Advancement of Latina/os members received their promotion and tenure to Associate Professors, and I am one of them. One of my sons already finished his business degree and is now employed by the same institution. The other one is graduating next spring.

Just like my sons, and other Latino students in the university, as a Latina faculty, I was only able to succeed with formal and informal supports. Some important factors for the success of both Latino/a students and faculty members included persistence, continuous mentoring, and family presence. Work-life balance for me was divided between developing a successful career as a professor and scholar, and in advocating for my sons' college life.

Latinos take the knowledge forward and help others. I am applying these lessons in the preparation of outstanding educational leaders committed to social justice, who are invested in children's academic and social success and their subsequent participation in society. I believe my sons, my Latina colleagues and I are all on a great path.

NOTE

1. Latinas is used here as the most accepted umbrella term of self-identification (Hayes-Bautista & Chapa, 1987). The term Latino/a, Hispanic, and Spanish has been used in the U.S. census since 2000.

REFERENCES

Alanís, I., Cuero, K. K., & Rodríguez, M. A. (2009). Research for the educational advancement of Latin@s: A research and professional development collaborative. *NASPA Journal about Women in Higher Education, 2,* 243-244.

Ek, L. D., Quijada-Cerecer, P. D., Alanís, I., & Rodríguez, M. A. (2010). "I don't belong here": Chicanas/Latinas at a Hispanic serving institution creating community through Muxerista mentoring. *Equity & Excellence in Education, 43*(4), 539-553.

Chronicle of Higher Education. (2010). Almanac of higher education 2010. Retrieved from http://chronicle.com/article/Percentage-of-Faculty-Members/123927/

Hatch, M. J., &Cunliffe, A. L. (2006). *Organization theory: Modern, symbolic, and postmodern perspectives.* New York, NY: Oxford University Press.

Hayes-Bautista, D., & Chapa, J. (1987). Latino terminology: Conceptual basis for standardized terminology. *Journal of the American Public Health Association, 77*(1), 61-68.

Murakami-Ramalho, E. (2009). La reina de la casa quieredemocracia: Latina executive leaders and the intersection of home and the workforce. In D. M. Beaty, W. H. Sherman, A. J. Muñoz, S. J. Mills, & A. M. Pankake (Ed.), *Women as school executives: Celebrating diversity* (pp. 192-202). Austin, TX: The Texas Council of Women School Executives.

Murakami-Ramalho, E., Nuñez, A., & Cuero, K. (2010). Latin@ advocacy in the hyphen: Personal and professional engagement in a Hispanic-serving institution. *International Journal of Qualitative Studies in Education, 23*(6), 699-717. doi:10.1080/09518391003641924

Nuñez, A., Murakami-Ramalho, E., & Cuero, K., (2010). Pedagogy for equity: Teaching in a Hispanic-serving institution. *Innovative Higher Education, 35*(3), 177-190. doi:10.1007/s10755-010-9139-7

Nuñez, A., & Murakami-Ramalho, E. (2012). Addressing the demographic dividend: Building inclusiveness for Latina/o faculty and students in higher education. *Academe, 98*(1), 32-37.

Oliva, M., Rodriguez, M. A., Alanís, I., & Quijada, P. (in press). At home in the academy: Latina faculty counterstories and resistances. *Journal of the Professoriate, 6*(1).

Padilla, L. M. (2000). Latinas and religion: Subordination or a state of grace? *University of California at Davis Law Review 33*, 973-1008.

Quijada-Cerecer, P. D., Ek, L., Alanís, I., & Murakami Ramalho, E. (2010). Transformative resistance as agency: Chicanas/Latinas re(creating) academic spaces. *Journal of the Professoriate, 5*(1), 70-98.

Rendon, L. (1994) Validating culturally diverse students: Toward a new model of learning and student development. *Innovative Higher Education, 19*(1), 33-51.

Thomas, D. A., & Ely, R. J. (1996). Making differences matter: A new paradigm for managing diversity. *Harvard Business Review, 74*(5), 79-90.

Turner, C. S. V. (2002). Women of color in academe: Living with multiple marginality. *The Journal of Higher Education, 73*(1), 74-93.

Turner, C. S. V., González, J. C., & Wood, J. L. (2008). Faculty of color in academe: What 20 years of literature tells us. *Journal of Diversity in Higher Education, 1*(3), 139-168.

The University of Texas System. (2010). Accountability and performance report 2009-2010. Retrieved from http://www.utexas.edu/academic/imasites/default/files/ UTSystemAccountabilityReport09-10.pdf.

Valencia, R. R. (Ed.). (2002). The explosive growth of the Chicano/Latino population: Educational implications. In *Chicano school failure and success: Past, present, and future.* New York, NY: Routledge/Falmer.

Yosso, T. J. (2005). Whose culture has capital? A critical race theory discussion of community cultural wealth. *Race, Ethnicity, and Education, 8*(1), 69-91.

CHAPTER 18

PIECES OF A PROFESSOR

Living With Limitations,
but High Expectations

Latish C. Reed

I have always loved musical lyrics that paint a picture and touch the soul. Ledisi, my favorite neosoul artist, sings a song entitled "Pieces of Me."[1] The song demonstrates the complexity of her life as a woman, with lyrics like, "People just don't know what I'm about." These lyrics ring true for me as well. Just like a puzzle, there are many "pieces" of my life that make up the whole me. As I have navigated my career as a teacher, administrator, and now a professor, some "pieces" have been more visible than others. One of the biggest "pieces" of me is that I have always been a go-getter, get-the-job-done type of person. In previous work (Reed, 2008, 2011), I have detailed my background and journey to the professoriate. As a former school teacher and administrator, my personal story has a backdrop of resilience in spite of many challenges due to race and/or gender or other circumstances. Cynthia Dillard (2006) noted the lack of scholarship that conveys the perspective of Black females and their research. Given this void, a major piece of my scholarship has focused on the intersectionality of race and gender for Black women principals. As a scholar, this same intersectionality is also a consideration in my own life.

Juggling Flaming Chain Saws: Academics in Educational Leadership
Try to Balance Work and Family, pp. 145–152
Copyright © 2012 by Information Age Publishing
All rights of reproduction in any form reserved.

The intersection of race and gender are visible "pieces" of me. Opinions, either positive or negative, are formed when people encounter me as a Black female professor. On the other hand living with Lupus,[2] a chronic illness is an invisible "piece" that completely affects my personal life and career. In what follows, I share an important "piece" of my life as I pursue tenure and live life with Lupus.

FINDING A HIDDEN PIECE OF ME

In the spring of 2000, I made one of my frequent attempts to "get healthy" again! At that time, I was a single school teacher whose life outside of work focused solely on me. I could do what I wanted, how I wanted, when I wanted, and where I wanted. So, I started my day by going to the local YMCA to exercise. After a few days, I noticed that my wrists were awfully sore. I brushed it off as perhaps I was holding the bars on the treadmill too tightly as I walked. After a few more days, I noticed that by second hour at school, I was completely drained. Yes, sixth grade is truly a challenging grade for overactive adolescents, but for the past 4 years, teaching had been my life and my love. I could handle my class. However, now by the end of second hour, I wanted to crawl under the table and just go straight to sleep.

After a few more days, I went to the doctor because I thought there had to be more to this fatigue. I thought he would probably give me some iron pills and send me on my way. A simple solution to a simple problem. Once at the doctor's office, he started asking me a series of questions related to my recent symptoms and some of the challenges I raised. After gathering some information, he looked at my chart and saw that I was only 27 years old. He solemnly looked at me and said, "You may have rheumatoid arthritis." I thought, "WOW! That is the stuff my grandma has. I didn't know that someone my age could get that." As I sat there bewildered, the doctor said, "This is chronic and you may not want to know that you have it. So let me know if you want to be tested for arthritis." I thought, "What kind of sense does that make to ask someone if they want to know what they have or not? Maybe it isn't so bad since he gave me the option for testing." After he down played this potential chronic illness sentence, I decided to just go home and rest up. I was young and used to bouncing back from most anything.

There was no bouncing back after a few days as my health continued to decline. One night, I came home late from work and could barely move. I was hot, then cold, then hot again with pain flowing through my body. I had an abnormally high fever. So, my best friend came to take me to urgent care. When I arrived at urgent care, I told the attending doctor my symptoms and he asked if I had ever been tested for Lupus. I said no, but my doctor thought I could have arthritis. He then ordered a battery of tests. A few days later I received a call from my doctor saying that it was likely that I had Lupus. What is Lupus? What does that mean for me? At the time, I was super ambitious. My lot in life was definitely to make a mark in the world. At that point, I barely had enough energy to make it to first hour to teach my sixth graders.

After consultations with additional specialists and more tests, Lupus was the confirmed diagnosis. For me, the first step in dealing with this diagnosis was to get educated. I read information from doctors and consumed anything I could find to learn more about this illness. In brief, I learned that Lupus affects many parts of the body including skin, joints, and internal organs. Normally, the immune system fights off viruses, bacteria, and germs. But with Lupus, the immune system is overactive and also fights healthy tissues, causing inflammation which leads to pain and damage to the body. The disease is considered chronic because it can last longer than 6 weeks. While there is no known cure for Lupus, the disease can have periods of remission where symptoms are almost nonexistent. Even though the disease can be deadly, it can be managed with medication and stress management. Another clincher was that Lupus affects women of color at much higher rates than anyone else. So, the race and gender "pieces" surfaced once again for me as I learned I had to face this disease diagnosed more commonly for women of color.

After learning about my uncertain life with Lupus, I struggled trying to figure out what the diagnosis would mean for my career as an educator. Since all of this happened in the late spring of the school year, I talked to my principal and we determined it best for me to take a longer term absence. For me, the worst thing for a teacher is to not be able to say goodbye to her students before summer vacation. But, I found myself in that predicament. My friend came to help me grade the final work for my students at home. I was so weak that I could not fill in the bubbles on the final grade sheets.

After a few weeks of educating myself on Lupus, a new medication regimen, and some real rest, I began to feel better. In fact, I was able to teach summer school. Based on all I had read and the doctors' advice, the key to remaining "better" was to keep the stress down in my life. What the heck was I supposed to do with that piece of advice? Unfortunately, being the intense person I had been my entire life did not lend itself to a stress-free disposition. At the same time, I knew that if I was going to make it through this situation, I had to embrace some new ways of living.

I made it through summer school. My principal also put me on a special project to streamline new curriculum for the upcoming school year. One day he called me to his office and asked me if I would be interested in taking an assistant principal position at another school where he had been asked to be principal. While I played it cool, I was ecstatic! Becoming a school administrator was in my career trajectory as my senior high school classmates had voted me "most likely to become principal". All of the happiness was interrupted by the new reality of my Lupus diagnosis. Yes, I was feeling better at that point, but I really did not know what the future held for me. So, I explained to my principal that I was extremely honored, but did not know if the duties and responsibilities of an administrator would be conducive to my new life with Lupus. My principal was truly one of the most compassionate people I had ever met. He assured me that I would be fine and because he was aware of my circumstance, he would work with my assignments to make sure that I was able to manage on a daily basis.

After much consideration, I decided to take the position. True to my boss's word, my assignments were suitable to my health challenges. I still had the daily grind of working with student discipline, but since it was sixth graders versus eighth graders, the offenses typically did not exceed minimal infractions (chewing gum, not having a pencil, and the occasional talking back to the teacher). My principal also capitalized on my ability to write. Throughout my 4-year tenure as an assistant principal, I led the charge to secure charter school status and more than $750,000 in grant funding for my school. This exposure and opportunity gave me the impetus to pursue my doctorate. Subsequently, I quit my full-time job to become a full-time doctoral student at the University of Wisconsin-Madison.

ADDING NEW PIECES TO THE PUZZLE:
WIFE, MOTHER, AND NEW OPPORTUNITIES

As a full-time student and newlywed, I found a different focus. Life with Lupus was not as stressful anymore. Working as a graduate assistant and balancing my course work proved to be manageable. For a while, everything was on cruise control, and then one of the most incredible things happened to me. I got pregnant with my son. For the first 7 months of my pregnancy, I considered myself in remission. For whatever reason, I had a lot of energy and I was extremely healthy during this time. However, in any good story there must be some bad turns. Since my pregnancy was labeled high risk, I was scheduled for twice as many check-ups. One day, I went in for what I thought was a routine check-up. I ended up being triaged and admitted to the hospital. After a week of declining health (vital organs beginning to fail and waning health of my son), the doctor decided to deliver my son 6 weeks prematurely. Despite the life and death challenges I faced, I completed the 6 credits that I enrolled in that semester.

The following fall after my son was born; I passed my proposal hearing and officially became a dissertator. By this time, I begin to face some critical challenges within my "blissful" marriage. My health challenges during childbearing, coupled with challenges that typically plague young marriages began to take its toll. During this same time, my dissertation chair began to talk to me about the professoriate. I always assumed that I would go back into administration after completing my doctorate. She and a couple other professors convinced me that perhaps I too could join the ranks of the academy. In the midst of my failing marriage and uncertain future, I applied for assistant professor positions all over the country.

To my surprise, I was hired as an assistant professor for the following academic year. My contract was scheduled to begin in July. Securing this job was pretty much the straw that broke the camel's back for my marriage. We ended up physically separated as I raced to complete my dissertation. While I had a contract with the university, it was explained that I would be a lecturer and not an official assistant professor if my dissertation was not completed. I decided that I would push to complete my dissertation so that I was classified as a regular assistant professor.

TRYING TO FIT THE PIECES TOGETHER: MANAGING LIFE WITH LUPUS

The work of a professor is rigorous. A few years ago, I was in a fireside chat given by Gloria Ladson-Billings where she said that as a professor, there is your "job" and there is your "work." The difference between the two is you have responsibilities on your job that include showing up for class on time, turning in grades, participating in committee meetings, and representing the institution where you are employed. Additionally, the teaching demands are high. Yet, while students are important, I don't believe that high teaching evaluations and low publications are the recommended combination to get tenure at a Research I university. Yet, delivering quality teaching takes time, energy and attentiveness. Your "work," on the other hand, is the part of your legacy. "Work" is your contribution to the world. Accomplishing your "work" takes hours to read, plan research projects, collaborate, and write. As a new assistant professor who moved halfway across the country for both a "job" and "work," it was difficult to make the transition. The uncertainty of how my health would hold up to the scrutiny and demands of my new position added to the stress.

With the excitement of a new life in a new city at a new job, I knew that I needed to make sure that I managed my stress. One factor I had not fully calculated was being a single parent away from the support of family and friends. In my "old town," even though his father and I were separated, he was still present in our son's life. I also had some friends and family that could provide some support with my son. In the new city, we were on our own. Sometimes the stress became too much and I became ill. The flexible nature of the professoriate allowed me to mask some of the mini-Lupus flares. Since many students communicate via e-mail, I was able to meet student needs. Since I was an assistant professor with mentors who truly advocated for my protection as a junior faculty member, I was not put on a lot of committees. So I had time to focus on my writing and manage some of my health challenges. This flexibility allowed for me to manage health and personal life with the demands of my personal life.

After a little over a year, I became aware that conversations were being held about my presence or lack thereof in the office. I have heard people refer to presence in the office as "face time." The flexibility of the professoriate can be up for debate. While as a junior faculty member, the main goal outside of teaching and service is supposed to be focus on your writing productivity. At the same time, the unique, unspoken expectation of face time engagement can be vague. Face time is not only time spent in the office, but it often happens at campus evening events or weekend activities. Additionally, it is important to travel to conferences to present your work and network with scholars. As a professional, these expectations are certainly not unreasonable. When I was a school administrator, I spent some 12-hour days at school. Your presence was the expectation and part of your "work." For my counterparts who work in corporate environments, frequent travel and face time are also a critical piece to success. So, I definitely understood the expectation, but physically it was increasingly difficult to manage. Further, in graduate programs, most classes are held at night or via weekend workshop formats. One semester, I had a class that ended at 9:50 P.M. I also had classes that were held an hour away in an all-day workshop format. I actually enjoy teaching the workshop format, but physically, it is quite strenuous. After many of these classes, I would be absolutely worn out, as if a Mack truck had hit me and left me for dead on the side of the road.

In between the schedule of my "job" and single motherhood, I still needed to find the inspiration to do my "work," It became increasingly difficult to be motivated to write. While the writing expectation is not clearly laid out for any assistant professor, I knew that I had better crank out some substantial publications in order to secure tenure. Given all that was going on, this expectation became harder to achieve. When I took the job, I never revealed to my colleagues that I had Lupus. I wrestled with sharing this "piece" of me. As an educator, I was fully aware of the 1990 Americans with Disabilities Act,[3] which protects the rights of the disabled. First, I don't think I have ever (and still have not) come to terms that I may be classified as disabled. As someone who studies inequities dealing with race and gender, I am sensitive to oppression of others. Individuals with disabilities have had a long standing history of oppression. In addition to facing the possible challenges of my race and gender, I was unclear as to how to manage this other uncontrollable challenge of health. With Lupus, I did not "look" sick, so I guess my strategy was to "pass" for being a healthy individual. The problem was sometimes, I was not well. During my second year, I had a serious Lupus flare to the point that I needed to move a class to an online format to finish the semester. In navigating this ordeal, I had to inform the dean and others of my health challenges. While accommodations were made, I was uncomfortable with the perception of my absence from face-to-face class, since I knew there were discussions about my lack of face time. As an untenured faculty member, you just don't know how you are being perceived. Of course, this uncertainty caused more stress, which manifested more in my health.

Fast-forward! I ultimately moved back home to the university in my native city. After a couple of years of trying to navigate the newness of a tenure-track professor position, single motherhood, and a chronic and potentially debilitating illness, it dawned on me that I may not be superwoman and I may need some support. Moving home definitely was a better scenario for my son and me. I had family and friends around whom I felt comfortable leaving my son with while I taught evening or weekend classes. I felt comfortable that if a flare-up happened, my son would be covered.

Even still, I was not comfortable revealing this chronic illness to my new colleagues. While I may not have wanted to reveal this "piece" of me, circumstances certainly forced the revelation. After an American Educational Research Association conference, I ended up hospitalized for 4 days. This hospitalization came during the same time that my materials were due for my third-year review. In a quandary, I had to let my chair and others know that my packet was incomplete and I was in the hospital. Again, everyone was accommodating, but I really did not want to be perceived as using Lupus as a crutch to justify why my packet was not done.

At this point, I live with uncertainty. I am constantly battling my innate drive to achieve professional and academic goals with the reality of my physical limitations. As I navigate this profession, both my "job" and "work," I struggle to reveal when it is important to share the Lupus "piece" of me. I certainly do not want to be perceived as using this challenge to my benefit, but in some instances it is important for me to do so. This constant battle leads to stress, the very thing I need to mitigate. After almost 12 years of living with this health challenge, I sometimes wonder what positive things have evolved from the struggle.

Lorraine Hansberry, a famous renaissance Black playwright, said, "There is always something left to love. And if you haven't learned that, you ain't learned nothing." I have learned to value the times I am in good health. The Lupus piece of me sometimes takes a central position in the complex puzzle that I am. Living with a chronic illness has forced me to focus on the "pieces" of me that are most significant. More importantly, my son is one of the most important pieces of me. He has given me a reason to continue striving on my "job" and to do good "work" that will hopefully make a difference in the world.

NOTES

1. "Pieces of Me," performed by Ledisi and written by Claude Kelly, Ledisi Young and Charles Harmon. The song was released in 2011 by Verve Music Group, a division of UMG Recordings, Inc.
2. For more information about Lupus, see the Lupus Foundation of America, Inc.'s website at lupus.org.
3. For a brief synopsis of federal employment protections, see *A Guide for People with Disabilities Seeking Employment*, located at http://www.ada.gov/workta.pdf.

REFERENCES

Dillard, C. B. (2006). *On spiritual strivings: Transforming an African American woman's academic life*. Albany, NY: State University of New York Press.

Reed. L. (2008). In an unfamiliar place: An expansion of a scholar's social justice perspective. *Journal of School Leadership, 18*, 164-187.

Reed, L. (2011). Star light, star bright: A Black female scholar seeks to find voice in the academy. In G. Jean-Marie & B. Lloyd-Jones (Eds.), *Women of color in higher education: Contemporary perspectives and new directions* (pp. 283-301). Bingley, United Kingdom: Emerald.

CHAPTER 19

CREATING SPACE

Martin Scanlan

For the past 2 weeks colleagues and friends have noticed my new wrist brace and inquired about this addition to my garb. "What happened?" they ask. I like to respond with the opener, "Well, I was at the dentist the other day ..." That usually elicits a quizzical look. I explain that when I went in with a toothache, the dentist told me it wasn't a cavity. He asked if I had any stress in my life, as he suspected my aching tooth was due to grinding. I laughed at his query. "Oh no, I have a charmed, stress-free existence. (pause) But now that you mention it, my thumb has been aching from all the typing I do. It's grading time at the university." My dentist responded by recommending that I get a wrist brace right away and get my thumb looked at, since small problems with the hand can get worse in a hurry. I left the dentist and went right to the drug store and got the brace. After a mouthful of fillings, I've learned to listen to my dentist.

So at dinner tonight as I shared with my wife that I'm writing a chapter about work-life balance, she looked at my wrist brace and couldn't contain a little jibe: "How apropos. You, who are probably going to end up getting hand surgery from all your writing, are going to write about balance! Is this a piece for 'The Onion'?" Alas, it's with a humble heart, and sore wrist, that I reflect.

LESSONS FROM THE "FIELD"

I grew up playing soccer, and have had many coaches over the years. As a White kid in a small Midwestern town, where "diversity" for many of us

Juggling Flaming Chain Saws: Academics in Educational Leadership Try to Balance Work and Family, pp. 153–160

basically referred to historical disputes between the Irish, German, and Polish Catholic churches (and don't even start in about those Protestants!), my soccer coaches provided my first glimpse of cultural pluralism. First, I had an English coach, then one from Belgium, then from Iran. I learned to understand their accents and temperaments and style. I learned that "bonehead" was a reprimand but with an endearing undertone, despite the gruff sound. My coaches transformed my teammates and me from swarming masses into players who understood the positions on the field and strategies of play.

One of my best coaches used to preach a strategic insight that I remember to this day: soccer is all about creating space. "Don't sit and ball-watch. Move to the space!" he'd cajole, especially at us pokier ones. And when we slowed the game down too much by playing it directly at a teammate, he'd correct us, "Play the ball to the space!" When you see the game of soccer as a game about creating space, it changes your perspective on how to move yourself, how to pass the ball, how to create an opportunity to score. As I reflect upon how I balance work and life, the voice of my coach returns: it's all about creating space. This image captures a lot of what I wrestle with as I strive to balance competing demands. Two stories are illustrative.

IT'S A BOY!

On October 22, 2006, I was on the run. The weather was frigid—upper 30s, rainy, windy. I was maybe on mile 8 or 9, chilled, already beat. Doubts crept in: would I be able to complete the marathon? Thinking about work-life balance brings me back to this cold, blustery morning.

In hindsight, this run strikes me as a point in time of surprising equanimity. At this time in my life so many different factors could have unhinged me. In the work category, it was just after midterm and the semester was already a long one. A rookie at the university, I was teaching two graduate classes—both new to me—and trying to make sense of my first position as full-time, tenure-track faculty. Fresh from completing my dissertation, I was chomping at the bit to publish, but didn't have anything of substance under review. Compounding my situation was the 90-mile commute to campus 3 or 4 days a week. In short, I was stretched thin on the job.

In the life category, my wife and I had a 4-year-old son—our first child—at home, as well as our nephew, living with us as he finished middle school. My wife was directing a nonprofit organization that she had founded, a job to which she brought great passion, but which also demanded tremendous time. Moreover, we had been struggling for more than 2 years to adopt another child and battered by being continually rejected, deemed "not a fit" in the open-adoption jargon. This combination of work- and life-related pressures could have been my undoing. So why, in the midst of this, was I running a marathon? And what does this have to do with creating space?

I'd run a couple of marathons before, first when I was a teacher in California, and later as an administrator in the Midwest. Each time, the most challenging aspect wasn't the marathon itself—when the crowds and adrenaline would take charge—but rather the lonely, tedious training runs. While these daily routines at times felt like the bane of my semester, reflecting now they seem to have paradoxically created space for work/life. The commitment forced me to take time each week to exercise—which of course was a positive for my cholesterol level—but was good for me in a multitude of other ways. The running gave me time to shed some of the stresses that I carried around, be those work—my self-doubts about pedagogy that I felt as I moved from teaching middle schoolers to adults, my anxiety about writing manuscripts without the guidance and feedback of my advisor—or life—my angst at the nebulous, never-ending waiting game that adopting a child can be. Amidst this, the space for solitary time running was truly a grace.

Which brings me back to that chilly, fall morning of the race. While I'd trained in the heat of the summer and early autumn, I found myself facing wintry weather. An hour into what would end up being a 4-hour slog, I hadn't shed my fleece, hat, or gloves. (As it turned out, I never would!) My head was obsessed with one thought: amidst this ordeal, would I see my family? My wife, son, and nephew, along with my folks, all had come as support crew, cheering me on. But finding them amidst the thousands of spectators, this would be no small feat!

I looked out and saw the swarming crowds, cheering us on in their encouraging, but generic roar. Most were bundled in warm coats and hats, rain gear and umbrellas, clutching hot coffee. I was looking for the familiar faces, my loved ones, scanning the crowds as I stumbled on. Then I saw the balloon. This was our sign. How was I to find my crew amidst the masses of anonymous voices? "We'll have a balloon. Look for a balloon." That was good, but still ambiguous. A balloon? What color? What would it say? We hadn't work out these details. Needless to say, many fans had similar thoughts, and balloons dotted the sidewalks as we ran down the soggy streets. I didn't know what to expect, but turning the corner—was it LaSalle Street?—I saw and knew in an instant that my crew was there. The balloon said it all. In the shape of a footprint, the blue balloon read in bright words, "It's a boy!" I saw it and broke into tears.

See, the week before the race, my wife and I finally heard the amazing news: we had a match! After years of waiting, praying, hoping, and despairing, we finally were going to bring another child into our family: Lucas would be able to come home in a couple weeks! While hearing that news brought me initial peace and gratitude, something about seeing it proclaimed on the balloon that morning was overwhelming. I recall a sense of peace washing over me amidst a time of great stress, an amalgamation of professional ambitions and personal, familial longings.

I don't think I want to say that I *needed* to run the marathon that morning to maintain my balance between the pressures of work and the rest of life. I know I don't want to imply that my grand planning led me to sign up for the marathon, knowing that the preparation process—those hours and hours and hours of training runs—would force me to make the space for solitary time to unwind, reflect, pray, release. But as I think about work-life balance, I am struck by how important this solitary space is, and how much it helped me navigate a difficult semester.

GOLDEN BIRTHDAY

Jump to April, 2009. It's now 2½ years later and I am in high gear as a junior academic, running the wheel like a hamster: teach and write and teach and write. Nary a day would pass when my nose wasn't pressed into the laptop with seven different windows open, me trying to simultaneously edit a paper, grade a student, respond to an e-mail, deluding myself that multitasking was somehow efficient and not, in fact, discombobulated. On this spring morning, however, I look balanced! I'm again on a run, this time on the beach in San Diego. (As an aside, I want to disabuse you of any illusions that I am some sort of svelte, swift, birdlike creature who's always running. The mirror doesn't hide the paunchier reality, and my calendar would indicate that my running habit is an on-again off-again thing.)

Alone on the run, I was not far from my family, still sleeping. We had arrived the day before on our first trip to southern California and were renting a condo on the beach. For the first time ever, we were transforming my typical solitary jaunt to an academic conference into a family adventure. Our 7-year-old had just had his golden birthday and, looking for a way to honor this, we managed—through a charmed alignment of schedules and frequent flyer miles—to parlay the conference travel into a celebration. My wife, a sleuth, found us digs that, for the same price as the conference hotel, gave us a kitchen and a separate room for the kids. Most important, they placed us a stone's throw from the beach.

If my first story of training runs for the marathon points to my struggles to find balance via *solitary* space, this tale of the family trip to celebrate the golden birthday illustrates my efforts to balance work and life through *shared* space. In my experience, striking a balance between competing demands isn't like baking a cake, a matter of having the right supplies and the wherewithal to fashion them together in just the right manner to a delectable end. That image is too sequential and cut and dried. It's not quite a juggling act either, where the balls (or flaming chain saws) are either all flying harmoniously or toppled. That image is too all-or-nothing. In my experience, striking this balance is more like navigating and negotiating a family trip, sharing the space together while moving ahead.

I think our stay at the beach that spring captures this well. It points to how space can be created that serves multiple, shared purposes. The beach created a space for me to be with the family and also close to work. I drove a few miles to the conference to present a paper, meet a colleague, then returned in a few hours to slide back into a family zone, looking for seashells, envying the surfers' skills. But the point is not to simply share a personal memory of a time, one in which I managed to mingle these two worlds of home and office to good effect. Rather, this golden birthday trip is an allegory for how, in the best of circumstances, creating shared space has allowed me to experience balance. Shared space is everywhere: my home office is also a guest room, my kitchen counter is where I grade papers and also make pizza. Rather than multitasking, this is creating space to embrace the competing demands of work and life and allow them to coexist.

Creating shared space allows me to recast the life/work dichotomy as a duality. Dichotomies are ends of a spectrum, where moving toward one inherently involves moving away from the other. By contrast, dualities are not "either/or," but "both/and." When I create space that embraces life and work I find myself drawing upon one to illuminate the other. By way of example, my scholarship of late has focused on how school leaders foster organizational learning by attending to communities of practice. As I teach my graduate students and present professional development for educators, I find myself making points in my work by incorporating examples from my life. When teaching about how to make tacit knowledge explicit, I talk about my son's skills at riding a skateboard (tacit knowledge) that he struggles to explain to his friend (explicitly). When teaching about learning in communities of practice, I discuss my home-brewing and my wife's bee keeping. I find such space that allows life to creep in and augment my work to be comforting, grounding.

Last week my wife took a writing retreat, working on her own scholarship. Instead of having to skip the end-of-semester happy hour of socializing with colleagues, I ended up taking my kids, getting them some Shirley Temples and hummus and hanging out for an hour to toast the changing season. Sharing the space took some risk on my part—going anywhere with a 2-year-old is always something of a crapshoot, let alone to a fancy urban bar—but it ended up working well, allowing me to stay connected to colleagues and, in a way, giving them a small window into some of the rest of my world. The point, simply, is that we can sometimes create space in which the competing pulls of home and work can coexist with begrudging acceptance, if not harmony.

TEAMMATES

I began this reflection by considering how creating space, a strategy guiding soccer, is a way of thinking about how I've strived to find and create balance in work and life. I want to connect the dots of my two stories of solo and shared space by returning to the soccer field, and one living legend of the game. Lionel Messi is a name familiar to practically anyone with even a modest level of interest in international men's soccer. This 23-year-old sensation is an incredibly gifted player whose ability to dribble, run, and score is bar none. Messi is frequently the indirect catalyst for scoring a goal: because of his prowess, he draws two or three opponents to cover him, thus creating space for his teammates to move unmarked. As often, however, Messi is a solo sensation. He creates space for himself with adept, darting moves and seems to single-handedly dismantle the defense, beating player after player, the ball ending up in the back of the net. As is the case when watching expertise of most types, seeing Messi play is a thing of beauty.

While the occasional individual is a superstar who can succeed independently, most of us need many others. I have been called many things, but have not yet, nor will I ever be, labeled a "Messi." On the soccer field I need many teammates to help me create the space to move the ball, seeking the goal. And in life, in trying to create space for balancing work and life, I rely on the help of many. Perhaps the most striking grace of writing this reflection is that the occasion has helped me not just recognize the solo and shared space that helps me seek this balance, but rather how utterly dependent I am on so many others in crafting this space. Whether it is the space for solitude and the solace that this provides, or the shared space for demands of work and life to abide together, I rely greatly on the generosity, forgiveness, and flexibility of my wife, family, and friends.

Creating space is on my mind more as time passes and life progresses. In terms of family, we have grown larger and more complicated. When I entered the academy we had one child, and now have three. Our nephew has been on and off in the abode and is just now moving out on his own, having graduated last weekend from high school. My parents and in-laws are aging and the inevitable aches and pains creeping up on them, and while all are still graced with relatively good health, I'm haunted by the last line in the poem, Memory, by William Matthews: "We all drink from a leaking cup."

In terms of work, the demands on my time at the university have steadily increased. Annual reviews, those regular reminders of the tenuous nature of assistant professorship, have in turn confirmed that I'm making steady progress and cajoled me to do more. The ticking of the tenure clock is a little like that one in the crocodile's belly as it pursues Captain Hook, always following me around, and giving me more than a little anxiety when it seems to be closing in. At times I find myself vexed with prioritizing the writing (which will weigh most heavily in my own job security) with the competing demands of teaching and providing service (which "count" for less in the promotion and tenure calculus, yet seem to impact the field in so much more meaningful, immediate manners).

At times it seems these demands of work and life pull in increasingly divergent directions. This brings me back to college where, among other matters, I studied dispute resolution. I learned about different perspectives one could take toward negotiating a conflict. Typically conflict is perceived as, and experienced as, a zero-sum game. Negotiations are a direct competition: the more one side gains, the more the other loses. Sometimes the game of balancing competing pressures of work and life strike me as a zero-sum game as well. There are only so many hours in a day, and the time I spend on one aspect of work (preparing for tonight's class) is time I won't spend on another (revising and resubmitting the article). All this work time will take away from time I spend on life, the mundane (fixing the fence) and the sublime (date night).

Back in college we also learned, however, that one could take alternate perspectives toward conflict, and that such perspectives might open up different possibilities for resolutions. Principled negotiation, by way of example, was an approach that emphasized focusing on interests instead of positions and creating options for mutual gain (Fisher & Ury, 1983). Perhaps resolving conflicts inherent in work / life conflicts requires alternative perspectives as well. Creating space for the solitude in the midst of a harried semester and sharing the space of a conference trip and a family vacation resemble, in this sense, new ways of approaching old conflicts.

Finally, the emphasis of this essay on creating space implies a more fundamental point: being present. When I recall that marathon run, and when I see pictures from the beach in San Diego, I am struck by how palpable the memories remain. These times stand in stark contrast to the many periods of life where I've tried to be too many places at once and ended up being distracted and absent. As I continue to make my own life journey, this reminds me of my aspiration to be *present* where I am.

Working at a Jesuit university does have some hidden perks. Last week I was meeting with my spiritual director, a benefit provided to faculty to foster their own spiritual development, regardless of faith tradition or nontradition. His office floor was cluttered with boxes of books, like he was in the midst of moving. "I'm trying to create some space," he explained. I had to smile, since the image worked so well. "Aren't we all?" I replied.

REFERENCES

Fisher, R., & Ury, W. (1983). *Getting to yes*. New York, NY: Penguin Books.

CHAPTER 20

A PHD IS A FAMILY AFFAIR

Douglas Wieczorek

My wife would say pursuing my doctorate was always part of the plan. She attests that she knew I was going to be a professor when we were dating in college. We took several history classes together (my major) and I would walk and talk, and relecture for Kate in my dorm room before every exam. She would joke that all I needed was the suit coat with patches on the arms and a pair of corduroy pants to fully assume the role. After 4 years of juggling school, work, family, classes, and conferences, I received some exciting news which brought me closer to wearing those pants—I am a doctoral candidate! We have to celebrate! I think we'll go out for iced cream sundaes, or maybe we'll go get some softball pancakes at Denny's—the girls love those. Things are really starting to fall into place.

I clearly remember the moment which spurred a change in the path of my educational career. I was an assistant principal at a small, private junior-senior high school. Our administrative team was meeting in the principal's office conference room to discuss plans to raise more money for a new, second gymnasium space. It was springtime, and as any administrator knows, is a difficult time of year. I was tired. My mind was elsewhere. I wanted to be outside. I wanted to plant my garden, mow the grass, and play with my kids at the earliest opportunity.

Mary was 5 years old at the time, and the twins, Sarah and Ellen, were just about to have their first birthdays. Mary was interested in playing soccer and had her first practice scheduled for the following Saturday after-

Juggling Flaming Chain Saws: Academics in Educational Leadership
Try to Balance Work and Family, pp. 161–168
Copyright © 2012 by Information Age Publishing
161

noon. She had her first pair of cleats, which she did not quite understand why they had so many bumps on the bottom, but she was excited and knew they were important to playing the game. As a Dad, I was excited too. The twins had us buried in a daily supply of bottles, diapers, and laundry. My wife Kate and I felt like we were running a 24 hour day care center instead of raising two infants; we were on autopilot, and having the opportunity to fulfill a different fatherly role and see Mary play soccer for an hour on a Saturday was a significant event for me.

My administrative team decided that we needed to schedule and host additional events at the school to solicit donations for the fundraising campaign. A series of three events were scheduled at different times over the next couple of months. Of course, the first alumni event was scheduled on the same day and time as Mary's first soccer practice. I went to Mary's soccer practice, but I know that I did not score any points with my administrative team, and I knew this issue would continue if I did not make a change.

The time and opportunity had come for me to pursue doctoral studies about 4 years ago. I was nudged in this direction because I spent an incredible amount of time at school as an assistant principal and I/we felt off balanced. (It is important to note this important point, I may write in the "I" or "my," but it will always be "we" and "our"). We sought more flexibility, we wanted the kids to have more of our time at home, and I sought more gratifying work in education, maybe as an academic. An amalgamation of inspirations, timing, resources, support, and opportunity came together and I threw myself in.

Some of the voices in my life were warning me right from the beginning that I had seriously misjudged my plan to become a member of the professoriate. When I initially notified one of my former academic advisors that I was applying to doctoral programs her reply was supportive, yet she warned: *Really think about if this is what you really want to do, the writing expectations are so very high. You know what they say, right? Publish or perish?* That same fall semester, during one of my first doctoral classes, the professor took some time during each class to discuss academia in very broad terms. I remember her saying: *Academia can be a lonely profession; it is you and your work, so build connections through this work. There is flexibility in your schedule; the institution will not care when you put in your 100 hours per week—just as long as you do.* I did want to be home to spend more time with my family, and to raise my girls. Pursuing doctoral studies has allowed us to achieve more balance at home, but the experience has come with many challenges for my family.

My family-student-emerging scholar balancing act cannot be fully explained by a specific strategy or skill, or the use of a planner, or a calendar, or solved by using Outlook. Balance for us includes constant communication, teamwork, and the support of family. This narrative account of my/our experiences as an emerging scholar is also coconstructed, where each of us contributed anecdotes, thoughts, and moments that jumped out as indicators of how we all work together. I am the emerging scholar in the family. As many families can probably attest, when there is a scholar in the family it is truly a family affair. Each member of my family should receive an honorary PhD degree and a yearly stipend, because it would not be possible for me to reach this goal without support. This support manifests itself in all types of ways: emotional, physical, financial, logistical, and psychological. I am so lucky to have the support that I have. A nod to critical theorists everywhere, I understand and acknowledge how I am in a position of privilege. I have a supportive spouse who earns a good living, a supportive set of healthy, vibrant parents who live down the road and will do anything to help out, a wonderful daughter who is the best big sister and extra pair of eyes a parent could ever hope for, money (for the record, dwindling at an exponential rate) in the bank, health insurance, supportive faculty, and continuous, multiyear financial support from the university through a generous graduate assistantship and tuition scholarship. Which begs the question, if I am having trouble delivering the goods, then how do others fare?

We are extremely close to my parents, and have developed a working routine over the years to make sure things run as smoothly as possible, so everyone gets what they need, and gets to where they need to go, and will be picked up to make it home. At the beginning of every month I download a free-use calendar program and start to fill in the days: meetings, classes, work time and other engagements at the university for me; running club, music, game club, Italian club, riding lessons for Mary; faculty meetings and appointments for Kate; pick up and drop off times for the twins at pre-K, gymnastics, doctor appointments, speech therapy, dentist, with the dates and times denoted by a (**) if Grandpa and Grandma will be picking up or dropping off, and other codes and notes at the bottom as reminders for snack week, when Mary has band, when the twins have library day, when money is due for which fundraiser, and notations for events that must be included on the next month's calendar. I save the document, name it, and I e-mail it as an attachment to my dad. My dad takes the calendar, prints it off and reviews it with my mom. Usually within an hour I receive a witty retort via e-mail from my dad: *We will be charging double the rate on the 10th for a pick up and a drop off.* Or, they will call to go over the calendar to clarify certain details to make sure we are all on the same page. Whenever I call their house, I usually call and ask for a specific department, like I am calling a multinational business switchboard operator:

Doug: *Uh, yes, hello, this is Rossland, I am calling to speak to the transportation department please.*

Mom: *Oh, hi honey, oh, I mean, yes sir, one moment please.* [calls out for Dad and hands him the phone, I hear him in the background, bellowing]: *I thought we were closed today!*

Dad: *Yeah, now what do you want?* [teasing tone]

Doug: *Hey, be nice or I will report you to your supervisor.*

We do have fun with it. I call and ask for an assortment of departments: transportation, child care services, maintenance (I am not very handy), counseling, barbershop, you name it. As a good-humored gesture, my Aunt Judy even bought my Mom a bright red T-shirt that reads in white letters on the front "Somewhere Special Child Care Center" with white handprints on it. We all know that my mom is the CEO of the operation. Sometimes (read, often) the support staff (my dad) playfully/seriously elbows me in the ribs about this arrangement. Like the day I drove up to my parents' driveway to find the twins' infant carriers on the sidewalk with blankets over them, with the diaper bag next to them, and the garage doors closed. The twins were not actually in the seats, but I got the message—the twins were a handful that day—and I roared out loud with laughter when I saw the setup. So, the next time I put the twins on the front porch in their carriers' and did a mock ring n' run—so all my parents saw were their two little faces in the side glass when they approached the front door. There is no possible way my family (the one under my roof) could be as healthy, happy, and as successful without my parents. Any conversation about work-life balance must include the sacrifices they have made, the love, the time, the support, the cheerleading, and the open arms that are always extended for any one of us whenever we need a hug. My wife and I know, without my parents, balance would never be possible during this period of our lives.

I have tried other ways to organize my life during my doctoral studies. The university gave me Blackberry this year to help facilitate and maintain communications as part of my graduate assistant position as a local school district tutoring coordinator. I never felt so stressed and lacking in organization despite using the user-friendly calendar feature. It never matched my wife's calendar, or my parent's calendar, or the calendar on our fridge, so it really did me no good whatsoever. My balancing act is multidimensional, where I am only one actor which plays a starring role in the production of my own life. From day to day it is choppy, it is smooth, sometimes I glide, and other times I cry. Sometimes the balancing act subtly cues me to check the scales through daily interactions with my kids while I am trying to work at home: *Daddy, can you come see this really weird bug that we found outside. Ellen wants to grab it but I told her no, wait for Daddy, it could be a bad biter bug.* Sometimes my wife and I are making it up as we go along: [texting to Kate] *Do u p/u MGW today or me? Or she takes bus to GG? Dunno.* Other times, the balancing act tips the wrong way when I lose track of things and fail to tell my parents a key details of schedule information: *Dad, can you pick up the twins?* [me, listening] *No, you were not supposed to pick them up.* [listening] *I know school is ending in 15 minutes, I forgot to ask you and to put it on the calendar. I am at the university at a meeting and I just remembered I could not pick them up today. I am sorry, and thank you.* [listening] *Love you too, bye.* Other times I am affirmed that my choices and the balance that I constantly fidget with and adjust are in the best interests of all of us: *Daddy, where is your next conference? Can you make sure you have another paper accepted for that one so we can all go? I'd really like to fly JetBlue if we can; I like how they name the airplanes.* Other times the balance is way off and ends with questions, doubts, and regret, like it did this past winter.

Just maybe, I thought to myself, I could steal an hour away while they are outside.

I went into the kitchen to fill the kettle to make myself a cup of coffee. I looked out onto the backyard through the kitchen window. My daughters were outside in the snow, a heavy, wet, snow-globe type snow. They really wanted me to come outside with them. I know I should go out there and watch them. I should go out and play. I always go. Just the other day I built them a snow fort. I have so much to do right now. I have two more qualifying exam questions to finish, two articles for a conference to write, and I still need to plan for classes that start next week. It is okay, really, they are older now and I am right near the window and can peek out and keep an eye on them while they are in the backyard. I don't want to keep them inside, the snow is so beautiful and they have been asking to use their new sleds. I remember days like this when I was little. They have been in the house so much lately, and they have been growing tired of the same games and toys. I sat down and began to type.

A loud crash, the door slammed open in the kitchen. My 9-year-old rushes in. She is screaming, crying: *It was an accident! It was an accident! Ellen, it's Ellen!*

I run outside in my socks and met Ellen in the driveway. Her face. Oh, her face. Her face is so bloody I cannot even see what is wrong. Her snowsuit is all stained like the color of red wine. She is crusted in ice and slush. She is so scared.

Well, I guess, now we can tell the twins apart. Ellen is the one with the missing tooth.

I had a productive time at the computer. I think. I cannot remember for sure. I do not even remember what I was working on. Who cares. I should have been there. If I was out there when they were sledding, this would not have happened. Kate says I should not shoulder the blame, at the time she could not go outside with them either. She was still recovering from an injury to her back and to her knee which left her a bit unstable. If she took one more tumble it could mean surgery.

I have many identities, as we all do, and I have had to rank and prioritize my identities accordingly: husband, father, son; emerging scholar comes in fourth place. Truth be told, I could probably put the title of "neighbor" in fourth place and bump "scholar" to fifth place because I help out my neighbor by regularly mowing his lawn and doing other odd jobs whenever he calls. He also has the best stories. I never tire of hearing about the time a mortar exploded and blew him up against a wall during a battle with the Germans in Europe during World War II, or how our neighborhood looked when he first built his house for his growing family 40 years ago, or when he used to chase teenagers who smoked pot in their cars at the dead end of the street by pretending to take their pictures with a camera. As I listen, or mow: *You really should be writing something right now.* I have recently started to share more of my frustrations with my academic advisor who has always supported me, and most importantly, allowed me to struggle and find my own way. This is the first time I have truly struggled with academic tasks. Like many graduate students, I have always been "good at school," and know how to play the game. This has been much different.

I meet with my advisor pretty regularly, about once a month during the academic year, except for the past fall semester when I went into hiding because I did not want to face him. I do not like making excuses or dragging my personal baggage around the department. Over the past 4 years I have tried to hide my fear and anxiety as best I could and maintain a firm, masculine, confident, and professional demeanor during our meetings. This past year, things have just not gone my way despite my level of commitment and attempts to juggle things more efficiently, to work harder, and to improve the quality and pace of my work output. I admit it was a self-imposed lockout, my pride and fears took over, and the negative self-talk consumed me. Deadlines and goals came and went. A conference commitment passed by. I know, I need to beef up the CV or nobody will look at me. *This must mean I cannot hack it, I am not good enough. Maybe I should bail out.*

You're freaking me out. There. I finally said it. There is no way I can get that paper out to review in 1 month's time. It is not going to happen. I have to mow the lawn, I have to go get cat food, I have the kids, I have my proposal, I have … (sigh). *How do you all do this?* The tug of academic work is always with me, it is haunting sometimes, but it is also motivating.

This past year I probably got a taste of what faculty life is really like. The challenge to maintain balance has become more difficult as my obligations as an emerging scholar have increased: teaching, working on a school-university tutoring program, shadowing an instructor for my next course, qualifying exams, dissertation proposal, multiple conferences, new conference proposals, volunteering for invited speaking sessions, and trying to become a published scholar. Part of me feels like I am on the outside looking in, especially when I see other graduate students who were invited to work on grant funded research projects, or working along-side faculty at sponsored on-campus professional development sessions, and are already published, and I am not. Instead, I am driving twins to preschool, or picking up twins from preschool, nursing a cold, making PBJ or mac n' cheese, waiting for the school bus to bring my oldest home, or taking twins to gymnastics and my oldest to riding lessons, or texting my wife: *What 4 dnr?* or *All good, got dnr.* I do not think I can put "Caregiver, driver, shopper, play-date, and father" on my CV. As a graduate student/doctoral candidate I am still negotiating the scholarly terrain and attempting to integrate this occupation into an overall lifestyle that works for my family going forward.

As I whittle away at the steps toward my degree, and submitting articles for publication, I make sure that I celebrate the smaller achievements in-between: finishing coursework; completing my first semester teaching a course on my own; working as a teaching mentor; and especially present-ing at my first conference. Presenting at the American Educational Research Association for the first time was an exceptional experience which gave me the boost I needed to know I was going to be successful as an academic. I presented to a great group of scholars in self-study; indi-viduals from all over the world listening to my work, and appreciating my thoughts and contributions to the discipline. They invited me to a busi-ness meeting and a reception afterwards—I felt like an eighth grader who found a "cool kids" table to sit with in the cafeteria. Kate saved a text on her phone from when I was leaving the convention center after the meet-ing: *I now know I belong here. Wow—I have stories for you. Will call soon.* I realized how the voices from the beginning of my program offered valu-able guidance; I was starting to build connections through my work and these connections extended far beyond any of my expectations.

Pursuing this degree has been the most challenging personal and pro-fessional journey I have undertaken thus far in my life, and many of my graduate school friends share the same challenges. Those peer connec-tions are very important to me—we cheer each other on—we share our doubts—we share our dreams. The prospects of improving balance when I attain a position in higher education do not seem particularly bright sometimes, as I continue to resist the numerous, foreboding warnings along the way. Fairly recently I was told by a faculty member: *Graduate school was the best time of my life, once you get a faculty position the pressure really takes its toll on you.* There are so many naysayers, but I just cannot allow myself to give in and listen to them. My family and I have put in too much effort and sacrifice for me to turn back now. And I love the work. When you get pumped up after seeing and almost meeting Ken Zeichner in person at a conference, you know you are hooked. It's like seeing Bono from U2, right? (I am glad Kate understands, or at least pretends to understand this).

Writing this essay has been a reenergizing exercise as I write my dissertation proposal and form my dissertation committee roster. I hope this short narrative glimpse into my personal experiences and the lessons I have learned resonates with graduate students at different stages and places in the academy. I have successfully persisted in my program by remembering and using two pieces of advice which two separate faculty members have shared with me:

The key is to stay in the game…. Keep doing good work and good things will follow.

PART II

MIDCAREER SCHOLARS

CHAPTER 21

WORKING TO LIVE
AND LIVING TO WORK

Finding Balance in the Academy

Floyd D. Beachum

In my first year in the academy, I attended a history conference in Florida. You could tell I was new because I did not even attend the UCEA (University Council of Educational Administration) annual meeting that year. At this history conference, one of the special guests was an American treasure, Dr. John Hope Franklin (who is now deceased). He was a respected, reserved, and venerable scholar. Although he was advanced in age, this was only matched by his advanced wisdom. He told a story about a young historian who visited him at his home. Dr. Franklin welcomed his guest into his home and they began to talk, and the young historian quickly got to the point of his visit. He wanted to know how to become a great scholar. What were the secrets and strategies to success in the academy? This was the essence of the visit. Dr. Franklin looked at the young man, smiled and said, "Follow me." Dr. Franklin took the young man to his flower garden and began telling him about different plants and flowers. By this time, the young man became impatient and said, "Dr. Franklin, I am sorry, but I do not see how this is related to my visit." Dr. Franklin gazed intently at the young man and softly said, "Do something else."

*Juggling Flaming Chain Saws: Academics in Educational Leadership
Try to Balance Work and Family*, pp. 171–179
Copyright © 2012 by Information Age Publishing

This true story highlights the importance of finding a work-life balance. Dr. Franklin clearly understood how academic work can be stressful, engrossing, and time-consuming. If not kept in balance, it can consume your thoughts and occupy far too much of your time and existence. Dr. Franklin's advice to the young scholar was to find a balance between the work of the academy and your personal interests. This is great advice, but difficult to heed, especially with the demands placed on today's tenure-track professors, especially at research universities. Even though these institutions often have work-life balance programs, it is still difficult to solve the problem due to the uniqueness of the role of the professor. It is synonymous with words like academic, scholar, and intellectual. Dyson (2004) wrote,

> An academic toils in the vineyards of higher learning, usually as a teacher who may also focus on research. A scholar is an academic whose focus is on research. An intellectual in higher education is an academic or scholar who swims beyond her specialty and embraces the surging waves of knowledge as they wash against entrenched disciplines. (p. xix)

Our work encourages us to embrace some or all of these roles, but the defining characteristic is that much of what we do takes place in our minds. Our charge engages us in intellectual heavy-lifting, which requires high levels of focus, imagination, analysis, synthesis, and strategy. This requires significant periods of reflective inquiry. This chapter will examine some of my own experiences in the academy trying to balance work with my personal life, as well as describe this is particularly difficult to do so, considering what is expected. I will also provide some insight with regard to lessons I have learned, and strategies for success and sanity.

LIFE IN THE ACADEMY

Life in the academy can be described as exciting, unique, multifaceted, dynamic, stressful, exhilarating, and complex. This description is especially true for faculty members who dedicate themselves to living a life characterized by teaching, research, and service. These people are indispensable to the college or university. According to Philipsen and Bostic (2010), "The faculty is the backbone of any college or university, and can be neither healthy nor productive if not cared for in ways that allow for a successful balance of personal and professional lives" (p. xvii). The problem in many cases is that the uniqueness of the faculty role subjects us to vague evaluative criteria and the paradox of flexibility. We are supposed to do high quality research, be effective teachers, and make significant service contributions to the university and external communities. The question is how much is enough? The answer is seldom clear. So in an effort to reach a standard that is vague at best, many faculty members dedicate inordinate amounts of time to their work at the expense of their personal lives (and sometimes families). In our time-honored system of tenure committees, there appears to be little interest in specifying exact requirements for promotion and tenure. Perhaps it is just a part of the payment for the privilege to get paid to think. Maybe the process is a form of academic hazing that all must endure and master in order to reach higher levels of scholarly self-determination. Whatever the case, it leaves pretenure faculty members in the wasteland of publication paranoia, always wondering if they have enough of the right publications to achieve tenure.

Some might retort that faculty members do not punch clocks or even have standard hours for which they have to be at work (besides teaching courses and meetings). Therefore, they have more than enough time to do all that is required of them. The problem here is the paradox of flexibility (Philipsen & Bostic, 2010). If expectations are unclear or undefined, then faculty members have all of this time to do what? How does one organize one's time if they do not know the standard? Colbeck (2006) quoted a colleague who said that faculty "enjoy the freedom to work themselves to death" (p. 8). In this way, the freedom ironically becomes a prison in some cases.

Publish or Perish

"Publish or perish" is the well-known mantra in many research-focused colleges and universities. It usually entails publishing scholarly works, such as books and/or journal articles. These publications are usually not just to be printed in any venue; the more prestigious, exclusive, and usually less read by most, the better. Many times these outlets have high rejection rates and relatively low readerships. The work-life problem here is that pretenured faculty members are expected to produce both high quality and quantity, while specific guidelines are usually kept unclear. At best, your tenure goal becomes a moving target, usually best defined by a committee that may not always agree on what is necessary and give conflicting information. This can make you become superfocused on publishing to the detriment of any kind of personal life, or superjaded, believing that the situation is rigged from the beginning and you do not really have a chance. Either option takes a heavy toll on your personal life.

Teach or Die

"Teach or die" becomes the expectation at more teaching-focused colleges and universities. In this context it is an important factor in tenure and promotion decisions. On one hand, teaching can be energizing, illuminating, exhilarating, and very rewarding. On the other hand, it can be time-consuming, depressing (if assigned to a course you do not like), and stressful (if you have too many, or particularly difficult, students). Unfortunately, the primary evaluative tool for teaching is still student evaluations; sometimes peer evaluations come into play. They can be particularly insightful, providing both quantitative and qualitative data sources. But they can also be flawed, as students can use them to even out a personal issue with a faculty member, as retaliation for disagreeing with the professor about an issue, and as backlash when having a negative attitude about course content which is inconsistent with their mental models (e.g., a diversity class). The work-life implications are the time needed for preparation, combined with too many or particularly difficulty students, compounded by a flawed evaluative system that ultimately can impact job security. Teaching preparation, improvement, and performance can become all-encompassing, to the detriment of family, outside activities, and a peaceful state of mind.

WORK-LIFE BALANCE PART I:
REFLECTION ON MY PRETENURE AND PROMOTION EXPERIENCE

As a pretenured faculty member, I remember being excited about my new job position, anxious about the research expectations, and ready to meet whatever challenges that were to come. This time period was filled with a lot of new things; new job, new place to live, new colleagues, new city, and new pressures. There were times when I felt like I had too much time on my hands. Unfortunately, I was unclear at that time about what was really expected of me, had no real research agenda, and had no concept of how fast the tenure and promotion clock was ticking. Thus, the precious time that I had was not always well utilized. At the same time, worries about tenure and promotion began to consume my thoughts and work essentially became my life. My stress level began to increase because my job worries were constant, I had new course preparations to do, and committee work slowly began to increase. I was in for certain doom if I did not find a balance in my life.

Finding a Balance: Part I

Over time, I discovered some strategies that provided some much-needed balance. These strategies are:

1. Take a break.
2. Physical activity.

3.   Go to social events.
4.   Stay connected to friends and family.
5.   Seek out mentors.

Take a Break

Sometimes it is helpful to just get away for a while. Although you may physically leave the campus, you must also take a psychological break. This is essential because we engage in "mind work," and it is not easy to stop thinking about concepts, approaches, analyses, new literature, and/or making new or different connections. Taking a break can ease the pressure and provide some rejuvenation.

Physical Activity

I found that working out was another good way to relieve stress and provide balance. I eventually began working with a personal trainer who encouraged jumping rope, lifting weights, running, and boxing. These activities kept me in shape and allowed me to meet other interesting people who were not in the academy. Furthermore, this increased my physical health and positively impacted my state of mind.

Go to Social Events

I began attending different social events; some were job related and others were not. The job-related ones were attended by university faculty and staff, so it was a good idea to get to know other people on campus, including faculty in different departments. I attended other events that were just interesting or fun in an effort to meet new people. This increased my circle of friends beyond the university.

Stay Connected to Friends and Family

This is incredibly important. These individuals can keep your focused and grounded. They are people you can confide in, lean on, and complain to about work. Then again, it is wonderful to talk to someone and just laugh. This provides a unique form of balance away from the sometimes rigid and seemingly monastic faculty lifestyle.

Seek Out Mentors

A mentor can be extremely helpful in giving advice with regard to finding a balance. They are usually more experienced academics who have navigated successfully and have wisdom to share. Sometimes it is a good idea to have internal mentors at your home institution and external mentors at other institutions. This allows you to have the benefit of multiple perspectives.

WORK-LIFE BALANCE PART II:
REFLECTION ON MY POSTTENURE AND PROMOTION EXPERIENCE

I have now been in the academy 9 years, have been granted tenure and promotion, and have worked as the program coordinator/director at two institutions. In addition, I am now a husband and a father. These responsibilities create new challenges with regard to work/life balance. I now have to deal with the dilemma of having even less time. At this point, it seems as if the expectation is to continue a steady stream of scholarly output, teach effectively, and do more service activities, while reviewing for journals, attending conferences, seeking out external funding, advising students, working with doctoral students, managing administrative paperwork, addressing state mandates and university requests, and negotiating institutional politics. And by the way, I did say that I have a family, so I need to figure out how to spend time with them too. Now, the juggling of all these things takes planning, skill, and coordination, but does not always happen neatly. I sometimes feel like if I give up too much time to my professional life, I sacrifice my personal life (mostly my family) and vice versa. This balance is delicate at best.

FINDING A BALANCE: PART II

What follows are some lessons learned from my more recent experiences. Admittedly, I do better at some of these than others.

1. Make family time sacred.
2. Find a way to unwind and reflect.
3. Make concerns known.
4. Organize your time.

Make Family Time Sacred

Family is very important. A concerted effort should be made to spend quality time with partners, kids, and other family members. They are one of the most important pieces of your life puzzle. They need your involvement, support, encouragement, and love. And you need theirs. Hopefully, your home life can provide you with a sanctuary away from the craziness of your professional life. Then again, home can be crazy too, but at least it is a different kind of crazy.

Find a Way to Unwind and Reflect

The aforementioned demands placed on your time and energy can be exhausting. Every once in a while, it is good to find a way to relax away from home and work. The two places provide their own unique challenges. In some cases, home can feel a lot like work, especially if you have young children. I find that spending time at a neutral place (e.g., coffee shop, favorite restaurant, cyber café, etc.) and allowing yourself to relax and reflect can be invigorating.

Make Concerns Known

The problems of work-life balance are probably best articulated by those tenured individuals who can bring such issues to the forefront and get them addressed. In other cases, when issues come up, faculty members or departments work together to cover classes due to pregnancy or illness for example. Institutionally speaking, it requires policies to influence greater numbers of people in the organization. Usually, tenured faculty members are some of the people who can best afford to serve on such committees (i.e., work-life) and bring the concerns of untenured faculty to the forefront.

Organize Your Time

With increased demands and responsibilities, time is of the essence. This requires greater organization of my time than in previous years. With everything from daycare, to meetings, and teaching all happening in the same day, it requires effective time management. Not to mention that it would be nice to still publish. Thus, time must be arranged, negotiated, or taken in order to get everything done. I find myself making lists (especially if I have a lot to do in one day), and watching my calendar carefully (thank goodness for the iPhone). Even with such organization and vigilance, life still happens, so you have to also be open to change.

WORK-LIFE BALANCE: A PROCESS NOT A PRODUCT

As it stands, the life of the modern academic is subject to increased demands for scholarly productivity and teaching expertise (Philipsen & Bostic, 2010). These demands are sure to keep rising as increased pressure from state mandates, shrinking funding sources, and competition impact colleges and universities. This usually places the greatest burden on pretenure faculty, but also influences other faculty members who are working hard to keep departments afloat by recruiting students, effectively teaching, serving the university community, and contributing to the field through scholarship and research dissemination. Therefore, finding a balance can be tenuous at best. As best as I can tell, it is a process that changes as our experiences and responsibilities increase. I doubt that there will ever be a time when I can say that I have it totally figured out. There is no silver bullet in terms of work-life balance; it is all about the process. As we learn more about how to unwind, arrange time, spend time with family and friends, and reflect we get better at the process. As we observe the time factor, we find that senior scholars (especially full professors) do not have the same levels of stress and have found a better balance than their colleagues at the associate and assistant levels (Philipsen & Bostic, 2010). The goal is to find the right balance between professional and personal life that allows the individual to optimally engage both areas for the benefit of others and oneself.

There are definite implications for colleges and universities as faculty members strive to find this careful balance. "Developing policies that aid faculty with work-life balance issues takes time, and yet it is increasingly seen as a necessary investment" (Philipsen & Bostic, 2010, p. 185). According to these authors policymaking committees should focus their efforts around the following topics:

- child care;
- spousal/partner hiring;
- child leave; and
- tenure.

Most of these policies need to be more flexible, well-defined, creative, and well-informed by institutional context.

CONCLUSION

"Do something else," the all-important phrase highlighted by Dr. Franklin at the beginning of this chapter leads us to the greater lesson captured in this statement: "Find a balance." This balance negotiates the terms of your academic commitments and balances them with personal commitments. You should not have to give up your entire life to succeed in the academy. At the same time you should not have to make the decision to be with your family at the expense of your career. Although many professionals have to deal with similar issues, the work of faculty at colleges and universities is unique. If we allow it to, it seems capable of consuming your mind, thoughts, and time beyond the borders of the institution. This is the peculiar gift and curse of the academy. A proper balance can be found, but it is up to individual faculty members to find out what works best for them, then share that information for the benefit of others. It is indeed a process.

REFERENCES

Colbeck, C. (2006). How female and male faculty members with families manage work and personal roles. In S. J. Braken, J. K. Allen, & D. R. Dean (Eds.), *The balancing act: Gendered perspectives in faculty roles and work lives* (pp. 31-72). Sterling, VA: Stylus.

Dyson, M. E. (2004). *The Michael Eric Dyson reader.* New York, NY: Basic Civitas Books.

Philipsen, M. I., & Bostic, T. B. (2010). *Helping faculty find work-life balance: The path toward family-friendly institutions.* San Francisco, CA: Jossey-Bass.

CHAPTER 22

HOW CAN WE BALANCE WORK AND LIFE? REFRAMING THE QUESTION

A Buddhist Perspective on Balance

Kathryn Bell McKenzie

Months ago I was asked to write this chapter on work/life balance, and it's now 1 month before it's due and I'm just starting on it. I couldn't get to it before because there was just *too* much to do—end of semester grading, University Council of Educational Administration proposal to get in, committee meetings, Mother's Day, summer trip planning, and so on. Sound familiar? Could it be that my work and life are not balanced? Balancing competing priorities is not easy. There are times when work needs a lot of attention and then there are times when friends and family relationships need to be nurtured. Oh yes, and then there are the day-to-day details of life like grocery shopping, exercise, dental appointments, trash and recycling, and on and on. So how *does* one balance it all?

I hate to disappoint, but I don't have an answer to this question. Hopefully, you haven't quit reading this chapter saying to yourself, "Great, someone writing about work/life balance who has no answer to the question—'How can you balance work and life?'" Hold on, I'm getting to the

Juggling Flaming Chain Saws: Academics in Educational Leadership
Try to Balance Work and Family, pp. 181–189
Copyright © 2012 by Information Age Publishing

point. I can't answer this question because I don't think the issue is one of work/life balance. It is about balance, but it's not about balancing two aspects of one's life. In fact, as a practicing Buddhist, I try to no longer think of work and life as two separate events that can be compartmentalized. Rather, I believe there is only "being." In other words there are not multiple compartments of one's self. There is just me. Well, actually in Buddhism there really isn't a "me," there is Buddha nature, there is no-self,[1] but these are discussions for another time.

> *To be a human being is to be a Buddha.*
> *Buddha nature is just another name for human nature*
> *—true human nature.*
>
> Shunryu Suzuki

For clarity, and because I don't want to confound the issue or pull a "Derrida," putting "me" under erasure, I'm going to have to use the not so accurate term "me" throughout this discussion. Continuing then, there is not the "worker me" and the "friend me" and the "family me," there is just me or more precisely my Buddha nature.

This may sound confusing or as if I'm trying to skirt the issue of work/life balance, but I'm not. I'm reframing the question. What I'm saying is that in my practice of Buddhism, and I'm certainly not claiming authority here, what I have come to understand is that the dilemma of balance is not about balancing the external world, that which is beyond or outside of us. It is about balancing the internal world, about balancing one's self, about equanimity. So, for me, the question is no longer, "How can one balance work and life?" but rather, "How can one stay balanced or equanimous in all aspects of one's life?" The question changes but the desired results stay the same, getting to a place of peace with our life, ourselves, or as the Buddha would say, freeing ourselves from suffering.[2]

EQUANIMITY AND THE EIGHT WORLDLY WINDS

It is difficulty to write about the Buddhist conception of equanimity or balance without discussing all the teachings because equanimity is a central tenet of, and is central to, the other tenets of Buddhism. I could write about the Four Noble Truths, the Eightfold Path, the Precepts, and much more. For this discussion, though, I am going to situate equanimity within the Eight Worldly Winds.[3] Hopefully, you will find this discussion useful; practicality and usefulness are foundational to Buddhism. This pragmatism, though, has some arguing whether Buddhism is a religion, a philosophy, or something else. This argument does not interest me. The importance of Buddhism in my life is that it offers strategies for daily living that can take one out of suffering. Moreover, the metaphor of the Eight Worldly Winds captures all the ways in which one may suffer or experience discontentment. These Winds are paired sets of opposites including pleasure/pain, praise/blame, gain/loss, and fame/disrepute. Each of these can blow one "off-balance," causing one to sway like a willow in a strong wind, moving from one side to another. Through practices like mindfulness one can learn to calm the winds and return to balance, to equanimity.

Although equanimity, from a Buddhist perspective, refers to balance of the mind, it is not about merely staying calm or repressing feelings. Rather, it is about identifying and experiencing the feelings, emotions, and thoughts that can cause one to get off-balance, to suffer, but then returning to balance, to peace. It's about being aware but *not* being reactive. In an effort to explain further, I will first expand on the discussion of the Eight Worldly Winds and identify the two that most often blow me off-balance. Second, I will provide a scenario from my life, specifically my "work life," that involved these Worldly Winds and challenged my equanimity. Third, I will introduce and discuss the Four Foundations of Mindfulness[4] and show, using my life scenario, the ways these strategies can be utilized to address the Worldly Winds and return to center, to equanimity. Ultimately, my goal is to offer at least *an* answer to the question I reframed: "How can one stay balanced or equanimous in all aspects of one's life?"

> *Equanimity contains the complete willingness to behold the pleasant and the painful events of life equally. It points to a deep balance in which you are not pushed and pulled between the coercive energies of desire and aversion. Equanimity has the capacity to embrace extremes without getting thrown off balance. Equanimity takes interest in whatever is occurring simply because it is occurring. Equanimity does not include the aversive states of indifference, boredom, coldness, or hesitation. It is an expression of calm, radiant balance that takes whatever comes in stride.*

Shaila Catherine
Equanimity in Every Bite, Tricycle Magazine

Returning to the Eight Worldly Winds, the two that batter me around the most are fame and disrepute, which are more easily thought of as acknowledgement and dismissal. There is a long history behind this, going back to my childhood and a less than nurturing home life. From childhood experiences, I have deeply grooved thinking patterns related to these two Worldly Winds—acknowledgement and dismissal. Hopefully, I won't conflate the issue by moving momentarily from the wind and tree metaphor to a Western psychological one, but I think this new metaphor may resonant better to some of us. The metaphor is a record, or if you're young "vinyl," playing in one's head that can get stuck on a song, a narrative, and play it over and over again. It represents habituating emotions and thoughts. It is often difficult to reset the needle and play a different song, particularly if the song has been playing in our heads for most of our lives. Early experiences in my life started my record going, and the song has played on and on and on.

THE RECORD: HABITUATING EMOTIONS AND THOUGHTS

My brother and I were adopted as infants, he first and then me. He is 4 years older than I and not my biological sibling. My parents adopted us when they were older, the age of grandparents. Unfortunately, my brother had severe psychological issues and was extremely violent. My parents were unprepared for this. At the time, in the 1950s-1960s, there wasn't much help available for children with psychological problems or parents with children who had these problems. As a result, our household was not a safe place, physically or psychologically. My brother was often violent; my mother was often scared and reactive; and like most fathers in the 1950s, my father went to work. As a result of my parents' frustration with dealing with my brother, I was often dismissed. "Kathryn, go to your room. We have to deal with your brother." "Kathryn if you will just ignore your brother, he won't tease you"—teasing was certainly a euphemism for what was going on. So, you get the context. From my view, I grew up being dismissed or disregarded. Thus, the "number one top hit" in my head is the song *You Don't Really Matter*, a tune about being dismissed. Thus these early experiences were the genesis of my struggle with the Worldly Winds of dismissal and appreciation. This struggle continues today as I will illustrate in an example from my work life.

The Eight Worldly Winds

Pleasure/Pain
Praise/Blame
Gain/Loss
Fame/Disrepute

I work at a large research extensive university. It has a history of being all male, nearly all white, and all military until the early 1970s. Since coming to the university, I have had many encounters in which I have felt dismissed by male colleagues, particularly some in leadership positions. My interactions with one of these leaders, who I will call Russell,[5] have been particularly challenging. I feel Russell is often dismissive. If I raise an issue in a meeting he is chairing, he will say, "Thank you for that comment," and then move along. Russell does not, though, respond this way to the men in the room. This is not necessarily an issue between Russell and me as I'm not the only woman he responds to in this way. Several of my women colleagues have talked to Russell about his dismissive behavior of women.

The point though is not about Russell and his behavior, it's about me. When one of these "dismissive" incidents happens, the record player in my head turns on. That old tune, *"You Don't Matter,"* starts to play. Often before I even realize the song is playing I react. I lose my equanimity; I get blown around by the Wind of dismissal. My first reaction is anger. I want to strike back. My second reaction is withdrawal. Both of these are an effort, albeit unconscious most of the time, to move away from the suffering associated with feeling dismissed. Conversely, this suffering is also caused by my clinging to appreciation. Therefore, at this point in the situation, I am being blown around—bending away from, or averting, dismissal while also bending toward, or clinging to, appreciation. I am out of balance. I am reactive. I am NOT in a place of equanimity.

So what does one do in a situation like this? Are we to ignore our feelings? Should we allow someone to treat us badly? These are the types of questions often asked of Buddhist. People wonder if the goal is to just walk around being calm and detached. The answer is NO! The ultimate goal is to be free of suffering. Suffering in this situation comes from being off-center, out of balance, lacking equanimity. In other words, I was not suffering because Russell was dismissive; I was suffering because I was clinging to admiration and wanting to avoid being dismissed. There are mindfulness strategies, though, that we can use to return to center, to equanimity. Next, I will offer a modest explanation of the Four Foundations of Mindfulness, knowing this is inadequate for deep understanding of these concepts and practices, and then return to my work scenario to apply this to my situation with Russell.

THE FOUR FOUNDATIONS OF MINDFULNESS

The Four Foundations of Mindfulness[6] are useful tools for helping one achieve equanimity and move out of suffering. When we are mindful, we know what is going on within us so we can better respond to what it going on around us. The Four Foundations of Mindfulness are mindfulness of the body, mindfulness of feeling, mindfulness of the mind, and mindfulness of the Dharmas. Using the first foundation, mindfulness of the body, one turns attention to the breath. If one's breath is tight and shallow, there may be anxiety or anger. One might ask "What is going on with my breath? What does this tell me about how I'm feeling, about my emotions, about this situation?" Beyond the breath, one might survey the rest of the body. Are the jaws clinched, is the stomach tight? What does this say about one's emotions or state of mind? Is there fear, nervousness? According to the Buddha what we call mindfulness of feeling (the second foundation) is a simple, nonjudging awareness of agreeable and disagreeable (even sometimes painful) feelings. Thus, one might ask, "What am I feeling now? Is this pleasant, unpleasant or neutral?"

Four Foundations of Mindfulness

Mindfulness of the Body
Mindfulness of Feelings
Mindfulness of the Mind
Mindfulness of the Dharmas

The third foundation, mindfulness of mind, is a practice of watching one's thoughts in a compassionate, nonjudgmental manner, asking, "What is arising here?" "What is my mood, the quality of my mind?" The practice related to this foundation is about identifying thoughts without "going with them," without getting caught up and obsessing. In other words, it is about recognizing the thoughts without developing an entire narrative or story around them. The fourth and last foundation is mindfulness of Dharmas. Gil Fronsdal, one of my favorite Dharma teachers, describes mindfulness of Dharmas as recognizing the fixations or entanglements one might get caught in. One might ask, "Am I resisting something here?" "Am I holding on or clinging to something?" "How is this entanglement affecting my body, my feelings, my thoughts?" Mindfulness of Dharmas, along with the other three foundations, can free one from habituation and provide clarity. This clarity, though, is not about discovering the true story, but rather it is about coming to understand what is going on within one's self, about how one gets entangled in emotions, thoughts, and stories.

To further illustrate the usefulness of the Four Foundations of Mindfulness, I'll return to the previous example of my interaction with Russell and replay that scenario applying the foundations. Starting with mindfulness of body, as soon as I noticed that I was not feeling right about the interaction with Russell, that I was getting off balance, I could "watch" and "label" what was going on with me. I might initially notice my breath—is it short and tight, is it being held? I might merely say to myself—"breath is short and tight."[7] Then I could survey my body. I might notice that my jaw is clinched, or my shoulders are tight, saying— "shoulders are tight." These physical manifestations usually signal emotions, taking me to the second foundation, mindfulness of emotions. I could then try to name my emotion—"There is anger" or maybe "There is frustration." Moving on to mindfulness of mind, I could pay attention to my thoughts, my mood—"There are feelings of being dismissed. This is unpleasant." And finally, being mindful of the Dharmas, I could look at the entanglements—"There is clinging. Clinging to admiration. There is aversion. Aversion to dismissal. This is an old pattern that has come up." By using the Four Foundations of Mindfulness in this interaction with Russell, I could bring myself to a level of awareness that could not only help me see what is going on, but could also stop the internal narrative, the compulsion, the record. It could move me from this narrative:

> He just dismissed me again. I can't believe it. He is such a jerk. He must think my opinion doesn't mean a thing. He doesn't do this to everyone. I've got to do something about this. I'm not going to let him get away with this kind of behavior. He can't treat me this way.

To:

> Something is going on here. Breath is short, stomach is tight. There is anger and frustration. Ahhh, the wind is blowing—dismissal/admiration are back. There is entanglement—clinging and aversion. Hmmm, interesting.

Some readers may be ready to scream right now thinking this is much too passive, are you really just going to let him treat you this way, are you are just going to sit there and be mindful? UMPH! No, not necessarily. There may be times when just sitting there and being mindful is what is needed. I might discover that what I thought was going on, my narrative, was just a fixation, an entanglement. Or I might discover that yes there are entanglements, but there is also a situation in which some action is warranted. The point is that if I stop and take the time to be mindful, to look at the situation without reacting mindlessly, I can come back to center. From this centered position, this place of equanimity, I will be better able to determine what is going on and what I need to do, if anything. If indeed, from a position of nonreaction, I think Russell is being dismissive then I might decide to go see him and discuss my concerns and desires. Or, I may decide that my reaction to Russell's behavior was unwarranted and somehow the record player in my head just got turned on and stuck on that top hit, *"You Don't Matter."* If this is the case, all I need to do is just notice the reoccurring pattern and appreciate the mindful insight. Either way, I can maintain my balance, my equanimity, my peace

CONCLUSION

Thus, in answer to my reframed question—"How can one stay balanced in all aspects of one's life?"—it is through mindful practice that helps us maintain equanimity in our day to day, moment to moment experiences. It may sound simple, but it is difficult to do. I have found that daily meditation and weekly Dharma practice with my sangha, my Buddhist community, helps. Returning to the original question I was asked to answer— "How do you balance work and life?"—my answer is—try to stay balanced, nonreactive, in all I do. Anyone who knows me well would say I often fail at this. Those winds are powerful and often blown me back and forth. Those records in my head are loud, and they get stuck and play the same old songs over and over and over. However, I am making progress. I am more and more mindful of when I am getting blown around, which helps me come back to center. I am more and more mindful of when those records start, and I can often just pick up that needle and change the tune. When my energies are not spent on battling the winds or trying to stop the music, I have more energy and time to give to my friends, my family, my work. Ultimately, I have more work/life balance because "I" am more balanced.

With Metta,

—Kathryn

I intend to cultivate equanimity and balance in 2011—not to panic when things appear to be off track, and not to relax when everything seems to be going smoothly. I intend to cultivate awareness and presence and not focus too hard on the outcome — paying more attention to the process and developing understanding and sympathy for myself and others.

New Year's Resolution
David Nichterm

NOTES

1. For an interesting discussion of the concept of no-self see Dennis Genpo Merzel's book *Big Mind/ Big Heart*.
2. In Pali, the vernacular language spoken in the Buddha's time, the term for suffering is dukkha. In the West, we think of suffering as something large like illness or loneliness. Dukkha does refer to these significant states of suffering, but it also refers to lesser states of suffering like the frustrations and disappointments we all deal with on a daily basis. Therefore, some

Buddhist scholars suggest that in the West it might be more helpful to think of dukkha as discontent or unsatisfatoriness (Keown, 1996).

3. The Eight Worldly Winds, pleasure/pain, gain/loss, fame/disrepute, praise/blame, are also called the Eight Worldly Vicissitudes. Equanimity is the protection against these winds.

4. See Gil Fronsdal's dharma talk. *Emotions, Thoughts, and the Four Foundations of Mindfulness.* Available at http://www.dharmaseed.org/talks/?q=&talk-sel=1&p=1

5. Russell is a pseudonym.

6. Also see: *An Introduction to the Four Foundations of Mindfulness.* Excerpt of a teaching by Lama Lhundrup in Dhagpo Kundrol Ling, November 2001, revised with the help of Lama Mingyur and Lama DorjeDrölma. Retrieved 5/20/2011 http://www.dhagpo-kagyu.org/anglais/science-esprit/chemin/medit/etat_esprit/mindfullness3.htm

7. I purposely am avoiding the use of the pronoun "I" to take the ego the self out of this discussion. For a thorough discussion of the no-self see Dennis Genpo Merzel's book, *Big Mind/Big Heart.*

SUGGESTED RESOURCES

Websites With Audio Dharma Talks

- DharmaSeed: http://www.dharmaseed.org/
- Audio Dharma: http://www.audiodharma.org/

A FEW GOOD BOOKS

Hagan, S. (1997). *Buddhism: Plain and simple.* Boston, MA: Broadway Book.

Keown, D. (1996). *Buddhism.* New York, NY: Sterling.

Krishnamurti, J. (1996). *Total freedom.* New York, NY: HarperCollins.

Merzel, G. (2007). *Big mind/big heart.* Salt Lake City, UT: Big Mind.

Salzbert, S. (1995). *Loving-kindness: The revolutionary art of happiness.* Boston, MA: Shambala Classics.

Suzuki, S. (1970) *Zen mind, beginner's mind.* New York, NY: Weatherhill.

Suzuki, S. (2002). *Not always so: Practicing the true spirit of zen.* New York, NY: Harper-Collins.

Trungpa, C. (1999). *The essential Chogyam Trungpa.* Boston, MA: Shambala

CHAPTER 23

BE KIND, BE CRITICAL, BE PRODUCTIVE

Nine Suggestions for Keeping Your Life and Work in Balance

Jeffrey S. Brooks

This chapter is based on my experiences working as a professor of educational leadership for nearly a decade. For better and for worse, I have worked at several institutions and I have learned lessons at each that I want to share with you as you consider the issue of working toward your own version of work-life balance. At the onset, I'd like to make three basic assertions that undergird everything else I will write here. First, being an academic is both a tremendous privilege and a great responsibility. I am privileged to be able to have a position that allows me to work in an exciting and stimulating world of the mind while also providing for my family. Given that privilege, I a feel responsibility to my students, colleagues, and people working and learning in schools to work hard helping us understand how we can positively influence the outcomes, processes and theoretical constructs that constitute work that is at once technical, conceptual and relational.

Juggling Flaming Chain Saws: Academics in Educational Leadership
Try to Balance Work and Family, pp. 191–198
Copyright © 2012 by Information Age Publishing
All rights of reproduction in any form reserved.

The second point I'd like to make is that all I can do here is share some of my perspectives on this topic. I know very well that every point I make here will be irrelevant to some readers and poignant to others. So ... I suppose what I mean to say is that I'm less concerned that you gain insight into my life here than I am interested in giving you a few things to think about—it's up to you to make one, two or 10 of them your own.

Finally, the fundamental insight I can offer with respect to work-life balance is that in my experience the more highly structured and productive my professional life is, the more I am able to enjoy my personal life. I do think it is useful, as some of the authors in this book suggest, to think about compartmentalizing these two areas of your life and to draw a line between the two. However, I find that the line is dynamic rather than static, and that as one recedes the other advances. Some people would have you believe that work and life have this kind of relationship:

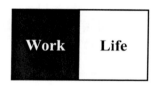

But I would suggest it's more like this:

Work and life are two forces in your life that are in dynamic tension—concordant opposition—and they exert reciprocal influence on one another. In the most basic sense, this simply means that balancing work and life is not a destination to be reached, but rather a state of existence that is in constant motion, something we must work to improve and change without ever attaining some perfect way of working and living. All that said, here are a few insights I've gained over the past decade.

1. DON'T TRY TO KEEP YOUR LIFE AND WORK IN BALANCE

An academic's life is not a balanced existence. There are many reasons for this, some Frankensteins of our creation and others endemic in the work we do. The beauty and danger of academic work is that it is on one level mental—we work with one foot in a world of ideas, and the other in a world of applying and testing those ideas in practice. This means we are asked to consider, challenge and refine intricate conceptual frameworks, philosophic arguments, and epistemological positions. Notions such as conscientizacão, weltschmerz, gesellschaft/gemeinschaft, community, leadership, learning, and zeitgeist not only mean something, these and thousands of other ideas are part of an infinitely complicated puzzle called "improved education" where the pieces are constantly changing shape. It's our job to help form those pieces into something concrete and try to understand how they fit in with the other constantly changing pieces our colleagues are working on simultaneously. This means the work is constantly changing and, really, that there is no single solution for almost anything we will ever do. The result? Even when we are away from the "office" the wheels in our heads are in constant motion, and this means that often when we are *physically somewhere* (washing the dishes, hiking in a park, talking with friends) we are *mentally somewhere else* (thinking about Foucault, trying to critique one theory using another, figuring out how theories can inform practice, wondering how we can decrease the opportunity gap, etc.). You can do mental work 24 hours a day, 7 days a week, 365 days a year. You can do it when your mind *should* be focused on cooking, cleaning, playing, loving, shopping, teaching, advising, etc. It's one of the reasons the cliché "absent-minded professor" is apropos. If you can find a way to compartmentalize things, or engage in other activities that are equally fascinating your mind will be more fresh and engaged in work *and* life. So … to me, finding balance as an academic has more to do with finding equilibrium with your personal imbalance—finding a space that allows you to do this work as happily, healthfully, and productively as possible.

2. BE PRODUCTIVE

There is a big difference between a scholar and a productive scholar; likewise, there is a big difference between a leader and a productive leader. Schools, colleges and universities are replete with brilliant people, but not all of them actually *produce* things. I urge you to be a productive scholar, not just a scholar, and I urge you to extend this to all aspects of your academic work. When you read, produce an EndNote file or a typed page of notes that you can easily use later in your writing. When you write, make sure you produce something at every sitting. Importantly, I'm not only talking about research or singing the siren song of vision, mission and goals. This habit of productivity extends to many other aspects of academic work as well. For example, in terms of teaching, think about how what you are doing can have a life beyond the classroom. Can you assign work to that leads students (and you) directly to publication or something they can share with their professional colleagues? Why? Can professional Learning Communities in your school actually produce something to share that might be a catalyst for change? Productivity is the name of the game in education. It is what earns you tenure and promotion, but more importantly it's how we make a difference in schools and in education.

3. DO SERVICE THAT MAKES A DIFFERENCE

One of the pieces of advice I've received many times is that it's great for an academic to serve on committees that never meet, to be an officer of something if it demands very little time and to add to your CV with as little effort as possible. Personally, I'm disgusted by this advice and by the assumptions embedded in it. Seeking out irrelevant and inactive "service" is tantamount to saying that service, *real service*, is something to be avoided rather than embraced and that there is a certain percentage of my time I should intentionally waste. Not only do I not buy this, I don't respect people who demean others by urging them to engage in this kind of nonservice. In my mind, the key is to do service that: (a) shares your unique gifts and talents; (b) helps people and organizations improve, and; (c) is meaningful for you and others. One of the wonderful things about being an academic is how ambiguous our jobs actually are, and this is especially true with respect to service. We have the space to create something from nothing when we see a need. Are you a good researcher? You can start a brown bag event and facilitate conversations among emerging and established researchers. You can start a writing workshop to help build a community of scholars around substantive inquiry. Do you have good philanthropic ideas? Start a foundation or mobilize an aid organization. Do you have good connections with publishers or journal editors? Build bridges by creating networks and opportunities of ideas and scholars. Do you see a need in your university or local community? Create something to address that need. Do you have an idea that would make a positive difference in a regional, national or international organization? If you don't see it, propose it! If a group has lost its "oomph," lead it! If you see something missing, build it! Make something new and positive, but whatever you do, avoid fake service activities. Fake service is one of the biggest soul-draining activities academics do—it suggests that our time isn't valuable and that service is a joke, not at the heart of what we do. I urge you to reject that dominant paradigm and bring your creativity, talent and perspectives to bear in your service activities the way you do in your teaching and scholarship. Also, service is fundamentally about lifting as you climb. I can't remember where I first heard this maxim, but I love it. As you focus on your own career, also be a positive influence on others. Your happiness, effectiveness, and influence on those around you will increase dramatically.

4. DO NOT MAKE TO-DO LISTS

The first 3 or 4 years after I earned my doctorate, I was a prolific writer of to-do lists. Every morning, I would drink my coffee and list several chores and errands that needed running, different things I needed to read, a dozen things I needed to write, and myriad other incidental things that came to mind. The result? I usually had a list with 15-20 items. On a good day, I would cross off 10 of them, on a bad day none or a few. Eventually, I came to realize that the items I didn't cross off remained in the back of my mind, taking up space and increasing my anxiety. It seems simple, but I made one change that both made me more productive, and allowed me to achieve much greater work-life balance—I stopped writing to-do lists. Now ... just like you I'm a busy guy. I still have many things to do, but instead of going into a list, when I have things to do they go directly into my calendar, where they are assigned a specific amount of time. Rather than a list I can't possibly finish, tasks are placed into my calendar, and when I get there they are completed, clean and simple. I try to schedule this in a way where I give myself more time than I think I will need, and from time to time this means that I actually get ahead in my work. Moreover, the great thing about moving to this system is that it means at the end of every day, I actually accomplish everything I set out to do. I don't have a half-complete list of tasks, I have a productive day on which I can reflect. Most days, this lessens rather than raises my anxiety and allows me to head home to my family each evening in a good frame of mind. I know that I've taken care of everything I needed to, and that the things I do have a place in my calendar; I'll attend to them in due time.

As you decide what you should do, make goals, then projects, then tasks. Dream big. Dream bigger than those of us who've come before you as scholars—it's the only way this thing is going to work. Every brilliant book you've read started as a vague idea. Every great article began as a general curiosity ... but then, writing them became someone—or some group's—goal. But, you don't "do" a goal. Every goal—every book, article, blog post, dissertation, etc. must be broken down into projects, and then those projects need to be broken into tasks. Tasks are something you can complete in a single sitting. For example, when I wrote my first book, *The Dark Side of School Reform*, I did the analysis and identified the themes that would become chapters. Once I had this table of contents, I started breaking down each chapters into an expanded outline. This meant that I basically broke each chapter down to the point where I planned every paragraph I would write. This allowed me to put "write two paragraphs about professional saturation" in my calendar—something I could really do, instead of "work on book" which is something you can never actually complete. Of course, as writing is a generative and creative process, sometimes I would end up with four paragraphs and sometimes one. The point is that I was able to finish what I started, every time, and that before I knew it the book was done. Goal achieved.

5. REEXAMINE YOUR ROUTINES

Don't confuse what you enjoy doing with what you need to do. If you are supposedly "writing" and at the end of the time you allotted for this purpose you have nothing to show for it, your routine is flawed. Staring at a laptop while thinking deep thoughts at the local coffee shop isn't writing, and although it's important to have time for reflection and relaxation let's not mistake nonproductive behavior for productive behavior. If your daily routine isn't productive, that means that eventually you will have nonproductive weeks, which will pile up into unproductive months and then eventually unproductive years. It's important that you consider the things you can and can't change about your routines and then experiment with them until you arrive at a routine that works for you, and only you. Are you a person who works best under deadline? Are you someone who needs to set aside a few mornings a week for writing? Do you do better work in the evening or the afternoon? Are you better after a coffee (or a beer)? Your routine is YOUR ROUTINE—look at it honestly and consider if it is getting you closer or further from where you aspire to be. You may need to sequester yourself from your friends or have them around you, you may need a mixture of these or even other concerns. Of course, you must also think about how your routines are structured in relation to your other responsibilities. I am half of a dual-career couple, and together we are raising three daughters and a son! My routine is no more important than theirs, and in many ways I feel strongly that theirs are more important than mine, but the bottom line is that we all have to compromise our flexibility a bit in order to be flexible enough to help and support each other.

6. CHOOSE FRIENDS AND COLLABORATORS WISELY

Enter into any writing or research project carefully and cautiously. I have watched a great many people innocently align themselves with unproductive and unethical folks. I have watched those same colleagues fail in their efforts to attain tenure, and I've seen even more of them spiral into dis-content as they give up their dream research agendas because they hitch their star to someone they believe is wiser and acting in their best inter-ests. I promise you that there are a great many wonderful people in higher education who do the right things for the right reasons. Many of the people like this I know are on the pages of this book ... but I also promise you that for every one of those there are five or six who would use you to advance their career or political capital without giving your best interests a second of consideration. I have been lucky enough to find a few colleagues whom I can trust completely. We built that trust over years of cautious collaboration, but now I know that they are as invested in my success as they are in their own—this is not something built overnight! Based on those relationships I've started to carefully branch out and establish new projects with new people, but I would urge you to not be impressed by a flashy presentation at a conference, a single heartfelt con-versation, or mutual research interests. You also need to know if your work habits and work ethic are compatible, you need to establish from day one who will be lad and second author on writing projects, what timeta-bles you will observe and how you might negotiate problems when they inevitably arrive.

Yet, while you have a *support* network, their existence is no guarantee—you must ultimately accept responsibility for your own success. Academe is one of those funny places, like most schools, where you may do some of your best work as a member of a group but you are often judged as suc-cessful or unsuccessful as an individual. Don't rely on anyone too much for your own success. Be in charge of it by designing and carrying out your own projects.

7. DON'T ABANDON THE THINGS YOU LOVE, BUT EXPECT THEM TO EVOLVE

I've met many people who pine for the life they had before they became an academic. "I used to love playing the bass guitar, but now all my time is consumed writing articles!" I love soccer, and while I don't have a lot of time to play at a highly competitive level I coach my daughters' teams. I recently discovered that I love cooking, and while I'm not at all accom-plished it's both relaxing, fun and improves the quality of my family's life. I'm pushing myself to learn new (to me) research methodologies, I read outside of education quite a lot, and I learn more from my wife, friends, and family than anywhere else. Don't forget the reasons you got into this in the first place, but let that passion evolve. Many people get into a doc-toral program in education because they love kids/teaching/learning/a particular subject area, etc. Don't lose sight of any of this! If you abandon this as at least part of your professional identity you are removing the passion from the work—share your passion and teach us new things—we NEED you.

8. YOU WILL GET CONSTRUCTIVE AND DESTRUCTIVE CRITICISM IN HIGHER EDUCATION, KEEP BOTH IN PERSPECTIVE

Don't get too high when someone tells you that you've done something amazing and don't get too low when someone blasts your work as irrelevant. One of the most-widely cited scholars in our field once wrote that the kind of research I do is not useful. I've also won awards and received high praise from colleagues—it's all food for thought but not anything that ultimately defines me. I didn't get into this for pats on the back or for kicks in the backside, but I've gotten (and probably given) both. Look, academics are not always the most socially gifted people, and some folks actually think it's their duty to be harsh. I guess that comes from some perverse "school of hard knocks" orientation, but you can't let any of it get you too high or low.

9. BE KIND TO YOURSELF AND EVERYONE ELSE

Above all, this is the most important point I can make and the one I will leave you with. I believe that education is fundamentally about caring, about the bonds we create and maintain with people, with ideas and with the discovery process. This demands work, it demands focus and it demands constant reflection on who we are and what we stand for—never lose sight of this.

CHAPTER 24

ACHIEVING WORK-LIFE BALANCE

Reflections of a Midlife Entrant to the Academy

Tricia Browne-Ferrigno

Becoming a professor emerged unexpectedly as my professional goal while I was enrolled in a required humanities course during my sophomore year at Florida State University (FSU). My instructor, Professor Anna Forbes Liddell, served as my inspiration. To a 19-year-old first-generation college coed, Professor Liddell embodied unimagined possibilities. Although she stood only 5 feet tall in her high-heeled shoes, she radiated power and authority, challenging us to question everything—to search for the truth. She required us to read extensively prior to class meetings and then provoked debate with her about the content of those readings. An adventurous world traveler, she enriched our class sessions with photographs and artifacts related to what we studied, bridging the past with the present through her artful teaching. She also revealed a softer persona by encouraging us to listen to our heart's response while she read us a poem she had written and then asking us to reflect upon its meaning.

Juggling Flaming Chain Saws: Academics in Educational Leadership Try to Balance Work and Family, pp. 199–206

I discovered many years later that Professor Liddell taught full time at Florida State College for Women and then FSU from 1926 to 1962 and that she was 74 years old when she taught my humanities course as an emeritus professor working part time. Based on the sources I read through a recent online search, she was remembered by her colleagues and students in the department of philosophy and religion as challenging, outspoken, and demanding. Through my online search, I also discovered that Professor Liddell not only wrote children's books and other fiction, but also advocated staunchly for both women's suffrage as a young woman and for passage of the Equal Rights Amendment as a senior citizen, even testifying for its passage before the Florida Legislature at the age of 90. I respect and admire her even more today than I did in my youth.

EARLY ADULTHOOD

As a young child, I often played at being a *teacher* with my dolls, stuffed animals, and occasionally complying friends and younger sisters as my students. I never imagined pretending to be a *professor* because the concept of higher education was unknown to me. My parents never attended college as traditional students or earned postsecondary degrees, but they made it possible for their three daughters to complete baccalaureate degrees as full-time resident students. As the oldest daughter, I was expected to find employment immediately following graduation to support myself; continuing my professional development through graduate studies was not an option. I complied with my parents' expectation and accepted a teaching position at the high school where I completed the required semester-long, full-time preservice internship. My becoming a professor thus became my soul's dream, lying dormant but not forgotten for 30 years.

During the ensuing 3 decades, I completed a discontinuous 15-year career as a teacher of college preparatory mathematics and earned a master of arts degree in special education/gifted. Due to cross-country relocations required for my husband's careers, I also worked in a variety of full-time positions outside the field of education—engineer aide for an international corporation designing nuclear reactors, corporate executive for a department store chain, national consultant for a textbook publisher, and legal assistant for a private partnership. For a short time following the birth of each of my two children, I also worked as a community volunteer. It was not until 1998, after settling into our new home in Colorado and gaining residency status that I was able to take active steps toward becoming a professor.

PREPARATION FOR THE PROFESSORIATE

Quite serendipitously, and fortunate for me, I chose the University of Colorado Denver (UCD) as the institution to complete my doctoral studies: The academic program and organizational culture aligned well with my needs as a midlife adult and with my learning preferences. The School of Education offered an interdisciplinary program leading to a doctor of philosophy in educational leadership and innovation with three options for focused study. The 70-credit-hour program required only six 3-credit-hour courses and 30 credits for dissertation preparation, thus providing students considerable freedom in program planning. Students were required to participate actively in at least one doctoral laboratory over several semesters in addition to two required research courses. The laboratories provided a structure for students to work closely with professors and peers in determining research foci, conducting literature searches, designing and conducting research studies, and disseminating findings.

As a full-time student, I had the opportunity to engage in two laboratories—one focused on adult learning, the other on P-12 education policy. Through the adult learning laboratory, I met a professor with whom I shared an interest in learner-centered and problem-based instruction. We have sustained our collaboration for over a decade, coauthoring numerous conference papers, journal articles, and book chapters. Through my engagement with the policy laboratory, I worked with individuals at the Educational Commission of the States and was hired as a research consultant to contribute to several projects. During both laboratory experiences, I was treated as a valued contributor, respected for the expertise that I possessed upon entering the program as well as for the emerging expertise I was gaining through doctoral studies.

My professional expertise was utilized in a variety of other ways at UCD. I was employed as a graduate assistant and instructor in preparation programs for aspiring teachers and school administrators, and I was invited to participate as the doctoral-student representative on school-wide faculty committees. I served as the coordinator of a multipartner teacher inquiry conference, member of a steering committee that designed and launched a graduate program for corporate trainers, advisor to action-research committees at two local elementary schools, and member of a high school accreditation review team. When faculty in the Division of Administrative Leadership and Policy Studies learned that I aspired to become a professor, they assured that I participated in diverse faculty activities intended as mentoring for a career in the academy. I graduated from UCD in May 2001 feeling confident, competent, and capable to be a professor.

EARLY YEARS IN THE ACADEMY

Upon arrival at the University of Kentucky in August 2001 as one of three newly hired assistant professors, I discovered a totally different environment from the one where I completed doctoral studies—and where I interviewed. Prior to hiring three assistant professors, the faculty in our department was composed of only tenured associate or full professors who had lived in Lexington for many years. The department had one graduate student hired solely to support publication of *Educational Administrative Quarterly*. The dean who hired us the previous spring had assumed the presidency of another university. Perhaps most startling was the practice of calling one's professional colleagues by formal titles (e.g., Professor Jones, Dr. Smith) whenever others were present.

As a midlife adult with 30 years work experience, I often assumed things that were not accurate. For example, while working as a corporate trainer for a department store chain, I developed the orientation portion of the 2-day training program for new hires. The orientation included a short history of the founding and expansion of the department store as well as an overview of the mission and vision of the organization, expectations for serving customers, and information about each of the 32 stores. While attending UCD, I assisted in the creation of an orientation notebook for new students. I thus anticipated a similar orientation as a new faculty member. However, our "orientation to the department" was basically an exhortation to seek external funding and publish extensively to assure that our promotion and tenure dossier, which would be prepared 5 years in the future, would be robust. When we were asked if we had any questions, I remarked that I anticipated our orientation would include such things as an overview of the department's instructional programs, a summary of departmental expectations concerning required meeting attendance, a roster of faculty members' office locations and phone numbers, and instructions for making copies and other such tasks. The response I received—that individuals holding doctorates could discover that information on their own—suggested to me that asking questions was something I should not do. Over the ensuing years, I unfortunately regularly forgot to remember not to ask questions and thus provoked the lasting ire of one professor.

Although I felt competent, confident, and capable to be a professor upon leaving UCD, I initially questioned my preparation and desire for a career in the academy. I fortunately learned that my two new peers responded similarly to our orientation. We scheduled an impromptu dinner the weekend following our first week as assistant professors. While enjoying our dessert, we vowed to support and mentor each other and to work collaboratively as often as possible to assure our success.

During our first year together, we designed, conducted, and disseminated research based on our experiences as educator mentors for first-year principals and discovered while presenting at a state conference that our work was unique. We collaboratively developed new syllabi for courses we taught; when two of us realized that we were teaching the same course on the same night, we merged the two sections into one class that we cotaught. A hallmark of our collaborative efforts that first year was our September 2002 award of a $500,000 three-year grant from the U.S. Department of Education School Leadership Program to deliver advanced leadership development for principals and administrator-certified teachers in a rural Appalachian district located 175 miles from the university. Every other week during the spring 2003 semester, we loaded suitcases and instructional materials into my car and spent 2-full days together, driving to the off-campus site where we delivered our collaboratively designed full-day seminar and then reflecting about the outcome and planning our next steps on the return trip.

Despite significant age differences and life experiences, the three of us became fierce friends and loving foes as we worked through stumbling blocks in our professional lives and addressed unanticipated events in our personal lives—death of family members, heartbreak and divorce, self discovery and new romances. We regularly ate lunch together and shared weekend and holiday meals together with our families and significant others. We provided a listening ear when one of us was angry, disappointed, or frustrated and gave critical feedback if asked—and sometimes when not asked. Our threesome provided us a safe haven to challenge each other's perspectives and ask tough questions to find meaningful resolutions to what puzzled us. When my two colleagues left the University of Kentucky in June 2003 for personal reasons, I lost kindred souls who helped me maintain a meaningful work-life balance during my first 2 years as an assistant professor.

BALANCE LOST AND RESTORED

Since our leadership development project was funded through September 2005, I continued traveling to eastern Kentucky. The grant did not have sufficient funds to pay a senior faculty member's salary; therefore, I hired administrative practitioners to assist with the training seminars. I often made the biweekly trips to the rural Appalachian district alone, without benefit of collaborative interaction and shared reflection with colleagues. And because I was often away from the campus, I had limited opportunities to connect with other faculty. Rather than taking time to relax and rest during lunch with colleagues as I previously done, I regularly ate lunch alone in my office, often seated in front of my computer. I began to live for work, not work for a living.

During a phone conversation with a professor at another university the following year, I mentioned how envious I was that she worked in a setting that was collaborative. She laughed and responded that she absolutely did not—that her department was truly dysfunctional. She explained that she intentionally developed relationships with professors at universities and colleges across the United States, hoping to make connections that would provide meaningful, supportive relationships. I determined that I had to do the same: Over time my professional life became enriched with long-distance collaborative connections with other professors. Attendance at annual professional conferences (e.g., American Educational Research Association, National Council of Professors of Educational Administration, University Council for Educational Administration) provides opportunities for face-to-face interactions with other professors. Although nothing has replaced the personal enjoyment of my first 2 years in the academy, I have linked with like-minded colleagues with whom I share similar interests and developed long-distance collaborations and friendships that I treasure.

During the 2007 University Council for Educational Administration annual meeting, a fellow member of a taskforce with which I have long been associated pulled me aside during a break. Although a dean who has been active in our field for decades, she is also a wise woman and observant friend. She whispered in my ear, "Now that you are a tenured associate professor, you no longer need to work as hard as you have these past 5 years. Take time for yourself and create balance in your life." Unfortunately, I could not act upon her advice immediately.

Upon my promotion to tenured associate professor in July 2007, I was appointed to a 4-year term as the director of graduate studies responsible for recruiting, admitting, advising, and scheduling oral examinations for students in our department. Although the position carries a course release for fall and spring semesters, my administrative duties spanned a calendar year because our department has a robust summer schedule. I was able utilize the course release only twice during those 4 years because our department had unfilled faculty openings that required my teaching a regular two-course per semester load—and sometimes additional courses. Since my duties as director of graduate studies ended in June 2011, I anticipate having more free time.

ACHIEVING WORK-LIFE BALANCE

Although neither of my sisters earned a graduate degree nor understand fully my career in higher education, they nonetheless are important contributors to my achieving work-life balance. The spring following my promotion to tenured associate professor, we reinstituted our lapsed tradition of an annual sisters' getaway. We collectively select a location for our vacation and make plans for must-do activities, while allowing time for serendipitous adventures. At my sisters' insistence, during my week with them I do not check electronic mail or phone messages and read only for pleasure, thus enjoying an uninterrupted period away from work. I recently decided that I do not need to check e-mail messages throughout the weekend, only on Sunday evenings to prepare for the upcoming week. The break has made my weekends more enjoyable and relaxing.

Like my inspiring FSU professor years ago, I plan to work full time well beyond what has traditionally been retirement age. I realized recently, however, that I needed to develop a hobby now that I can enjoy after I retire. I wanted an activity that would not only feed my too-long-dormant creative spirit but also support work-life balance. During the past 12 months, I participated in four oil painting workshops and am registered for two more scheduled during the coming year. The artist who facilitates the workshops reminds participants that the purpose of painting is purely for our enjoyment. She asserts that like handwriting, our art is distinctly ours—not to be judged by others. After years of conforming my academic writing to critiques by peer reviewers and editors, I now have an outlet that does not have to conform to others' expectations. How refreshing to write, "I am an artist, and my work only matters to me."

The final stage in my achieving work-life balance is completion of a decade-long home remodeling project. I recently admitted to my husband that I often stayed late at campus to postpone returning to a house that has been continuously in some phase of construction. We agreed to devote time this coming year to work together toward completing our house renovation within the year.

ADVICE BASED ON LESSONS LEARNED IN THE ACADEMY

I entered the academy as a midlife adult whose husband fully supported my career change and whose two grown children were living independent lives in other states. I understood professorial responsibilities through the mentoring I received while engaged in full-time doctoral studies. As a new assistant professor, I utilized professional expertise gained through working in diverse careers and understood that P-20 education is not the same across the United States. My first advice for aspiring and assistant professors is to assess the knowledge and skills that you possess and then to use that expertise in your professional work as a professor.

Throughout all my previous careers, I regularly used data to inform my practice and thus intentionally selected a research extensive university as my work site. I also understood, as did my husband, that seeking external funding regularly and publishing regularly would be required. We both knew I would have to work long hours, including weekends and holidays, in order to have required credentials for promotion to associate professor. My second advice is to understand clearly the work expectations at the institution where you are seeking employment or are currently employed: The *fit* between employer and employee is critically important. And although professorial work must often be completed independently and privately, it can be enriched considerably through working with others. Thus, I also advise building an extensive network of collaborative relationships with other professors and with P-12 practitioners.

For those who need a sanctuary away from work in which to relax and rejuvenate, I advise strongly against beginning a new career in the academy while simultaneously launching a major home renovation—the combination can be exhausting.

CHAPTER 25

SEEKING MORE THAN BALANCE

An American Indian Female Scholar's Attempt to Navigate the Perceived Work-Life Divide

Susan C. Faircloth

Perhaps we need to find ways of taking our life to work, instead of just taking our work home with us. Perhaps if work/life were not represented as slashed, as balancing or colliding, there could be room for other conversations and policies

—Bartlett (2006, p. 23).

INTRODUCTION

In this chapter, I explore the ways in which my time within the academy has been shaped in large part by four critical life events. Each of these events has empowered me to find, and at times create, my place in the academy in a way that is authentic, meaningful and productive. Each of these events is described in brief below.

Juggling Flaming Chain Saws: Academics in Educational Leadership
Try to Balance Work and Family, pp. 207–214
Copyright © 2012 by Information Age Publishing
All rights of reproduction in any form reserved.

FOUR LIFE EVENTS THAT HAVE SHAPED MY CAREER PATH

Event 1: Coming to Terms With the Responsibility of Earning a Doctoral Degree

In December 2000, I earned a doctoral degree in educational administration. I was the first in my family to do so. My mother is a high school graduate who worked for 37 years at one of the largest pork processing plants in the nation, while my father earned an associates degree and worked in law enforcement. Growing up in an American Indian community in the rural south, I always knew that what the educational system expected of me and many of my peers was that we would graduate from high school, get a job and live lives very similar to those of our parents, with few of us venturing outside the community for extended periods of time. However, I also knew that my parents had different dreams and expectations for me. For them, there was never a question of whether or not I would go to college; the question was where I would go. I chose a small college in the mountains of North Carolina where I studied Latin American history, political science, and anthropology; not the most employable fields but ones that I was deeply interested in. Armed with a bachelor's degree, I returned home only to find that there were few jobs for which I was qualified. After much searching, I found myself working in an American Indian education program in a large urban school district, followed by a 2-year appointment with a student support services program at a local community college where I began working with students with disabilities. Little did I know that these jobs were setting the stage for my master's and doctoral studies.

The day I was hooded and received my doctoral degree was one of the most bittersweet days of my life. All I wanted to do was cry, but I couldn't explain why. I eventually came to realize that my tears were an outward symbol of my inner fear that I would not be able to live up to the expectations of previous generations of scholars who had worked to establish the American Indian Leadership Program at Penn State. With this degree came the knowledge that I was expected to make significant contributions to the lives and education of Indian peoples and communities. As one might imagine, this level of responsibility had the potential to be both empowering and overpowering. I had the desire to make a difference, but lacked the initial confidence to believe that I actually could make a difference.

Over the years, I've come to terms with the fact that a large part of giving back and making a difference involves engaging in service-related activities. This means sometimes making a conscious decision to engage in service when the academy tells me to write or taking time to talk with parents and families about their rights in the special education process when the academy tells me I should be using this time to collect data. In the end, I attempt to do it all. I engage in service, I collect data, and I write. I meet the expectations of the academy, but foremost, I strive to do so in ways that are honoring to Indigenous peoples and communities.

Event 2: Working in the Best Interests[1] of Our Beautiful Little Ones

The second critical event was the birth of my niece, Kanani, which means "beautiful little one" in Hawaiian. In an earlier publication (Faircloth, 2009), I wrote about Kanani and her ability to navigate the cultural divide between my family's home community in rural North Carolina and her home community in an urban area outside Honolulu. What Kanani has taught me is that the work I do is not just for this beautiful little one, but for all of our beautiful little ones. What is so striking about her birth is the constant reminder to me that our children benefit or suffer as a consequence of the work that we do and its impact on the educational system. I often use pictures of Kanani in presentations to demonstrate the ways in which our family works to ensure that she is able to blend her cultures (Hawaiian and American Indian) with western conceptions of education and academic press (e.g., pictures of her dressed in her regalia while holding and reading a book). Seeing these pictures of her reminds me that I need to spend time listening to and learning from the little ones, as well as to my elders, for they have so much knowledge and wisdom to share that is not written down in text books or academic/scholarly journals. Stopping to listen is an enormous challenge for an academic who is always on the go and never seems to have enough time to complete the endless to-do lists. Yet, I'm learning that listening is as important as reading or researching. One way I do this is by spending Tuesday evenings typing a column, titled "Under the Shade Tree," that my mother writes for her local newspaper. The column chronicles her work with a senior citizen center and includes old-fashioned remedies, recipes and folk tales. After a late night of teaching, one of the last things I want to do when I get home is to type this column, but I remind myself each week that there are lessons to be learned from this task. So, I sit, type, and listen.

Event 3: Making Family a Priority

The third event that helped to shape my career path was the diagnosis of my father with a chronic neurological disorder. This occurred during

2007, in the midst of my tenure as a Ford Foundation Postdoctoral Scholar at the University of California at Los Angeles. Driving out to California, I viewed this as Susan's great adventure—a time to focus on my work and myself and engage in total academic self-centeredness. This was the year that I would research, read, write and refresh, something I had not been able to do in my dual roles as a faculty member and codirector of a personnel preparation program for aspiring school leaders. Unfortunately, that was not meant to be. By late November, my dad was experiencing a loss of sensation from the soles of his feet to his shoulders. He had no reflex in his legs or arms. He was scared and so was I. This was something new for our family. My dad is a big, strong ex-Marine, always in charge, never one to back down from a challenge, and here he was calling me and asking me to talk to his doctors. He said to me, "You know the right words to say and questions to ask. I don't." So, as one might imagine, I was soon on a plane bound for North Carolina. For 3 weeks, I sat with my parents as I watched their lives change forever. This once strong man couldn't feed, bathe, or change himself. All of the academic stuff that I had planned to do seemed so unimportant compared to the loss of my dad's mobility and independence. So, I stayed until he was settled and then I returned to California, with the fear in the back of my mind that his condition would worsen, that his breathing would be impaired and that I might lose my dad. Four years later, he's walking, driving, working, and gardening. His disease has not gone away, but it's manageable. The work that I left behind in California was completed; new projects have been started, and the world did not end because I stopped doing my work for a few weeks. As my parents get older, I move forward with the knowledge that situations like this may occur again and that my work may have to be placed on hold again. In the end, I'm OK with that because I know that while my parents may not always be here, my work will always be here in some form or fashion.

Event 4: Becoming a Mother Posttenure

The fourth critical event involves the birth of my daughter on January 16, 2010. For more than a year, my husband and I had been trying unsuccessfully to adopt. The week our daughter was born began with three failed matches and a sinking feeling that perhaps I was not meant to be a mother. After hearing that the third match had failed, I began to clean house like a mad woman, finally settling down to sleep well into the night on the 15th. Little did I know I had begun the process of nesting. The next morning, my husband and I were awakened by the sound of my cell phone. It was our lawyer calling with the news that a baby was being born as we spoke. We did not know the baby's gender or if he or she was healthy. All we knew was that we had been chosen and we would need to fly across the country later that evening to meet our child. Both of us were stunned. How do you prepare to be a parent with just a few hours notice? After an hour or so of denial and disbelief, we finally decided that we should make airline reservations and pack. By 4 P.M. that same day, we were in the air. Two diverted flights and a day later, we met our daughter, a beautiful baby girl, who we named Journey. At that moment, our lives were changed forever.

All of this happened during the second week of the spring semester. What we expected to be 1 week waiting for clearance to return to Pennsylvania turned into 3½ weeks filled with freezing rain, freezing fog, thunder snow, postponed court dates and more, before we finally returned home in February with our daughter. As I sat in a hotel room in Oklahoma City, I struggled to balance the demands of motherhood, with a looming deadline to complete a book chapter on working with urban American Indian parents and families (Faircloth, 2011), and to make arrangements to teach a graduate seminar on inclusive education at Penn State. In the midst of all of this change, I found myself typing with my daughter snuggled safely in my arms, reaching out to colleagues and friends to cover my class, and hoping that my students would be patient with me during my absence. In the end, the book chapter was slightly late, but it was finished, and, my class went on as planned.

LEARNING FROM OTHERS

Last year, I had the opportunity to attend a conversation session at the annual meeting of the University Council for Educational Administration. This session was focused on work-life balance issues. As a new mother and an associate professor of educational leadership at a research I institution, I found this session quite timely. What I learned most from this session is that I am not alone in my attempts to balance the demands of parenthood, research, teaching and service. In fact, I am among good company —a vibrant and productive group of male and female scholars striving to create and preserve spaces for their life work. Two years ago, I would not have found myself attending this session. I was a newly tenured faculty member, married, but childless, overworked, but not overly conflicted in terms of how to manage or allocate my time. A typical day for me was working from midmorning well into the night, sleeping 4 to 5 hours, and starting over again the next day, with occasional breaks to spend time with family and friends. I was happy, but not content. I had a longing to nurture and mother, but I hid this desire from many of my colleagues because I thought it said something negative about my commitment to my academic and scholarly work.[2] I struggled silently. I cried. I prayed and then, I waited.

GUIDING PRINCIPLES

As these stories demonstrate, family has played a central role in my personal and professional lives. Fortunately, I have been blessed with a job that allows me the flexibility to work wherever I may be rather than being place bound. This means that my work can and does travel with me wherever I go. The challenge is being careful not to be overwhelmed by the intensity of or passion for this work. Reading this, one might ask, how I have been able to create or maintain balance in my personal and professional lives and what lessons have I learned from this process?

As outlined below, there are a number of principles and beliefs that have helped to shape who I am and how I work. Although I'm not sure that a true work-life balance can actually ever be achieved, I do feel that these principles and beliefs help me to make sense of an often chaotic lifestyle.

1.   The assurance that my work will always be there. That's one of the benefits and challenges of being an academic.
2.   Belief in the importance of quality versus quantity of time spent with family and friends. This is a belief, reinforced by husband's gentle reminders that spending time with my daughter means more than sitting on the floor with her with my laptop in hand.
3.   A strong desire to be known as more than just a good scholar. Foremost, I want to be known as a good person, mother, wife, sister, daughter, aunt and friend. I firmly believe that If I am successful in my attempts to achieve goodness as a person, I will be successful in my attempts to be a good scholar.
4.   The overarching desire for my life to have made a difference. I struggle with this quite often. When I'm in doubt, my husband reminds me that the biggest difference I can make is in the life of my beautiful little one. To have failed her in my attempt to be a good scholar, is to have failed at the most important job of all.

SOURCES OF STRENGTH

I would be remiss if I did not acknowledge that I am not always successful in my attempts to balance work and life issues. It's an ongoing process.

I'm coming to terms with the fact that I may not be the academic super-star that I once aspired to be, and that's okay. Instead, I now aspire to be what my husband describes as a session player. In the world of music, a session player is one who has longevity in the field, and who, in essence, has the ability to make a steady, lasting impact on the field. So that's my goal. In doing so, I find strength and encouragement from a number of sources as outlined below:

1. I have always been motivated by an urgency to do something meaningful. My goal is to give back to all of those who have gone before me and made it possible for me to achieve my goals and do I what I do. I owe it to my academic, intellectual, and cultural/spiritual elders to do good work. If I don't, they owe it to me to hold me accountable and to demand that I do better work.

2. I am strengthened and comforted by a strong sense of spirituality and belief in a higher power. Even though I have my moments of doubt and questioning, I believe that the Creator, however one chooses to define this term, is with and in each of us, and the work that we do.

3. In my home community visitors are often asked, "Who are your people?" In the academy, my people are those who are committed to improving the education of disenfranchised children and youth, particularly those with disabilities, and those from American Indian and Alaska Native communities. On those days when I'm struggling to connect with that community of scholars, my immediate and extended family remind me of who I am, where I come from, and why I'm doing what I do. They are my grounding force.

4. Engaging in the art of laughter. One of the things that first attracted me to my husband was hearing him say that I was funnier than he ever imagined the professor type could be. What he didn't realize was that he is one of the few people who truly gets to see the relaxed, joking, big kid that I really am. Most importantly, he allows me to be myself. When I'm tired and stressed, he reminds me that I still have a lifetime of work ahead of me. This gives me the freedom to take a moment to relax, refresh, and play.

5. In addition to my family, I've benefitted from the support and encouragement of my mentor, friend, and colleague, Dr. John Tippeconnic. As a doctoral student, he saw something in me that I did not see in myself—a scholar. More importantly, he modeled for me the importance of putting family first. To him, I will always be indebted.

6. Finally, I am motivated and energized by a love for and commitment to the work that I do. In the end, I'm not certain that we ever create a real work-life balance. What I do believe is that if we truly are in love with our work and our work is done in the best interests of the communities for whom and with whom we work, the struggle to attain balance will be eased.

CONCLUDING REMARKS

Each day, I am reminded that the life of an academic is challenging; marked by fleeting periods of sleep and rest, never-ending deadlines and demands for my time and energy, and the elusive search for balance. In spite of these challenges, the academic life is a great life, and I wouldn't have it any other way.

NOTES

1. For an in-depth discussion of the term "best interests," see Stefkovich (2006).
2. For additional discussion of this topic, see for example, Aisenberg and Harrington (1998).

REFERENCES

Aisenberg, N., & Harrington, M. (1998). *Women of academe: Outsiders in the sacred grove.* Amherst, MA: University of Massachusetts Press.

Bartlett, A. (2006). Theory, desire, and maternity: At work in academia. *Hecate, 32*(2), 21-33. Retrieved from Proquest Research Library.

Faircloth, S. C. (2009). Re-visioning the future of education for Native youth in rural schools and communities. *Journal of Research in Rural Education, 24*(9). Retrieved from http://jrre.psu.edu/articles/24-9.pdf

Faircloth S. C. (2011). American Indian and Alaska Native students with disabilities: Implications for practice and research. In M.C. Sarche, P. Spicer, P. Farrell, & H. E. Fitzgerald (Eds.), *American Indian and Alaska Native children and mental health: Development, context, prevention, and treatment* (pp. 63-88). Santa Barbara, CA: Praeger.

Stefkovich, J. A. (2006). *Best interests of the student: Applying ethical constructs to legal cases.* Mahwah, NJ: Erlbaum.

CHAPTER 26

MOMMY GUILT AND CHICKEN COOPS

Work/Life Imbalance on the Tenure Track

Bonnie C. Fusarelli

"I've got the greatest job in the world. I won't ever retire ... I'll work until I drop." This was the response my husband of 6 months gave to our new financial planner when he asked, "At what age do you plan to retire?" Stunned by his response, we peppered him with questions. The planner was focused on "what if's." "What if you are no longer able to work? What if you change your mind?" Mine were more pointed and infused with a bit of panic: "Have you lost your mind? How can you think this is the greatest job in the world? Do you realize that I plan to be kicking back on some beach as soon as I am eligible to retire?"

I could not comprehend how it was possible for two people in the same line of work to have such different views of the job. As I reflect back over the last 8 years as an academic couple, the answer becomes clear: Our experiences continue to be very different.

The differences between how men and women experience life in the academy play out in real time in our home. Fortunately, I have a husband who is a tad bit of a feminist and can see the gender inequity. On a number of occasions he's said, "Read this," as he has handed me articles/

Juggling Flaming Chain Saws: Academics in Educational Leadership Try to Balance Work and Family, pp. 215–221 advice on gender inequity from Ms. Manners' column in the *Chronicle of Higher Education*. He knows that no matter how much he strives to be an equal partner, he didn't have the morning sickness, he didn't have to leave meetings early to go pump breast milk and he fully recognizes that when our kids are sick they want their mommy. In his typical self-deprecating manner, he will even jokingly admit to having taking full advantage of this when the kids had stomach bugs!

While being married to another academic is a blessing in many ways, it also creates a unique set of challenges. The most stressful of which was the incredible pressure I secretly placed on myself to earn tenure out of the fear that two academic careers would be negatively affected if I failed.

TRAILING SPOUSE?

My future husband, Lance, and I met at an academic conference. We were both assistant professors at research intensive universities; I was in my first year, he was in his fourth. Lance was on a discussion panel with my former dissertation advisor, Dr. Bill Boyd, who introduced us after the session. We hit it off right away, a long-distance romance ensued and we were married a little over a year and a half later.

Once we were engaged, we went on the job market; purposefully targeting institutions with two openings in a naïve attempt on my part to avoid the stigma of the "trailing spouse." We were both offered jobs at the same university, in the same department. Lance accepted an associate professor position and I accepted an assistant professor position. Many people assumed that I was a "spousal accommodation" hire. We were often referred to as "Dr. Fusarelli and his wife Bonnie." Although eventually I became known as "the other Dr. Fusarelli," it has been a long journey to get to this point.

Within the first 12 months of our marriage, we could tick just about every item on the list of life's most stressful events: we got married, sold a house, moved, started new jobs, a close family member died, bought a house, got pregnant, had a baby, had major medical problems, my dog died, and my mother had a serious health crisis, all while my tenure clock was ticking.

HONEYMOON BABY

We were surprised when we discovered that within a month of being married, I was pregnant. I was both thrilled and terrified. The joy of becoming a mom was clouded by my fear that having a baby would destroy my chances for tenure. I had just started a new job. I found out through the grapevine that no one could recall anyone ever taking maternity leave. I was not sure how my department head and dean would react to the news.

Fortunately, they seemed genuinely happy for me, especially after I told them that since the baby was due in late May, I wasn't going to take maternity leave. The decision to not take maternity leave was one of my biggest professional and personal mistakes.

It turned out that getting pregnant was a whole lot easier than my staying pregnant. I had a very high risk pregnancy that required frequent visits to maternal-fetal medicine specialists at a hospital that was over an hour away. I struggled to keep up with my work, but thought I was doing fine. In retrospect, I was a complete wreck. The night before the doctors planned to induce my labor, I worked feverishly to finish the references and do a final edit on a manuscript so it could go out for review. Around 3:00 am my husband realized I was still awake and gently but firmly demanded that I get some sleep. We left 2 hours later for the hospital, we didn't return home for over 10 days.

The experience at the hospital can be summed up best by what the chief of maternal fetal medicine said to me: "No one could have predicted that things would go the way they did—but when things go so terribly wrong, there is nowhere better you could have been than right here." Things went very wrong, but thanks to some incredible doctors, our son was born healthy. It took a whole different team of specialists however, to address the multiple complications I experienced, some of which I continue to contend with.

After about 10 days in the hospital, there was a flurry of activity trying to make arrangements so I could go home (Our baby had been released 8 days earlier, but was allowed to stay with me in my hospital room). A hospital bed and other equipment were delivered to our house and home nursing care for me was arranged. Our home coming was bittersweet. Our beloved dog of 13 years died a few hours before we made it home. The joy we felt as new parents was overshadowed by the sorrow of losing our beloved pet and the uncertainty about my prognosis.

Six weeks later, I was strong enough to walk from my bedroom to the living room without help. As the start of the fall semester drew near, I couldn't imagine how I would ever be able to go back to work. About a week before classes were to start I received a phone call from my department head. He said he had heard from the dean that I was in really bad shape and that she told him to call and offer me a course release. I was delighted, relieved, and then he said "I never would have done this because I wouldn't want to offend you by not treating you like everyone else in the department. I thought you might be offended, but the dean told me to call you." I assured him I was not offended and readily accepted the course release. "Great." He said. "Now you can concentrate on your writing. You can use the time to get *additional* publications."

When I hung up the phone I couldn't help but think about how my colleagues would have acted or what accommodations would have been made if a male colleague was bedridden from a major medical trauma? Was it really special treatment simply because my injury was related to my pregnancy? Did he really expect me to write additional manuscripts when I was on prescription pain medication and trying to care for a newborn?

The short answer was clearly, yes. The tenure clock did not stop. The demands of my master and doctoral students did not suddenly go away. The timelines for grants did not get extended. The only thing that slowed down was me, and I was going to be held to the same expectations for tenure.

I didn't take maternity leave because I thought that I would be perceived as not committed enough, as not a team player, as not carrying my load. One of the many lessons this experience taught me was that taking maternity leave or not, people have preconceived beliefs about working mothers that impact how they relate to you, both positively and negatively. Either way, the work doesn't stop. You can't turn off from the academy for any extended amount of time. You still need to read and stay current with the research literature. Your doctoral students still want to graduate. You must have publications in the pipeline or you will have gaps in your curriculum vitae. I didn't fully appreciate this until I experienced it. I never thought I would feel so much pressure to write that I would nurse my baby while typing a manuscript. Looking back, I missed many magical moments because I did not live in the moment. I was too focused on the "next" (tenure), that I failed to enjoy the journey.

I now actively advise colleagues on how to better negotiate leave (maternity or paternity). Since the work doesn't stop, I suggest they take intermittent Family and Medical Leave Act (FMLA), and treat the time as a whole as a buy-out (like for a grant) to get course releases or released from other duties. The fact that every department in our college does leave differently creates both challenges and opportunities. The challenge is that some individuals are better able to negotiate for themselves resulting in vast differences in leave arrangements. The opportunity comes from the flexibility that allows for innovative solutions to surface. As we make progress in this area, we will need to formally establish faculty-friendly policies that will take root, grow, and become normative.

CHICKEN COOP

A few years into motherhood I thought I had the balance thing down. There were no longer tears (from me) at day-care drop-off and I was having a productive year with my publications. I was working long hours putting together a grant proposal and my tenure dossier. Then, "it" happened. On an early spring day, I took my 3½ year-old son to the local feed store to buy dog food. It was a week before Easter and they had day-old chicks for sale. My son was mesmerized by the chicks and asked, "Mommy, can we please get some chicks." I said, "No." He kept pressing the issue and asked over and over if he could have some chicks. Exasperated, I finally blurted "Drew, what on earth would you do with chickens?" He quickly replied, "Mommy, they can be my friends when you are working so much." My heart sank. He wasn't being manipulative. He was being honest. With tears in my eyes, I asked, "Baby, how many chicks do you want?" With great excitement he replied: "Four. One for each member of our family." I bought the chicks. My mommy guilt was somewhat alleviated, but in truth, I was working long hours. When I was at home, I was often on the computer and checking e-mail. I fooled myself into thinking that by being at home while doing my work, I was there for my kids. I was physically there with them, but not fully present.

It turns out that getting chickens, though in violation of our neighborhood ordinances, was a great decision for our family. They are delightful to watch chasing bugs through the yard and bring us much joy. We give our neighbors fresh eggs and so far, they haven't ratted us out to the homeowners association. Our boys collect the eggs after school and race into the house with that day's production. As I place the eggs in the refrigerator, I have a daily reminder of the need to be fully present in my boys' lives.

Recently, after a day of fishing on a local pond, my boys (now 7 and 4 years old) and I were joking back and forth on the drive home about who caught the biggest fish and how cool it would be to feed the chickens the extra worms! Then "it" happened again. After a long belly laugh, Drew said, "Mom, you're my best friend!" His younger brother piped in that I was his best friend too. I smiled so much the rest of that day that my cheeks hurt. Three years later, I think I am finally getting closer to my ideal work/life balance.

LESSONS LEARNED AND LOOKING AHEAD

When I put together my dossier for tenure, it was surprisingly a very emotionally painful experience. I was unprepared for the introspection that the process evokes. While intended to be a documentation of my professional work, it was in fact a representation of my life choices. Should I have spent the time writing the article that I finished at 3:00 A.M. the night before I gave birth, only to have to have to revise and resubmit it months later? Should I have missed the kindergarten field trip to attend a grant proposal planning meeting for a grant proposal that ended up not being funded? Did I make the right choices? Was it worth it?

I am now at a point that I can say, "Yes, it was worth it." Tenure provided a new degree of intellectual freedom. I landed the largest grant in our department's history and that has enabled me the freedom to pursue the work I find the most personally rewarding; preparing aspiring school leaders. I feel like I am, making a difference in small but significant ways.

As the only woman in my program and for a long time, the only woman in my department, I give advice to similarly situated colleagues on how to avoid some of the negative experiences I had to navigate. Now, more attuned to the struggles of new mothers, most semesters I leave my office at certain times to allow it to become a "lactation room" for nursing grad students who need a private space.

While everyone may not hit all the top stressors in a single year, every individual will face their own challenges; challenges that are very real and intense to them at that moment. Navigating life in the academy is not easy. You can find myriad of books written on the topic. Some are full of brutal stories of inequity. While many of us have experienced some of the less glamorous side of the academy, I chose not to discuss or expand on it in this chapter because the truth is; I know I had it better than the women who came before me. They were the original pioneers to whom I am tremendously thankful. They made it possible for me to engage in rewarding work and stretch myself to become the type of public servant I hope my children will respect.

Therefore, the hopeful news is we are making great progress. Things are getting better. I recently found out that the newly renovated student union building will have lactation rooms. Male colleagues are taking paternity leave. My university's strategic planning task force included a subcommittee on campus culture and work/life balance on which I was honored to serve. Baby steps perhaps, but they add up to real progress.

In the end, the simple truth is that while I felt undervalued and overwhelmed at times, I know that it is a privilege to be an academic. That privilege comes with responsibilities. Responsibilities to maintain high standards for myself and others and to pay it forward and help the next generation. If I am ever blessed with grandchildren, I hope my sons' wives will not have the "mommy guilt" that I experienced. I hope they will have increased opportunities to pursue work they find as rewarding and personally enriching as I find my work. In whatever profession they may pursue, I hope they will live more balanced lives because of the progress we are making in the academy.

Now, almost 8 years later, I must admit, that although our paths remain very different and we experience different challenges, my husband was correct. Academics really do have the "greatest job in the world." While I still plan to retire and sit on the beach, I now embrace the journey—and enjoy fresh eggs every morning!

Postscript: My Catholic roots have compelled me to make a small confession here. I am still very much "a work in progress!" In a feverish attempt to meet the submission deadline for this chapter, I was late to my own son's birthday party! His party was held on the last day of school at Monkey Joe's (an indoor funhouse full of inflatables). I showed up with my store bought cupcakes about 10 minutes after the party's start time. My husband had arrived early and had everything under control. I apologized profusely to him, my son, and the other moms who were nearby. Lance just gave me a knowing wink and said, "It's alright, just remember to make us all omelets in the morning!"

CHAPTER 27

FINDING COURAGE AND CHOICE ON THE JOURNEY TO A BALANCED LIFE

Mark A. Gooden

My name is Mark Anthony Gooden and I have been married since 1998 to Angela Gooden. We have a daughter together and her name is Nia Ayanna, which is roughly translated from Kiswahili as "beautiful flower with a purpose." She is 4 years old and I am sure one of her many yet to be revealed purposes on this earth has been to teach me new lessons about life, including giving me a compelling reason to strive for balance between life and work.

I am an associate professor at The University of Texas at Austin (UT), a top-tier Research I institution. I was promoted to associate professor in 2007 at University of Cincinnati (UC) and recently changed jobs and started at UT in January 2009. Transitioning into my new role as associate professor and program director has made the search for balance even more elusive. In fact, I have found that despite my fantasy that my job would become automatically more manageable after I earned tenure, it appears to have gotten busier, but without the pressure to get tenure. Lately, I have reflected on why this is the case. That is, why has my life not taken a more manageable, though still busy, form? There is a complex answer to this rather simplistic question. However, the major reason is that I continue to

Juggling Flaming Chain Saws: Academics in Educational Leadership Try to Balance Work and Family, pp. 223–229

take on too many projects even though many are good ones. Of course there are other factors but the one that is most compelling is to work to improve the state of education for children who have been marginalized because of race, class, culture, gender, language, ability, sexual orientation, or religion. That work continues to conflict with the many aspects of my personal life, as I continue to achieve better balance and fulfill my need and obligation to serve. However, it is a privilege to have this job.

PRIVILEGE

Many mornings I get to take Nia to her daycare. Before I drop her off, I get to take my time focusing on her on the drive to school where we listen to all kinds of music, NPR, and/or talk. I even get to prepare breakfast for her and sit down and speak to her in the mornings before we leave. This also helps my wife, who really is much better than I am at getting our routine started in the morning. I feel really blessed to be able to do these things, especially when I notice some of my fellow daycare parents who are frantically moving quickly to do their drop-offs to avoid being late to work. It is nice not being so restricted by a clock and I also realize that this is a wonderful privilege for me as I have time to speak to the teacher if necessary. I can also schedule times to visit Nia's class and read a story or just check to see how she is doing. During the afternoons it is also a privilege to pick Nia up from daycare and carve our time to eat dinner with the family three or four times during the week. I am also thankful for things like being flexibility to work at home I don't take any of these privileges for granted. However, to carry out these activities without guilt, I had to develop the courage and make the choice to enjoy these privileges even before I earned tenure. I had to make the choice that whether I made it or not as an assistant professor, I needed to hold on to something that was going to be a consistent part of my identity as I worked to succeed in the academy. That consistency is my family. Of course, even now, there are always things to do and demands on my time. I could easily fill this special time with my family by sending off more e-mails, editing more articles, or finishing at least another review. However, I would be unhappy and unfulfilled in the end, and alienated from my family. That does not mean I am not regularly asked to show up at one meeting or another during these small family moments. The simplest way to keep these familial obligations is to choose to schedule this time and just be courageous enough to stick to it.

OPPRESSION

Though being a professor affords me many privileges, it also requires that as a conscious[1] Black[2] man I remain aware of the fact that there is a paucity of African American scholars in the field of educational administration. That means in addition to my typical research, teaching, and service obligations, I have additional personal responsibilities to scholars who are of African descent and have committed to work in the academy. I realize this is largely a personal interpretation but I know that there were many who helped me along the way and I believe it is incumbent upon me to do the same by offering time, advice, or just listening to scholars of color as they struggle to survive in the academy. I have known several Black scholars who have taken up this same burden without complaint, or have avoided it, sometimes with a fair amount of guilt. That means two things for me. First, when I travel to conferences, I already know that a part of my responsibility not documented in my dossier involves scheduling face time with junior professors of color. These meetings do not show up on the tenure/promotion review ticker or my curriculum vitae but they are necessary and sometimes therapeutic for the scholars and for me. These gatherings allow me time to listen and be present to listen to familiar concerns that the academy is not designed for people like us. These scholars share a belief that they have to simultaneously work to survive within the academy and to change it. Second, in between conferences, I continue these conversations with these scholars over the phone and via e-mail. Mentoring and support are often needed between conferences. I do what I can to encourage others and continue to encourage myself that there is good work to be done in the academy by scholars of color. There is resistance but there is a place for the work we are doing that will enhance the lives of black children in particular.

When considering the academy as a system that privileges and oppresses, it is important to note that I recently recognized that though I have been predisposed to stand up for myself, I have chosen to work within a system that just does not work for a significant number of people of color. If we believe that racism permeates all aspects of American life (Bell, 1992), then we have to concede that the academy is no exception. I agree that racism is defined as a system of advantage based on race (Wellman, 1992). That means if you white, you are going to be accorded certain advantages in the academy. This plays out in ways that make work-life balance even more difficult for people of color. For example, I have the same requirements as my White colleagues, but I often feel I have more responsibilities because I have to spend time helping to keep scholars of color engaged in a system that frequently, and sometimes boldly, questions our presence in the academy.

STRENGTH, COURAGE, AND WISDOM

For scholars of color, work-life balance can be tricky. I want to avoid generalizing to all scholars of color, as all of our experiences are clearly not the same. However, I have noted some common experiences in the academy for some scholars of color who are conscious of them. Any scholars of color who are faced with these realities as they strive to develop a balanced life can employ what I offer below.

During the times of my first years, it was priority one to establish myself as a scholar by reserving significant amounts of time to do research, reading, and writing. Achieving this goal is particularly strained in the case of scholars of color because often we are asked to serve on department, college, or even national committees as the only one (tokenism) or one of a small number. We are asked to take on students of color who have not been supported well (sometimes all of them) by the institution or we are expected to interface with ethnic programs and services on campus, and we tend to have research and service obligations to our cultural communities as scholars of color. To be clear, all of these can and may likely be noble goals. Nevertheless, managing these obligations and opportunities well as part of work-life balance can completely overcome even the most organized and focused scholar, and interfere with first goal to publish and establish ourselves as scholars first. Regardless of what is said to scholars of color, publishing is what counts. Moreover, I have heard the story more than once that when these scholars go up for tenure, no one seems to take the service work seriously.

To stick to a regimen of conducting research and publishing takes courage. As I reflect on the story of my start in the academy, I wish I had more insight and courage then, even though I still got tenure. As I noted above, there were mentors along the way who helped tremendously. I have always found myself in some type of administrative position because in the recesses of my mind I saw myself as someone who could in fact work within the system to improve it. I may have been misguided in trying to do this as an assistant professor. To be sure, I understood that at the University of Cincinnati there was a need to distribute the work of this type of service. However, doing administrative work can really wreck your balance and/or adversely impact your career and should be avoided if possible. Be aware that sometimes politically you may have to do it, especially if you have a small program and a limited number of tenure-track professors. If that is the case, then be sure to ask for accommodations that will support your research like course reductions, stipends, time off in the summer, etc. That was the route I took and while not ideal, it helped me survive as a scholar and maintain more balance in my life. It is also important to have an understanding of the publishing, teaching, and service expectations and the type of institution in which you choose to work. After I had served as a program coordinator for 3 years, I decided it was time to pass it on to someone else. My division head (department chair) really wanted me to continue but had told me in the past that there was no money for stipends or course reductions. I naively thought this was still the case. However, interestingly, she found money for a stipend and gave me a course reduction. Having these concessions helped me take time to focus on my research and to have more time with family. Having this kind of support was instrumental because at the time I was still an assistant professor without tenure. The lessons I learned were that you need to be courageous, push your research agenda, and attempt to make as many connections as you can between your research and your service. This was an important lesson for me as an African American scholar. I was just not as experienced at asking for what I needed from the academy and I had to rely on the wisdom of many mentors. Without their guidance, I would have been even more stretched and it would have really thrown my work-life balance out of sync. Even when they told me what to ask for, I still had to muster up the courage to do it. I am certain that you have to be smart (and/or have good mentors) to survive in the academy, as it is not a place that was designed for folks with families and it is also a system that is unfriendly to people of color. When I make this statement and most of what I tell here, I am referring to my experiences in Research I institutions, which can be tough places in which to work. There are those institutions out there that are friendlier to families and people of color. However, we have to be courageous enough to make the choice to work in those places. Next, I will share a story about a leadership opportunity and work/life balance.

Once I was asked to consider serving in the role of the division head. In fall of 2007, I started the year as a tenured associate professor. I was excited about the work that needed to be done and somehow thought I would be able to focus more on the writing and research with a reduced amount of pressure since being untenured no longer hung over my head. However, soon obligatory opportunities to lead came my way. With the exception of my first year as a faculty member, I noticed that in 2007 I had been in some type of coordinator or director role for the last 5 years. The level of responsibility necessary to be successful in these roles varied but one thing was common, they all took time away from the focus to conduct research and publish. As noted earlier, this does not include the other formal and informal obligations I had as a faculty of color. Though my colleagues were supportive of the service in leadership I offered, they still fully expected me to produce as a scholar. Thus leadership responsibilities over the past 5 years added more pressure and challenged my ability to keep things in balance. The prior 6 years were important times for my wife and me as we were both going through the tenure process. That made it easier to focus on work as it was just the two of us then, and we supported each other as we went through this process, and forgave each other for working longer hours than we should have.

In August 2007, our daughter was born and during that upcoming academic year, I applied for a sabbatical. I planned to work the following fall of 2008 and go on sabbatical January 2009. During that year, our department was also experiencing some growing pains. The dean developed a search committee for a new division head (chair) and a respected colleague approached me and asked if I would consider applying as it was only going to be an internal search. I was quite honored that he thought I should apply but was convinced there were many reasons I should not. First, my life had changed dramatically with the birth of Nia. Next, it was much too early in my career to even consider this opportunity. I had not before, but I started to think of it after that conversation. I pondered what would it mean for someone like me aspiring to leadership to apply for the position now. I got excited and felt like this could be a great opportunity to jumpstart my career on the administrative track. I needed time to think about this and discuss it with my wife.

Shortly thereafter and before I reached a decision, another respected colleague and mentor in the department, mentioned that he wanted to speak with me about the prospect of putting my name in the hat for division head. I listened intently and followed his rationale closely and agreed with much of what he offered as good reasons that I should apply. He noted in his strongest reason that many folks respected me and felt as if I had no or little political aspirations, thus making me a great candidate for the job. I told him I would think about it but life was pretty hectic now with a new baby, an approaching sabbatical (which I would lose if I were to get this position). In the end, after mulling it over and having several conversations with my wife, I started to reason that becoming division head would take me away from research I know I still needed to conduct. It would throw my life out of balance I thought. My wife and I, working together, eventually concluded that this was not a good time for me to take this position. That took courage on my part, but we know the quality of our lives were better for it. In the end, decisions I make now continue to throw my life in "frenzy mode" frequently. Still, usually, I can look back to see if I have the strength, wisdom, and courage to make the choice to achieve better balance in my life and my work. What about the work that drives me to support marginalized students while sometimes making it difficult to be present for my family? In conclusion, I believe work/life balance is about doing those things that are important, meaningful, and difficult and that is the work. Seeking work/life balance is understanding that as a scholar of color I sometimes work on behalf of those who may not have a voice in the academy. In sum, I have to be courageous enough to choose to engage in those assignments, activities and projects that are relevant to this mission and that work.

NOTES

1. Conscious as used here implies an awareness of the impact of race and racial issues
2. Black and African American will be used interchangeably in this chapter.

REFERENCES

Bell, D. (1992). *Faces at the bottom of the well: The permanence of racism*. New York, NY: Basic Books.

Wellman, D. (1992). *Portraits of White racism*. Cambridge, England: Cambridge University Press.

CHAPTER 28

GEN X IN THE ACADEMY

Liz Hollingworth

In many ways, the professorate is a good career for balancing work and family: we can schedule our own office hours, work on a grant from home if a child is unexpectedly sick, and are typically not tied to a 9 to 5 work day. In educational leadership, we have the added bonus of getting to know many of the teacher leaders and school administrators in our neighborhood schools outside of the parent-teacher context. But the work of a professor is mentally challenging, time-intensive, and oftentimes requires absences from family to travel to academic conferences several times a year. It is not surprising that many professors struggle with work-life balance.

I am one of the 51 million children born between 1965-1980: Generation X. In 1993, I read *13th Gen*, a book that posits that we are the thirteenth generation of Americans, and that historical trends and events have affected the way we see the world. At the risk of making gross generalizations about millions of people, the authors accurately predicted what my generation, who were then recent college graduates, would be like as adults: "Dedicated spouses, they will work hard to shield their marriages from the risk and stress of their work lives. Around the year 2000, these efforts will be reflected in a marked downturn in the national divorce rate" (Howe, Strauss, Matson, & Williams, 1993, p. 221). Their prediction has turned out to be true not just for me personally, but for our generation as a group. For whatever reasons, Americans experienced the lowest

Juggling Flaming Chain Saws: Academics in Educational Leadership Try to Balance Work and Family, pp. 231–236
Copyright © 2012 by Information Age Publishing
All rights of reproduction in any form reserved.

**Table 28.1.   Provisional Number of Divorces
and Annulments and Rate: United States, 2000-2009**

Year	Divorces and Annulments	Population	Rate per 1,000 Total Population
2009[1]	840,000	242,497,000	3.5
2008[1]	844,000	240,663,000	3.5
2007[1]	856,000	238,759,000	3.6
2006[1]	872,000	236,172,000	3.7
2005[1]	847,000	234,114,000	3.6
2004[2]	879,000	237,042,000	3.7
2003[3]	927,000	245,200,000	3.8
2002[4]	955,000	243,600,000	3.9
2001[5]	940,000	236,650,000	4.0
2000[5]	944,000	233,550,000	4.0

Source: National Center for Health Statistics (2011).
[1]Excludes data for California, Georgia, Hawaii, Indiana, Louisiana, and Minnesota.
[2]Excludes data for California, Georgia, Hawaii, Indiana, and Louisiana.
[3]Excludes data for California, Hawaii, Indiana, and Oklahoma.
[4]Excludes data for California, Indiana, and Oklahoma.
[5]Excludes data for California, Indiana, Louisiana, and Oklahoma.
Note: Populations are consistent with the 2000 census.

divorce rate in modern history in 2009, according to the Center for Disease Control and Prevention (see Table 28.1).

But our devotion to our families is not at the expense of a passion for our work. Like many other professors of educational leadership, I believe my research, teaching, and service will change our K-12 schools for the better. This is consistent with what has been written about Generation X in the work force. In his book *X Saves the World*, Gordinier (2008) writes that our generation is patient about change and that we do not necessarily jump on the bandwagon of new reform movements:

> We're wary enough to see through delusional "movements"; we're old enough to feel a connection to the past (and yet we're unsentimental enough not to get all gooey about it); we're young enough to be wired; we're snotty enough not to settle for crap; we're resourceful enough to turn crap into gold; we're quiet enough to endure our labors on the margins; we're experienced enough to know that change begins on the margins. (p. 170)

So, academically, Gen X is skeptical and determined. Personally, however, I believe our generation has learned from personal experience as to what happens when work becomes more important than family.

I am a child of divorce raised on the *Brady Bunch* and *Happy Days* who watched families on TV that were very different from the ones we knew. By the time I was in junior high in the 1980s, I watched grownups both in my life and on television go through the "me generation" phase. Like many of my Gen X brothers and sisters, I didn't have role models for how to balance work and family; I had role models for how *not* to balance work and family.

My parents (who were married in the summer of 1969) ran an advertising agency in Southern California in the late 1970s and 1980s. Every day after school, my brother and I would hang out for a few hours in some of the empty office spaces in their building, waiting for it to be time to go home. We could play darts in the break room, use the vending machines, draw, or listen to music, but we were not allowed to bother mom and dad while they were working. For lots of reasons, my parents divorced and dissolved the agency when I was in sixth grade. When I got married, I knew that I did not want to put my children in a position like the one in which I had grown up: with busy parents who struggled to find time for each other and for their children.

It was in 2007 when I first realized how to better compartmentalize work and family. I was a meeting with the Wallace Foundation about the School Administrative Managers project. I was part of a team developing curriculum to train preservice administrators about awareness on how they spend their time in schools as instructional leaders. I was the only Gen Xer on the team, and the youngest participant by at least a decade. After several people had mentioned how hard it had been for them personally to balance their administrative jobs with their families and how many of them had been divorced as a result, I realized there was something different about the way I keep work and family in two distinct categories in my mind. It's not that I'm not busy; it's just that family does not typically get ignored because of work obligations in our household.

I have been happily married for 16 years and have a teenage daughter, Emily, who is preparing for high school. My husband, a fellow Gen Xer, is also a professor. While the three of us work at home after dinner with our laptops (each of us doing our "homework"), that time still functions as family time, not work. Work is something that happens during the day, and family time begins when we are all home together at the end of the day—after school, dissertation meetings, volleyball practice, driving the carpool, oboe lessons, a bucket of balls at the driving range, or yoga. The internet is probably the biggest reason we can do so much of our work from home: correspondence via e-mail has certainly changed the amount of time this generation of professors needs to be available for office hours to communicate with students. We were the first people we knew to get rid of our land lines and just use cell phones in 2002. Upon reflection, that has really done quite a bit for making sure that work does not intrude on family time. It would be very unusual for any of us to take a work-related call after dinner, and the caller ID features on our individual phones makes that possible.

When I am teaching, I tell my students on the first day of class that if they need to sneak out of class to take a personal call on their cell phones, I totally understand. Some of my students leave their children with baby-sitters so the parents can be free to come to class. Most of my students take me up on this offer, but I cannot think of a student who has abused this policy. For the most part, graduate students in our educational leadership program are full time educators with families who, like me, are balancing multiple responsibilities.

Boomers seem to be baffled by Generation X in the workplace. There are a myriad of online articles written to decode the mysterious behavior of people my age looking to mix business with pleasure. We tend to confuse older colleagues with our desire to have fun at work and to socialize with our coworkers afterhours. Another junior faculty member and I tried to start a Friday afternoon happy hour in our department, and a senior faculty member told our department chair that it was inappropriate and out of line and we had to be stopped. Luckily, the chair did not agree, but the two of us decided it was politically easier to join the intercollegiate new faculty happy hour rather than start our own within the department.

In an online article written for About.com to explain to readers how Gen X views the work and life balance, Kane (n.d.) writes:

> **Value Work/Life Balance:** Unlike previous generations, members of Generation X work to live rather than live to work. They appreciate fun in the workplace and espouse a work hard/play hard mentality. Generation X managers often incorporate humor and games into work activities. (Kane, n.d., para. #8)

One of the first things we did in our new faculty cohort is to exchange e-mail addresses at orientation to create the aforementioned New Faculty Happy Hour that met every Friday for about 5 years. Senior faculty did not join us. This observation is consistent with research conducted on Generation X and work/life values. Gerkovich (2001) surveyed 4,500 Generation X professionals about their expectations for work and family. She found:

> Members of Generation X appear to place a much higher priority on personal and family-related goals than on their career-related goals: 84% of the respondents stated that it was extremely important to them to have a loving family, 72% indicated that it was extremely important to have a relationship

with a significant other, while 79% responded that it was extremely important to enjoy life. (Gerkovich, 2001)

Unlike my family when I was a child, we travel together as a family several times a year. Sometimes it's because we have frequent flyer miles and want to go somewhere new. We also have family friends from graduate school who are also in the academy, and each summer we head to a water park in the Midwest as a group and the golfers golf while everyone else experiences extreme slides. Seldom do we travel to one another's academic conferences, but sometimes (for example when my husband was asked to speak in Japan) we make a family vacation out of it. Our vacations are planned up to 14 months in advance, and we try not to bring work with us when we are together as a family. We have never canceled a family vacation for a work commitment. But of course the lines between work and home blur.

Being a professor in educational leadership has provided me with the unique opportunity to teach my daughter's teachers at the university. Rather than being an uncomfortable arrangement, I find it very rewarding to go to parent-teacher conferences for my daughter at the middle school with her teachers, who are graduates of our leadership program. In addition to being involved in Emily's school life as a frequent volunteer in the school and as a Girl Scout Leader, I have also found ways to include Emily in my work. As a fifth grader, she illustrated a book I wrote for reading teachers. I described to her a model I have for all of the different academic tests that are used to make instructional decisions in schools. I explained that it is like our Jacuzzi in the backyard: if I put my finger in to see if it's hot enough, that's not enough to know if it's safe to go in. We also have to test the chemicals and look for algae. My model shows all of the different data points from assessments that are used to determine a student's academic abilities and aptitudes. So Emily drew a picture of our hot tub so I could use it in my book.

In the same way, Emily also is recruited into service to pilot computer-based tasks my husband creates for his visual cognition lab in the psychology department. Usually these tasks happen after dinner when he has put the finishing touches on a three dimensional scene he wants to use with his eye-tracking device back in the lab, or a computer game he has created to test visual memory. She takes great pleasure in telling him how to improve his work if she thinks the games are too easy.

So even though we have been known to blur the lines between work and family, I can't imagine any of my friends missing every single one of their kid's baseball games for work. I do not mean to suggest that Generation X has figured out the work-life balance; but the need for balance is certainly not as much of a factor in my relationships with my friends and family as it was for my parents and their friends.

REFERENCES

Centers for Disease Control and Prevention. (2011). National marriage and divorce trends. Retrieved from http://www.cdc.gov/nchs/nvss/marriage_divorce_tables.htm

Gerkovich, P. (2001). Generation X and work/life values. Retrieved from http://wfnetwork.bc.edu/The_Network_News/08/The_Network_News_Interview08.pdf

Gordinier, J. (2008). *X saves the world: How generation X got the shaft but can still keep everything from sucking.* New York, NY: Viking Penguin.

Howe, N., Strauss, W., Matson, R. J., & Williams, I. (1993). *13th Gen: Abort, retry, ignore, fail?* New York, NY: Vintage Books.

Kane, S. (n.d.). Generation X. Retrieved from: http://legalcareers.about.com/od/practicetips/a/GenerationX.htm

CHAPTER 29

MAN, I WORK LIKE A WOMAN[1]

Eric Houck

I wish that I could have others write this chapter for me, because in some sense the perspectives that my friends, spouse, and children have on the way I work is a primary lens I use to consider my success as a scholar and a human.[2] Upon hearing of the topic of this chapter, my daughter recommended writing in large letters, "I don't know how—I just do it." In some ways that sentence is perhaps truer than she thinks. My wife enjoys telling friends and relatives about how I simply forget many minor holidays and invariably end up locked out of my building or calling home with the observation that "no one seems to be on campus today." "Yes," my wife will dryly note, "Memorial Day is often like that."

So just because I work to develop a work/life balance does not mean that I am actually doing it well. There may be a tenure vote or a family meeting in the near future to remind me that I have been living a life out of balance in some important aspect. But I know that I have developed a commitment to being a good colleague, a good researcher, a devoted spouse, and a present parent.[3] And working to maintain those commitments feels good to me.[4]

How did this chapter title come to be? Well, if they get ready for school and we have some time to spare, I'll let the kids watch some TV in the

Juggling Flaming Chain Saws: Academics in Educational Leadership
Try to Balance Work and Family, pp. 237–243

mornings before they go catch the bus. They can pick between two educative options: "SportsCenter" or "Morning Joe."[5]

It was a "Morning Joe" morning that we watched Mika Brzezinski plugging her latest book, *Knowing Your Value: Women, Money and Getting What You're Worth* and I came to discover an anchoring metaphor for this reflection. Part of Brzezinski's thesis was the notion that the very things that currently devalue women in the workplace and depress their salaries—the fact that women are often juggling career and family responsibilities—requires a skill set for multitasking and efficiency that should actually be rewarded.

And, at the risk of displaying a vast ignorance in my readings on women's issues and feminist perspectives,[6] this thesis resonates with me. Part of my journey in the academy has been a journey of integrating my responsibilities as a spouse and a parent with my responsibilities as a scholar. Unwilling to short change either, I have come to see my work and life struggles as an intricate play between personal and professional responsibilities. While periods of this journey have been difficult, the lessons learned thus far have served to strengthen my skills in both arenas. The sections that follow provide a general overview of my particular context and reviews my struggles with work/life issues beginning with graduate school and continuing through my positions as an assistant and associate professor. Finally, I will attempt to synthesize any strategies or approaches that I have found particularly helpful.

INITIAL THOUGHTS

Pat Conroy's narrator in *The Prince of Tides* concludes his reflection upon his Whiteness, maleness, and general tone deafness on social issues by sighing, "I seem to embody everything that is wrong with the twentieth century." While I am loathe to equate my social outlook with this character's', I include this sentence to acknowledge that there are aspects of my position within the academy that have knowingly and unknowingly advantaged me relative to my female, non-White, single, and lesbian, gay, bi, and transgender peers. I feel it is important to position myself in this conversation as a White, married male with two children who came of age, like many in my generation, with two working parents as a latch-key child.[7]

Like many of my peers, I saw the role of breadwinner came with a price and desired to create a more balanced existence. In some respect, then, I had to create a space for myself to actually assume more of a traditionally female role by consciously taking responsibility for doctor's visits, practices, teacher meetings, housework, and other domestic and/or child-rearing tasks.[8] Later, as my wife moved back into the workforce, taking on these roles became even more critical. It is amazing sometimes no note how few dads are around at some of these events.[9]

My appreciation for the notion of balance also stems from the fact that I was a part time graduate student for 2 years before entering a doctoral program full time.[10] This has given me perspective on the manner in which graduate work represents a third sphere for many students—one that often has to be prioritized after professional and family considerations. And it was my inability to conduct quality work in that degree program that helped in part to my move toward full-time graduate study. While this decision had immediate and profound negative economic implications for my family, it also represented the only way that I could see to create an opportunity to move into a career as an academic at a research I university. Especially during my matriculation and early career, when my spouse was at home caring for our young children, I feel as if this advantaged position actually threatened to upset the type of work/life equilibrium I was struggling to define for myself. To the outside world, my positionality gave me a pass on many domestic responsibilities. As a man and breadwinner, there were expectations that I would concentrate on my work and leave much of the relationship maintenance and child rearing responsibilities to my spouse, thereby replicating patterns of work and home that have existed for middle class American men for generations.[11] But that was not what I wanted. I wanted to be a fully equal partner in the domestic and child-rearing dimensions of my life.

In one sense, I was lucky to have work/life balance issues thrust upon me, as I began my doctoral program with a 9-month-old daughter. Early on, graduate school confronted me with a series of choices about a number of issues that addressed the tension between work and family: what study groups to get involved with (how late do they meet?), what courses to take (when are they offered?), and even what to choose as a preferred methodology.[12] These choices had a direct cost—I clearly remember turning down an offer to collaborate on a class assignment (which became part of a major grant award) because it would eat up too much of my evenings. Clearly, a more aggressive response would have resulted in a direct financial benefit to me. However, these issues acculturated me to what I now refer to as a "culture of compromise," in which I am much more comfortable understanding that every decision—whether professional or personal—will carry a cost. The trick then becomes determining if I am willing to bear that cost at that time.

As a result, I have avoided what I have observed to be a sometimes—difficult transition for my colleagues: the shift from a professional life without children to one with children. I have been making these trade-offs since day one. While it was difficult, I feel that I have developed my professional career around my family and have not had to adjust my career too dramatically because of family issues. Nevertheless, graduate school confronted me with many opportunities to establish the important of taking time to tend to personal and relationship needs in addition to studying for exams, writing papers, and working as a teaching and research assistant. Communicating clearly about deadlines, informing students that I would not be available to answer questions late into the evening, and other methods of carving out time for my personal life became important exercises in self-assertion that would benefit me when I moved into the role of an assistant professor.[13]

SCHOOLED TO WORK

In many ways, my relationships with mentors in the academy not only one of academic preparation but one of professional preparation. I was fortunate to observe many models: some faculty with a 9 to 5 blue collar approach to their work, while others squeezed in work whenever possible. Some relied on technology to integrate their workflow and maintain communications with friends and family. Some took aspects of each of these main approaches. It was here that I developed my basic strategy of professional compartmentalization: dinner time is sacred, no work on the weekends, only work at home when deadlines demanded it, be fully present in the home to the best of my abilities, include the kids whenever possible.[14]

Perhaps the most profound impression made upon me, however, was when my (male) advisor took a semester of family leave upon the birth of his first child. His decision and the resulting discussion of that decision among faculty and students illustrated both the possibilities and pitfalls of an academic career. On one hand, all agreed that this was an important move which they supported personally and institutionally. However, a number of questions arose regarding the timing of taking a semester off. Should leave be taken so close to third year review? How would this leave be calculated when examining my adviser's contributions to research, teaching, and service? I was further fortunate that a number of faculty in my graduate program would take time to discuss and answer questions about their work and families.[15]

MOVING INTO THE MIDDLE

Taking my first academic position placed greater stress upon my work productivity as I gingerly stepped upon the tenure track. The additional demands of serving on student committees, contributing to faculty governance and the scholarly community placed additional pressure upon my time. Often, the boundaries between work and family or personal time strained under this pressure. However, the basic structure of allocating time into one of two binary areas continued to serve as the foundation for almost all of my time management decisions. While work more appropriately took on a greater role in my daily life, I found that it was also important to set precedents with my faculty colleagues. Early decisions and discussions served to signal my commitment to be fully present as a spouse and parent as well as a contributing faculty member. Informing committee members that I would be taking my son to the doctor or that I would not be able to have dinner with a job candidate because of my daughter's school performance served both as methods of signaling how I drew boundaries between my professional and familial obligations and as a method of sharing my life with my colleagues. Once established, these boundaries were relatively easy to maintain.[16]

CONCLUSION

One acknowledged bias I profess, therefore, is that I do view the work and family spheres of my life as separate, even though they intersect from time to time. Defining, understanding, and protecting these boundaries have been, therefore, a critical aspect of my conception of maintaining work/life balance. While I do not claim that many in my generation maintain this same position, I would assert that numerous colleagues have expressed to me a desire to strike a better balance between professional and personal obligations as a reaction to the manner in which they themselves were parented. For some, this expresses itself as a more integrated and organic approach to work and family, while others (myself included) take a more bifurcated and mechanistic approach to defining and enforcing boundary areas between the professional and the personal.[17]

There is an old chestnut in policy to the effect that you know a policy is good when both sides of an argument are unhappy with it. This is somewhat analogous, I find, to maintaining a work-life balance: one is probably doing it right when it feels like you are short changing both. Many of one's daily decisions create discomfort as one realizes the opportunity costs on both sides of the work/life balance. However, the idea of a professional and personal life in consistent dialogue has the opportunity to be an energizing discussion that provides for a more fruitful fulfillment of both spheres of one's life.

NOTES

1. Having lived in Nashville for 3 years, I am contractually obligated to make reference to a country music song or performer. For those of you in the Northeast—it's Shania Twain.

2. I did not edit this sentence and find it interesting that I typed "scholar" before "human." Perhaps this is a signal to move along to the next essay ...

3. After receiving reviewer feedback, I tried to crowdsource this chapter on Facebook. A former roommate (and the best man at my wedding) reminded me in no uncertain terms that this work is far too dichotomous—that considering balance as an act that only engages me as a scholar and a parent leaves out important dimensions of my personality, such as, for example, drinking beer with, perhaps, a former roommate or the guy who was the best man at my wedding.

4. After I submitted the first draft of this chapter, a kindly reviewer recommended that I include more personal stories in my narrative. I would offer two observations about that: (1) relating personal stories makes quantitatively oriented researchers break out in hives, and (2) much of my time as a grad student and early career professional are a blur precisely because I was trying so hard to strike an appropriate work/life balance. I actually don't have many stories to relate. Nevertheless, the idea was a sound one. I hope the paragraphs that follow relay my reflections upon finding a work/life balance and also include illustrative [shudder] personal stories.

5. Hey—I get to enjoy morning TV too, right? Besides, what is there that they can learn from kids TV that they can't also learn from sports or politics?

6. I am not well versed in feminist scholarship, but I will take the opportunity to self reflexively insert the following citation: Longino, H. E. (1988). Review: Science, objectivity, and feminist values. *Feminist Studies*, *14*(3), 561-574. doi:10.2307/3178065

7. Yes, I had a house key on yarn around my neck.

8. It seems so antiquated to even use this language.

9. I think our kids' dental hygienist believes me to be unemployed.

10. It is interesting to note that my wife and I basically saw graduate school as a better option that both of us working, me attending grad school, and us having a baby. We disadvantaged ourselves economically, but gained a lot in terms of time and space.

11. When told I was going home to take my daughter to ballet practice while I was in grad school, a fellow student responded, "But your wife is at home ... right? So ..."

12. "Data never sleep," intoned a wiseful professor.

13. Of course this rigid compartmentalization does not always work. I have called into dissertation defenses from the passenger seat of the family minivan on multiple occasions. I have taken conference calls at the beach. The bleed-over goes both ways. My children have written on university white boards in permanent markers. I have sat in committee meetings while my daughter watched DVDs in my office. I have clicked out of a conference call to speak with a pediatrician.

14.   This strategy has had interesting consequences. To this day, my daughter blanches in horror as I recall how she—as a toddler and in a case of mistaken identity, whacked former Vanderbilt and now Ohio State chancellor Gordon Gee on the bottom during a departmental Christmas party.

15.   I remember the first time we drove past my new office building on a Saturday in Athens. Noting the empty parking lot, my wife observed, "It's a Saturday and your parking lot is empty. I'm going to like it here."

16.   It is still painful at times. I was out of town at a conference when the dog died, for example.

17.   In discussion with a friend who works for a major U.S. corporation about this article, he noted that the corporation terms this issue "work/life integration." When I asked what that meant, he jokingly responded, "Answering e-mails while cooking dinner, I guess." This gets at my fears of not maintaining work and life as separate spheres; that the integration of both of these aspects of my life necessarily correlates the diminishment of both.

CHAPTER 30

WHY BALANCE ISN'T THE BEST OPTION

Changing Our Perspective to Work-Life Integration

Audrey J. Jaeger

In one of our foundational graduate classes at North Carolina (NC) State, I talk about the idea of work-personal life integration (Rapaport, Bailyn, Fletcher, & Pruitt, 2002). I have chosen to reframe the conversation of work and personal life, consistent with other scholars (Burke, 2004; Rapaport et al.), and remove the idea of "balance" from the discussion. The term balance implies an equal separation or a 50-50 division, which according to scholars (Rapaport et al.) and practitioners is not necessarily realistic, doable, or even desirable.

Striving for an equal separation of our work and nonwork lives creates expectations for workers and their families that focus on equal time and treatment rather than fulfillment, happiness, and enjoyment. Burke (2004) notes that the term balance separates the work and personal life into two domains, treating work as if it is not part of life. "Not everyone wants to give equal weight to work and personal life, and choosing one should not mean sacrificing the other" (p. 300). Integration, according to

Juggling Flaming Chain Saws: Academics in Educational Leadership
Try to Balance Work and Family, pp. 245–251
Copyright © 2012 by Information Age Publishing

Burke, implies that individuals can engage in and attain satisfaction in their work and personal life no matter how much time they choose to invest in either domain. The concept of balance sets up an either/or situation. NC State's current strategic plan states, "For our students, faculty, and staff to reach their full potential, they must strike an effective work/life balance" (see http://info.ncsu.edu/strategic-planning/pathway-to-the-future/#goal-4). This language suggests that work is not part of life and life does not include work. It also suggests the goal for everyone is a 50-50 split. If an individual chooses work, then s/he must not be choosing what falls outside of work, which is often family. For me, it is about reframing the conversation so that we treat all aspects of life as contributing to the greater whole, regardless of percentage of time spent. As any parent can attest, one aspect may be more important or demanding at one point in our lives. The ultimate goal is integration by connecting our work and nonwork lives yet not necessarily overlapping these.

A relatively new term—"weisure time"—also suggests that work and personal life are not easily separated. Coined by Dalton Conley, a professor at New York University, weisure time suggests that the line dividing work and leisure is blurring as there is no longer a 9-to-5 workday but instead a 24-7 life of weisure. In an age of technology and social media, Conley notes that the expectations of work and fun are not clearly separated (see http://articles.cnn.com/2009-05-11/living/weisure_1_creative-class-richard-florida-leisure-time?_s=PM:LIVING). We know this to be the case for both our students and ourselves as we tend to be technologically connected to our work and personal life at all times (e.g., social media and mobile phones). Conley's use of the terms leisure and fun may not be typical words associated with working parents as the role of managing a family schedule can at times be anything but fun and leisurely.

Although the conversation about work and personal life must be reframed it is inadequate to suggest that technology and today's blending of work and nonwork activities is the answer to work-personal life integration. Being able to have a face-to-face conference call on your smart phone while at a swim meet is not the only strategy to consider in work-personal life integration. Clearly defining our work and personal life roles and expectations within those roles will help us be more successful at integrating them.

Work-personal life integration for me begins with knowing the place at which I work. Being a successful faculty member is different at different places. History and culture create the rules, unwritten and written, about what is expected in relation to how we spend our time. I am an associate professor of higher education in the Department of Leadership, Policy, and Adult and Higher Education at NC State. My partner and I have two young children, both were born before I attained tenure. My partner has spent most of his career in higher education as well and has a good understanding of the rewards and challenges of a faculty member. My research focuses on the social and organization factors that influence the careers of faculty and future faculty. In my own research on graduate education (Haley, Jaeger, & Levin, 2012; Jaeger & Haley, 2011) it is evident that work-personal life integration is a strong consideration in whether graduate students choose careers in academe. The conversation is also apparent in the lives of contingent faculty, which includes part-time faculty and full-time nontenure track faculty (Washington & Jaeger, 2010). In my research and practice I have identified four strategies of my own that help support the idea of work-personal life integration.

Since each institution of higher education is unique, it is critical to adapt work-life integration strategies to the environment in which you work. This coupled with the uniqueness of individuals, makes broad suggestions beneficial only if we apply them to our own situation. Each institution has important gatekeepers, including department chairs and deans. These individuals have access to resources, often manage teaching loads, provide incentives, and can ultimately determine your fate at an institution. Building relationships with the gatekeepers can be critical to success within an institution.

My first suggestion to integrate our work and personal lives is to *set clear expectations*. When expectations are clear with our colleagues, students, and administrators challenging situations that arise are easier to address. I was once told by a senior colleague that I spent too much time teaching (e.g., grading, preparing, nurturing, etc.). Although I was first alarmed by the comment, I quickly realized there was much more to her suggestion than my commitment to teaching. She wanted to make sure I was also allocating sufficient time to research as was expected of me at a major research university. Making wise decisions in how we allocate our time is important to being able to integrate our lives. Many institutions have some type of statement of mutual expectations or means to engage in dialogue about expectations. Work-personal life integration is only possible when we are aware of our own expectations and the expectations of others. These expectations may also change thus renegotiating our roles and expectations are necessary.

Asking for specifics in regard to those expectations is also important. Although the specifics may not be codified in policy and administrators may be reluctant to share exact details; they exist, so our job is to know them. Understanding the expectations of our work environment can help us set clear expectations in our personal lives. Expectations we have for ourselves and others as well as the expectations others have for us cross over work and personal life. Who is expected to drop off the kids affects what time someone can get to work. Expectations about who makes dinner, reads bedtime stories, and pays the bills cannot be separated from article journal articles, teaching class, and serving on committees as they are bound to come in conflict with one another throughout our career. The goal is integration so that our work and personal worlds do not have to be in opposition to each other. This does not mean that our work and personal lives are blended and inseparable. It does mean that we do not need to separate them so as to provide equal time to both. For example, I am clear at work that between 3 P.M. and 8 P.M. I am rarely available, as this time includes picking up my daughters, family dinner, piano lessons, homework, and many other activities that go along with having children. Yet, I am also clear that responding to e-mail at 10 P.M. is appropriate for me as this weaving of work and personal life works for my situation. Again, each individual has to identify what works for him or her; seeking equal balance between our work and personal life will likely only cause us to fall short in one or both areas at some point.

My second suggestion is *be a policy expert*. Rules and regulations governing our institutions can have dramatic effects on our ability to integrate our work and nonwork lives. Polices about paternity leave, promotion and tenure, teaching loads, as well as others, vary by institution. Being our own policy expert puts us in the position to get what we need. I was the first to seek maternity leave in my department thus it was a new experience for all involved. I took the time to research all the policies that affected my leave and return to work as well as how the policies were implemented in other departments and colleges. When I presented what I wanted to my department head there was little to discuss as I offered a valid case that had precedent at the institution. Of course some aspects of policy are nonnegotiable; yet, much of what we do can be adapted to fit the situation. Policies not only affect us, they affect our colleagues. Taking leave time to care for a parent or having a child can add to the workload of our faculty colleagues. Although we are not responsible for other's reactions to our decisions, we can be mindful of how our work affects the work of others. Policies can affect everything from what we put on our syllabi to tenure decisions. If we are not aware of the policies and how they have been interpreted we may miss opportunities. Also being aware of who develops policy, who has the authority to change or amend policy, and who is the final authority on policy interpretation is as important as the policy itself. I have often been told, "We can't do that?" or "That's not possible." The rationale behind these statements is likely guided by someone's interpretation of policy. Building a network of colleagues throughout campus can be helpful when responses received to questions have something to do with limitations based on policy. Many policies are meant to support faculty and nonwork lives (e.g., paternity leave), but can become obstacles to our achievement when we lack knowledge about them or the individuals work with them. Unofficial policies can often be more powerful than official policies. University policies may be inconsistent with department policies. Being our own policy expert helps us take the lead in better integrating our work and personal lives.

Above all, I believe it is important to *role model work-personal life integration* for our students and our colleagues. Last fall my husband's father died suddenly in a vehicle accident the first week of classes. My course started the following week; the day before my father-in-law's funeral. The first meeting of any course is a critical time to set expectations and begin to develop community. Since I had prepared for the first day several weeks in advance, I asked my doctoral student teaching assistant to lead the first class, while I drove the long distance to the funeral. It turns out that several students attempted to get in the class on the first day thus making the class too large to facilitate some group activities. One of the texts was not available, which made the students anxious and contributed to a challenging first session. Upon returning to work and learning about the difficulties of the first session, I empathized with my doctoral student teaching colleague about having to teach the first class alone. Even though it was an important class to miss, it was the right decision for me. I recall the teaching colleague saying she appreciated having a role model for work-personal life integration; an example of someone who made difficult choices and was still successful. Choosing to attend the funeral and miss 2 days of work and then talking about the decision with the teaching colleague and students in the class provided a real example of making tough choices in pursuit of work-personal life integration.

During the semester I seek guest lecturers who represent different capacities for work-personal life integration; some who do it well and others who fail miserably. After each speaker we talk about the content area of class then we also talk about the personal lives of the presenters. We openly ask our guest speakers how they make work and personal-life decisions and how they effectively or ineffectively integrate these two worlds. Students become more confident in the possibilities as the semester progresses, challenging the notion of an equal 50/50 split in our work and nonwork. One student recently e-mailed me saying he had spoken to someone in collegiate athletics who did not believe work-personal life integration was possible in this area. The student's response, "Perhaps it's because they are unwilling or unable to try or that they are choosing to do something else instead. It's only possible if you try, right?"

At the end of every semester, I invite my students to my home. I introduce them to who keeps me busy between 3 P.M. and 8 P.M. when I am not available for work commitments, who paints the pictures on my office walls, and who processes with me after a long class. I offer them an opportunity to see my life, not as the "other part" aside from work, but the parts of my life that make me whole. My goal is to not only provide them with an example of someone who integrates her roles in life but who also talks about the challenges and opportunities along the way. My work and personal lives are not inseparable, which often means for some individuals that they are working via technology all the time. It does mean I bring work home and home to work so that I am not seeking this definitive separation. The challenge with separation

Finally, I add to this conversation the important element about *individual choice*. Each person comes to this discussion from a different place with a different set of values and goals; thus, integration allows each of us the opportunity to connect the various aspects of our life as is appropriate for us. This book includes rich individual stories as to why "balance isn't the best option." Readers will be able to identify multiple strategies that may differ from one another, but are appropriate for the individual telling the story.

Accepting others' approaches to work and nonwork life can be difficult for me. I am challenged by how often we over use the term "busy." I find it difficult to understand how someone without children or significant nonwork responsibilities can be "busy." At the same time, understanding that everyone approaches their work and nonwork lives in different ways helps to support the idea that an arbitrary 50/50 split is likely difficult for everyone. If we envision a scale or a seesaw, in order to achieve balance we have to be exact, precise and cannot change the composition of our work and personal lives as needed. Each of us is unique and thus considering a visual that is often in motion, such as a windmill may be better. There are distinct aspects of our lives (the blades on the windmill), and they work together. They sometimes look inseparable, but when we slow down we know there are various parts of our lives.

Reframing the conversation about work-life balance will, at a minimum, allow us to reflect on our work and personal lives, our expectations, our actions, and the possibilities.

REFERENCES

Burke, R.J. (2004). Work and personal life integration. *International Journal of Stress Management, 11*(4), 299-304.

Haley, K. J., & Jaeger, A. J., & Levin, J. (in press). Not all going in the same direction: The effects of social identity on graduate student career choices. *Journal of College Student Development*.

Jaeger, A. J., & Haley, K. J. (2010, April). *Choosing a faculty career: Voice of students of color*. Paper presented at the meeting of the American Educational Research Association, Denver, CO.

Rapaport, R., Bailyn, L. Fletcher, J. K., & Pruitt, B. H. (2002). *Beyond work-family balance: Advancing gender equity and workplace performance.* San Francisco, CA: Jossey-Bass.

Washington, K. E. P., & Jaeger, A. J. (2010, November). *Community college part-time faculty perceptions of roles and expectations.* Paper presented at the meeting of the Association for the Study of Higher Education, Indianapolis, IN.

CHAPTER 31

TAKING CONTROL?

The Struggle to Balance
Professional and Personal Life

Gaëtane Jean-Marie

Two weeks before my dissertation defense, I received a phone call from
my physician's nurse informing me that I needed to schedule a magnetic
resonance imaging (MRI) because of an abnormality in my recent blood
work. I panicked and thought, "Not now." Knowing that I needed to focus
on my upcoming dissertation defense, I asked the nurse, "Can I schedule
the appointment after my meeting?" Emotionally, I wasn't prepared to
face the outcomes of what the MRI might reveal. After hanging up the
phone, I prayed, drawing from my spiritual source of faith, courage, and
hope. Echoing bell hooks (1999), in moments like this I am reminded
that, "there [is] always available a spiritual force that could lift me higher
and give me moments of transcendent bliss wherein I could surrender all
thought of the world and know profound peace" (p. 116). I was in need of
a spiritual uplift after this troublesome phone call.

   As serious of a matter this was, I decided not to tell my family until
after my dissertation defense. Although my family is very supportive, I
didn't want to cause unnecessary worry and couldn't deal with the constant phone calls that would ensue once I told them. I also couldn't face

Juggling Flaming Chain Saws: Academics in Educational Leadership
Try to Balance Work and Family, pp. 253–260
Copyright © 2012 by Information Age Publishing
All rights of reproduction in any form reserved.
                                                          253

the pressure so close to my defense date because everything was weighing on finishing my doctorate. I successfully defended and had already accepted a professorship position at the University of Oklahoma. But, I had to face the immediate health scare and follow through on my appointment for the MRI. It was at that point I told my family.

When the test results came, I learned that I had a small benign brain tumor which affected my pituitary glands. The stress of working full-time as a university administrator and attending graduate school sometimes enrolling in 12 hours started to impact my health in ways that I could not have imagined. Unfortunately, living a stressful life was a precursor to what my life in academe would be like for many years. I was on a fast moving train and did not know how to slow it down. Ambitious and driven to succeed in my academic career, I committed to working more and longer days at the expense of my health. In retrospect, there are several things I would have done differently to balance my professional and personal life.

In this chapter, I chronicle two periods in my life on the journey to achieve success as a professor in educational leadership. Almost 10 years since entering academe, I offer lessons on the importance of creating a balance between one's professional and personal life. As the first in my family of Haitian descent to pursue a PhD and go on to be a professor, I learned through trials and errors, and mentors and colleagues who provided guidance and helpful insights along the way. Myers (2002) identifies three streams of support system that African American women in academe draw from as part of their development and maintenance of self-esteem: family, close friends, and colleagues and other African American women faculty. The combination of these three streams of support played an instrumental part in my journey to achieve success as a woman of color in academe.

WHAT HAPPENED TO PLAY?: WORKING PROFESSIONAL AND FULL-TIME GRADUATE STUDENT

In 1996, my life changed forever. At the age of 59, my father, Joseph after 3 months of being diagnosed with gastrointestinal cancer died a month after his birthday. The doctor gave him 6 months to live but he died in 3. I was devastated. I felt cheated of my father's wisdom, love, and support he always provided me. Being the first in my family of nine siblings to pursue my doctorate, I did not know what to expect when I decided to follow this path 2 years after his death. Ironically, I am writing this chapter on what would have been his 74th birthday.

The year that my dad died, I felt a tremendous loss because of the many years I was robbed to share and celebrate many dreams with him. I expected he would live much longer to see me and my siblings accomplish many achievements and make him proud. The death of my father made me reflect on my life (i.e., take stock of what I have accomplished and what I wanted to do next). I was 24 years old, had a master's degree, and just ended a relationship. Further, while my position as assistant director in a precollege program was wonderful, it was time to move on. My decision to move out of state and pursue my doctorate was terrifying because I would be leaving behind my support network—close-knit family, friends, and community. Since emigrating to the United States in 1979, Newark, NJ was home.

When I relocated to Greensboro, North Carolina, I was charting a new path, one with uncertainties. I initially planned to be a full-time graduate student and live off-campus. After the first semester living in a 250 square foot room, I pursued full-time work so I can have a steady income and spacious living arrangements. I was hired in the dean's office in the college of education and was promoted in less than a year to a higher level position with more responsibilities. Now that I was working full-time and attending graduate school 3 nights a week, I slowly gave up my social life albeit it was difficult to develop as newcomer to North Carolina. When I lived in New Jersey, I worked but always made time to socialize and have a personal life. With five sisters and friends, that was not difficult to do but I was slow in developing a supportive network in my new hometown and I attributed this to working and going to school full-time.

The long work and school days had taken a toll on my health and I experienced some health issues in my second year in Greensboro. It did not start out that way when I first moved to Greensboro. In the first year, I was deliberate in establishing a routine of eating healthy, exercising regularly, and going out on the town to learn more about the city. My desire to have a steady income led to my pursuit of full-time work while simultaneously going to graduate school. Play went out the window and all I did was go to work and attend school. I lost sight of what it meant to balance work, school and personal life. I was also driven by the notion that this would only be for 4 years and my normal life would resume. What I did not realize was that I was conditioning myself to a stressful life and possible burnout. Fatigue, weight gain and female related issues were warning signs that I failed to pay attention to until much later. When I took heed to the warning signs, I had already encountered some health issues that resulted in ongoing doctor visits to diagnose what was wrong. Given the demands of my job and graduate school, I adopted a delayed gratification mentality in my personal life and as a way to cope with the stress, I held on to the belief that things will get better when I enter the professoriate (Shanafelt, 2007).

While I did not alter working and going to graduate school full-time, I committed to having a social life and nurturing my personal well-being. It was around the same time I met two African American women on campus, one was a doctoral candidate in the counseling program and the other an administrator in student affairs. In meeting them, I was introduced to the Greensboro Crew, a diverse group (e.g., race/ethnicity, gender, age, and marital status) of 12 individuals who were affiliated with the university in some way and most of us were from out of state. Every month, one of us hosted a potluck and we played cards or games, or engaged in conversations along a number of topics. At times, the women would have a movie or spa day while the guys had their own event. We celebrated birthdays, anniversaries, milestones, and would get together during holidays. They became longtime friends and a strong support network, proxy family.

As my work and job were consuming more time at the expense of my social life, the Greensboro Crew was an outlet in my attempt to achieve balance in my life (Sirgy & Wu, 2009). Sirgy and Wu (2009) maintain that balance in life contributes significantly to a subjective well-being which is attainable when both survival and growth needs are met. During those years, I was in survival mode and would often feel guilty for setting aside work that demanded my attention to go out with the Crew. When I attempted to decline an invitation, my friends were persistent in their efforts to convince me to go out. I sometime declined; other times, I gave in. So, I struggled with achieving balance in my personal and professional space.

Building on Seligman's (2002) theory of authentic happiness, that is people have to experience a pleasant life, a good life, a meaningful life, Sirgy and Wu (2009) argue that individuals must also have a balanced life. On a continuum, I was living a more imbalance than balance life. Imbalance is defined as a state of reflecting satisfaction or fulfillment in a focused domain (e.g., work, family) that ultimately leads to negative effect in other domains. For me, that was work and graduate school. I enjoyed my job and was happy about my pursuit of a doctoral degree but I failed at allowing myself to experience satisfaction in my personal life domain. Work and school consumed a lot of my time and during the weekdays, I was too exhausted to devote to socializing and my weekends were often committed to work-related or doctoral studies tasks. Conversely, balance is defined as a state reflecting satisfaction or fulfillment in several important domains with little or no negative effect in other domains (p. 185). Ideally, I would have liked to have balance in my work, graduate school and social life domains. However, I was emotionally invested in my work and graduate school domains. I often sacrificed the social life domain; and unfortunately, I maintained this imbalance once I entered academe but was hopeful it would change. Being diagnosed with a benign tumor during the last semester of my doctoral program was a wake-up call to live a less stressful life. For 4 years, living a demanding life was part of my repertoire and that was difficult to abandon.

ENTRY TO ACADEME: DRIVEN TO EXCEL BUT AT WHAT COST?

By the time I walked on the stage during commencement to be hooded by my advisor in May 2002, I had leased an apartment, obtained new phone numbers and scheduled my moving date to relocate to Norman, Oklahoma. After 4 years on my fast moving train of work and graduate school, I was looking forward to a more balanced life in my personal and professional domain. I was excited about the move, meeting new people, and working towards tenure and promotion. What I soon learned after relocating, I would be starting all over again, similar to what my life would be like when I first moved to North Carolina. Once again, I was at a farther distance from family and friends and was to begin anew. But I thought, "I'm sociable and in no time, I would develop a social network through people I met at work, church, and in the community." That didn't exactly happen that way. But I quickly scaled back such effort because I needed to get off to a good start in academe—publish, publish, and publish, especially at a research university.

Driven to obtain tenure and promotion, I was determined to be productive as an emerging scholar in my field. Research and scholarship productivity are two key areas in the professional lives of faculty at research universities (Jarmon, 2001; Jean-Marie & Brooks, 2011). The proverbial "publish or perish" was a resounding message on my mind. Being at a research university, I felt an added pressure to excel in teaching, researching and scholarly writing. So, I focused my efforts to doing that and assumed I would have a balance life. After all, I was no longer in graduate school and had more flexibility with teaching two courses per semester. Why wouldn't I have a personal life? I chuckle thinking about this.

Life in academe was a rendition of survival. As the only Black female faculty in my college, department, and program area, I was acutely aware of the heightened exposure to scrutiny, performance pressure, potential bias in the assessment of performance and being viewed as a woman of color rather than as a professional (Alfred, 2001; Jean-Marie, 2009). These are what I call academic stressors. Several incidents during my first semester gave me insights on the challenges I would confront due to my race, gender, and age (Jarmon, 2001; Jean-Marie, 2011). I recalled one incident in my first semester in an instructional leadership class of 31 master level students. On the first night of class, one middle-aged, White male student who on several occasions in class referred to my colleagues as Dr. so and so stayed to talk to me after class ended. On our way to the parking lot, he turned and asked me, "Can I call you by your first name?" I did not respond to his question but instead said, "Have a good evening and I'll see you next week." On my 10-minute drive home, I reflected on his question and was curious as to why he felt it was appropriate to want to call me by first name but referred to my White male colleagues by Dr. so and so in class. Was this about race, gender, or age?

When I arrived home, I sent an e-mail to a mentor who was a former professor in my graduate program and taught classes on gender, politics, and ethics. In the subject line of my e-mail, I titled it, "What's in a name?" In short, I interrogated why this student might felt it appropriate to ask to call me by my first name. Under a different circumstance, I would be receptive to being called by my first name but this was different. The undertone of his question suggests that I did not merit the title, Dr. or Professor Jean-Marie. My disposition is to always address an issue directly so it doesn't fester because it was unaddressed. The following week, I returned to class and stated that since the common practice in our department is that students refer to my colleagues by their professional title (i.e., Professor X or Dr. X), the same applies to me.

In another incident that semester, the department secretary engaged in a conversation with me and another colleague about a particular matter. When she mentioned my colleague's and another person's name, she referred to them as Dr. so and so but when it came to me, it was Gaëtane. It was so noticeable that my colleague responded and said, "Well, Dr. Jean-Marie should have access to the online portal." It was another one of those moments that I pondered, "What was that about?" Over the years, I've encountered subtle practices that intended to undermine my credibility or challenge my authority in the classroom as a woman of color in academe. So, life in academe as an assistant professor made me more aware of racism and sexism. The steady stream of microaggressions just wears one down and I often reflected on my experiences.

In addition to working on fulfilling the tripartite expectations of teaching, research and service, I had a heightened sensitivity to incidences that related to my race and/or gender. I contended with questions such as, "Would I succeed in academe?" Would the academic environment be supportive? This consumed my pretenure life in academe. It was at the expense of having a meaningful personal or social life. My work was my life which created an imbalance that pulled me farther away from what I desired—a healthy balance of my professional and personal life.

CONCLUSION: LIFE LESSONS ON WHAT I KNOW FOR SURE

As I reflect on my life after obtaining tenure and promotion, I learned that old habits are hard to break or die. I still struggle with balancing my professional and personal life. As I approach my 40th birthday, I am going on a journey in pursuit of a more balanced and fulfilling life. In reflecting on this, I offer the following lessons. First, *self-preservation is important*. You can't be all things to all people. I am relearning to do what I love, be selective, and make time to play. Recently, I made an appointment for a body massage. My body was so tense that the massage therapist asked, "Did you just fall off a horse?" I'm taking heed to that and will find different outlets to destress (e.g., commitment to daily exercise, meditation, journaling, enjoying the simplicities of life such as gardening, walking the dogs, gourmet cooking etc.). Second, *develop and nurture support networks in and outside academe*. My networks became my lifeline at different times in my life. It may be a phone call to my sister, a friend, colleague to share good news or moments of frustration. In reciprocity, I reach out to new faculty at my institution and other universities to pay it forward. Third, *saying no is okay!* For a long time, I would agree to serve on a committee, participate in a project or avail myself to things that I really should not have said yes to. But, I wanted to help and be a team player. I'm practicing to say no and it has helped me to not over commit. Lastly, *celebrate life* because you are only here for a short time. Because my plate is always full, I don't spend enough time with family and friends, travel or entertain as I would like to do. I have started to add fun things on my calendar so I can "live life passionately, laugh until my belly hurts, and love unconditionally." While these lessons may not get a person tenure and promotion, I wished someone would have whispered them to me.

REFERENCES

Alfred, M. V. (2001). Success in the ivory tower: Lessons from Black tenured female faculty at a major research university. In R. O. Mabokela & A. L. Green (Eds), *Sisters of the academy: Emergent Black women scholars in higher education* (pp. 57-80). Sterling, VA: Stylus.

hooks, b. (1999). Embracing freedom: Spirituality and liberation. In S. Glazer (Ed.), *The heart of learning: Spirituality in education* (pp. 113-131). New York, NY: Penguin Putnam.

Jarmon, B. (2001). Unwritten rules of the game. In R. O. Mabokela & A. L. Green (Eds), *Sisters of the academy: Emergent Black women scholars in higher education* (pp. 175-181). Sterling, VA: Stylus.

Jean-Marie, G. (2009) "Fire in the belly": Igniting a social justice discourse in learning environments of leadership preparation. In A. Tooms & C. Boske (Eds.), *Educational leadership for social justice. Building bridges, connecting educational leadership and social justice to improve schools* (pp. 97-119). Charlotte, NC: Information Age.

Jean-Marie, G., & Brooks, J. (2011). Mentoring and supportive networks for women of color in academe. In G. Jean-Marie & B. Lloyd-Jones (Eds.), *Diversity in higher education: Vol. 10. Women of color in higher education: Contemporary Perspectives and new directions*. Bingley, United Kingdom: Emerald.

Myers, L. W. (2002). *A broken silence: Voices of African American women in the academy*. Westport, CT: Bergin & Garvey.

Seligman, M. E. P. (2002). *Authentic happiness: Using the new positive psychology to realize your potential for lasting fulfillment*. New York, NY: The Free Press.

Shanafelt, T. (2007). A career in surgical oncology: Finding meaning, balance and personal satisfaction. *Annals of Surgical Oncology, 15*(2), 400-4006.

Sirgy, M. J., & Wu, J. (2009). The pleasant life, the engaged life, and the meaningful life: What about the balanced life? *Journal of Happiness Studies, 10,* 183-196.

CHAPTER 32

A PERSPECTIVE OF WORK-LIFE BALANCE IN THE ACADEMY FROM A SINGLE MALE

Carlos R. McCray

TREPIDATION AND HESITATION

As a single male who became a college professor at the age of 29, the art of balancing life and work has been at times somewhat tumultuous. I make this statement with much respect to those who have a spouse and children. I must admit that I begrudgingly took on this writing assignment with a little trepidation and hesitation. The consternation or insecurity came from a place deep within side of me due to the fact that I have not earned the right to talk about the notion of work-life balance. In fact, as I vacillated back and forth on whether to proceed with this essay, I communicated with a close colleague as to "what the hell do I know about work-life balance." I confided with him that my concern was that I am single and do not have any children. Alas, his answer to my inquiry was not necessarily the response I was looking for to validate me taking on such a personal endeavor. In short, his answer was "yeah, I know … right" followed by "I am just kidding." I should point out that my colleague is married and has a toddler who is 3 years of age. When I juxtaposed my narrative against his with regard to work-life balance, it almost seems a

Juggling Flaming Chain Saws: Academics in Educational Leadership
Try to Balance Work and Family, pp. 261–269

262   C. R. McCRAY

foregone conclusion as to who has earned the right to undertake such a difficult writing assignment. Nevertheless, as I begin to deconstruct and problematize my journey as an academic for over the last 9 years, I soon realized that I too had a narrative to share.

Perhaps my story is not as compelling of a narrative as those narratives from scholars who have other responsibilities in their personal lives. Yet, I have hesitantly come to the conclusion that there is something captivating about my personal journey over the last 9 years. I will not be presumptuous in this essay as to propagate a form of certitude with regard to having a clear understanding of normalcy. But nevertheless, this is my journey within a profession that I am truly blessed to be a part of; this is my story with regard to work-life balance in the academy.

THE BEGINNING OF THE JOURNEY

My journey into the academy started when I finished my doctorate from Bowling Green State University in 2003. Upon finishing my doctorate from Bowling Green, I took a nontenured track position at a historically Black university in the South. I was 29 at the time when I decided to go teach in the department of educational leadership at this particular university. When I decided to take my first position as an instructor, I was determined to be a great teacher as well as a service oriented colleague. At this particular time, I did not have any aspirations concerning making an impact in the field with regard to scholarship. This particular disposition was mainly due to the fact that this university was regarded as a teaching institution—and a really good one I might add. Thus, all my time was entirely focused on preparing for my courses and engaging in departmental and collegewide service. As I engaged in these specific duties, the work-life balance for me was somewhat manageable. I was able to connect with family and friends as well perform the very important tasks that came with being an instructor/professor at the university level. However, I would soon begin to travel to conferences in order to stay informed of the latest research in the field and continue to cultivate meaningful relationships with colleagues from other institutions.

As I begin to travel to two specific meetings, the University Council of Education Administration and the American Educational Research Association, I begin to immerse myself in the latest research as well as make my own contribution to the knowledge base in the field. Thus, I begin to develop a line of research at a very early stage. Although my research agenda would eventually expand to include other areas of interest, it originally was centered on multicultural education and school- building-level research. Thus, from 2004 up until now, I have spent an enormous amount of time crafting my pedagogical techniques, engaging in service activities and conducting research.

TEACHING, RESEARCH, SERVICE, AND THE [WOULD BE] BALANCING ACT

When I received the call for papers on this topic and peeled back the essence of what the assignment should include, I have to admit that I did not see myself as a raconteur. I also wondered should I place such pressure on myself if I decided to take on the topic of work-life balance and what it means to me. As I once again vacillated, this time on how to proceed, I surreptitiously came to the conclusion that such pressure had undergirded my entire time in the academy; thus why should this endeavor be any different from the last 8 or so years. The essence of this essay is undergirded by the notion of what it means to engage in teaching, research and service at a cogent level and continue to enjoy a balanced life outside of the academy (i.e., a relationship with friends and family and an authentic sense of self).

Unequivocally, the role of a college professor is a challenging endeavor. I will not attempt to engage in pertinacious debate concerning where this line of work ranks with other professions in terms of impacting the balancing act of my work and my personal life. I can only elucidate on the time commitment required for this profession. And for the purpose of this essay, I would like to focus my attention on the balance that is needed to achieve success in a field that is truly rewarding on multiple levels.

As I mentioned briefly, being a college professor requires three particular skill sets. The three particular skill sets I am referring to are the skills of teaching, conducting research, and engaging in service. These aforementioned aspects of the profession are often times carried over into the sanctuary of the home from the office. As I continued to work at my first college position, I started to engage in more research endeavors along with the heavy teaching I was doing. Consequently, this required me to bring my students' papers home and make cogent comments that would inform their writing on future assignments. To this day, there are many times when I am up past midnight reading over my students' papers. And inevitably there are distractions that come my way and tempt me to take a break from grading (i.e., family members calling to say "what's up" or the urge to take a break and catch a football or basketball game). As all academics know, the art of giving strong feedback on students' assignments is not the only aspect of strong teaching. As an academic in my current position at Fordham University in New York, I find myself putting in enormous hours preparing for class. At Fordham University, I teach doctoral students, which is the highest level of teaching an academic can engage in at the university level. This level of teaching demands that I spend multiple hours preparing to engage students in theory as well as praxis. Most of our students who are seeking their degrees are in very high level educational leadership positions. Thus, when they come to us seeking their doctorate, they seek out theory as well as ways to put theory into practice. As an academic teaching at a university that places emphasis on teaching and research, it is an enormous challenge to provide my students with meaningful content each and every class and conduct research at a high level. As an academic who greatly cares about the quality of teaching my students are exposed to within the classroom, considerable time and effort are required to make classes worthwhile and meaningful. The corollary of such efforts is there is not always time for friends, family, and recreational outings that tend to be therapeutic and often brings a balance to the job and my personal life.

In addition to the vast amount of time required to ensure that authentic and responsible teaching is being delivered to my students, I also have to engage in heavy research due to the fact that I am at a research university. I conduct research for multiple reasons. First, as I just mentioned, producing research is crucial if I expect to be successful at this level. Each year I am evaluated on the amount of research I have produced. Second, I also believe that research and teaching are two of those skill sets that overlap. In many instances, my teaching informs my research and my research is connected to my teaching. Thus, in order for me to continue to become a better teacher, I thoroughly believe that I have to continue to become a better scholar and contribute to the field's knowledge base. This part of my profession also requires a considerable amount of time as well. Countless hours are spent in the library outside of "traditional work hours" researching and reading articles. I am hesitant to use the phrase "traditional work hours" here due to the fact that in this field I am not entirely sure as to what constitutes such hours. Nevertheless, the scholarly activity that is conducted in the library ultimately carries over into my personal space—the home. Countless hours have been spent writing articles, book chapters, as well as my coauthored book, *Cultural collision and Collusion: Reflections on Hip Hop Culture, Values, and Schools* in order to contribute to the knowledge base in the field and climb the latter of academic success.

But to add more pressure on my work-life balance as an academic, I have recently begun to think of another reason to engage in scholarship. This reason is similar to the premise of adding to the body of knowledge to the field but in many ways goes somewhat deeper. This other reason that I am referring to deals with the notion of a legacy I would like to leave in the academy. When I first started out researching and writing, I was mostly engaging in it because I enjoyed the endeavor. It was fulfilling to write with other colleagues from around the country and share your research with likeminded scholars at international, national, and regional conferences. I was also committed to this activity because it was a major requirement for academic success (i.e., tenure), which is one of the ultimate pinnacles for any academic. However, as I have gotten older and more established as a scholar, I have had these somewhat hair-raising concerns as to what type of legacy I will leave in the field of educational leadership. These concerns are undergirded by the thought process as to will I produce the type scholarship that I care about in order to have an impact in the field of educational leadership. Alas, this thought process has complicated work-life balance in more ways than one. The corollary of such a thought process is I am constantly thinking about the next article, chapter, or book dealing with my research interest. Thus, when I make it home from the "traditional office hours" at work, there is the strong desire to pick up a journal article or academic book to read or pull out my laptop and continue to write on the manuscript that I started on earlier in the office. This intensive focus on scholarship and teaching makes for a complicated work-life balance. However, there is one more skill set that is critically important to me as a college professor.

This other skill set that I am referring to involves the notion of service. As a new professor at Fordham University, it has been vital that I present myself as a team player while also balancing the other aspects of the job. Thus, I make myself available for a multitude of service opportunities in my own department as well as the college of education. Even though many academics might not rank the notion of service as high on the priority list as teaching and research, I feel that it is something all academics should aspire to be involved in at some level. Service opportunities at the department level consist of serving on curriculum and program review committees, helping out with National Council for Accreditation of Teacher Education reviews, and serving on interdisciplinary doctoral programs. Each one of these service opportunities are personally rewarding and help build collegiality with my colleagues. And there is also service to the field of educational leadership. Currently, I am serving on three journal editorial advisory boards as well as a reviewer for multiple major journals, where I review manuscripts that are in consideration for publication. I also work with our major governing bodies (i.e., American Educational Research Association and University Council of Education Administration) in various capacities. And certainly not least, I feel obligated to serve my surrounding community by being a guest speaker at certain events and taking up the task of mentoring individuals within the community. These are but a few of my service endeavors that I engage in at any given time.

Without a doubt, the conflation of teaching, research, and service at a high level complicates the work-life balance that all academics try to attain. Nevertheless, a balance must be achieved for my own personal sanity. When I think of what it takes to achieve this delicate balance, I often think of the venerable Dr. John Hope Franklin who insisted on not giving his entire self to his field. As a prolific historian, Dr. Franklin found many avenues and outlets to achieve his work-life balance. One of those outlets consisted of working in his prized garden. Dr. Franklin often talked about his love to work in his garden in order to achieve a therapeutic outlet away from his prolific teaching and writing. I remember reading this aspect about his life some time ago. Alas, I can't say that it had an immediate impact on me as a junior faculty member as I read his story. At the time I was determined to work as many hours as it took to achieve my goals. I remember thinking that I could take up a therapeutic outlet once I had achieved a fraction of what Dr. Franklin had achieved in his lifetime.

Throughout my journey as a college professor, I have begun to understand that an academic such as Dr. Franklin does not make the mark on his or her field by waiting later in life to attain a work-life balance. In essence, it is actually the opposite; I believe prolific people in the field are able to become prolific by achieving a work-life balance as early as possible in their young careers. As I look back on my relatively few years in the field, I am somewhat disappointed that I was not more diligent in pursuing the work-life balance that so many of my colleagues have managed to attain. In the past, I perceived that a good work-life balance consisted of catching up on all my work though the week and freeing up my time on the weekend to catch multiple college and professional football games. Even though I found this somewhat therapeutic; I have come to the realization that there isn't much substance that undergirds this style of work-life balance. In the meantime, a majority of my friends and family members are off to exotic vacations and preparing for nuptials and the idea of raising a family. As I now reflect back on Dr. Franklin, I realize that gardening was one of many outlets he probably had in order to bring stability to his life. And as I also reflect on the light-hearted conversation that I had with my good friend and colleague concerning what do I as a single male know about achieving a clear and thorough work-life balance, I have come to the realization that I have learned much over the years. Now it is just a matter of putting what I have learned into practice.

Thus, here is what I have learned over the years from being in the academy. First, the work never stops. When an academic has provided a plethora of research and writing to his or her field and has secured enough publications for tenure, there is something inside the academic that keeps calling his or her name—something that motivates the academic to not only have an impact on his or her field, but to also leave behind some type of legacy. The same is true for teaching and service as well. It has always been my goal to provide the best teaching and service possible to my department. Thus, I have come to the realization that the work in the academy is not a fast pace sprint to see who can get to the finish line first. At the end of the day, the work of an academic reminds me of a marathon—where those who are most successful have purposefully chosen to conserve some of their energy in order to go the distance. In order to truly have an impact in teaching, research, and service, one has to have a work-life balance.

I started this essay off by proving some personal details about my life—that I am a "relatively" young African American male professor who is single. I can remember some time ago perceiving that the ultimate goal in my life was to obtain a doctorate by a certain age and then proceed with ascertaining tenure at a major university. Embedded in this goal was also the aspiration of becoming known in the field and to make a difference in the issues I was passionate about pertaining to education and educational leadership. Along the way I told myself that I would make time for family and friends and perhaps find a wonderful woman who was compatible with my ideals, goals, and aspirations. But there was always another article to write or another class to teach as well as some service to be done. As I think back to my undergraduate days in college, I distinctly remember coming across professors who seem to have immersed themselves completely in their work. You could see in their eyes that they were somewhat exasperated from all of the writing, teaching, grading papers, and service activities. Although I completely had the utmost respect for them, I told myself that if I were to go into this profession, I would definitely have a more balanced approach to life. Now, it seems as if I am on the verge of becoming an inductee into the nonbalance academic club.

As I vacillated back and forth as to whether to write this essay, I came to the conclusion that if I chose to write this essay I had to be completely honest concerning my work-life balance. The truth is that I have probably not been as balanced as I would have hoped for a little over a decade ago when I started out working on my doctorate. As I have matriculated through my career, I have heard individuals from other professions communicate how they decided to change jobs because their previous jobs were just too demanding. I have known a few attorneys who started out working for corporate law firms who walked away from enormous salaries because they were working at the office long into the night. They ultimately decided to continue to practice law but in venues other than corporate law. This is a luxury that I simply do not have as a college professor. People often ask me if I feel as if I am in my dream job. And I tell them with pride that I feel I am doing what God placed me on this earth to do. Even though this profession is truly demanding, it is unacceptable for me to even consider being in another profession or line of work. Thus, I have come to the conclusion that in order for me to become as productive as possible in this line of work that I cherish so much, I have to become committed in balancing my professional and personal life.

LESSONS FROM OVER THE YEARS

The following are some my ideas and thoughts that I have learned throughout the years with regard to having a balance of work and a personal life. First, I have learned that it is somewhat problematic for me to be successful in any endeavor without a healthy dose of family and friends embedded in my life. I have learned throughout the years that I have an affinity for relationships. I am truly at my best when I have authentic interaction with family and friends. I left a host of family and friends behind at my last place of employment in Atlanta, GA. Since moving to New York City, I have had to make new friends, which is not that difficult for me. Nevertheless, I did come to the realization that I might have taken relationships left behind for granted—assuming that they would always be there. As of yet, I have not had the pleasure of exchanging marriage vows with a wonderful bride. Thus, I find that keeping in touch with my family (i.e., mother and father, aunts and uncles, and many cousins) as well as my friends help me to stay grounded and is the most therapeutic outlet I have as of now.

Finally, in keeping with the advice from the late Dr. John Hope Franklin, I also truly believe that it is somewhat critical to have other outlets such as the one he so often identified with—his gardening activities. I can remember growing up in Alabama and watching my paternal and maternal grandparents work in their gardens. I now see why Dr. John Franklin found so much joy in this activity. Even as a child I thought to myself "wow, this seems like such a wonderful activity." Even though I have not had the opportunity to take up gardening as of yet, it is critically important that I continue activities that allows me to escape the teaching, research, and services aspects of the job. As of now, I have found that escaping into sports related activities is what works for me—whether I am watching or playing. I cannot deny that I am an avid sports fan. I love football, basketball, baseball, soccer, hockey, and even NASCAR racing. But I must admit that even when I sit down to watch a sporting event, I find myself thinking about the next article or book chapter that needs to be written. I am almost certain that when Dr. Franklin worked in his garden, his mind was not preoccupied with the work of the academy. Nevertheless, this brings me to my next point. Perhaps the reason I am still thinking of work is due to the fact that I need to find more substantive activities in order for me to truly balance my work and personal life.

In the summer of 2010, I took a trip to Miami and Key West Florida for a vacation. I learned from a mentor that AERA and UCEA conference trips were nothing close to a real vacation and shame on me for thinking such. Consequently, I took her advice and traveled to the Keys with a close friend. Thus, I told myself that I would make it a priority to take a trip somewhere each summer in order to improve my work-life balance. But at the end of the day I know there is something more enjoyable than keeping in touch with my friends, watching my favorite sport teams, and taking a vacation to an exotic place. This type of substance and joy is derived from starting my own family. Thus, I am just hopeful that when the time arrives, I will have truly mastered the art of balancing my work and personal life like so many other scholars I have had the pleasure of knowing.

CHAPTER 33

MILITELLO & SONS, INC.

A Family Business

Matthew Militello and Dominic Militello

We are told to stay balanced. Work, family, health, spirituality, and so on. However, balance is difficult to attain. James March (1999a) poignantly stated, "Balance is a nice word, but a cruel concept" (p. 5). Given all the hyperbole associated with balanced lifestyles, living balance is a murky and complex production.

Our professional and personal selves become blurred at a very young age. We are taught balance early in adolescence, but our professional (work and/or school) expectations soon supersede and subsume our lives. This instability is formally and informally learned. That is to say, the pressures that surround us—family, media, peers, government, mentors—all preach diversity and balance of knowledge, skills, and experience; However, there are clear and present forces of competition and attainment that create instability. In Table 33.1 we highlight a list of counterforces we brainstormed together.

These countervailing forces begin in child rearing into adolescence and continue through adulthood. Throughout life we face multiple pressures, often competing and confusing. For instance, schools are to teach democratic principles, yet the relationships in schools and the school handbooks that drive policy are wholly undemocratic. Outside of schools

Juggling Flaming Chain Saws: Academics in Educational Leadership Try to Balance Work and Family, pp. 271–279

Table 33.1. Anchors of Disequilibrium

Countervailing Forces	
Fun	Serious
Play	Competitive sports
Learning	Schooling
Independence	Obedience
Democracy	Dictatorships
Individualism	Assimilation
Equality	Marginalization
Humility	Hubris
Risk	Security
Process	Outcome
Interests	Obligations
Originality	Conformity

social forces (e.g., media and peers) continue to compete with our mores pressing us for what we ought to do and be. Moreover, economic forces paint a bleak future for those not taking responsibility and becoming college "ready." These forces create confusion and disharmony. As a school administrator I recall a teacher-student meeting where the teacher told the student, "Wait until you are in the real world." The student replied, "My world is right now. It does not get more real than that!" I could hardly contain a smirk.

Wrestling with balance is also played out in how people and organizations make decisions. Binary opposition theory, promulgated by philosophers such as Jacques Derrida, stipulates that we tend to embark in dichotomous thinking. This polemic thinking can have isolating effects (e.g., ignorant thinking) and at worst it can become routinized marginalization (e.g., institutional racism). Table 33.2 highlights a number of theorists' depiction of these false dichotomies. This table illustrates how the pressures we identified in the previous table can become institutionalized in our society.

Both tables above mark the bipolar world we exist in. We submit that these extremes have promulgated a way of life centered on pure craft-

Table 33.2. Balance Dichotomies From a Theoretical Perspective

Binary Systems		Theorist
Lifeworld	Systemsworld	Habermas (1984)
Exploitation	Exploration	March (1999b)
Discovery	Enactment	Daft and Weick (1984)
Command	Commit	Rowan (1990)

based productivity for efficiency. This chapter does seek balance between the extremes, but rather strategies to intertwine them. We do so by providing perspectives from a midcareer professional and a high school student. Throughout the chapter we incorporate both our collective voice for context and our individual perspectives for content. We also attempt to make a clear and compelling case for going beyond balance. That is, we offer a new model—one that moves away from the hyperbole of balance and toward a model of inclusion and integration.

A FAMILY BUSINESS

The term "PK" is a term for people who were raised in households where a preacher was the patriarch or matriarch—the PK acronym refers to a *Preachers Kid*. We are both "EKs," *Educators Kids*. Both of us have been raised in an environment with professional educators. Being an EK brings with it privilege. The most striking privilege is the commonality of language and experience. While many father and sons share the experience of *schooling*—knowing how and why schools function allows for a more advanced dialogue when it comes to the broad term *schooling*. Figure 33.1 illustrates how we are each surrounded by professional educators (parents, in-laws, and kids).

DOMINIC AND ME

We would like to provide three specific examples of how we have infused family and work. We are writing together for two reasons. First, we have had the most experiences binding work and family together. Additionally, we are currently involved in project where we are working collaboratively. Second, Luke (second oldest son) has previously worked on an article about the pressures of school assessments (see, Militello & Militello, In Press). We offer three examples of our work together: Educator Needs Assessment in China, School Leadership Development in Northeast North Carolina, and National Community Learning Exchanges.

Educator Needs Assessment in China

In 2006 we traveled to China for 16 days. The trip was funded by the University of Massachusetts at Amherst and their partner Shaanxi Normal University in Xi'an, People's Republic of China. The grant focused on

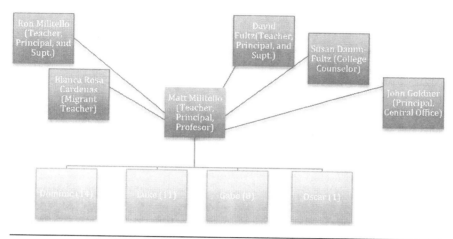

Dominic's Perspective	Matt's Perspective
I am used to going to work with my dad. I remember going to numerous school functions from sitting in boring meetings to going into the locker room after a high school basketball game. Funny how I knew my dad as a principal and now as a professor—I was too little to remember him as a middle school teacher. But I have been to a few of his classes at NC State. They were boring, but the students seemed to like him. My dad is not the only educator. All my grandparents were as well. They ask me lots of questions about school—And, because they "know" schooling I can't get away with anything!	My dad was my high school principal. Do I need to say more? Thank goodness for my brother who was a grade ahead—he got in trouble a lot. By the time I got my drivers license I knew it was not a good idea to take the family car out of the faculty lot for lunch. Dad missed a few central office meetings from that—made for interesting dinner conversation. My dad brought me to school all the time. I begged him to take me to varsity football games and to take me into the locker room at halftime. He also took us to conferences with him. I remember driving from the Upper Peninsula of Michigan to New Orleans to a National Association of Secondary School Principals conference. A conference I would later attend and present at! I also remember visiting migrant farms in northern Wisconsin where my mom taught English. While she does not possess a high school diploma, she was a professional educator.

Figure 33.1.   The Militello education profession family tree.

developing a needs assessment of educators in basic and higher education in five northwestern provinces (Shaanxi, Xinjiang, Gansu, Qinghai, and Ningxia). We spend time together in Beijing and then apart while the research was conducted. We met up again in Xi'an.

Dominic's Perspective	*Matt's Perspective*

China was my first introduction to the work that my dad does as a professor. At first I thought that it was just going to be a vacation—just getting away and having an experience out of the county. But I was wrong. This trip ended up being one of the best learning experiences and one of the most inspiring things that I have ever done. The amazing thing is that I was only in fourth grade.

There was a lot to remember—climbing the Great Wall of China, seeing the Terracotta Warriors in Xian, and visiting the Leshan's Giant Buddha in Chengdu, but I remember most was the first morning in Beijing. We woke up at 4 A.M. because we were messed up from the 12-hour time change. My dad needed coffee so we walked the streets neat Beijing Normal University on a search. Coffee is hard to find in China! We finally found a McDonald's and we sat down and talked about what we had seen. I admit I was a bit afraid of being in a new place so far away from home. I can see now that this experience created a sense of adventure in me—always wanting to do new and different things.

When Joe Berger and I began this work I never thought of the possibility of bringing family members to China. We knew that our first trip would be at least 3-weeks long. Joe told me how he took his wife and three kids to rural Africa while he conducted research. He pushed me to think about taking Dominic. It helped that Joe's family was going and they would stay together in Chengdu with members of Joe's sister-in-law's family who were Chinese. Nonetheless, this was a difficult decision for my wife and I to make. Take our 9-year old 12,000 miles away from home for 3 weeks—not even with his family for half of that time. We took a risk and asked Dominic if he was interested. Without hesitation he said, "Of course, I'm in!"

I was so proud of Dominic's ability to be so independent at such a young age. At one point we flew from Beijing to Chengdu. We were meeting Joe's family at the airport. I would then fly on to Western China to conduct interviews. Dominic got sick on the plane and I had a hard time leaving him at the terminal and jumping on another plane. It was Dominic who relieved my fear—he said, "go on Dad, I'll be all right." Indeed son!

Photo by Xiao Zhou (2006).

Figure 33.2.   Dominic and Matt in Tiananmen Square, Beijing, China.

Dominic's Perspective	*Matt's Perspective*

NELA is moving a step up from my China experience. This is because I am now not only observing what is going on but also taking an active role—I have been taking videos for each of the gatherings. I am now working on creating two videos that document the NELA Fellows' experiences. At the Fellows' orientation I set up all of the technology including Smartboards and video editing stations. I felt really good that so many of the Fellows—who are current teachers—asked me to help them make videos. I am used to the teachers helping me!

In August 2010 I had the opportunity to meet the North Carolina Governor, Bev Perdue. She invited the NELA Fellows (and me) to visit the Governor's Mansion after graduation in May, 2012—I can't wait!

Dominic has been hanging around our NELA project since the orientation for Cohort I. But the most powerful moment came this year when Dominic, my father, and my father-in-law were all helping us run the Cohort II Candidate Assessment Day. The Assessment Day took 33 candidates through a number of scenario-based activities. Each activity was assessed by an evaluation team consisting of high school students, teachers, professors, and school administrators. My dad, who recently moved to Raleigh, and my father-in-law, who was passing through town, were members of evaluation teams. During the introduction to the day I told the candidates that "there are three generations of Militello's here … we believe in learning from elders and from youth… we want candidates with the same dispositional qualities." This was a powerful moment for me professionally.

Photo by Matt Militello (2010).

Figure 33.3.   Dominic with Governor Bev Perdue.

School Leadership Development in Northeast North Carolina

Both of us are involved in a Race to the Top funded grant ($7 million) aimed at developing school leaders called the Northeast Leadership Academy. The grant will train three cohorts of leaders in a high-poverty, underperforming schools of North Carolina (2011-2014). The first cohort just completed year one and we recently hosted an intense Candidate Assessment Day for Cohort II.

National Community Leadership Exchange

The Community Learning Exchange (CLE) is designed to help vulnerable communities build their local capacity to address equity issues and improve lives. The CLE is an outgrowth of the Kellogg Foundation's Leadership for Community Change initiative (2002-2009), a leadership development and capacity building endeavor which brought new people into leadership roles while crossing boundaries of race, culture, age, gender, etc. The original national evaluation team included a youth evaluator. This apprenticeship model proved extremely valuable to the project. As such, the inclusion of youth evaluators to the CLE Evaluation Team was a given. We were honored to have included two youth to our team: Emiliano Guajardo (college student) and Dominic (high school student).

CONCLUSION: A NEW MODEL

James March was right about the cruel concept we perpetuate called balance. March often taught courses using such divergent books as Cervantes' *Don Quixote* and Tolstoy's *War and Peace*. The former is a comic treatment of the need for play and folly while the later depicts the stringent aspects of high culture and military life.

Life exists not at the poles of play and folly or exacting science. Rather we think that work and family should be infused, integrated, merged,

Table 33.3.   Link's to Videos Created by Dominic

Youth Summit CLE, Washington, DC, February 2011	http://www.communitylearningexchange.org/ group /dcyouthsummit
CLE, Seattle, WA, May 2011	http://www.communitylearningexchange.org/ group /seattlecle/forum/topics/dateline-seattle-feedback

Dominic's Perspective	*Matt's Perspective*

In China I learned what my dad did. With NELA I started to participate. In the CLE, I am a full participant and member of the evaluation team. This experience has allowed me to take and make digital stories based on questions and interviews that I help conduct. I also have lots of experiences talking in from of groups. If you are interested in seeing a few of the videos I made go to the links below.

It is also very fun working with friends, not just coworkers. For example the person I work very closely with is Emiliano Guajardo. Emiliano is a college student and also a member of the evaluation team. We have come to be very good friends. Together we work side by side with adults and are able to combine our thoughts—using adult and youth perspectives. I am happy that the adults respect what youth like me have to say and do. At the Youth Summit in Washington, DC, many of us had the chance to ask Secretary of Education Duncan questions. Many of those questions were not fully answered by him. The youth voice is important and should not be ignored. A lot of adults I know don't like to going on business trips, especially my mom. Mostly because they don't want to be away from their families. But now my dad is not, if anything he is excited. The reason for this is that he is now taking part of his family with him. My dad and I have always had a very close relationship and if anything these has made it even closer and stronger.

I have been involved with KLCC and CLE from the beginning. I was a graduate assistant on the project while at Michigan State University (2002-2004), a project consultant (2005-2009), and now the national evaluator (along with Dr. Chris Janson) for the CLE (2010-2014). Throughout the project we have always honored intergenerational learning. Now this includes my own son. There are three CLE's each year. Dominic and I will have the opportunity to travel the country working with vulnerable populations. I cannot think of a better life lesson.

* * *

By this time the reader must be asking (1) why do I do this and (2) how did I convince everyone to take such risks? One of the best life lessons I learned was from Dr. Rick Price at the University of Michigan. He was one of the lead evaluators on a Kellogg grant that I was involved with as a graduate assistant. He told me on one of our numerous trips about some advice he received while he was a GA and had a young family. I recall him encouraging me to take my kids with me when I did my work. More specifically, he advised me to take only one of the kids with me. He said that his grown kids today do not have fond memories of family trips, but warmly reminisce about trips with individual parents. Such sage advice from a social psychologist must be worthy! Although there was not a lot of convincing to be done—only explaining to others unfamiliar with our family.

Photo by Miguel Guajardo (2011).

Figure 33.4.   Kellogg CLE Evaluation Team.

united—in short, one. Moreover, the field of education affords us with this opportunity. While many professions do not lend themselves to such infusion, in the education profession we have a unique confluence of organizational ability and the technical core of what we do—improve teaching and learning. These affordances lend themselves to access the youth voice in meaningful ways.

We enjoy the charms of home at home and work at work. Yet we must constantly toggle between them. Our desire to taste the delights of work and family should not be relegated by time and space—these are merely artificial barriers. We found the time and space to move beyond balance and toward working side by side—shattering the myth of time. In the end, we learned from one another. We learned about the content of what we were writing about. More importantly we opened new portals of context—learning about one another.

Time and space are excuses and balance a utopian end. The real heart of a new reality of work and life resides in the real engagement with one another. A lesson we learned long ago, a lesson that will continue with a father and his sons.

REFERENCES

Daft, R. L., & Weick, K. E. (1984). Toward a model of organizations as interpretive systems. *The Academy of Management Review, 9*(2), 284-295.

Habermas, J. (1984). The theory of communicative action (T. McCarthy, Trans., Vol. 2). Boston, MA: Beacon Press.

March, J. G. (Ed.). (1999a). Introduction. In *The pursuit of organizational intelligence* (pp. 1-10). Malden, MA: Blackwell.

March, J. G. (Ed.). (1999b). Exploration and exploitation in organizational learning. In *The pursuit of organizational intelligence* (pp. 114-136). Malden, MA: Blackwell.

Militello, M., & Militello, L. (in press). Fear and loathing in elementary school: Lessons about better assessments from a third grader. *Educational Forum.*

Rowan, B. (1990). Commitment and control: Alternative strategies for the organizational design of schools. In C. B. Cazden (Ed.), *Review of research in education* (Vol. 16, pp. 353-389). Washington, DC: American Educational Research Association.

CHAPTER 34

NAVIGATING A WORK-LIFE BALANCE IN THE ERA OF HIGH-STAKES ACCOUNTABILITY

Stacey A. Rutledge

If asked why we have chosen our line of work, I believe the vast majority of educational researchers would identify two fundamental reasons for pursuing the occupation. First, we care deeply about helping to improve educational opportunities and experiences for all students. Second, we are fascinated by students, classrooms, schools, and the system in which they are embedded. Certainly in my experiences as both a middle and high school teacher and researcher, I understand education to be a source of social improvement and I am motivated by a curiosity about the infrastructure of schools and schooling. While issues of subjectivity exist for all researchers, in the field of education we all experience a version of Lortie's (1975) apprenticeship of observation. Because we have all been students in schools and many of us have worked in the K-12 system, we enter with preconceived ideas about how schools and classrooms work. In my graduate program, professors taught us to be wary of these prior beliefs and motivations, warning that our efforts to improve the system would color our objectivity as researchers. In methods courses, we learned

Juggling Flaming Chain Saws: Academics in Educational Leadership
Try to Balance Work and Family, pp. 281–287
Copyright © 2012 by Information Age Publishing

techniques that would help us identify our biases and help us acknowledge how our preconceived opinions, ideas, and values shape our research. As a qualitative researcher, I employ these strategies to identify and address biases. Given my attention to these issues, it was particularly unsettling to have a new subjective dimension emerge, namely, my role as parent.

I am married to a historian and we have two children. In terms of work-life balance, being married to a fellow academic has distinct advantages. We both have very flexible schedules and we are committed to supporting one another as we overcome academia's many hurdles. We have negotiated a particular work-life balance that has included single-parent weekends as one of us (usually me) has toiled at a computer. We have also had our lines-in-the-sand moments when one of us (usually him) cannot take another second of carpooling. It works most of the time.

In my research, I have focused largely on understanding test-based accountability and its effect on the work of administrators, teachers and, by extension, students. I have been particularly interested in how school administrators and teachers make sense of curricular and instructional standards and the related high-stakes standardized assessments and how implementation is shaped and shaping their knowledge, beliefs, and experiences. As a policy researcher who draws on sociological frames, I draw on research and theories that highlight social stratification, tracking, inequality, and equity. This research finds that schools stratify children from the moment they enter school, within classrooms (Barr & Dreeben, 1983; Gamoran & Nystrand, 1994), within schools (Nye, Konstantopoulos, & Hedges, 2004; Oakes, 1985) and between schools (Clotfelter, 2004). This, in turn, shapes students' educational opportunities and academic attainment with low-income and minority children disproportionately negatively affected by this stratification.

We live in Florida, the state with arguably the most intense version of test-based accountability at the moment. In the last 12 years, state and federal policies have been passed that grade schools on student performance as measured by the state standardized test (the Florida Comprehensive Achievement Test or FCAT), tie teacher merit to test scores, and, of course, measure schools based on their Adequate Yearly Progress. Given my beliefs about education, I wanted my children to have a public school education and I was not overly concerned about the testing environment. I knew that test-based accountability was different, but I also thought, teachers have always taught to tests; how different would this be? Our neighborhood school is multiracial and represents almost a perfect U-curve on the FCAT. The school has a strong academic and artistic reputation and serves a spectrum of students from different socioeconomic backgrounds, from those on free and reduced lunch to children of professionals. It fit my own worldview that my children should go to a school that mirrored a version of the general population.

The first major disruption of my particular work-life balance occurred with my oldest child's first-grade teacher, a young and organized teacher with 2 years prior experience (which of course is consistently found in the research to be less then optimal; more on this later). The historian and I went to the first parent-teacher meeting fully expecting to hear about our enthusiastic and bubbly 6-year-old. We sat in the tiny chairs facing the teacher. With her gradebook open as a reference, she began the conference by saying, "Well, your daughter started first grade knowing 72 sight words, she now knows 95 with a gain of 23 words. My class average is 34." The first thought to come to mind was that my daughter was bringing down the average.

I should say here that I have interviewed administrators and teachers from approximately 40 schools in two states about test-based accountability. I have found that administrators and teachers will tell you that standardized tests are but a snapshot of a child's ability and then, within the same minute, describe students in terms of their standardized test scores. In Florida, students receive a 1 to 5 score on the FCAT with 5 being the highest. This practice of referring to "the ones and twos," the "threes," and "the fours and fives" has always struck me as interesting. On the one hand, the teachers report that they do not put too much credence on a test students' take for 5 hours of their school year; on the other, they are classifying and referring to their students by their test scores.

As I listened to the teacher talk about my daughter's sight words, I felt a concern I had not experienced up to that point, namely, that my child was being reduced to a numeric indicator. I had been expecting the perhaps now clichéd "Your child is a pleasure to have in class, but" that I remember from my own report cards, a version of which was taught in my own teacher-education classes where we were told to always start with something positive when talking to a parent. The teacher continued by going through her progress monitoring binder and informing us of our daughter's scores on assessments such as reading fluency and standards-aligned math. Not once did she comment on the socioemotional development of the child or, identify her strengths. It was all extremely "professional."

Three years later, I experienced a version of this with our son, this time more informally. Seven weeks into the school year, I was volunteering at the school and asked his first grade teacher, "How is he doing?" I fully expected a short summary of his adjustment to first grade. His teacher, an enthusiastic woman who had also come of age in the era of test-based accountability said, "Let me see." She went to her computer and pulled up a university-based website on her electronic Smartboard.

Within 30 seconds she had accessed the scores of his reading assessment on the 3 by 5 foot screen. She proudly announced, "Well, this program says that he has an 80% chance of meeting the first grade benchmarks."

When I am in researcher mode and a teacher or administrator reveals a particular worldview—in this case a quantitative, assessment-based explanation of a child's achievement—I feel the thrill of having that telling quote or example that exemplifies how that person is making sense of their occupational demands. As a parent, I feel confused. I had not been concerned about the sight word acquisition of my curious and creative daughter nor had I been worried that my loquacious and inquisitive son would fail to meet the first grade benchmarks. Why were they being reduced to a percentage? Should my daughter have known more sight words by October 2nd? What did the 20% chance my son would fail to meet the benchmarks mean? I am a highly educated mother who is in the field of education and I was confused. If I am confused, how about the 20-something single mom who is working her way through nursing school? How does she make sense of this kind of information?

In my daughter's first 4 years of elementary school, I volunteered weekly for an hour and a half in the classroom. I was working toward tenure and did not participate in the School Advisory Council or the PTA. While I was introduced to the principal and the assistant principal, I was quickly forgotten. My husband and I had no real reason to go to the administration and we were not concerned. Our child was doing fine. I was steeped in the research on middle-class White privilege (Brantlinger, 2003; Lareau, 2000, 2003; Lee, 2002) and did not want to exert any undue power or influence. At the same time, however, I was teaching courses in my university's educational leadership program and I noticed that the administrators did not remember me or my children. When our daughter was tracked in first and third grade math because of her math scores (and put in classrooms with students scoring similarly to her), I did not complain, even though I knew of studies that showed that if a child was not in the top group, they were exposed to less subject matter content. I was satisfied with her academic and social progress. These seemed like reflections of the larger testing culture that, I assumed, she would navigate.

At the end of third grade, my daughter took the FCAT. While there was some decontextualized test preparation, it largely occurred in the 2 weeks prior to the test. My daughter reported feeling fine during testing, however, 2 weeks afterwards she came home with an "FCAT Journal" in which she had recorded the anxiety she had felt during testing. She had written, "At first when I got the test, I couldn't stop shaking, but then I started working and it was ok," complete with a drawing of her trembling at her desk. This was all news to me. When her scores came out in June, we were alarmed at the discrepancy between her grades and the test scores. Informed by my experiences as a researcher, I began to take a much more active role in navigating the testing world of my children. In the 2 years since receiving those scores, I now make a summer appointment with the principal to discuss their annual progress. I advocate for their math group placement commensurate with grade performance, not just standardized test scores. I find myself fighting the contradictory world of "the test is just a snapshot" and "my fours and fives." While I have never been a parent in another policy environment, I am mobilized by the testing environment to be more assertive for my children.

All the while, I agonize over this new role. In particular, I now feel that I have to navigate a new dimension in the area of research objectivity. I had always been highly conscious of the encroachment of objectivity by the focus in the field on educational improvement. This strikes me as a particular work-life balance issue related to the field. As researchers, we are versed in the findings and debates in the field. We know the optimal number of years of experience for a teacher, the successes of different kinds of interventions used in the classroom. We debate the benefits of different class sizes and critique educational leadership practices. Put differently, we bring our knowledge base to our perceptions and interactions with administrators and teachers. We also bring those experiences to our research.

Nowhere has this been clearer to me than with this case of standardized assessments and their related scores. In the field, we are well aware of the myriad of problems related to standardized testing. We know the difference between criterion and norm-referenced tests and the measurement issues related to them. We are taught in graduate school that it is unfair to test children on material they were not taught, that tests are but one measure of student achievement, and that they need to be free of socioeconomic, racial, ethnic or gender bias. We know that there are validity criteria to gauge the quality of different assessments (Herman & Baker, 2009). Yet still, the large quantitative study that shows causal link between a policy, program, or intervention and student test score gains is the gold standard in the field. We are caught in a paradox where we know that the assessments that we need in order to make large-scale causal claims have important limitations. Children are not numbers, yet it is also useful to reduce them to numbers. Further, we are living in a moment in which testing and standardized assessments are only becoming more pervasive. Given increased technological capacity, a system enamored with the promises of rationalizing education through data-driven decision making, and a policy environment satisfied by the numeric evaluation of schools, this system is only growing and intensifying.

Which brings me back to the work-life balance question. I did not expect that being a parent to school aged children would encroach on my work world. I realize that this was naïve. Given that my children will be in primary and secondary school for 18 years, how could being a parent not affect my work-life? While, of course, I will employ my research skills to remain as objective as possible in my own research, it is interesting to see the creep of my children's experiences at school challenge earlier assumptions and conclusions about standards and assessment policies. As researchers in all contexts, we need to be aware of threats to objectivity. They can come from many sources as age and experience shape our worldviews. Yet, with something as deeply personal as children, I find that becomes yet another element to attempt to leave at the door.

My older child enters middle school next year. The 2011-12 FCAT scores aren't in, but I am bracing myself for the "grades versus test score" tension as computers are increasingly using test scores to determine course placement. She will attend a magnet school that resides within our neighborhood school. I am intent on being supportive of administration and faculty as well as an advocate both for her and for all students. I recently went to talk to one of the administrators. As part of the conversation, I raised the topic of my daughter's writing skills. "So how did she do on the writing assessment?" the administrator interrupted and she began typing on her computer. Soon, my daughter's fourth grade class photo appeared on the left hand corner of her screen. The administrator said, "Cute picture!" as she scanned for my daughter's scores. Indeed, there was my daughter, grinning away.

REFERENCES

Barr, R., & Dreeben, R. (1983). *How schools work*. Chicago, IL: University of Chicago Press.

Brantlinger, E. (2003). *Dividing classes: How the middle class negotiates and rationalizes school advantage*. New York, NY: Routledge Falmer.

Clotfelter, C. T. (2004). *After Brown: The rise and retreat of school desegregation*. Princeton, NJ: Princeton University Press.

Gamoran, A., & Nystrand, M. (1994). Tracking, instruction, and achievement. *International Journal of Educational Research, 21*, 217-231.

Herman, J. L., & Baker, E. L. (2009). Assessment policy: Making sense of Babel. In G. Sykes, B. Schneider, & D. N. Plank (Eds.) *Handbook of education policy research* (pp. 176-190). New York, NY: Routledge.

Lareau, A. (2000). *Home advantage: Social class and parental intervention in elementary education*. Lanham, MD: Rowman and Littlefield.

Lareau, A. (2003). *Unequal childhoods: Class, race, and family life*. Berkeley, CA: University of California Press.

Lee, J. (2002). Racial and ethnic achievement gap trends: Reversing the progress toward equity. *Educational Researcher, 31*(1), 3-12.

Lortie, D. C. (1975). *Schoolteacher.* Chicago, IL: University of Chicago Press.

Nye, B., Konstantopoulos, S., & Hedges, L. (2004). How large are teacher effects? *Educational Evaluation and Policy Analysis, 26,* 237-257.

Oakes, J. (1985). *Keeping track.* New Haven, CT: Yale University Press.

PART III

SENIOR SCHOLARS

CHAPTER 35

THROWN OUT OF BALANCE TO FIND TRUE BALANCE ...

Kathleen M. Brown

"Before" adopting two small children with special needs as a single, middle-aged woman, my life seemed in balance. I worked hard, played hard, and slept well! I published versus perished, was promoted versus demoted, and succeeded versus failed. I fulfilled my personal and professional obligations, met internally and externally imposed deadlines, and avoided interruptions and chaos at all costs. As a Type A, anal retentive, self-diagnosed "obsessive compulsive" personality, I remained in control versus out of control at all times. In essence, I "thought" I was living a rather healthy, well-adjusted life. And, from all external appearances, it appeared that way as well! In hindsight (and on a much deeper, personal level), I was actually living a warped sense of balance.

STORY I: TENURE, PROMOTION, AND FAUX BALANCE

Life is good! After years as a 24/7 middle school principal, the life of a tenure-track assistant professor is a piece of chocolate cake! New game, new rules—but time, flexibility, and freedom are pure gifts. Rekindle the drive while recharging the discipline and tenure and promotion are within sight. That's the goal, right? Reach for the golden ring? Or reach for the sky? It all depends on how each is viewed and defined.

Juggling Flaming Chain Saws: Academics in Educational Leadership Try to Balance Work and Family, pp. 291–295
Copyright © 2012 by Information Age Publishing
All rights of reproduction in any form reserved.

For the first 10-plus years of the professorate, I thought I was living a rather balanced life. I taught my classes, wrote my papers, and presented my research. I advised my students, supported my colleagues, and served my field. I reviewed articles, submitted proposals, and attended committee meetings, conference proceedings, and district hearings. I took to heart my 40/40/20 contract of research, teaching, and service and tried to be the best assistant and associate professor I could be. And, in retrospect, I'm proud of the work that I have accomplished. For me, it has true meaning and merit. As a scholar-practitioner, I firmly believe in effective, site-based servant leadership that connects theory, practice, and issues of social justice in breaking down walls and building a unified profession of culturally aware educators working toward equitable schooling for all. As a spiritual person, I wholeheartedly believe in approaching education from an ethic of social care and working toward changing the metaphor of schools from hierarchical bureaucracies to nurturing communities. And, as a life-long educator, I sincerely believe in never-ending learning, growth and development for all!

The irony is that I often told myself and others that I did not and would not define myself by what I do. Yes, I am a professor but that isn't who I am; it doesn't define my being. Or did it? Had I fallen into the fateful trap of self-definition according to career role? Had the road (aka "track") to tenure and promotion actually lulled me into a false sense of actualized self? As a model professor, did I unconsciously, subconsciously, or even consciously mold myself into the ideal worker norm? Was I a workaholic without balance? I was definitely working hard but was I really playing hard too or just telling myself that I was? I was achieving but was I enjoying? In other words, was my outer persona (aka social role based on conditioning) controlling my inner self? And, if so, what was my true identity? As a person? As a professor? As both?

Getting tenure actually precipitated a mini midlife crisis. Now what? Getting promoted to full professor precipitated yet another? What's next? Both events triggered a journey into deeper self-discovery. Was I living a balanced, independent life according to my priorities or was I living a life of "shoulds" without even knowing it? Okay, maybe I knew it. And maybe I knew that it was time for introspection and rediscovery of what is important to me and why—time to question all previous assumptions and actions. No Catholic guilt allowed … just lots of courage, creativity, and candor needed to turn inward, to reflect, reassess, realign, redesign, regroup, renew, and reenchant the joy within.

Life is short and we are called to live fully! What does that mean and what does it look and feel like for me? Authentic wisdom gained from living thus far told me that to realize my dreams, I must give them some breathing room. I the groundwork (tenure and promotion afforded me a sense of security and stability). Now it was time to step back and let life unfold! It was time to release the fear, lose control, and take a chance! It was time to go with the flow ... to go where the current took me rather than manically micromanaging every detail of my existence. My inner compass told me that, to really live, it was time to do more, give more, be more. It was time to meet chaos head on. And so, I adopted two small boys with special needs. They had been in the foster care system for 4 years in four different placements (through no fault of their own). They were looking for a forever mommy and I was looking for something ... perhaps genuine balance in life! I allowed my life to be thrown out of balance to experience true balance. Be careful what you ask for J.

STORY II: ADOPTING CHILDREN AND GENUINE BALANCE

Luis and Diego have literally "rocked my world" (and it hasn't always been welcomed and/or appreciated). Before kids, I lived a rather charmed, blessed, self-centered life. Since kids, we still live a life of privilege but it now has more purpose, power, and depth! I met Luis Enrique Martinez (age 5) and his brother Diego Ramon Martinez (age 4) for the first time on January 6, 2009. Their biological father is Mexican and their biological mother is African American. I am Caucasian. The boys moved into my adult townhome full-time on January 30, 2009. Yes, just 3 weeks later. They were in a bad placement (i.e., foster parents inattentive and overextended with older several older children) and the social workers wanted them moved as soon as possible. When asked when I'd be ready to welcome foster children into my home, I clearly responded "any time after April 1" as February and March were already overbooked and jam-packed with scheduled work. I was chairing the department, teaching classes, advising dissertations, supervising interns, leading a distinguished professor search, completing a book manuscript, writing conference articles, and preparing promotion papers for external review (due March 15).

Did I mention that Luis and Diego moved in with me (i.e., a single, middle-aged, workaholic perfectionist) full-time on January 30? Ugh! I was not prepared in any shape, form or fashion. Two and half years later, I'm still not sure I'm prepared! The boys transitioned well, I did not! The first 3 months were hell. The next 6 were not much better. My happy, seemingly stable, composed life was tossed into complete and utter turmoil and I was struggling mightily to find a way to right the balance in our lives without tumbling completely into disarray. I was vulnerable, out of control, and completely overwhelmed! Externally, everyone was so solicitous and so delighted for me/for us. Internally, I was an emotional wreck. So much so that one of my best friends often recalls the image of me laying on her floor in a fetal position crying inconsolably. What had I done? I had these two tiny human beings staring at me, literally clinging to me, testing me, pushing me, needing me more than anyone else and I couldn't handle it. I didn't want to handle it. I wanted to give them back. I wanted my old life back (where I was comfortable and in control).

For 9-plus months I embarrassingly flailed around in opposition, mourning the death of my old life! Instead of going with what was presented to me as gracefully as possible, I resisted versus accepted, I resented versus embraced, I reviled versus appreciated. Fostering to adopt two little boys was creating a life out of balance for me (or so I thought). For the first time in a very long time, my personal life was clashing with my academic job expectations. I was tired, conflicted, and even late. I missed meetings, deadlines, and expectations. I wasn't focused, coherent, or even rational at times. I was behind schedule instead of ahead, running to catch up instead of soaring above, and under prepared instead of overly organized. Needless to say, my equilibrium was thrown out of whack! I desperately needed a recovery process! I needed to muster inner strength, to regain control, to embrace a new norm! I needed others (i.e., family, friends, and colleagues more so than ever before and in a much different way)! I needed time, support, and help (and I had to ask – ugh). I had to admit that I'm not Wonder woman; I can't do it all, and it's okay! I'll survive!

Following this 9-month metaphorical gestation period, I officially adopted Luis and Diego, sold the townhome, and moved to Mayberry. Trust me, I'm not exactly the Mayberry type mom and Luis and Diego are not the typical Mayberry type kids. And yet, we all landed in the suburbs in a ranch-style house on a cul-de-sac with a fenced in backyard and neighbors who water their plants, feed the birds, and greet us daily! Only our golden retriever named Bogey (I actually used to play golf J) is the Mayberry type dog. In fact, she is the hit of the school bus stop every morning where close to 20 people gather on any given morning. We are surrounded by a great village now. I'm still working on transitions (both physical and psychological) between work life and home life but I now have much clearer boundaries and some degree of separation between the two. Instead of reading only educational journals, I now read kiddie books, instead of running into the office for a few hours on Sunday afternoons, we now go to the park, pool, or play dates, instead of working late in the evenings, I now go to bed early too exhausted to think.

I still work hard but now I play hard too and sleep really well (except for the occasional premenopausal symptoms that is)! The house is a little dirtier, the clothes a little more wrinkled (can't remember the last time I ironed), and the e-mail inbox is a little fuller. But, through patience and adaptability, I am now living honestly in alignment with my personal values. It is a much more mindful, intentional living! I don't think we can live a life in true balance all the time. I don't think I want to ... it would not be interesting! I'm having fun. I'm still achieving but I'm also enjoying as well! I schedule downtime to recharge, I exercise to clear my head, I go to the office to get away, and I hire babysitters to get out and about! I'm also much more strategic about how I spend my time, dropping activities that zap my energy while adding activities that boost it!

In an effort to prepare educational leaders committed to eradicating issues of injustice and advocating for issues of equity, I often talk with my graduate students about the "isms." On a professional level, we trace how the themes of racism, classism, heterosexism, and ableism have been constant themes throughout the history of education in the United States and then discuss how such oppressive attitudes and behaviors are still relevant today. On a personal level, I now feel as though I am experiencing these issues from a very different vantage point (moving from book knowledge to experiential knowledge—from an objective, theoretical, cognitive awareness to a much more subjective, maternal, affective consciousness). Luis and Diego have global developmental delays, learning disabilities, and IEPs. They are often judged by the color of their skin, by the poverty they were born into, and by the lack of literacy, nutrition, and stimulation they were exposed to. We have already experienced the soft bigotry of low expectations, the nonverbal communication of nonacceptance, the sting of being prejudged, and the silencing of self-expression (especially as Diego explores issues of gender, orientation, and preferences). As a family, we don't fit the "norm." Unfortunately, as a society, we are reminded of this often in subtle and in not-so-subtle ways. And, although my new lived experiences are actually a natural integration of my research interests (i.e., good combination of work and life if you will), I am reminded daily how much easier it is to read and write books versus navigate the world of difference and otherness. Having been a teacher and principal, sitting on the other side of the desk as an elementary school parent isn't very comfortable either. Many have said to me that Luis and Diego are lucky little boys! In actuality, I'm the lucky one! They have already taught me so much ... including humility, patience, gratitude, simplicity, and childlike self-expression.

In *Lion King*, Simba's father Mufasa explains to his son that "everything you see exists together in a delicate balance ... we are all connected in the great circle of life." In physics, scientists explain that balance is a desirable point between two or more opposite forces. In our family, I explain to Luis and Diego that the secret to maintaining a great work-life balance is to achieve and enjoy daily in multiple areas of your life!

CHAPTER 36

SE HACE EL CAMINO AL ANDAR/ WE MAKE THE ROAD BY WALKING

Ruminations on Work, Love, and Struggle in a Latino Academic Household

Gerardo R. López, Marina Nayar López, and Cora Lucía López

When I (Gerardo) was initially asked to contribute a chapter to this edited book, I immediately thought that it would be a great idea to coauthor the chapter with my two children, particularly given the theme of the book. I pitched the concept to Kathleen Brown, and she immediately embraced it. When the school year was over, my girls and I embarked on a month-long journey that included numerous informal discussions, a few group interviews, and countless dinner table discussions of possible ways to approach our chapter.

By inviting my children into this process, I not only gave them a brief glimpse into my academic world of research and writing, but I was also treated to a rare glimpse of their world and got a chance to talk to my children in ways that provided new understandings and insights about

Juggling Flaming Chain Saws: Academics in Educational Leadership
Try to Balance Work and Family, pp. 297–316
Copyright © 2012 by Information Age Publishing
All rights of reproduction in any form reserved.

297

how they viewed their world as children in an academic household. It was a fascinating and eye-opening experience, to say the least. My girls had dozens of questions about what I did during a typical day, how I spent my time, and why I went to so many meetings. Implicitly, they knew mom and dad were always busy, but they had very little knowledge of how we actually spent our time. In the same vein, I was treated to a fascinating perspective of our family from our children's point of view and what life was like for them growing up in a dual academic household where both parents were on the tenure track, and how family life is for them now that my wife and I have received tenure.

As a way to embark on our writing project, the three of us talked informally about the book project—what it was about and why people studied issues of work/life balance in the first place. We read the book prospectus together, and engaged in informal discussions about work/life balance in our own home. During a 2-week period, our informal discussions flowed organically. We would talk during lunch and dinner, share our ideas with friends and visitors, and would take brief notes about possible themes we felt were important about how we balanced "work life" and "home life" within our own household.

We then separately identified three to four questions we wanted to ask each other during a more "formal" interview and we sat around the kitchen table with a digital recorder to interview each other in a more semistructured format. In true qualitative fashion, however, we quickly realized that our conversations were quite lengthy and elaborate, and that we would need more time to get through all the questions we initially identified. As a result, immediately following each recorded interview, we would collectively determine whether we would need to set more time to continue our conversation.

We met for 5 days following our initial recorded interview. Our shortest interview lasted about 60 minutes, while our longest interview took about 2.5 hours. After all the interviews were over, we had a long conversation about what we thought were the main themes that emerged during our interviews. We identified the top five themes we felt were most important to share in our chapter, and then set off to independently write about each of the themes.

Below are our individual and independent thoughts about each theme. As a researcher, I felt it was important not to edit, revise, or amend the narratives written by each author, so that each voice can speak in an authentic and independent fashion. As a father, however, I was often torn by this decision, because I constantly felt the need to supervise and "control" the process—fearing that my children might air some of our dirty laundry, or worse: not say anything particularly interesting. In the end, to allay some of these concerns, I asked my girls how they felt about interspersing a few quotes from our tape recorded conversations throughout our narrative in order to give readers a better idea about each of the themes. They thought it was a good idea.

Overall, we had a great time preparing and writing this chapter and we think it truly captures various "slices" of family life in our household. It is important to note that the chapter was written during a time of transition prior to making an academic move to a new city. When Cora, my 10-year-old daughter, asked me what I thought New Orleans would be like, I replied that I simply didn't know and that we would have to find out once we got there. I told her that we had to "make the road by walking," paraphrasing Antonio Machado's (1912) famous poem. I believe the mental image of a "road" not only serves as an appropriate title for our chapter, but also as a metaphor for our next family adventure.

THEME #1: FAMILY FIRST

Gerardo: I can honestly say that my role in your lives didn't really happen until after I got tenure. Do you know how sucky it felt, as a parent, to tell your babysitter, "Here's some money go to Michaels and buy some glitter glue to help my daughter with her third grade project"? You feel like a total failure! You don't feel adequate as a parent. And here I am writing about parents and parent involvement and the importance of being involved. You know? There was a sense of absolute hypocrisy. And so after tenure, it opened up a space for me to say "That's not the type of relationship I want to have with my kids." I wanted to put family first, and I think I've tried to stick to that philosophy every single day since tenure.

Marina: Yeah. You're always telling us that family is important.

Gerardo: Not just your immediate family, but your extended family as well.

Cora: I did notice that you kinda got more involved in school projects and stuff after tenure.

Marina: Like that shark. Remember that shark that we built? I was so proud of that shark!

Cora: And that Andrew Clements project? Remember that?

Marina: And my solar system!

Cora: And my cereal box project.

Marina: And Jimmy! We can't forget Jimmy!

Gerardo: What on earth is Jimmy?

Marina: Jimmy! My molecule.
Cora: And my hamburger valentine's box!
Gerardo: That hamburger box was awesome!

One of the ways in which we find balance in Casa López is by putting family first—perhaps above everything else. Now I know that the notion of putting family "above" work is anything but a balance between the work sphere and the family sphere. However, I find that since parent/family involvement is the center of my research and writing, there needs to be a balance between what I preach and what I practice. In other words, I find that the more my everyday world is in concert with my research agenda, the easier it is for me to feel as though I am being true to myself and my convictions.

But coming about this insight was not particularly easy. In fact, there was a significant period (especially prior to receiving tenure) when my "work world" and my "family world" were, indeed, very separate. There were days I would literally lock myself in my home office 24/7 away from my wife and kids, working *ad nauseam* trying to write the next brilliant piece on parent involvement. In fact, and quite regrettably, there were times when I honestly felt my kids were a distraction and a burden on my scholarship.[1] I remember days when Marina would enter my office asking me to read a book to her and I would literally shoo her away, telling her I was too busy working on an article, prepping for class, or grading papers. I also remember days when Cora would ask me to play a board game and I would tell her that I would get to that as soon as I was done sending an e-mail or writing that last paragraph on my conference paper. My poor kids! They suffered through so much when I got lost in my academic world.

When I was going through the tenure process, the situation in Casa López was particularly tense. I wanted so badly to achieve the "grand prize" of academia, that there were days when I lost all perspective of the world around me as I immersed myself in my work. Of course it didn't help that both my wife and I were both going up for tenure at roughly the same time. That made things particularly contentious. In fact, there was a period when it seemed as though we were always in a heated competition for that scarcest of resources—time—and that our children were often caught in the middle of a work/life tug-of-war. To be certain, "war" is an excellent metaphor to describe our pretenure household because the stakes were high across the board: We either "published or perished" in our careers, "succeeded or sank" as parents, or "continued or collapsed" as a couple. There seemed to be no compromise; no middle ground.

Not surprisingly, after we both received tenure, it was as though a heavy burden had been lifted. But ironically, instead of ushering in feelings of joy and triumph, I experienced deep sadness and regret. Although I had "made it" as a scholar, I felt I had failed miserably as a parent.[2] I felt cheated and resentful. I was angry not only at my university, but at the entire *institution* of academia. On the one hand, I had achieved what I most desperately wanted: Tenure at a Research I institution. On the other hand, my accomplishment came at a high psychological and emotional "cost."

In the blink of an eye, my kids had grown up and I had missed so many wonderful and significant moments in their key developmental years. To make matters worse, they now had grown accustomed to "stay away from daddy while he's at the computer" and, therefore, no longer asked me to play games or read them books with as much frequency. Sadly, I came to the realization that I had pushed my children away so often that they had become detached, hardened, and somewhat distant.

Tenure is a time of transition, and like all transitions, it forces one to seriously rethink one's role and purpose in life. For me, tenure brought forth a painful realization that for the first 7 years of my professional career, I was living a lie. As an academic, I wrote about the importance and centrality of parent involvement, yet as a father, I was not "involved" in my own children's lives. I was not the father that I wanted to be, and certainly not the parent that I wrote about in my articles and research manuscripts. I wasn't being true to my ideals and beliefs, and it was this cognitive dissonance that made me realize that I needed to make a change.

Vowing to never let this happen ever again, I began to consciously, aggressively, and unapologetically, put my family first, and at least try to recuperate the many years that were taken away from me and my family. That's why today, I try to spend as much time as I can with my kiddos, and enjoy those special moments as much as possible.

Cora

My parents always tried their hardest to spend as much time with us (my sister and I) as possible. The thing they always went out of their way to do was, and still is, is to have dinner as a family. And I didn't realize how rare that is, to be eating as a family most of the year. Just by eating dinner as a family, they gave up an hour of writing an overdue blog entry, or grading a paper. I never knew what it felt like to not have dinner as a family, so I took it for granted. I always did love having dinner as a family because of all the interesting conversations we have. Except for the boring conversations, in which my parents have entered another world, talking about the gossip at work, and the new professor. And this is the only world my sister and I don't understand.

Another thing that my parents always tried to always do is take the whole family to other countries or states for their teaching trips, and for trips to visit our relatives. Usually on the teaching trip, Mom's the one teaching. So far, just on teaching trips, we've been to England, Brazil, Spain, China, other cities in the United States, and probably some more countries that I don't remember because I was a baby.

My dad's side of the family lives in Los Angeles, CA, so my family goes to see them every once in a while. My Mom's family lives in Puerto Rico, and yes, I get to go to beaches as well as visit family when I go there.

Marina

In a two tenured professor household, life can range from the crazy to the borderline insane. Both Mom and Dad are in an environment that requires lots of time and energy. I soon realized that there had to be a way to balance both the home aspect and the work aspect of my parents. A mantra soon came into being: Family first. Family had to be the first in line in order to create a harmony between work and home.

One way that my parents make sure that family is a constant, is dinner. I have always had the pleasure of eating dinner together daily, and have never realized how many families do not use dinner as an opportunity to ensure that they are still working as a unit. It keeps us together. Dinner is a chance for the family to talk and communicate. Without this, many families cannot sustain a healthy relationship between all members. We try as hard as we can to make sure that nothing interferes with our family's time at dinner.

THEME #2: RELISH THE SMALL MOMENTS

Marina: So what would you say are most important things for us to do as a family?

Gerardo: I'd say that spending time as a family unit as much as possible is something that I personally value. Because during the day it's just absolute craziness. There are so many things happening in your mom's world and in my world, that to try to balance it all is really tough. I think that's part of the reason why we try to make those small moments really matter as much as possible.

Cora:	I like it when we play games, or go to a movie together.
Marina:	I like it when we read together.
Gerardo:	Do we do that very often—like read or play games?
Cora:	Well not all the time, but when we do it, it's a lot of fun.
Gerardo:	Yeah but finding the time to do it is pretty challenging.
Marina:	We have dinner together. I like that.
Cora:	Me too.
Gerardo:	Me three!
Together:	[laughter].

Gerardo

Another one of the ways we make it work at Casa López is that we embrace those small moments that "connect" us to each other each and every day. It might be eating dinner as a family (which we do every night, with the exception of teaching nights and days we are at conferences), playing a board game together on weekends, or reading a chapter of a book with the girls during those rare moments of family "downtime." While we try to maximize "formal" family time, the moments I relish most are those spontaneous moments where we just let down our guard and be silly: cracking jokes, clowning around, and taking turns "diving" onto the king size bed. Indeed, laughter is important at Casa López, as is having a good sense of humor. Those moments of childlike distraction bring us together, break the monotony of our daily routine, and help remind us of the importance of recreation and having a good time.

Because our days are extremely busy and typically jammed with meetings and academic responsibilities, we've come to really enjoy those small moments that connect us to each other as family. I'm not going to lie: most of the time, work still consumes us and makes it quite difficult to pull away from the computer. However, I find that I always need to remind myself that "work time" can always be made up (at night, early in the morning, after lunch, etc.), but "family time" can never be recuperated.

Unfortunately, this philosophy often puts me at odds with editors, coauthors, colleagues, and even students—especially when I am running behind on deadlines, am late in returning e-mails, or cannot respond in a timely fashion. To be certain, I'm not in any way suggesting that I (or anyone for that matter) just blow off professional responsibilities and colleagues. Rather, I'm merely stating that "work" can wait a little— certainly not indefinitely, but perhaps briefly—to enjoy time with family.

Clearly, most of us can't "do it all" (though I do secretly marvel at those individuals who seem to find that balance effortlessly!). In the past, I tried to "do it all" and found myself quickly burning out. There were times when I was so tired from lack of sleep/energy, that I would literally fall asleep while trying to read to my girls. In the same vein, I cannot begin to count to the number of times I've fallen asleep in front of my computer at 3am! I soon realized that I couldn't continue in a zombielike state all the time—not only because I was burning out, but because I wasn't "present" with my children nor with my work. I came to the conclusion that it was better to be present and awake for smaller moments, than to be sluggish and lifeless trying to "do it all" in my work and parental roles.

Cora

It's the little things that really matter. Like last summer, my dad, my sister Marina and I read all the seven *Harry Potter* books together and watched the movies just to get ready for the movie that was about to come out. And we had a pasta-making day where we invited Miss April Bruce and Miss April Meade (who share a duplex along with Miss Kelly and have the same name and both love cooking!) to our house to make handmade pasta with my Dad's pasta-maker and we also made two different sauces to go with the pasta (let's just say my arms hurt SO much from cranking the pasta out of the machine that day).

My family is very musical. My mom is mostly classical, but the other three people in my family love all music of all sorts. That is, except for all those pop types like Justin Bieber, Lady Gaga, and Ke$ha. In my opinion, they are a disgrace to music.

Marina

It is virtually impossible to find us all together in one spot other than dinner. We have to find time to bond in the time that we have available. I forced my sister and my dad to read the *Harry Potter* series aloud with me. We squeeze in a chapter here and there and before I knew it, we'd finished the seventh and final novel. We would have intense discussions about the movies versus the books. We have, through the magical world of Hogwarts, created memories that are irreplaceable.

Music is another constant in our lives. We share new finds or old favorites. We talk music theory or just music itself. Mom tends to favor classical and Juanes [a Latin singer]. Dad's music tastes cannot be classified with a few terms, meaning he likes a little of everything. [Cora] Lucía and I are somewhere in between the two, blending both tastes into one. I think music plays a big role in our lives because it provides a slight respite from the otherwise crazy lives that we lead.

THEME #3: BABYSITTERS ARE A GODSEND!

Gerardo: Let's talk about tenure.

Cora: Man that was insane!

Marina: Wicked!

Gerardo: Yeah, it was pretty intense.

Marina: That was when we saw the sitters more than we saw you guys.

Cora: It was like "Good morning dad!" [then imitating dad] "Good morning kids!" You'd get your coffee, and go right upstairs!

Gerardo: Yeah, they came in during really critical times, like tenure.

Marina: And your third year review.

Cora: And UCEA

Marina: And AERA

Cora: And your book.

Marina: The book! That was another crazy time.

Cora: And LatCrit [The Latina/o Critical Race Theory Conference].

Marina: And teaching.

Gerardo: Yeah, we rely on our sitters a lot. They're like our guardian angels. They come in at critical times. They're like our Keebler elves. They help us make our shoes when we get bone-tired.

Marina: They're my favorite!

Cora: They're the bomb!

Gerardo: Basically, they're the supporting cast members that allow us to do everything we need to do in our house.

Cora: They're the backbone.

Gerardo: Why would you say they're the backbone?

Cora: Because whenever you're working, and mom is doing something, they're just there.

Marina: Like tonight, you're busy teaching, so Miss April's coming in to help.

Gerardo

When we decided to be a dual tenure-track household, we instantly knew that the only way we were going to "make it" was by bringing in help. With research, teaching, service, and countless other responsibilities on our respective plates, it was important to accept the fact that we couldn't "do it all" and still tend to our home and family responsibilities:

The house needed to be cleaned, clothes needed to be laundered, kids need to be picked up, homework needed to be reviewed, dinner needed to be made, etc. On top of that, we still needed to research, write, publish, teach, provide service to the profession, present at conferences, supervise dissertations, and attend to a host of other duties. Therefore, to lighten our load, we hired people to clean our house, mow our lawn, trim our hedges, maintain our house, and we also recruited a team of dedicated and loving sitters to help us with our kids.

Now, our sitters are absolutely amazing and we consider each of them an important part of our family.[3] Our sitters have not only helped us during "crunch time" and times of sheer insanity (e.g., dossiers, writing projects, conferences, etc.), but they also have been there during times when we just needed an extra pair of hands to help us out. They've picked up our girls from schools, have eaten dinner with the kids when we couldn't be together as a family, and have even invited our girls over for sleepovers during those times when intense deadlines were looming and we needed extra time to focus. Indeed, our sitters have been there through thick and thin. They have supervised homework assignments, worked on school projects, served as tutors, and have taken our children to extracurricular activities such as piano practice, volleyball, and soccer. Our girls have practically "grown up" with these sitters, and our girls view them more like big sisters or older cousins than actual sitters.

Our relationship with our sitters has developed over time. We hired most of them in 2003-2004 when they were first-year law students and our girls were very young. Most of our sitters stayed on well after graduating from law school and after passing the bar exam. Our kids were probably the only ones in the entire state of Indiana to have attorneys as babysitters! Yet, despite their personal and professional interests, our sitters continue to have a wonderful relationship with our girls and our family. The fact is, we love our sitters, and we know they have a deep love and affection for our girls. In fact, at least three of our sitters—April Bruce, April Meade, and Melody Goldberg—regularly attend our girls' school performances, ceremonies, and other important events such as piano recitals and competitions. We know it brings tremendous joy to our girls knowing that their sitters are there along with us at these important functions and events.

It is precisely this kind of *familismo* that we value as parents and as caregivers. As Latinos, having an extended kinship network is critically important. It is the backbone of our culture as well as an important mechanism of interpersonal trust and support. In this regard, our sitters are like coparents or *comadres*.[4] We trust them wholeheartedly and entrust our children to their care. Knowing that our children are safe, loved, and with "family" allows us to let go and focus on our work.

Cora

Ah, babysitters. That, ladies and gentlemen, is the reason we (get used to that word: we. It means my family and I) remain sane. They're there for all those, "Gosh, I forgot about that meeting, and I NEED to go!" moments, and all those times you need to grade nine papers and your wife's [mom's] on a trip, and your kids want to play Clue and the times when you've been in a meeting all day when you check your watch and tell yourself, "Oh no, I'll never make it in time to pick up the kids!" My parents have had lots of those [moments].

I don't remember a lot of my babysitters, but here's a few off the top of my head: Miss Erin, Miss April Bruce, Miss April Meade, Miss Kelly, Miss Melody, Miss Leslie, Miss Sally, Miss Kristen, Miss Miranda and Miss Angie. Notice they all have "Miss" before the name because my parents insisted on [me and my sister addressing the sitters formally].

I remember when my parents were writing their collaborative book, *Persistent Inequality*, and every weekend, a babysitter would come to play with us, and either Dad would be shut in his office, typing madly, or Mom would be in the living room corner, in the big red armchair, in her own world, typing not very loud, not minding how much noise we made. They were so absorbed in their writing, if you asked them something like, "Can we watch *Elf*?" You would have to repeat the question about three times before they turned to you and said, "Eh?" and you would have to repeat the question yet again, and then you finally got a yes or no out of them.

Marina

At the López-Pabón household, we LOVE our babysitters. They are the foundation that keeps the world working as smoothly as it can be. My parents were both up for their Promotion and Tenure almost the same time. My dad was up first. This meant that Dad was upstairs in his office working nonstop. This also meant that Mom had to take care of us by herself and continue with her work. When she needed her time during the weekends, she hired one babysitter to come Saturday afternoons and another to come on Sunday mornings. This continued for most of the semester. They are the lifesavers that make sure that all of the work gets done.

At first, they started off as the ones who played games with us for an afternoon. Now they are friends who are almost family. For my birthday last year, I even chose to have a sleepover with two babysitters so we could watch the long version of *Pride and Prejudice*. They are confidants and best friends. They come to movies with us because they want to. Because they are a constant, I have come to realize that my parents work extremely hard. The babysitters are the ones that are there when my parents need time to work.

THEME #4: TIME IS UNYIELDING

Gerardo: What's a typical day like?

Cora: We don't have a typical day!

Gerardo: What do you mean by that?

Marina: No two days are exactly alike.

Cora: Yeah, it's crazy!

Gerardo: So what makes it crazy?

Cora: There's just like no routine.

Marina: We just have so much going on. Every minute of the day is taken. Work, school, driving, homework, dinner, showers, more homework. It's just crazy.

Gerardo: But you just said that there are no routines. That sounds like a routine to me.

Marina: It's just that every day is different. Mom's at a meeting. Dad's at a board meeting, Mom's in California. Dad's in Pittsburgh. Mom's in Florida, or L.A., or Nevada, or San Francisco. Dad's at UCEA.

Gerardo: Would you say that your parents are always running around?

Cora: No. It just seems that way.

Marina: For us, it seems like it's like that every other day.

Gerardo

One of the lessons we've learned along the way is that there simply aren't enough hours in the day to do it all. María and I both have teaching, research, and service commitments, so we really need to carefully plan and coordinate our calendars religiously in order to manage our lives. The fact is, we're always planning in our house; whether it's simple things like what to make for dinner (and who will make it), to more complicated matters, like when one of us will be out of town and whether we need to bring in the sitters to help out. It's critically important to plan *everything* in our household, because if we don't, something is bound to fall through the cracks. As a result, María and I spend considerable time coordinating our calendars to ensure that there aren't any holes or gaps in coverage.

For example, our respective course schedules have to be planned at least two semesters in advance so that we don't teach on the same days. Likewise, our faculty and student meetings have to be coordinated to ensure that at least one parent is available to pick up a child (or to make sure a sitter is on call to do it). Our travel and conferences have to be planned so that the nontravelling parent can plan accordingly, et cetera. This is more than just a courtesy "FYI" or a note on the family calendar. Rather, because our schedules are so filled with academic and nonacademic responsibilities, it is essential that our calendars are in sync; otherwise, things can fall apart quickly. In like fashion, our home lives also require a certain amount of planning to ensure that everyone—parents and children alike—can effectively manage all of life's stresses.

Although we consider ourselves to be a "typical" family, admittedly, what is probably "typical" in most families is probably not very typical at Casa López. For starters, María and I rarely sleep. We both average less than four hours of sleep per day (I sleep about 4 hours per day and María sleeps considerably less). We are also both actively involved in local/community affairs—with María serving on the State Board of Law Examiners, State Supreme Court Advisory Panels, and numerous legal associations, and myself serving on the school board of a private independent school as well as on the board of our mayor's office responsible for charter school approval, renewal, and policy oversight.

All of this "additional" service can only contribute to our lack of sleep. To complicate matters, in addition to these activities, our children attend an independent school located an hour away from our home.[5] Unfortunately, my university office is located *in the opposite direction* of my children's school. This means that on any given morning, I might leave my house by 7 A.M. to drop off my kids on the north side of town, only to drive two hours south in order to make it to my office by 10 A.M. While the "windshield time" can make for a welcome respite from the madness of our daily lives, it also takes away precious moments from working on other things (e.g., reading, responding to e-mails, returning phone calls, etc.) on a daily basis.

With so much going on, it is critical that we have a "routine." Below is a typical, nonteaching, posttenure day in Casa López. I've contrasted it with a typical, nonteaching, pretenure day so that readers can compare and contrast the differences:

On most days, María and I will usually alternate the drop off/pick up schedule. We usually drive back home after picking up the girls from school to supervise homework and get started on dinner. Some days, however, if there are after school extracurricular activities, or if there is an evening activity at the school (performance, meeting, conference, etc.), we will eat dinner at a nearby restaurant to avoid the additional commute.

Table 36.1.   Typical, Nonteaching, Pre-, and Posttenure Day

	Typical Posttenure Day		Typical Pretenure day
6 A.M.	Wake up, iron clothes	6 A.M.	One parent wakes up (Parent who has stayed up longest, gets to sleep in). Iron clothes, wake up kids.
6:15	Wake up kids. One parent helps kids get ready, other parent prepares breakfast.	6:15	Kids get ready on their own while parent prepares breakfast.
6:30	Kids come down for breakfast.	6:30	Kids come down for breakfast. Parent serves breakfast. Kids eat alone while parent takes "power nap" on sofa.
6:50	Kids finish breakfast. Parents clean up. Kids get ready for school.	6:50	Kids finish breakfast. Parent cleans up. Kids get ready for school.
7:00	Leave for school.	7:00	Sitter arrives to take kids to school. Parent goes back to sleep.
8:00	Arrive at school/drop off kids.	8:00	Both parents wake up and get ready for work.
9:00	Arrive back home after dropping off kids (or 10 A.M. if heading to office).	9-4:	Work/meetings/etc.
9-2:30	Work/meetings/etc.		
2:30	Parent leaves to pick up kids from school (leave at 1:30 if driving from my office)		
3:30	Kids picked up from school	4:30	Parent arrives in time to greet children, and then works at home, checks emails, etc. Kids arrive home with sitter. Sitter supervises homework.
4:30	Arrive at home. Kids start homework/Parent starts dinner.	5:30	Parent starts dinner.
6:00	Eat dinner as a family	6:00	Kids eat dinner
6:30	Clean up. Kids finish homework/do extracurricular activities	6:30	Clean up. Kids finish homework.
7:30	Kids off to bath.	7:30	Kids off to bath.
8:30	Kids in bed.	8:30	Kids in bed.
9:00	Lights out for kids.	9:00	Lights out for kids.
9-2 A.M.	Parents continue with work.	9:30	Second parent arrives from office. Parents eat dinner together.
		10-3 A.M.	Parents continue with work. One parent usually in bed by 3 A.M.
		3:30 or 4 A.M.	Second parent to sleep.

Regardless of what happens after school, one of the things our family agreed to do is to try to have dinner as a family as much as possible. At Casa López, dinner is a special time; it's a time to be together as a family, and time to talk to each other about our respective days. Homemade/non-restaurant dinners are important and preferred. While we realize that going out to dinner, or buying "semihomemade" or "preprepared" dinners might be a huge time saver, we actually prefer making dinner ourselves. I fully realize that some of our choices are highly personal, and perhaps a bit time consuming, but we feel it adds to the special moment we share as a family each day.

Notwithstanding, after dinner, we try to get back to work as soon as possible. Time is uncompromising; it's the one thing we can't afford to waste. Though we relish our family time, we also realize that we need to keep those moments concentrated and "bracketed" so that we can enjoy them when they happen and not feel rushed to get back to the grind.

Cora

Every weekday at 6 in the morning, I wake up to either Dad doing something silly, or Mom trying to get me to fall out of my bed. I groggily get dressed in my neatly ironed school uniform (thanks, Dad). Then, I eat something like a half of a bagel or a bowl of cereal, both accompanied by a banana, because my parents insisted on that. About 30 minutes later, at around 7:00, we load up our things in either the light blue Honda CR-V, or the small, black, toaster-shaped Toyota Scion XB, or sometimes, Miss Erin's dark red Chevrolet Cobalt. We arrive at my school, Park Tudor, around 7:55, which gives my sister and me just enough time to be in class by 8:00. That is our weekday morning routine. Whatever my parents do the rest of the day nobody knows. We only know that the morning routine and the pickup time will always stay constant.

I don't know what my parents do all day, but I do know that at school, they say that we have a certain schedule and that we actually follow that schedule. Well, that's a very rare thing, with last minute music practices for the Young Strings Program that's at our school, and sudden assemblies. We also have to incorporate extracurricular activities, such as piano lessons, piano competitions, Indiana State School Music Association, piano recitals, school recitals, and when my sister and I were younger we used to do ballet and sports.

Marina

Our lives can be most compared to a train schedule. We cannot be late and we are constantly running. We have a secret weapon that is the one piece that keeps our family running: Calendars. Our lives are constantly going which means that coordination is necessary before anything happens. The calendar is what determines who's going to pick [Cora] Lucía and me up from school or if a babysitter will be needed. Calendars are the key to the López family planning.

"If it doesn't make the calendar, it's off my plate." These words of wisdom were from my dad when I mentioned that I had a recital 2 days before the event. My parents have to know about things in advance to make sure that all items will be attended. The constant running around that we do make extracurriculars hard to plan. My friends know that all things have to be planned at least 2 weeks in advance. We have to do only what we have complete interest in because time is a limited resource that has to be used wisely.

THEME #5: ALWAYS STAY GROUNDED AND NEVER LOSE SIGHT OF WHAT'S IMPORTANT

Gerardo: One of the things that's unusual about an academic job is that the work never ends. You're always on. Every day of the week. Every day of the year. Any other job, you can punch in at nine and you punch out at five and you're done. But for us, we go into work in the morning, work during the day, come home, have dinner, and we're back on. And it's one of those jobs that can consume you if you let it. And we try not to let it consume us. But there are times when it does. When that happens, we always try to remind ourselves that we're parents first and academics second.

Marina: Do you think that your colleagues make that distinction?

Gerardo: What distinction?

Marina: Being parents first and academics second?

Gerardo: Some do. Unfortunately, some do not.

Cora: Why not?

Gerardo: Like I said, it's hard being an academic. This job can just eat you up. And for some people this becomes their lives. It's not that they don't have balance, or that they don't care about their families, but that the job becomes primary. I've always said, that for me, it's not about "balance" it's about being grounded and knowing what's important.

Gerardo

One of the lessons we learned though our discussions, is that life in Casa López is pretty intense. Every day can be unpredictable, and each member of the family has learned to adapt to this uncertainty in his/her own way. As the old adage goes, "life happens," therefore we need to be able to roll with the punches as best we could whenever something arises. In the past, when our carefully laid plans didn't go quite as anticipated, I've had to reschedule meetings as well as take the girls with me to classes or dissertation defenses. Likewise, María has taken the girls with her to lectures, classes, and countless meetings with judges, lawyers, students, and even some of her clients. While some readers may view this as simply the ability to be "flexible" or "accommodating," we also find that learning to live in the present is an important part of our family functioning and well-being.

Living in the present is a way of seeing the world and an approach to life. It is more than an attitude or predilection, but a way of existing and "being" with and in the world. It engenders the importance of being secure in family and the ability to be grounded in faith, love, and support for each other regardless of life's challenges. As such, living in the present necessitates being "emotionally present" as well as "environmentally present" with what is happening in our daily lives.

When my father passed away 4 years ago, I felt as if my world had been turned upside down. I struggled in my writing; I couldn't focus. And despite my emotional state, there was a constant pressure from the institution to publish, write, and produce. In fact, one of my dear UCEA colleagues tried to be supportive by earnestly encouraging me to write a research paper as a way to "deal" with my emotions. However helpful my colleague was trying to be, I honestly felt that writing was not what I needed at that point in time. I needed to feel. I needed to grieve. I needed to cry.

The problem with academe is that we don't "feel" or cry very often. In fact, we're not a very "feely" profession at all. Too often, we hide our emotions behind our papers, our conferences, and our research, and we don't let ourselves be connected to our own emotionality. As a result, we fail to be connected to ourselves, and thus, to each other. Academia can be numbing. We can get so caught up with our research, writing, and institutional commitments that we become anesthetized to the world around us. In all honesty, I cannot write a research paper as a way to "deal" with grief. I cannot bracket or table my emotions—though admittedly, that's probably what I did to "survive" during my pretenure years. Now that I have tenure, however, I've learned a powerful lesson about what I sacrificed to get it and I don't ever want to go back to that place of insensitivity and coldness.

I now try to teach my children to stay grounded—to love and support each other, to struggle for what's right, and to leave the world a better place than they found it. These are the lessons that my parents taught me, and what I hope my children will teach their own children and/or loved ones in the future.

Cora

Being a López isn't easy or simple. A lot of days Mom will send me off, saying that she'll pick me up, and when I get to the pickup line at school, I don't see her car. So I look around until I spot Miss Erin's familiar car. This happens very often. Occasionally, if all the babysitters are at work, she'll get her friend Magdalena to pick my sister and me up.

Sometimes, Mom will say something like, "Better clean up your room, Cora, because Tia Angie is going to be sleeping in it tomorrow" and I had no idea she was even coming over. People come over to our house a lot, and sometimes I have to clean my room because it is also the "guest room" when people sleep over. I don't mind though, because whenever we have guests, I get to sleep in my parent's room!

One time, dad forgot he had a meeting with a student the next day, and mom was out of town, so my sister and I sat there for what felt like forever waiting for the meeting to end. That's actually happened twice this year, once when mom was out of town, and once when Marina was on a school trip. I don't like waiting very much, but most of the time it's not that bad. At least I get to be with dad, and I like that very much.

Marina

We live on a routine that is always changing. We live on variations of the same day. Because of this, we give a lot of ourselves. In my parent's case, they barely sleep. In my and [Cora] Lucía's case, we've had less play dates and extracurricular activities. We all had to give a little (or a lot) in the pursuit of finding the balance between work and home. In many ways, we still struggle to find this balance.

These experiences help us grow closer together. No matter what, family is the one aspect of my life that is most important. Our lives do not allow us to look too far ahead or too far back. Life in an academic household means working in the present because plans can change and things are constantly going on. We have to be closer because we have to be strong to survive as a family.

CONCLUSION: "SE HACE EL CAMINO AL ANDAR"

When we first started the journey on this chapter, we had no idea where it would lead us, or how it would turn out. We knew it had to focus on broad themes about work and life balance in our home, but had no idea it would turn out to be a reflective journey of love, struggle and sacrifice. Throughout this process, we've learned some very powerful lessons about life as an "academic" family, and were reminded about our own convictions, values and beliefs.

Being an academic household isn't easy. It can be intense and difficult, especially during those "pressure-cooker" moments when it feels like the weight of the world is on one's shoulders. During those times, we relied on each other; testing each other's patience, love, faith, and support along the way. To be certain, no one taught us "how" to be an academic family or how to balance work and life in a dual tenure-track household. Fact is, we had to learn some painful lessons along the way. Although we're pretty sure we didn't get it "right" off the bat, we made some adjustments and are a happier family because of those changes. Now that María has been named Dean of the Law School at Loyola-New Orleans, we know that new hopes, new dreams, and new adventures await us in our new academic home. We will continue to adjust and make a new road as life takes us down its precious journey.

POSTSCRIPT

It has been 3 weeks since the three of us arrived in New Orleans (Note: María has been here for 10 weeks to transition into her administrative role). Suffice it to say that it feels as though our world has been turned upside down! Since our arrival, we've unpacked and settled into our house, Cora and Marina have started at a new school, and Gerardo has started his job at Loyola University. Our family hasn't figured out a routine, we have no sitters to rely on, and María's new role has introduced new challenges and time constraints into the family dynamic. As such, we find ourselves struggling once again to find that work/life balance in our lives. As we reconfigure our schedules and try to get used to life in a new city, we realize that we will need to reevaluate "what works" in our household in order to find that stability once again.

NOTES

1. Trust me, the irony of writing about involvement yet feeling burdened by my own children, doesn't escape me! Moreover, I speak as though all this were in the past. In all honesty, sometimes I occasionally, and unconsciously, slip back into "work" mode. I'm still a work in progress. I'm not perfect.

2. I also felt that I had failed as a husband, but that's another issue altogether. Suffice it to say, that both my wife and I now realize how much academia estranged us from each other.

3. This is not a tired cliché. Trust me, as Latino father, I really wrestled with the sheer *thought* of hiring someone to "help us" with our kids! I truly felt we needed to be able to do it on our own—balance work *and* family—the same way our parents did back in the day. For my parents, seeking external help wasn't just taboo, it was an admission of their own inadequacy. They instilled within me the idea that hard work and sacrifice were all that was needed to raise a family. I guess that's why it took years for me to even warm up to the thought of having sitters.

4. For more information about Latino extended kinship networks, see Portes (1998), Stanton-Salazar (2001), and Wilson (1998).

5. Our decision to enroll our children in an independent school was not easy. Marina and [Cora] Lucía were both enrolled in public schools until the third grade, but two separate racial incidents (including one where a teacher called Marina "Little Miss Mexico" on a bullhorn), made us think hard about the type of learning environment we wanted our children to have. As a public school advocate it was a difficult decision to enroll my children in a private school, but one which I don't regret, given the racial climate of some of our local public school options.

REFERENCES

Machado, A. (1912). Proverbios y cantares, XXIX. In *Campos de castilla* (pp. 147-169). Madrid, Spain: Renacimiento, S.A. Editorial

Portes, A. (1998). Social capital: Its origins and applications in modern sociology. *Annual Review of Sociology, 24*, 1-24.

Stanton-Salazar, R. D. (2001). *Manufacturing hope and despair: The school and kin support networks of U.S.-Mexican youth*. New York, NY: Teachers College Press.

Wilson, T. D. (1998). Weak ties, strong ties: Network principles in Mexican migration. *Human Organization, 57*(4), 394-403.

CHAPTER 37

NOT EVEN *BUILT* FOR BALANCE

Catherine A. Lugg

I am lying on a table, tightly strapped into two back braces. The top brace is threaded around my shoulders and then strapped just as tightly to the table. The straps of the lower brace are attached to a rope, which in turn is attached to a device with a pulley and an electric motor. While I can move my lower arms and head somewhat, I can't move any other part of my body to any meaningful extent. Before things begin, I am handed a "kill switch" to stop the machine if something goes wrong during this treatment—or I freak out. Then, the device is switched on and the lower brace is gently pulled at 30 pounds of torque for 30 seconds, then it lets go for 10 seconds of release. The device then repeats the pull, but this time at 60 pounds of torque, again for 30 seconds. After the second pull, the physical therapist releases the lock on the table. With the next pull of the machine, which is at 95 pounds of torque for 30 seconds, the middle part of the table and my lower spine … move downwards. The physical therapist makes sure I'm okay, waits for the fourth pull, double checks everything, and then he leaves me alone to contemplate life with this modern-day "rack" for the next 30 minutes at 30 seconds per pull.

This chapter maps my imposed change toward trying to live a more balanced life, something I've really never quite believed in. I grew up in rural Pennsylvania, in a strongly working class, Appalachian environ-

Juggling Flaming Chain Saws: Academics in Educational Leadership
Try to Balance Work and Family, pp. 317–323
Copyright © 2012 by Information Age Publishing
All rights of reproduction in any form reserved.

ment. When I was born, a neighbor welcomed me into the world by bestowing my mother with two squirrels that she had just shot. As a teenager, I would play catch with my father with 60 pound bales of sugar as we unloaded a tractor-trailer filled with groceries for his store. It was always hard times and people worked extremely hard to hopefully avoid even harder times. Consequently, to me, striving for a "balanced life" sounds like so much middle-class whining. Who has the time to goof off when *there's all this work to do?* That is how I still feel, but the reality is I am trying to find some sort of balance quickly before I land on permanent disability.

I GET OUTED BY MY MOTHER

My elderly mother has been in New Jersey and living in an assisted living facility since 2009 after a spectacular health crash and the subsequent nightmare of Appalachian heath care. While she was highly resistant to moving to New Jersey and having me coordinate her health care, she wasn't keen about dying of stupid—which she was experiencing in spades before she moved out of rural Pennsylvania (see misdiagnosed colon rupture, being treated with counterindicated medications, her portable heart monitor missing batteries and losing 24 hours of data, a car crashing into the wall of her room at the nursing home, and so forth). Since that traumatic move, she's adjusted to a new life with greater aplomb than I could have ever imagined. That she has experienced world class health care and actually feels good on most days have softened the blow of a forced relocation. Best of all, she even likes her doctors, including her spinal doctor who manages her severe osteoporosis and occasionally gently chides her on her choice of footwear.[1]

In the early fall of 2010, my mother *outed me* to her spine doctor as "having a bad back." This doctor then proceeded to shoot me "the hairy eyeball" every time I came in with my mom or my partner Mary, who also has back problems, for their respective appointments. But mom did have a point. I have long had a "bad back" and it had gotten much worse over the last few years. I was already on a drug regimen for pain management (spinal arthritis, scoliosis, and a smashed-in tailbone), but I was lousy at following any exercise program. Long ago I was warned not to do any seated exercise because of my smashed-in tailbone so bicycling was forbidden, running was out because of the spinal curvature, and given how nearsighted I am, swimming terrifies me. That left me the option of using the ultimate instrument of pain and torture, the ski machine, which had as much appeal as unmedicated dental surgery. While I used to love the ski machine, over the last few years I had felt increasingly worse after exercising with it—so I stopped. In the fall of 2010, after a fairly painful conference season and two miserable plane landings that jarred my back to the point I thought I was going to vomit everything that I had eaten in the last 3 weeks, I finally agreed to be evaluated by mom's spinal doctor.

The evaluation was pretty straightforward: x-rays, balance and mobility tests, and visual inspections of my spine and legs. The x-rays basically confirmed some long-standing problems including spinal arthritis, scoliosis and the smashed-in tailbone, but there were no surprises. Then, the spine doctor had me sit on top of the exam table and she pulled on my legs.

Doctor: "Did you know that your left leg is significantly longer than your right leg?"

Me and my mature response: "No, it's NOT!" At this point, Mary is laughing quietly in the corner. The doctor repeats the test and says:

Doctor: "Did you know that your left leg is significantly longer than your right leg?"

Now, Mary outright guffaws. *SIGH!*

Being flung out of my denial by this gently persistent doctor and totally busted by my partner who was laughing out loud is not one of my fonder moments. Mary had long suspected that one of my legs was longer than the other, but I had been adamant that this wasn't possible. My reasoning? I had played varsity basketball in high school, which seems like "mission impossible" if I had a seriously short leg. Additionally, part of my resistance and denial was and is that for all of my radical queer politics that longs for major social change, *personal change* is not something I do with particular grace or equanimity. So, contemplating and then implementing major life changes make me more than a tad cranky. Denial is so much easier. That said, Mary is a New Jersey licensed clinical social worker who has a private psychotherapy practice. In other words, my partner is a shrink who isn't about to tolerate a partner in denial—about anything. So, I dutifully, if more than a tad sullenly, routed myself for some fairly extensive and intensive physical therapy (Three hours a session, three times a week and this included time with "the rack" for each session, for roughly 5 months), accepted the change in medications, and steeled myself for the upcoming MRI of my lower spine.

The MRI went very badly. If you've ever had one, the trick is to lie perfectly still on your back, resting on something as comfortable and plush as a flatbed scanner, while it sounds like the U.S. Army is having artillery practice overhead your head at the distance of an inch. I haven't been able sleep on my back in over 15 years because it simply hurts too much, much less been able lie *perfectly* still on my back for 20 minutes. After 10 minutes into the MRI. I nearly bolted from the machine and the technician had to end the scan. I was sternly chided by the technician for wiggling around so much and potentially spoiling the exam. Nevertheless, the results that the radiologist was able to read indicated I had managed to damage every lumbar disc in my spine—a 5 for 5 batting average. The other finding was that I have stenosis or the narrowing of the spinal column in the lumbar region, which can slowly compress the spinal cord if it progresses. Since the test was incomplete, there might be even more disc damage and stenosis in the lowest parts of the spine. But I was not up to being sedated and then having everything repeated just to receive possibly more bad news. That said, the report was definitive enough. Working class "yah best do it yourself" cultural norms aside, my days of schlepping endless boxes of books, shoveling show, and carting large grocery bags were over.

My mom's response to all of these findings was fairly expected. While she's seen the memo on not saying "I told you so" to her children since it tends to hinder open communication, she's filed that piece of information under the category of "parenting practices for wusses." So, when I informed her of my own experience with her spine doctor and the results of all the diagnostic testing, her response was, "I *told you* that you are too old to shovel snow." I actually laughed out loud and said, "Yes, you're right." There's no point in me being sullen about things since mom *is* right about that.

Ironically, the leg length discrepancy has been easy to remedy through the introduction of oh-so-clever lifts that are inserted into my right shoes, and then gradually expanded to minimize the discrepancy over a period of several months. The lifts now have me standing up straight for the first time and my life—instead of tilting to the right, my sense of balance has vastly improved so long as I'm wearing shoes,[2] and even my field of vision has been slightly altered.[3] But the spine damage is a bigger hurdle, particularly because of the bulging discs, arthritis and stenosis. Chronic back pain is one the most commonly cited reasons Americans either retire early or go on permanent disability. In my case, the damaged discs are not "fixable" per se, but the damage can be managed through physical therapy, regular exercise, and a reduction of physical and other stress. Similarly, the spinal stenosis is irreversible and could progress. Consequently, if I'm not careful, all of this could get much worse leading to possible permanent disability. So, besides making the medical changes and being compliant about physical therapy, exercise and adhering to the dreaded "don't lift list," I was going to have to "rethink" my job. Great, just swell, more personal change—just what I love doing.

"I'M JUST A GIRL WHO CAN'T SAY 'NO'"

One of the wonderful things about being a professor in educational administration and policy is that I get to work with really smart students who care deeply about their own students, their schools and colleagues, as well as the larger society in which we all live. Many of my colleagues at Rutgers and elsewhere are similarly oriented to the greater good. Consequently, I have one of the best jobs in the world since I am surrounded by people who give a damn about other human beings, our communities and our institutions. For someone who leans toward working compulsively, this is a fabulous, if potentially volatile mix, since having a life full of fabulous people committed to the greater good has a major downside: how can you say "no, I can't help you" or "no, I can't do that?" It gets even more agonizing when the project involves issues of social justice and students whom I'm supposed to serve. Of course, Mary will quickly remind me, "you can NOT and should NOT do it all" and "you're trending toward seriously crazy if you think you can." I'll solemnly agree with her, but then worry that if I do say "no" to some invitation for more work, I'll miss out on a potentially fabulous experience as well as the potential to make itsy-bitsy social and political changes. I also worry about losing my job—a highly improbable situation for a tenured full professor. But I spent many years as a working class American, and the industrial collapse wrought by the Reagan era did leave some interesting scars.[4]

I do cause my partner endless consternation with my seemingly inability to say no. But the situation becomes even more complex in an era of chronic faculty shortages. When does "yes" become enabling behavior on my part—particularly when universities are tempted not to hire tenure-track faculty to keep costs down? I am still wrestling with these questions and concerns and so far have no real answers, though I'm starting to get some strong indicators.

That said, I'm tinkering with technology to help with my job. I've moved to all e-mail submissions for student papers and working dissertations, and I only required a hard copy for dissertations that are ready to be defended. I've also started to move my professional library to e-books. The move to e-books has the additional virtue of being able have copies on my work computer and back-up computer (in case of crashes). While the historian in me cringes as I dispense with actual books, I really can't schlep any weight. This task is going to take a number of years, and I won't be able to replace everything. But at this point less is more.

An easier issue to tackle has been professional and personal travel. My idea of hell is to take an airplane—to anywhere. In particular, take offs and landings are the pits because of the bouncing and pressure on my spine, and the ride itself isn't fun because I can't get up and move around too much.

Prior to 9/11, I could at least stand in the back of the plane with other members of the "bad back" club, where we would amiably chat about various spinal disasters for the majority of the trip. But in a post 9/11 world, the airlines and the U.S. federal government want everyone seated and strapped in for the duration of the trip. All I can say is "owww!"

To compensate for my aching back during conference season, I try to pack in extra time to literally cushion the blow of traveling. For example, if a conference begins on Thursday, I'll travel to the locale on Wednesday to give myself enough time to stretch out, rest, settle in, and be ready to go the next day. Similarly, if I get home on a Sunday from a conference, I'll stay home from work the next day to give myself time to recover. During the conference, I try to not to stand too much, sit too much (the chairs are designed to be stacked, not sat upon for any length), to have back-to-back sessions, or go to bed too late (after 10 P.M.). I try to carve out time so I can stretch and do my daily back exercises, and if I've been sitting too long, I now will pace in the midst of a business meeting or conference session. At this point, I don't care about how potentially rude this behavior might seem. After spending a few years actually debating with myself whether or not it would be faster to crawl or walk somewhere because my back hurt so badly, I'm working hard to completely avoid that internal debate.

And finally, whether I'm home or traveling, I strive to be uber-compliant on my pain medications. This is something that many patients, regardless of malady, have a hard time with drug compliance. One really does have to take the medications *exactly* as prescribed, or else. In my case, if I'm not timely on one specific opioid medication, I'll go into withdrawal, which is as jammed-packed and fun-filled as portrayed on the TV. I've only gone there once, by mistake, but it was and remains a harsh lesson learned. While some friends have been horrified that I'm "addicted" to medication, the correct term is "dependent." My body "depends" upon this medication to keep the pain at bay. Without it, I'm a big old lump of miserable. So, it's far better to be "dependent" on a drug than to be mean as hell and on disability due to unmanaged or poorly managed pain. Effective pain management means I can actually go to work. Ineffective pain management, because I'd rather be pious about not taking the supposedly evil opiates/opioids, is seriously counterproductive. No thank you.

LEARNING TO SLEEP WHILE
BEING STRETCHED IN NEW DIRECTIONS

Much to my utter shock, my disconcerting experience with "the rack" has had one more unexpected development: I can fall asleep while lying on my back during the "rack sessions."[5] Since I haven't been able to sleep on my back in over 15 years, it's an astonishing development.

Besides being physically stretched in some new directions, I've also started to be stretched in some interesting directions both personally and professionally. One interesting development has been the need to just "let go" when I can't do something physically. I used to charge ahead and do it (lift luggage, shovel snow, etc.), but now, I either hire out the task (like steam cleaning our carpets) or break the physical task into smaller components (carrying groceries). I'm also starting to pack in time for breaks, exercise, and just "drool time" where I can let my brain pan drip and my back unwind. While I'm literally not built for any sort of balance, I think I'm slowly moving toward some sense of stability in maintaining my professional life and personal life. At times, both do go "upside down," but if I better manage the chronic physical stress associated with my problematic back, the rest should hopefully sort itself out.

NOTES

1. If mom could cram her shattered then rebuilt titanium ankle into a 5 inch heel and then totter out of her apartment with her rolling walker, which she needs because of her complete vertebrae collapse, her world would be complete. She is Jackie Onasis on Fosomax.

2. The balance issues have been most problematic since I have a long and spectacular history of falling down complete flights of stairs, followed by trips to the emergency room at a local hospital. Like wearing glasses, this has been a constant theme in my life. I'm hoping with the change in balance, this bone crunching history is at an end.

3. For those without this "structural blessing," having a leg length discrepancy is like going through life with one shoe on and one shoe off. The torque on the back, as well as the hip, knee, and ankle of the short leg all take their toll after 4½ decades. So far, I've not blown out my hip or knee and the ankle is more stable than it's been in years. But those joints are being monitored.

4. I did my student teaching in Elmira, NY, in instrumental music at Broadway Elementary and Junior High School, and Southside High School. In March of 1985, after spectacular collapse of the area's industrial base, the unemployment rate soared to 21%. The teachers at Broadway Elementary were clobbered both economically and socially. Their husbands' incomes from industrial wages had been far greater than their salaries. But by March of 1985, they were filing their family income tax returns as head of household. This last point was quite traumatic for both the teachers and their spouses, who had previously taken great pride in their capacity as chief breadwinners. These faculty conversations were quite strained and painful.

5. Why I can sleep is that the stretching of the spine allows the bulging discs to slide back into place—hence pain goes away and I fall asleep. The benefits last until I hit a pothole driving home.

CHAPTER 38

ROLE OF VALUES IN WORK-LIFE BALANCE

Restoring Harmony and Reclaiming Purpose

Anthony H. Normore

I begin this chapter with words of wisdom from John Ruskin, English writer and critic of art, architecture, and society, 1819-1900, who at the beginning of the Industrial Revolution said: "In order that people may be happy in their work, these three things are needed: they must be fit for it, they must not do too much of it, and they must have a sense of success in it" (cited in Thinkexist.com., 2011, para.1). There was a time in my life when the boundaries between work and home were fairly clear. Today however, and if I were to allow it to happen, the expectations of my work could easily invade my personal life and take complete control. Having spent 29 years in the work force I continue to battle the work-life balance. I do believe however that my work-life balance isn't out of reach and as a result I engage in regular evaluations of my relationship to my work. And yes, I continue to strive for ways to strike a healthier balance by engaging in meaningful daily accomplishments and enjoyment in my life around work, family, friends, and self. And I think that's true for all of us. McDaniel (2011) said it best: "Life will deliver the value and balance we desire ... when we are achieving and enjoying something every single day ... in *all*

Juggling Flaming Chain Saws: Academics in Educational Leadership Try to Balance Work and Family, pp. 325–333

the important areas that make up our lives" (p. 2). To quote Winston Churchill, "We make a living by what we get, but we make a life by what we give" (cited in quotedb.com., 2012)

Recent research indicates that consistently working long hours and not taking respite away from work can have a damaging and negative effect on personal life (Helms, 2010; Jacobs & Winslow, 2004; Perna, 2005; Ward & Wolf-Wendel, 2005). I learned a long time ago when I first entered the work force how tempting it was to rack up hours at work, especially during times when I found myself trying to earn a promotion or manage an ever-increasing workload. However, what I didn't realize at the time is that with increased expectations at the work place came more responsibility. In other words, I was quickly becoming my own worst enemy and perpetuating the very practices and behaviors I vowed earlier to never succumb to. Like any snowball effect one thing lead to another and pretty soon more concerns and challenges surfaced. While overtime was never expected—at least not contractually—there were many times when it appeared to be a requirement. As a result, I spent a large chunk of my time engaged in work-related activities while my personal relationships took a hit. The language at home and at work seemed to revolve around deadlines, 11th-hour work habits, the midnight oil lamp along with alarm clocks soon became my good friends. As a result, I was forced to consciously alter my sense of priorities due to a loss of personal time and commitments to friends and loved ones. Not one to shift my responsibilities on the shoulders of other, I realized I needed to take back my life —to restore its harmony and reclaim its purpose. It's been iterated time and time again in management circles that working long hours and not taking personal downtime makes for a more productive workforce. In my view, this notion is a managerial myth, with no foundation to support it. Our bodies are complex biological machines, and like all machines they can wear out long before intended—if not cared for (Cooper, 2011).

In order to share my thoughts on work-life balance it's critical that I first share the essence of who I am and how I've come to be that person— my personal and professional experiences, my values and the role these values play in my work-life balance, my philosophy of education (my work), and how I've been influenced by strong mentorship.

IN THE CONTEXT OF A PERSONAL WAKE-UP CALL

It was 1989—a turning point year in my life. After having just returned to Canada from a 1 year care-free "working holiday" in Europe and North Africa I was headed to a new teaching job in a rural out port eastern Canada. I had planned a stopover to visit with my sister who was 9 months pregnant at the time. She was scheduled to deliver her first baby any day now. It just so happened that she went into labor during my stay and her baby was on the way. Thrilled with the excitement of the moment and coupled with some anxiety about the first baby in the family I sat in her home with a couple of friends while she and her husband went to the hospital. We waited for the news. The news came. In a matter of moments, our worlds turned upside down. My niece Janine was born with a birth defect known as Microcephaly.

In our little corner of the world, little was known about microcephaly. We learned later that it's a birth defect caused by cytomegalovirus. Cytomegalovirus is a virus that infects 50-85% of adults in the United States by age 40 and is also the virus most frequently transmitted to a child before birth in the first trimester of pregnancy. My sister was 29 at the time and after two ultrasounds up to the day of delivery there was no indication that Janine was underdeveloped or that any kind of birth defect was expected. Janine weighed in at two pounds, jaundiced, and severely underdeveloped leaving her blind, deaf, and immobile with minimal communication ability. She was given 24 hours at most to live. Two families were completely unprepared for this day. If it weren't for the family, friends, the medical community, and support groups in the greater community Janine would not be reaching her 22nd birthday on August 31, 2011.

As I continue to witness the importance of love, patience, nurturance, and compassion for Janine's care throughout these last 22 years I am grateful to be part of this experience. I continue to see resilience take precedence with Janine's parents as they move forward despite the many setbacks they've faced as parents of a child who has undergone numerous surgeries, infections, regular bouts of pneumonia due to a weak immune system, and hospitalization. The parents have become experts in how to change a feeding tube, how to operate a ventilator, how to cope with daily "unknowns"—all while maintaining two jobs as educators and raising two sons who are now 18 and 20 and in college. I am grateful for the opportunity to learn more about disabilities, how society treats people who are different, and what it truly means to contribute to the learning of those around us who are less informed about issues that do not directly affect them. One major lesson learned for me is that family and friends matter most at the end of the day.

Values have always played a central role in my life. It's the essence of who I am as a human being and my professional life's work as a scholar-educator. My professional values act in sync with my personal values and serve as my moral compass to having a sense of direction or purpose. As humans we have the freedom of choice to make decisions but decisions about right and wrong constitute only a subset of all the valuations I make. Above all else, it's the true essence of my "being"—my heart and soul and my ability to decide about what is good, true, just, and beautiful. With a debt of gratitude to my parents, grandparents, siblings, friends, professional colleagues, and to the larger national and international community, my core values are centered on hope, love, respect, benevolence, goodwill and concern for the welfare of others, doing good deeds, trust, respect for self and all people, and an appreciation of the genuine relationships in society for which I hold myself and others responsible.

Anything I do that could jeopardize my relationships sets me up for failure as a human being. I continue to work hard but I also play hard. I realized a long time ago that my work will very likely always be there with or without me. I am not indispensible. Family and friends have always played a pivotal role in my life. As I reflect on my core values and how I continue to live my life several significant lessons/expressions I've heard over time resonate with me and continue to be pervasive in determining my daily personal and professional interactions as I search for balance.

- I have a contribution to make to the world.
- It is not my right to criticize, judge, condemn, or try to control others.
- I am not indispensable.
- It is not the things I say that really matter; it is the things that I do.
- I can't always control what happens to me, but I can always control how I react to it.

We are all shaped by our experiences. I am shaped by my experiences as a child, as a youth, and throughout my adulthood. From an early age my parents, grandparents, and extended family taught me the importance of never taking anything for granted and extending love to *all* people of the world, regardless of race, religion, nationality or any other artificial distinction. I was taught that we should never fail to do the good things we would expect of others and that humility is a quality of being courteous and respectful of others. Acting with humility does not in any way deny our own self worth. Rather, it affirms the inherent worth of all people. My upbringing focused on the importance of humility—and that humility is what is needed to live in peace and harmony with all persons, and that slander, greed, deceit, and arrogance had no place in the home or the community.

ON A PROFESSIONAL LEVEL

One of the hallmarks of a stellar organization is when its culture is characterized by a shared belief that the organization contributes to the health and livelihood of its members into the future. It accomplishes this mission by integrating its activities into a set of values that act as bell weathers across communities and generations. My work launches from a perspective that every interaction I have as a member of the education community must be consistent with my personal values system in supporting personal and professional growth, respect, integrity, compassion, competence and responsibility. I do this in my daily interactions with others, in my role as teacher and mentor, in the seriousness that I give to my professional productivity as a facilitator of learning, scholar and researcher, in my duties as a member of various professional learning communities and in my ability to integrate my professional skills into the important work of learning organizations within the community, within the country, and throughout the world.

Throughout my years in education as a public school teacher, school site and district level administrator, and a professor of educational leadership I have relentlessly supported and encouraged individual talents and strengths of my students and colleagues; facilitated student skill development needed to succeed as professionals and scholars; have devoted time and effort to support professional and personal development of graduate students by encouraging them to engage in the professional/academic community; and, have a long-term commitment to the mentor-protégé relationship with my students. Most of all, I continue to hope that my moral character has influenced and continue to influence the manner in which those who surround me exercise integrity, courage, fortitude, honesty, conviction, respect, kindness and loyalty to the communities in which we/they serve.

My professional practice is guided by a philosophy that has guided my entire professional career. It provides me with a platform for reflective practice and directed self-improvement which ultimately documents my progress toward, and attainment of, established goals as an educator. My primary motivation is guided by my values system to help create an environment for restructuring sound education directed toward the provision of the best quality of education for ALL students. I want to see people learn, grow and make contributions to improvement of our society. My work as a professional educator allows me to take on this responsibility for myself and encourages me to help further these possibilities in others. I have been most fortunate in academe in that I have two brilliant, caring, supportive and compassionate friends (also colleagues who I'll call GJ and JB) who I rely on constantly to remind me of my work's purpose in those moments when I may be pondering about "why I do what I do." They are my support network and always there when and if I need them to be. They work hard, and like me, are guided by the essence of who they are as human beings when reflecting on the work-life balance. Every faculty member in academe should have a GJ and a JB. And every nonfaculty member should have one too.

EDUCATION PHILOSOPHY AND PRACTICE

My philosophy as an educator reflects a learner-centered orientation. I think of myself as an educator who facilitates learning opportunities rather than as a teacher of a subject. I believe that effective education does more than educate students—it also acts as a working model of civil society, and thereby helps to create, sustain, and improve our communities. Accordingly, I believe it is the responsibility of all educators at all levels to focus on educating and encouraging communities of students to develop into responsible, caring and contributing citizens. Effective education is inclusive, from the classroom to the boardroom, because supporters of education believe than an inclusive education is best for students and for the community, and an inclusive democratic government for education is best for the community. Education must be barrier free, values driven, and respectful of every student, every worker, and every citizen. My belief is that an effective educational system provides a quality education by guaranteeing that every child will have a place in a jurisdiction or in the care of that jurisdiction by making a habit to help, or at least to do no harm, to any child. This belief is governed by a democratic process that is open to every member of the community regardless of disadvantage or difference. As such, I believe it is my moral imperative to promote civil democracy in preference to any sectarian perspective as the basis for thriving communities; and, celebrate diversity among students and in our communities by working with communities, colleagues and students from different backgrounds, outlooks and experiences. In my early years as a novice educator I believed the same to be true. In those earlier years however, while I acknowledged the existing perils in the world in blind conformity and indifference I did little to prevent them. I found myself sometimes locked in my immediate sphere of interest, losing sight of the larger picture. Today, my social justice advocacy has become more intentional and meaningful as a result of having a niece who lives on the margins of society. A long as Janine is considered a child on the margins, then I, too, live on the margins. It's been personal for quite some time.

MENTORING AND BEING MENTORED.

While in graduate school, I was fortunate to receive a true "servant mentor" as my dissertation supervisor. Through his continued guidance and support I was able to feel much less overwhelmed, disoriented, and frustrated with the expectations graduate students often experience in graduate school. My dissertation supervisor taught me the importance of creating a mentor-protégé relationship between professor and the student. While helping me to adjust to the many nuances, idiosyncrasies, and unwritten codes of the institution, he provided me with leadership and mentoring characterized in the form of coaching, guidance, assistance, advising, sharing, and sponsorship. This relationship has lasted over time and marked by a substantial emotional commitment from both of us. The true mark of a mentor is seen when the protégé continues the legacy of the mentor who encourages students to "pay forward."

In my role as an educator it is my responsibility to provide the guidance and sponsorship to my students by speaking or writing on their behalf, or simply "being" there on a spiritual level. I further believe that as a professor I should stand for the best that university life can exemplify —having a warm presence coupled with a deep personal integrity that spreads trust. A student should never need to worry about my position on issues that affect human welfare—that I am there for people, for building and nurturing relationships, that my word is true, and that I teach all students by example—that I am ultimately guided by a strong sense of values, morals and guiding principles.

With courage, conviction, self-efficacy, and a powerful integration of faith and learning, we can further mould and stimulate keen intellects that enhance and promote student-centered learning, we can create and support scholar-practitioners; we can further build and enhance innovative communities of practice that foster lifelong learning, social responsibility and justice; we can further lead by example in the exercise of integrity and ethical standards of conduct, and; further embrace a diverse culture that is compassionate, caring, and respectful for the dignity of all in the community. With an open mind and heart I believe we can all embrace the human spirit of multiple backgrounds and perspectives and further make a difference in the world while maintaining a healthy work-life balance.

SOME STRATEGIES TOWARD STRIKING A WORK-LIFE BALANCE

As long as I work, juggling the demands of my career and my personal life will probably be an ongoing challenge. Like most people, my hope is to keep a balance between paid work and personal attachments without being victimized at work. With much effort and time I have managed to find coping strategies within my control that helps find the work-life balance that's best for me. It may not work for others however. As Joshi (2011) indicates, "There is no perfect, one-size-fits-all, balance we should be striving for. The best work-life balance is different for each of us because we all have different priorities and different lives" (para. 1). Returning to my values system, I learned that if I don't invest in strategies and personal disposal time in my relationships outside, with my family and friends, I'm at risk of undermining the very social support systems I may need in difficult and stressful times. I intentionally seek out strategies that: nurture my personal life with family and friends that are separate from professional work (i.e., visits, lunches, dinners, outings, family gatherings, and special occasions); maintaining a weekly physical exercise routine that helps boost my energy level and ability to focus; and enjoying creative leisure activity (museums, reading, walks on the beach).

In my professional work I tend to take advantage of my options by exercising more control over my work hours while fulfilling the needs of my institution and my students; engage in tasks sharing; telecommuting; and other scheduling flexibility. I've learned to say "no" at my work place (especially for committees that only sometimes or never meet) and think it's perfectly acceptable to respectfully say so. As a result, I've learned to make more room in my life for the activities that are meaningful to me and bring some personal fulfillment. I tend to manage my time reasonably well by organizing household tasks more efficiently, such as running errands when necessary rather than saving it all for a particular day. I keep a weekly to-do list. I do what needs to be done and let the rest go (although sometimes reluctantly and not always successfully). I've also learned to bolster my support system. At work, I tend to join forces with coworkers who can cover for me if and when necessary—and vice versa. At home, I've enlisted a trusted neighbor to check in on my home when I travel for extended periods of time. Further, I've heeded the advice of Marilyn Puder-York (cited in Douglas, 2011) who indicates that "Many people waste their time on activities or people that add no value—for example, spending too much time at work with a colleague who is constantly venting and gossiping," (para. 3). She recommends "taking stock of activities that aren't really enhancing our career or personal life and minimizing the time we spend on them" (para. 2, cited in Douglas, 2011).

Striking a healthy work-life balance isn't a one-shot deal for me. Creating work-life balance is a continuous process as my personal obligations, interests and work life change. I continue to reflect and examine my priorities—and make changes, if necessary—to make sure I'm staying on track. I'm almost certain that we would all agree that a substantial increase in our work is due, in part, by information technology and by an intense, competitive work environment. Sometimes however, the pressures at work are self-inflicted so to avoid allowing these pressures to take its toll on our well-being my suggestion is to reflect and reprioritize

REFERENCES

Cooper, C. (2011). *Well being: Productivity and happiness at work*. New York, NY: Palgrave Macmillan.

Douglas, N. (2011). *Good living – figure out the secret to work-family balance*. Retrieved http://www.ultimate-health-fitness.com/healthy-living/good-living-figure-out-the-secret-to-work-family-balance.html

McDaniel, V. (2011). New year' resolutions with a twist. *Administrator, 2*(1), 2

Helms, R. M. (2010). *New challenges, new priorities: The experience of generation x faculty*. Cambridge, MA: Collaborative on Academic Careers in Higher Education.

Jacobs, J. A., & Winslow, S. E. (2004). Overworked faculty: Job stresses and family demands. *The ANNALS of the American Academy of Political and Social Science, 596*(1), 104-129.

Joshi, S. (2011). *Balance: Calling the bluff*. Retrieved from http://completewellbeing.com/article/calling-the-bliff/

Perna, L. (2005). The relationship between family and employment outcomes. *New Directions for Higher Education, 130*, 5-23.

Quotedb.Com. (2012). Retrieved from http://www.quotedb.com/quotes/3185

Think-Exist.com. (2011). Retrieved from http://thinkexist.com/quotation/in_order_that_people_may_be_happy_in_their_work/146362.html

Ward, K., & Wolf-Wendel, L. E. (2005). Work and family perspectives from research university faculty. *New Directions for Higher Education, 130*, 67-80.

CHAPTER 39

BOOMER BRED

Professional and Personal Reflections and Strategies to Survive in the Professoriate

Rosemary Papa

As a member of the Boomer generation, I entered higher education believing I could do it all, *I am woman hear me roar*. As a second generation Italian Mexican American and of the first generation to go to college, I lived the 1970s and 1980s as a super woman believing I could "bring home the bacon," and raise my children happily and keep my home amazingly clean. The balance act was work in a man's world by day and be the wife, mother, daughter, sister by night.

I entered higher education in my mid 30s. I had been successful as a teacher, principal, and a chief school administrator prior to being hired in a tenure track position at a large public regional comprehensive university in central California.

Moving back to California from the Midwest in 1986, I had 3 small daughters in tow, a not too healthy mother and a husband who decided to seek his fame and fortune overseas. My girls were 8, 6, and 3. My success in the Midwest in the K-12 arena had led me to believe I would be fine in higher education. I was born and raised in Los Angeles and was excited to

*Juggling Flaming Chain Saws: Academics in Educational Leadership
Try to Balance Work and Family,* pp. 335–342
Copyright © 2012 by Information Age Publishing

be back in progressive California. During this time I was being divorced by my first husband.

HIGHER EDUCATION IN CALIFORNIA CIRCA THE MID-1980S

To my surprise I was not warmly embraced by the other Educational Administration faculty—all White male and former superintendents, in 1986. I was later to discover I was the university's first female tenure track hire in educational administration and one of only a few in California. My surprise was coming from the Midwest, I thought California was not as progressive as I had remembered. I expected to be valued for being a former chief school administrator. My program coordinator took me for coffee the week before classes began, August 1986, and told me he did not want me in the program and that he had resigned in protest from the search committee prior to my coming in for the interview. He went on to say that he did not believe in former, female superintendents period. It was a man's role and certainly not one with three small children. I felt stunned at hearing his perspective. And, my recalcitrant program director also told me he had changed my textbook order for his book selections and gave me four different course preparations all at the 7 P.M.–10 P.M. time slot. With some resistance I at least managed to change my book orders back to the books I had chosen.

Thus began my time in higher education. I had just moved 2,000+ miles and wholesaled my vehicle to buy beds for my children and mother. We were in a rented 900-square foot condo within a half mile of campus. So, I walked my children to school, walked to the bank, the market and took cabs to the pediatrician when my kids were sick.

All universities in the California State University system were exploring in the mid-to-late 1980s joint doctoral degrees with the University of California system. I had chosen my university over two other offers as it was nestled in the beautiful San Joaquin Valley, the growing food garden of the west coast. Two other universities had offered me tenure track positions as I was a published former chief school administrator from the midwest.

It was an interesting time in California higher education and I was fortunate enough to be at the center of the drama provided by the Commission of the Master Plan in 1987. The Master Plan of the state (a type of strategic plan) distinguished the doctoral granting universities from the regional comprehensive universities and the community college system. The trifurcation worked in some ways and naturally not in others. As is the case when dealing with a document that was over 50 years old, institutions began through population growth and employer needs to outgrow the three distinct categories of universities under the master plan.

The California State University system began to become sensitive to the K-12 arena's need for an advanced degree for school district leaders. All of the CSUs were hoping for the ability to offer a practitioner degree, the EdD, in educational leadership. So, as I was returning to the state I was met with great zeal to be hired.

However, the reality of this position was: I was the colleges' first female hire in educational administration. As I looked around the college I noticed quickly that there were only two females that were full professors and around the state through the CSU system and across the University of California system, females were rare to find in my discipline.

SO, HOW DID I SURVIVE?

I found an immediate mentor by putting myself outside of the rather parochial setting which existed. There was a call for a researcher to work with a strong name in the field of education administration from back east. Dr. Charles Achilles, a professor with expertise in class size, was working a consultant job in a nearby school district and needed local help. I was the only one to answer the call and that colleague became a career long mentor to me. I worked with him on his research project, got involved in the nearby district working with all the administrators and teachers, so my local research efforts began.

Dr. Charles Achilles led me to my first NCPEA, National Council of Professor of Educational Administration summer conference, in 1987. And, NCPEA has played a very important role in how I grew into my professional life. At my first summer conference in 1987, I met Dan Griffiths, Charol Shakeshaft, Jack Culbertson, et cetera, just to name a few. I was one of four female professors in attendance at Chadron, Nebraska. In the picture depicted two wives joined their husbands, hence the six women. I found this to be quite telling to what I discovered with the paucity of women in higher educational leadership in California.

It was an amazingly embracing organization. The professorial colleagues were great. The spouses (mostly wives) were supportive and it was a kid-friendly environment. I brought my 8-year-old daughter and thereafter, all three of my girls would grow up at NCPEA summer conferences. And, today, my granddaughter, Josephine, attends with me.

The inclusive nature of NCPEA helped me write many articles, critique my research and guided my entire career. As a former K-12 administrator, it reminded me of NASSP (National Association of Secondary School Principals) and AASA (American Association of School Administrators)

Figure 39.1.

conferences for the camaraderie. And, my children could come too. As a single parent this was very important to my life.

I became the first female president of NCPEA, 1991-1992, and it is the acknowledgement in my career for which I am still most humbled. In a man's environment, educational administration, I was accepted for my experience in K-12 and higher education. I would be able to mentor more females and professors of color into the hierarchy of a national organization.

Other important mentors emerged from the University of California. I was open to working with all and tried not to show my fear of difference: female and from a regional comprehensive institution. The first four strategies relate most to those new in the professoriate.

Strategy #1:   A willingness to work with others, be mentored by others is a key strategy. And, finding an organization, such as the National Council of Professors of Education Administration, that nurtures your scholarship and research is critical.

Strategy #2:   Internal to the university, I developed female colleagues both for writing and for my personal ongoing friendships. There was one female colleague who had children that were young. Otherwise, I developed lots of "older sisters" who surrounded me with their wisdom of surviving in the university environment and helped me with my children, especially when I was sick. We were a very tight knit group and without their support I may not have survived.

Strategy #3: Female and minority graduate students became a focus to give support to that I have kept through today. Mentoring became a personal and professional obligation. Being a mentor to students and junior colleagues actually became a support system for me.

In 1991, I was the founding codirector of the first joint doctoral program in Education Leadership between a CSU (California State University) and five UC's (University of California). It was a regional doctoral degree with participating professors from UC Berkeley and CSU Sacramento in the north to UC Los Angeles in the south, including UC Santa Barbara and Davis. Faculty from the six campuses came into the San Joaquin Valley to deliver a doctoral program for school practitioners. I was fortunate to have founded this program and it became my first *Camelot* experience in higher education. At times, I had more UC administrators supporting the development of this program, at the time Dean Henry Trueba, UC Davis, than I would have envisioned. He worked tirelessly on this doctoral degree with me. And, this program would not have been possible without my female colleagues internal to the university and NCPEA colleagues and friends. They gave me the support and courage I needed to fulfill this major accomplishment in California.

Strategy #4: My work-life balance was essential to my success. So, many aspects of the founding of this degree in my professional life were balanced by my personal life and *my belief in myself to be a good scholar and a good mother.* When UC faculty came in to teach, many stayed at my home, sharing many dinners with my children. When NCPEAers came into Central California, they too stayed at my home.

My children were/are an integral aspect of who I am and I had to find a balance in my work and home lives. In 1991, I married for the second time and found a life partner that embraced me, my work life and especially my children.

OPEN TO CHANGES, STUMBLING AND PICKING MY SELF BACK UP

My career in the CSU led me from the single campus to a central office position in academic affairs, working creatively with the University of California on joint degrees across disciplines. I was fortunate to have strong mentors who gave me the sense I could bring this program to fruition in the then chancellor of the CSU and the president of the UC. When the CSU Chancellor left his position, I left to pursue a private industry opportunity. My curiosity with business began when I was working with the CA Business Roundtable and its desire to impact K-12 education. I always wanted to know if I could be successful in the business world. So, I took a leave of absence while still maintaining some of my systemwide duties and joined a company that sent me to many school districts around the country. The position I found was with a major educational company located back east and I became their teacher expert and was given the title of vice president.

My girls at this time were either in high school or just beginning college so I thought working nationally would not be a problem. They now had a father who adored them and gave us all great stability. Little did I know that I would spend the next 12 months traveling over 150,000 miles going back and forth across the country. When my youngest began to refer to me as the *absent mommy* I realized I had created a huge imbalance in my life. A big stumble!

Strategy #5:   I found the work I was doing quite fulfilling and exciting in the corporate environment focused on for-profit and philanthropic educational products. But, my family was more important. When you choose a path that turns out not to be best for those you love, stop, reevaluate, and make a change. I did and never looked back.

I still had the 'fire in the belly' to keep achieving in my field. Located in a town with only one public university and married to a high level administrator at that university posed a problem for career advancement at that institution. I sat down with my spouse and looked at what might be possible, focused on an administrative position on the California coast and was offered the job. They guaranteed me 1 week a month home. This position geographically was 6 hours by car or two plane stops away from my home.

My husband was not thrilled. My youngest child was even less thrilled. She refused to move with me. I declined the offer with quite a heavy heart. I felt that this was the end of my administrative ambitions. It was very tough to return to my 'husband's' university.

Strategy #6:   Jobs come and go. Families are forever. Change is constant. It is one's outlook that becomes primary in how to view one's success or failures. You hold your own cards. How you feel about them says a lot about your ability to handle disappointment and move on to find your next dream. So, a brief pity party is okay. Get over it and see what is next coming your way.

Returning to a single campus environment is interesting. I found it hard at first. Happy for my husband's career, but tough on my sense of work self. My girls were happy and my husband fulfilled in his work. I too, felt that choosing my family over my own ambitions was the right decision. It just felt tough when I was at work.

As life has a way of working out, within a few days of being at the university I was approached for a faculty position that had been nationally posted but not filled. I was spoken to by "board" members of the Center for Teaching and Learning wooing me to take the position. It would keep me low on the radar from my husband's work and yet let me work with all faculty across the disciplines. Not quite like the state of California former academic affairs for the CSU, the UC, or the national work within corporate America, but it was at least campus wide work.

I grew to love this job. It was a center that worked in a nondeficit way with faculty to improve their teaching. And, I intertwined technology into helping faculty change their teaching strategies which became a win-win. I began to travel worldwide (China, West Africa, Taiwan, etc.) based on my adult learning theory and practices I created while in this position. I was very lucky to work in a job I loved while home with the family!

Strategy #7: Know yourself. I knew a department would seem too parochial in my work life and though the director position was still humbling to take it was campuswide in its work focus. Reflection is critical to giving yourself permission to explore other options in your work life and examine the limits we place on ourselves through preconceived notions of worth and value.

In late 2006, my husband casually mentioned to one of my colleagues at a UCEA conference that he was considering retirement. He was curious of what potential there might be for me in my career if I was free to move. The word soon spread that I might be "available" to leave California. Within a short time I was offered two endowed chair positions and subsequently accepted one of them. I was fortunate that during my time in other positions I had kept up my writings, research, and connections in my field. Now, I have a position that allows me to research and publish with "abandon."

Strategy #8: Life is about change. Enjoy it. Attitude, curiosity and actively embracing what is real and in front of you are aspects of knowing who you are and accepting yourself as you are while focusing on all you can be if only you let yourself try.

IT IS WHAT IT IS

Changes happen often. We directly control very little. Clearly, *our* attitude is something we do control. If you choose a path that turns out not to be best for those you love, stop, reevaluate, and make some changes. And, stumbling is ok and *is* to be expected. Self-reflection is critical to giving yourself permission to explore other options and lets you embrace what is real in front of you and with mentors to guide you, your family circumstance and professional career will be all you wish and hope it to be. So, remember:

- Be a mentee and mentor
- As you are mentored, *pay it forward* to your students
- Keep your personal *life* foremost
- Stumbling is to be expected.
- Know yourself. Be brave.
- Life is about change. Enjoy it!

REFERENCE

Commission for the Master Plan Renewed. (1987). *The master plan renewed: Unity, equity, quality and efficiency in California postsecondary education.* Retrieved from http://www.ucop.edu/acadinit/mastplan/MPComm1987.pdf

CHAPTER 40

DON'T STOP BELIEVIN' IN THE IMPORTANCE OF WORK-LIFE BALANCE

Linda Skrla

Since 2004, I've met everyone who's currently in or who has ever been a member of the U.S. rock band Journey except two former drummers and legendary former front man Steve Perry. I have countless autographs, dozens of guitar picks and drum sticks, an assortment of cheesy pictures with band members, a drawer full of tour T-shirts, and a bulletin board covered with ticket stubs—in addition to the entire music catalog from the band's 35-year career on CD, MP3, and DVD, plus a raft of additional music from various band members' other bands and side projects. Founding guitarist Neal Schon routinely waves at me in my customary spot in the front row on "his" side of the stage at several concerts each year.

Over these past 7 years, I've met hundreds of fellow Journey fans from across the United States and around the world, several of whom have become close friends. We turn up in various configurations at concerts and at pre- and postshow parties and interact with each other on music fan sites and on Facebook. Among this new group of friends and acquaintances are engineers, psychologists, teachers, doctors, nurses, physical therapists, musicians, business owners, groundskeepers, military personnel, students, retirees, and homemakers. What they all have in common—

*Juggling Flaming Chain Saws: Academics in Educational Leadership
Try to Balance Work and Family,* pp. 343–348
Copyright © 2012 by Information Age Publishing
All rights of reproduction in any form reserved.

in addition to their love of all things Journey-related—is something they've all figured out that I wish I had clued in to much, much sooner. That is, these rock and roll aficionada/os understand the importance of leading a life that has balance, one that includes a space for nonwork-related activities/interests/avocations that are significant sources of positive energy (happiness) in one's life.

As a scholar and professor of educational administration who holds multiple leadership roles and who has an avowedly social justice-oriented research agenda, it is not unproblematic for me to come out as a major classic rock and roll fan. Regrettably, there is not a positive social construction available at present in U.S. society for a middle aged White female who really enjoys live rock music. While at least one group of ethnographers (Krenske & McKay, 2002) have studied rock fans and suggested categories for female fans, including *metal wench, glam chick,* and *hardcore bohemian,* complete with dress codes, body types, and general modes of participation (p. 271), none of those quite work for someone in her 50s with a PhD, a responsible and demanding job, three grown sons, and an encyclopedic knowledge of 1970s and 1980s rock bands.

In fact, for the first few years of my reinvigorated interest in screaming guitars, leather jackets, and sappy lyrics, I didn't mention my concert adventures to anyone except my children and closest friends. I kept the fun I was having to myself because the first few times I did bring it up outside my most inner circle of confidants, the comments I received were almost always disbelieving, sniggering, or downright insulting. "Groupie" was a term tossed out around a lot. Apparently, even though the band members of the groups I follow are almost all older than I am, for some reason it is socially acceptable for them still to be out there rocking, but it is definitely not okay for me to be still rocking out to their music.

As a feminist scholar in educational administration, I certainly understand the narrow range of acceptable social constructions for middle aged femaleness and the balancing act all women perform in "doing gender" (Butler, 1990) in ways coded as appropriate. I also understand the paradox apparent in my choosing a swaggering, macho, sexist culture like the rock music scene (Krenske & McKay, 2002) in which to hang out for fun and entertainment. However, like Audre Lorde (1982), I've come to understand and accept myself well enough to know that the position furthest out on the margin is often the place where I am most comfortable. So, I now worry less about the codes and judgments others might assign to my enjoyment of classic rock and roll and, instead, try to embrace it as a valued part of a balance life.

OVERACHIEVEMENT AS THE DEFAULT SETTING

This understanding and acceptance, though, was extremely tough to acquire while working under the pressure of the normalizing culture of the educational administration professoriate. This culture developed from a history described by Mertz (2009) in this way:

> Pressure to legitimate the field of school administration and ground it in the growing scientific movement nurtured the growth of university-based program to prepare school administration, school superintendents in particular (Blount, 1998; Campbell, Fleming, Newell, & Bennion, 1987). From their inception, such departments were almost exclusively male, mirroring the their administrative counterparts in schools.... But the professoriate was even more tightly gendered than its counterpart in the schools.... Professors of educational administration taught and then joined their former students in projects and organizations developed for school administrators, forming a neat, companionable network of knows, a proverbial "good old boy network." (p. 3)

Though women have infiltrated this network in increasing numbers over the past 2 decades, the culture of the professorate in our field continues to bear the imprint of this history—making it a particularly difficult place for many women to fit in and to achieve professional success while maintaining a healthy sense of work/life balance.

Thus, women join the ranks of the educational administration professorate (often from the practice of school administration) in tenure-track roles and unknowingly and unreflectively get caught up in a cycle of trying to please others, to get everything right, to overcome obstacles with hard work, and to self-silence with respect to unfairness, discrimination, and disrespect. We tend to strive to do more and better amid constant reminders that we won't get tenure if we don't—don't publish more in higher ranked journals, don't get more grant money, don't chair more dissertations, don't serve on more committees, don't take on national leadership roles, don't present at more conferences, don't serve on more editorial boards. And, most important of all, we must always, always "be nice" while doing all these things. Furthermore, with the advent of the internet and, more recently, social media, we are literally in constant reach and are always in touch with our colleagues and students, potentially turning our jobs into 70-80 hour a week positions. How many of us reach for the iPhone or Blackberry immediately upon awakening to check work e-mail and also look at it last thing at night before going to sleep?

The pressure to be right and to be correct and to be high performing (while being nice) isn't, of course limited to the work environment. As has been documented elsewhere (Hochschild & Machung, 2003), women have a second shift to work, where the expectations by others and those we place on ourselves to be perfect are just as fierce as they are in the workplace. We think we should be perfect partners, perfect parents, perfect daughters, perfect members of our faith communities, perfect friends, and so forth. And we think if we somehow just work harder and somehow get everything right that we won't have to face discrimination, we won't be criticized for our choices, our children will be magically well-adjusted, our relationships with our partners will never fail, and on and on. In our rush to do ever more and to do it all perfectly, our work/life balance becomes severely unbalanced, often without our awareness.

RESETTING THE BALANCE

Unfortunately, the overachievement and perfectionism strategies that many women in professional settings, including the educational administration professoriate, default in to do not really work well over the long term. People will criticize you anyway, you will experience discrimination and unfair treatment, your children will encounter the typical difficulties of growing up, and your relationships will struggle.

I distinctly remember looking up from my computer one day and realizing that, after having devoted 6 years to the single minded pursuit of tenure, I was newly divorced and had completely lost touch with most of the things that had brought joy into my left in earlier days—women friends, travel, hiking, movies, novels—and, yes, rock music. Other women faculty members in our field have noted similar patterns. Carolyn Wood (2009), for example, found herself facing a diagnosis of clinical depression after having won an extraordinarily bitter battle for tenure and wondering, "Why would anyone be depressed after winning?" (p. 47).

I'm not sure what Wood did after realizing that having won the tenure battle didn't cure her melancholy because her chapter in Mertz's excellent book chronicling pioneering women professors in our field does not report that part of the story. As for me, I made a conscious decision to enter the next phase of my academic life with a different approach than the one I had taken on the run up to tenure. That is, I made a concerted effort to figure out what sorts of things (other than my work) upped the joy factor in my life. This was far more difficult than it may at first sound. I had to spend considerable time sorting out what actually made *me* happier, as opposed to what sorts of things were supposed to make me happy according to societal gender scripts or what things made my children (or parents or ex-spouse) happy.

Like Gretchen Rubin (2010), the author of the currently best-selling *The Happiness Project*, I applied the same sort of focus and deliberate effort that I use in my work life to identifying and choosing to participate in non-work-related activities that I enjoy. Although the list of things I eventually came up with that are outside of the work sphere and that up the happiness factor in my life included many more items than rock music, attending live concerts by favorite artists was high up that list. Luckily for me, there has been a renaissance for 1970s and 1980s rock bands over the past 10 years, and many of them have produced new albums and hit the tour circuit nearly every summer.

I wish it hadn't taken so long for me to figure out that work/life balance wasn't just important for other people and that it was something to which I should pay serious attention. Or perhaps it was only after having achieved tenure that I was able to relax sufficiently to give myself permission to care for myself by allowing nonachievement activities back into my life. I can say with confidence, however, that the addition of such activities has not diminished my productivity. If anything, it has enhanced it by reducing the length of the trips I routinely take to self-doubt hell when trying to produce scholarly work. The music soundtrack now often playing in my head seems to drown out the negative messages from old tapes of self-doubt that sometimes still load and autoplay.

Of course, having a "second life" as mega rock fan has created its own new set of challenges. I no longer try to hide this aspect of myself from colleagues or students; in fact, I've become somewhat of a zealot for the work-life balance cause. I often tell my students about my rock and roll adventures as a way of illustrating the importance of not neglecting care of self while they pursue their doctoral degrees. Communicating the importance of work-life balance to my students is part of my ethical stance toward my work. It is not only the nuts and bolts of school administration, theory, and research that these students will need to have successful and productive lives in our field. I am, though, sometimes unsure of how effectively I am communicating this message, as illustrated by the comments of a student in my models of epistemology and inquiry class.

This class is the introductory course in our six-course doctoral research sequence and is basically a philosophy of knowledge course. Students, especially those without a prior experience with the content, find the class extraordinarily challenging. During one summer session of teaching this course, I was teaching on a Friday afternoon and had to leave immediately after class to drive to Fort Worth, Texas, for a concert. Our class was deep into a discussion of postmodern approaches to research in educational administration when I noticed a student with his head in his hands who had stopped participating in the discussion. When I paused the class discussion to ask if he was doing okay, he said, "Dr. Skrla, you are standing up there talking about things I don't understand using words I can't pronounce wearing a Def Leppard T-shirt. You are making my head explode."

REFERENCES

Butler, J. (1990). *Gender trouble: Feminism and subversion of identity.* New York, NY: Routledge.

Hochschild, A., & Machung, A. (2003). *The second shift.* New York, NY: Penguin.

Krenske, L., & McKay, J. (2002). Hard and heavy: Gender and power in a heavy metal subculture. In S. B Merriam (Ed.), *Qualitative research in practice* (pp. 262-282). San Francisco, CA: Jossey-Bass.

Lorde, A. (1982). *Zami: A new spelling of my name—a biomythography.* New York, NY: Crossing Press.

Mertz, N. T. (Ed.). (2009). Framing the stories. In *Breaking into the all-male club: Female professor of educational administration* (pp. 1-12). Albany, NY: SUNY Press.

Rubin, G. (2011). *The happiness project: Or why I spent a year trying to sing in the morning, clean my closets, fight right, read Aristotle, and generally have more fun.* New York, NY: HarperCollins

Wood, C. J. (2009). Nothing except a battle lost can be half so melancholy as a battle won: A fight for tenure. In N. T. Mertz (Ed.), *Breaking into the all-male club: Female professors of educational administration* (pp. 37-50). Albany, NY: SUNY Press.

CHAPTER 41

AVIS LA FIN
AT THE DOWNTOWN GRILL
AND BREWERY

Autumn K. Tooms

I write this from the front porch of the Downtown Grill and Brewery in Knoxville, Tennessee. In front of me is my standard glass of cranberry juice mixed with iced tea and a soft pretzel. This makes it a typical Sunday afternoon as I always have good luck writing on Sundays and in rather odd places. I learned this skill as a doctoral student and wife of a football coach. He would coach his game; I would sit in the stands and write on a legal pad the outlines for papers and projects. When the game was over, coaches from around the city would gather with their wives at a watering hole and kibitz into the wee hours of the morning. I would sit with the wives, my cranberry elixir, and a pile of cocktail napkins waiting to be scribbled on with ideas and paragraphs. While my marriage to the coach did not last, the odd ability to generate an idea and write in the midst of a chaotic bar or playoff game did.

The sporting events celebrated at my hometown brewery are football, basketball, scrabble, people watching, or some combination thereof. In between pretzels, one of my colleagues, an architect who teaches for the University of Tennessee asked, "What are you working on?" I replied, "A chapter about how I balance work and life." He laughed and wondered

Juggling Flaming Chain Saws: Academics in Educational Leadership
Try to Balance Work and Family, pp. 349–357
Copyright © 2012 by Information Age Publishing
All rights of reproduction in any form reserved.

aloud if any consideration had been given to the irony of *where* I was writing and thinking about balancing my work and life. Of course I had. But until his question, I was too much of a coward to admit a most painful truth: I am a workaholic and my work as a scholar is inextricably linked to the other contexts of my life. This affliction is common among academics because of the unique nature of our job.

Junior professors learn quickly that the quest for tenure and promotion is the only thing that matters for the first several years of their career. Building a vita to withstand the specter of faculty ballots continually looms until young academics are coronated as tenured, associate professors. I can tell you the thrill of holding the congratulations letter from the university president lasts about a day; only to be replaced by a hypnotic quest for a higher rank, a deanship, or the vita of a rock star. The first lesson in how to be a professor begins with knowing the crucible of three responsibilities: Teaching, writing, and service. The faculty handbook and "Welcome to our university "brunches never mention the importance of balancing work and life. Why? Because the nature of our profession merges the two together. Such nuances make it difficult to understand what we *do* in the professoriate. A friend once lamented:

> Even my wife doesn't understand what I do for a living. No one really understands the pressure to build a vita unless they are professors too. If the people at my job become unbearable or if the state cuts funding and I need to move to a new university, my vita is the ticket to help me get the next job. Building my vita isn't about my ego, it is about job security. Protecting my vita haunts me every day. It has to because that is how I can provide for myself and my family.

With this universal truth in mind, I begin again by offering a series of axioms that have helped me to find balance as both scholar and human being.

AVIS LA FIN

There is one equalizer among all academics: time. How it is spent is what makes the difference between successful, balanced academics and mediocre scholars struggling to find a moment's peace. It is important to realize there are all kinds of career paths in the professoriate. You must decide what kind of academic you wish to be and how to build a trajectory towards that goal. Do you wish to serve a college that primarily values teaching? Is writing and research something you do not feel ready to be vexed by? Then a large research oriented institution is probably not a good choice for you. Do you want to become a department chair or a dean? Then you might consider a path that includes a great deal of service to your university.

Another question you must answer is what kind of lifestyle do you want? I was once stuck in the Atlanta airport with a senior colleague who was quite famous in her field. I asked why she chose to stay at a relatively small university in the Midwestern United States. She said, "Its simple, I am a big fish at my university and I don't have to work too hard. The president trots me out as a prize to behold and I get to travel all over the world." My colleague is known internationally and she could easily teach at a place like Stanford; but then she would have to put much more energy into her writing and not into her travel. Her insights are to be admired because she knows the kind of life she wants. The first step in balancing work and life is deciding what kind of life you want beyond the title of academic. Understanding where you want to go is the driving force behind a successfully balanced existence.

The Kennedy Clan of Scotland sums the above lesson by way of their motto, *Avis la Fin* (Latin for "Consider the end").[1] A colleague expounded on the idea of *Avis la Fin* during my first year at Kent State University. He said the key to being successful was "getting from Point A to Point B". The trick is deciding what Point B is. Once you have identified Point B, the second step is to realize your goals are not the same as others in your department or college. In many circumstances, they may actually be in direct conflict with the goals of your colleagues'. That's all right because we are independent contractors working in a shell commonly known as a university. Recognizing this dynamic helps us protect our investments of time. It allows invulnerability to guilt trips wrapped around requests for our time and talents related to a project that is of value to *someone else*. Ultimately we are the only ones who can protect ourselves from exhaustion and a career out of balance. The key to such effort rests in consistently maintaining fidelity to your priorities.

SET YOUR GPS

I use the term *Global Positioning System* (GPS) as a metaphor for analyzing your day-to-day responsibilities as they relate to getting to Point B. Often we get sucked into daily projects that winnow away focus on our trajectory. We struggle to complete these projects and our myriad of efforts spill over into the little time left to enjoy life outside professional responsibilities. My GPS is simple; I first identify what Point B is. Then *every single time* I am asked or given the opportunity to do anything professionally I ask myself if it will help or hinder my trajectory toward Point B. Why? Because everything I do should get me from Point A to Point B. Collins (2001) describes this as the "Hedgehog Concept" (p. 25). My exhusband would describe this as keeping your eye on the ball. Focusing on the path to Point B should be the contextual framework for all the choices you make.

I decided early in my first year as an academic that my Point B was to emulate the professors I admired the most. Those scholars had a national presence and were involved with The University Council for Educational Administration (UCEA). Shortly after I had been chosen to serve as a plenum representative to UCEA, I was also nominated to serve as a senator for the Kent State University Senate. The thought of being able to put "senator" on my vita seemed rather prestigious until I sought advice from a senior colleague I greatly admired. She explained that the role of college senator took a great deal of time. If I wanted to invest my time in becoming well known at my university this was a good idea. However, if I wanted to raise my profile outside of my home university I needed to rethink where I was investing my time. And I needed to build a robust vita and publish in international and national tier one journals. This was not easy advice to hear and I sadly withdrew my nomination as a senator. To date, I have never served as a senator. However, I have taken advantage of every opportunity to serve in any capacity as it relates to UCEA, and have enjoyed fruitful collaboratives with colleagues and coauthors from around the world. I still think it would be fun to be a senator, but I simply do not have the time to put towards such an important responsibility.

FIND A MENTOR

I argue that the word mentor has lost its potency because it's definition has been blurred by sloppy discursive use. A mentoring relationship requires chemistry similar to parental-child or even sibling relationships. It is a mutually beneficial relationship between someone older, wiser, and more experienced, and someone younger and less experienced (Browne-Ferrigno & Muth, 2004; Collins & Scott, 1978; Jeruchim & Shapiro, 1992). Such a relationship requires honest dialog, mutual trust, and the willingness of the mentee to reflect on the insights of the mentor (Tooms, 2010). Part of how I look for balance in my life is to trust the insights of my mentors. The way to find a mentor is to look for people who model the values that you admire. Seek their advice, follow it, and build a relationship. A true mentor finds gratification in your success and loyalty (Tooms, 2010). They are a precious force because they serve as both mirror and fulcrum. I have found the most difficult thing to endure professionally is the honest critique of my mentors. Yet following their advice has made a significant difference in my career and life.

My dissertation chair at Arizona State University, Dr. Robert Stout, has been retired for more than 15 years. He has patiently mentored me through several administrative positions and an entire career in academia. He is of paramount import because I always know he will tell me the hard truth, I trust his political analysis of everything, and if he believes I can do something, then I believe it too. In sum he remains the greatest professional inspiration I know. Such is the enchantment of mentoring.

USE THE 5-5-5 RULE

One of the differences between being part of a work force and being a professional is what happens after 5 o'clock. Unlike other noble workers, we do not stop thinking about a project or a deadline after a certain hour and we do not require and office to perform many of the tasks of our job. Paramount to our responsibilities is the interdependence of reading, writing, and research. Because of this I have made the decision to invest the majority of my time reading things that will benefit me the most as a writer and researcher. Thus I sacrifice reading for pleasure many novels because I simply do not have the time. When I hear about a new book I ask myself "Will reading this help me in 5 days, 5 months, or 5 years?" If the answer is, "Yes, what I am reading will end up in a literature review or a paragraph I am writing" then I purchase and inhale a book without hesitation. As a reader I tend to finish a book in one setting because of my obsessive nature. Because I know this, I make a novel wish list and save those books for pending airplane flights and vacations. Magazines are a different story. They are require very little time to read and I can easily put them down and return to them. Over the course of 5 days a magazine provides a nice break from the tasks at hand. Thus, the 5-5-5 rule helps me to structure my reading time into an investment in my writing time.

The 5-5-5 rule is also helpful in conducting a cost benefit analysis when life and work inevitably collide. During my second year as a professor I had the opportunity to ride a horse across the Canadian Rockies in Banff, Canada. The trip lasted 14 days and started on the second day of the fall semester at Kent State University. If I went, I would miss the second and third week of class. I made some nonspecific inquiries with my program coordinator and department chair about missing class. I was told that having someone cover a class was generally frowned upon. I decided to go to Canada anyway. I did not ask permission. I simply gave my students a field exercise to do during my absence instead of meeting me for class. I went without telling my coworkers. A secretary tried to contact me via e-mail and I was eventually found out for missing a class. The program coordinator was not pleased and my department chair did not speak to me for a few days when I returned. I felt horrible. That was 10 years ago. The program coordinator retired. The department chair became a dean at another university and my vita and classroom evaluations never suffered. Five days after my trip the incident was eclipsed by other dramas in the department. Five months after the trip, I no longer felt any twinges of guilt. Five years after the trip I remember fondly the fantastic adventure I had. Did I break a rule set by my program coordinator? Yes. Did I suffer? Not really. I did make a point to work very hard in the classroom and I never took another trip like that again. But asking myself how I would feel in the 5-5-5 helped me to carve out some balance in my life that I greatly needed in order to remain a productive scholar.

FIND A COMFORTABLE WAY TO SAY NO AND USE IT OFTEN

One of the dangers of our profession is that we can be seduced by exciting opportunities and we do not know how to set a boundary. Junior professors are often asked to serve on all sorts of committees because senior professors know that their tenure allows refusal of such service without ramification. In other words, the higher you go up the food chain, the more you can tell people to leave you alone while you pursue your Point B. For junior professors Point B typically includes tenure and the hallway ethnographies of coworkers that play out on a tenure and reappointment ballot. If you are a junior professor do not be afraid to invoke "no" when asked to serve on a committee by using your quest for tenure as the excuse. There is no better reason to turn a request down. For example:

- "No, I am afraid I can not teach an overload class as I am getting my file ready for external tenure review this year."
- "No, I am afraid that I can not serve on the library committee for the department as I am working on a deadline for an article that I have to get in for my tenure file."
- "No, I can not serve as the program coordinator this year because I have to get my tenure file ready."

Another way to say no is to carve out time for your writing away from the office and your colleagues who may take up your time with chatting. I marveled at a colleague who had a 1-year-old baby. She and her husband worked out a schedule so she could write and work in her office undisturbed on Saturdays and her husband would look after the baby. Some days the husband would take their baby with him to work so she could stay home and work undisturbed. I have several colleagues who will occasionally lock themselves in their university offices after dinner and work into the wee hours of the morning. While this is not necessarily the most convenient arrangement, it allows for time with their children in the evening and then time focus on their research or meet a deadline. I find it helpful to carve out time in my weekly schedule to write at home, or in a coffee shop, free from the interruptions of the day. When asked if I can attend a meeting scheduled during a block I have designated for writing, I will respond my schedule is already full because it is: *With writing*. I understand that publications are the key to getting to my Point B. As such I protect that time to the expense of everything else.

Another dynamic many do not recognize is the importance of both writing and reading. I see my writing as constructed into two distinct and sacrosanct phases: Writing, which is the actual putting of ideas or facts to paper (or computer). And prewriting, the process that involves reading, thinking, and organizing the flow of ideas. I give priority to both. So some days when I have calendared "writing" I may actually read all day, as I am engaging in a prewriting activity. Most importantly, I honor both as far away from my campus as possible because both require concentration.

DECLARE YOURSELF A "NATIONAL HOLIDAY"

Midway through my career as a principal, I began waking up at 3 A.M. worrying about work. I did not look forward to anything, and I was too tired to exercise. I finally got so irritated about my life I decided I would do the unthinkable: I would ditch school. So I called in sick and went to see a matinee movie 15 miles away from my school district. As I stood in line for popcorn the principal from my sister school walked up behind me and started laughing. I was mortified at being caught and stammered, "What are YOU doing here?" He said, "Its National Hugo Martin Day at my school, so I could not go to work. Apparently it is also National Autumn K. Tooms day." I giggled and said yes it was. I asked my dear friend Hugo Martin if he ditched school often and he told me,

> I can tell when the stress gets to me. I lose my sharpness with details and I get cranky. When that happens I do something for me to escape. Not for my family, just for me. It is important to spend time with family, but I need to be the best me I can in order to serve everyone else. National Hugo Martin Day does not mean I stay home to do yard work, and it does not mean I stay home to help with the kids. Those are wonderful things to do but when I declare a national holiday it means I am doing something just for myself. That way when the day is over I can return to my work reenergized, rested, and refocused.

Doing something that energizes *you* is the reason why the "National Holiday" is declared in your name. So choose distractions with care. "Autumn K. Tooms Day" typically involves a movie, ignoring all e-mail, reading anything but something for work, tripping through a flea market, and perhaps refinishing an old piece of furniture. The point is that I engage inactivities that lift *my spirits* and give *my mind* a rest. One person's round of golf is another's day refinishing an armoire.

So go forth! Declare a "National Holiday" in your name. Bear no guilt, as it is the best way to recalibrate your sites on the path to Point B. You will be more creative, more focused, and more energetic when you do. Which brings me back to this porch on an early summer's day at the Downtown Grill and Brewery. The clock on the street tells me it has been 3 hours since the architect and I laughed together. Fraternity boys are swilling beer and loudly jeering. Downtown locals are arguing about who dated Johnny Cash before he married June Carter. The scrabble tournament just claimed a new winner, and my drink coasters are scrawled with six truisms: (1) *Avis la Fin*; (2) Set your GPS; (3) Find a mentor; (4) Use the 5-5-5 rule; (5) Find a comfortable way to say no and use it often; (6) Declare a "National Holiday."

To my great joy, the revelry escaped me entirely. Yesterday was "National Autumn K. Tooms day." Clearly it worked. For I have heard nothing but the clicking of my keyboard and the wheels whirring in my head, perfectly realigned.

NOTES

1. I know this because the "K." in Autumn K. Tooms identifies my family's clan the Kennedy's of Eirshire, Scotland.

REFERENCES

Browne-Ferrigno, T., & Muth, R. (2004). Leadership mentoring and clinical practice: Role socialization, professional development, and capacity building. *Educational Administration Quarterly, 40*(4), 468-494.

Collins, J. (2001). *Good to great: Why some companies make the leap and others don't.* New York, NY: Harper Collins.

Collins, E. C., & Scott, P. (1978). Everyone who makes it has a mentor. *Harvard Business Review, 56*(4), 89-101.

Jeruchim, J., & Shapiro, P. (1992). *Women, mentors, and success.* New York, NY: Ballentine Books.

Tooms, A. K. (2010). *Socializing aspiring school leaders: The politics of a grow your own administrator program* (pp. 169-190). In W. Hoy & M. DiPaola's (Eds.), *Analyz-*

ing school contexts: Influences of principals and teachers in the service of students. Charlotte, NC: Information Age.

ABOUT THE AUTHORS

Noelle Witherspoon Arnold's research agenda includes analyses of life history and narratives documenting and analyzing leadership and work issues for people of color. Other aspects of her research agenda explores how various belief systems emerge and impact the (re)interpretation of policy and practice, social justice and advocacy, ethics, and the intersection of gender and race. Recently, she has worked with organizations in the area of African Americans in STEM fields. She is currently working on a project regarding medical access and school leader advocacy for students and families through the creation of school clinics. She has also undertaken research on African Americans and medical care, particularly in the areas of counseling and psychology. Other areas of strength and expertise that provide grounding for much of her teaching and research include womanisms and feminisms, cultural studies, African American spirituality, history, critical geography and narratology. Dr. Witherspoon-Arnold's most recent articles have appeared in the *International Journal of Qualitative Studies in Education*, *Journal of Educational Administration History*, *Equity and Excellence in Education*, *Journal of Negro Education*, and the *Journal of Educational Administration*. She is also completing a series of books on race and education and education and spirituality for Information Age Publishing and a textbook entitled *Leading for Learning Through Personnel Administration* for Pearson Education.

Lisa Bass is an assistant professor of educational leadership and policy at the University of Oklahoma. She completed a postdoc at the University of Vermont, and a dual major PhD at The Pennsylvania State University in educational leadership and policy studies, and comparative and international education. Her primary research interests are ethics, specifically the ethic of care in educational leadership; leadership in high poverty contexts; and urban school reform through alternative approaches to schooling. Her goal is to positively impact urban education and the perceptions of urban youth.

359

Floyd D. Beachum is the Bennett Professor of Urban School Leadership at Lehigh University. He is also an associate professor and program director for the educational leadership program in the College of Education. He received his doctorate in leadership studies from Bowling Green State University with an emphasis in educational administration. He also holds a master's in education and a bachelor of science in social studies education from Alabama State University. He has a total of 16 years in education (K-12 and higher education) as well as experience as a substitute teacher, student teacher, classroom teacher, and lead teacher for social studies. Before coming to Lehigh, he served as associate professor and program coordinator for educational administration at the University of Wisconsin-Milwaukee. His research interests include: leadership in urban education, moral and ethical leadership, and social justice issues K-12 schools. He has authored several peer-reviewed articles on these topics in journals such as the *International Journal of Education Policy and Leadership, Journal of School Leadership, International Journal of Qualitative Studies in Education, Multicultural Learning and Teaching, Urban Education,* and the *Journal of Cases in Educational Leadership.* In addition, he is coeditor of the book, *Urban Education for the 21st Century: Research, Issues, and Perspectives,* a coauthor of the book *Radicalizing Educational Leadership: Dimensions of Social Justice,* and coauthor of the book, *Cultural Collision and Collusion: Reflections on Hip-Hop Culture, Values, and Schools.* He is married and has one son.

Karen Stansberry Beard is an assistant professor of educational leadership at Miami University of Ohio where she teaches organizational theory: culture, climate and change, educational administration/leadership theory, and school and community relations. She's developed three courses including: leadership for the public good, curriculum and instruction for principals, and leadership, policy and politics, the latter two, she also teaches. Her research interests include: educational administration/organizational theory, positive psychology, flow, academic optimism, principal development, and achievement and diversity. Her experiences as parent, teacher, principal and researcher permeate her long time interest and inspired her work in the achievement gap. She has authored several peer-reviewed article on these topics in journals such as *Educational Administration Quarterly, The International Journal of Qualitative Studies, Teaching and Teacher Education,* and *The Journal of School Leadership* (in press). Correspondence information: beardks2@muohio.edu

William R. Black is Gabriel and David's dad and Jessica's husband. Although his parents are from Lubbock and San Antonio, Texas, one of the many reasons he cannot become president of the United States is because he was born in Costa Rica and lived there until he was almost 7. He grew up in New Orleans and have lived in Durham, NC, Miami, Austin, Indianapolis, and now Tampa. He has taught English in Costa Rica, worked on immigrant rights projects in Florida and Texas, been a bilingual elementary teacher and assistant principal in Austin, and after graduating from the University of Texas with his doctoral degree in December, 2004, he became an assistant professor at the Indiana School of Education, teaching in Indianapolis and Bloomington. In the fall of 2007, his family moved to Tampa and this year submitted his tenure application at the University of South Florida, where he is a recently tenured associate professor in the Department of Educational Leadership and Policy Studies. His scholarly work focuses on leadership preparation, bilingual education, and now special education policy and politics, and he is interested in critical perspectives on policy implementation and leadership. His years in New Orleans and Austin have helped him learn to appreciate dancing with his kids, good music, good beer, and good food.

Christa Boske is an associate professor in educational administration at Kent State University. She works to encourage school leaders to promote humanity in schools, especially for disenfranchised children and families. Christa's recent work is published in the *Journal of School Leadership, Journal of Cases, Journal of Research on Leadership Education, Multicultural Education and Technology Journal,* and the *Journal of Curriculum Theorizing.* Her scholarship is informed by work in residential treatment and inner-city schools as a school leader and social worker. She recently coedited the book titled *Bridge Leadership: Connecting Educational Leadership and Social Justice to Improve Schools* with Autumn K. Tooms in 2010 with Information Age Publishing. Christa has two more edited books scheduled for publication in 2012: *Educational Leadership: Building Bridges Among Ideas, Schools and Nations* (Information Age Publishing) and *Global Leadership for Social Justice: Taking it From the Field to Practice* (Emerald Publishing).

Jeffrey S. Brooks is associate professor and program coordinator of educational administration at Iowa State University. His research focuses on sociocultural and equity dynamics of educational leadership practice and preparation, and his most recent work examines how globalization and racism influence leadership in schools. Dr. Brooks has conducted case study and ethnographic research in the United States and in the Philippines, where he studied leadership for social justice as a J. William Fulbright Scholar. He is author of *The Dark Side of School Reform: Teaching in the Space Between Reality and Utopia* and coeditor of the forthcoming edited volumes *Instructional Leadership for Social Justice: What Every Principal Needs to Know in Order to Lead Equitable and Excellent Schools* (with

George Theoharis) and *Educational Leadership and Racism: Preparation, Pedagogy and Practice* (with Noelle Witherspoon Arnold). Dr. Brooks' work has appeared in many peer-reviewed educational research journals. He is editor of the *Journal of School Leadership* and series editor of the *Educational Leadership for Social Justice* book series.

Melanie C. Brooks is an assistant professor in the Department of Educational Leadership and Policy Studies at Iowa State University. She was a Peace Corps volunteer in Thailand and holds a PhD in sociocultural international development education studies from Florida State University. She began her career as a high school library media specialist and transitioned to working in academic libraries in the areas of instruction, reference, and collection development. She has also coordinated international education programs for students and teachers and has passion for travel. Her research uses sociological theories to understand issues related to education. Her work has been published in *Educational Policy, Etc: A Review of General Semantics, Encyclopedia of the Social and Cultural Foundations of Education,* and the *International Journal of Urban Educational Leadership.*

Kathleen M. Brown, EdD, is professor and chair of educational leadership at the University of North Carolina at Chapel Hill. As a scholar-practitioner, her research interests include effective, site-based servant leadership that connects theory, practice, and issues of social justice in breaking down walls and building a unified profession of culturally aware educators working toward equitable schooling for all. Dr. Brown approaches education from an ethic of social care and works toward changing the metaphor of schools from hierarchical bureaucracies to nurturing communities. Her most recent publications appear in *Educational Administration Quarterly, Journal of Educational Administration, Journal of School Leadership,* and *Equity & Excellence in Education.* Her most recent book, *Preparing Future Leaders for Social Justice, Equity, and Excellence,* was published as part of the Christopher-Gordon School Leadership Series.

Tricia Browne-Ferrigno, PhD, is an associate professor of educational leadership studies at the University of Kentucky. She directed two rural-based leadership development programs funded by the U.S. Department of Education: Principals Excellence Program for principals and administrator-credentialed teachers, and Team Development for Instructional Leadership in Restructuring High Schools for principals, teachers, students, and parents. She served as senior researcher on the recently conducted Wallace Foundation evaluation study, *Districts Developing Leaders:*

Lessons on Consumer Actions and Program Approaches from Eight Urban Districts. Dr. Browne-Ferrigno is past chair of two AERA SIGS (Leadership for School Improvement, Learning and Teaching in Educational Leadership) and a founding member of the UCEA/LTEL SIG Taskforce on Evaluating Leadership Preparation Programs.

Leslie Hazle Bussey is director of strategy and development at the Georgia Leadership Institute for School Improvement. In her role, she is responsible for evaluation of leadership development in districts across the state of Georgia; advocacy of leadership development policies; and for nurturing relationships with corporate and private foundation partners to sustain school improvement work in Georgia's most remote and impoverished regions. Drawing on her experience as a teacher of middle grades students, Leslie's research interests are located at the intersection of school leadership development and leadership for equity, excellence, and social justice. She is a member of the UCEA/AERA Task Force on Evaluating Educational Leadership Preparation and, in April 2011, completed her 2-year term as the secretary/treasurer of the AERA Leadership for Social Justice SIG. Formerly the director of research at the Southern Regional Education Board, Leslie oversaw a 16 state policy study of indicators of cohesive leadership development systems, and was lead evaluator on a federally funded grant studying teacher induction. She has been recognized by AERA Division H for innovative program evaluation reporting, and has conducted numerous program evaluations in K-12 and higher education settings. Leslie received her PhD in educational leadership from Saint Louis University and resides in Atlanta with her husband and two daughters.

Bradley Carpenter is a former public school teacher, assistant principal, and principal. Bradley is now an assistant professor of leadership, foundations, and human resource education at the University of Louisville. His research focuses on issues pertaining to education leadership, with a specific focus on school improvement/turnaround, the politics of educational leadership, and the ways in which democratic and deliberative theories are enacted to shape educational policy. Bradley is also interested in how educational leadership programs prepare future school leaders to participate in and facilitate conversations surrounding race, racism and race related issues. Bradley received his PhD in education policy and planning from The University of Texas at Austin.

Sarah Diem is an assistant professor of educational leadership and policy analysis at the University of Missouri. Her research focuses on the social and cultural contexts of education, paying particular attention to how the politics and implementation of educational policy affect diversity outcomes. Sarah also examines how conversations surrounding race and race relations are facilitated in the classroom and whether these discussions are preparing future school leaders to be able to address critical issues that may impact the students and communities they will oversee. Sarah is the coeditor of the forthcoming edited volume, *Global Leadership for Social Justice: Taking it From the Field to Practice* (with Christa Boske). Sarah received her PhD in educational policy and planning from The University of Texas at Austin.

Susan C. Faircloth is an associate professor of education (educational leadership) and the director of the American Indian Leadership Program at the Pennsylvania State University. Her work focuses on the factors that account for the disproportionate referral and placement of American Indian and Alaska Native students in special education programs and services in the early grades, the role of early childhood programs and services in the education of young Native children, and the moral and ethical dimensions of school leadership. She has been published in the *Harvard Educational Review, the Journal of Special Education Leadership, International Studies in Educational Administration, Values and Ethics in Educational Administration*, the *Tribal College Journal of American Indian Higher Education*, the *Rural Special Education Quarterly*, and the *Journal of Disability Policy Studies*.

Bonnie C. Fusarelli is an associate professor of educational leadership at North Carolina State University, she earned her PhD in educational administration from The Pennsylvania State University. Dr. Fusarelli's research focuses on educational leadership and policy, the politics of school improvement and organizational change, with a particular focus on state-level education reform and leadership development. To support her research, Dr. Fusarelli has received funding from the U.S. Department of Education, The National Science Foundation, The Bill and Melinda Gates Foundation, and the North Carolina Department of Public Instruction. She has authored over 40 articles published in various research journals and is the recipient of numerous teaching awards at both the K-12 and university level, including being an inductee of NC State's Academy of Outstanding Teachers. Her current work is primarily focused on her role as principal investigator for and director of the Northeast Leadership Academy, a Race to the Top funded initiative to prepare innovative school leaders for rural schools.

Mark A. Gooden serves as an associate professor in the Educational Administration Department. He is also director of The University of

Texas at Austin Principalship Program (UTAPP). His research interests include the principalship, antiracist leadership, issues in urban educational leadership, and legal issues in education. His research has appeared in *Brigham Young University Education and Law Journal*, *Education and Urban Society*, *The Journal of Negro Education*, *Educational Administration Quarterly*, *The Sage Handbook of African-American Education* and *The Principal's Legal Handbook*. Mark is also a member of the University Council for Educational Administration Executive Committee (UCEA).

Kathrine J. Gutierrez received her PhD from The Pennsylvania State University and is currently an assistant professor in the Department of Educational Leadership and Policy Studies, Jeannine Rainbolt College of Education at The University of Oklahoma. She is a mother to a young energetic and curious toddler, and her husband is also a faculty member in the same college and department. Her research interests include ethical and democratic leadership, curricular and instructional considerations for educational leadership preparation, organizational theory, and policy implications of legal school case decisions. She can be contacted at kjgutierrez@ou.edu.

Kristina A. Hesbol is an assistant professor in the Educational Administration and Foundations Department at Illinois State University. In public schools, she has served as a teacher, principal, and assistant superintendent. Hesbol's research interests focus on leading change, using issues of equity and power as a conceptual framework to filter and analyze data to inform the improvement of teaching and learning for every student. She recently completed a study of entrepreneurial teachers and principals, and is currently examining the behaviors of principals whose leadership strategies include the use of data in high performing high poverty schools that demonstrate high math achievement.

Liz Hollingworth is a professor at the University of Iowa in the Educational Policy and Leadership Studies Department. She grew up in San Diego and went to UCLA for her undergraduate studies. After moving to Northwestern University for her graduate studies, she taught in Chicago Public Schools and then at a middle school in Michigan. Her research centers on issues of social justice, instructional leadership, and assessment policy.

Eric A. Houck is an associate professor of educational leadership and policy at the University of North Carolina at Chapel Hill. A specialist in school finance and educational policy, Dr. Houck's work has appeared in numerous academic and legal publications including the *Journal of Educa-*

tion Finance, the *Peabody Journal of Education*, *School Business Affairs*, and *The School Administrator*. His research interests include intradistrict school finance and student assignment policies. Dr. Houck received his bachelor's degree in education from the University of North Carolina at Chapel Hill, his master's degree in educational policy studies from the University of Wisconsin-Madison, and his PhD in educational leadership and policy from Vanderbilt University. She previously held an academic position at the University of Georgia and has also worked in North Carolina with the Wake County Public School System, Wake Education Partnership, and the Charlotte-Mecklenburg Schools.

Audrey J. Jaeger is an associate professor of higher education and coexecutive director of the National Initiative for Leadership and Institutional Effectiveness at NC State University. Dr. Jaeger's research examines the roles of current and future faculty with emphasis on STEM faculty and part-time faculty. Dr. Jaeger's recent research explores how cultural and social identity influence the career choices of doctoral students of color. She is a member of the Academy of Outstanding Teachers and Academy of Outstanding Faculty in Extension and Engagement at NC State. She received her PhD from New York University. Her research appears in such journals as the *Journal of Higher Education, Research in Higher Education*, and *Journal of College Student Development*. Prior to NC State, Dr. Jaeger worked in higher education administration at New York University's Robert F. Wagner School of Public Service and Bucknell University (PA). She was also an adjunct professor at Baruch College (CUNY). Her professional experience includes both academic and student affairs positions include academic advising, student activities, community service, and leadership development.

Gaetane Jean-Marie is an associate professor of educational leadership at the University of Oklahoma-Tulsa campus. Her research focuses on leadership development and preparation, effective leadership for educational equity in K-12 schools, women and leadership, and urban school reform. She recently published two coedited books, *Women of Color in Higher Education: Turbulent Past, Promising Future* and *Women of Color in Higher Education: Contemporary Perspectives and New Directions* (w/ Brenda Lloyd-Jones). She is also coeditor of *Educational Leadership Preparation: Innovation and Interdisciplinary Approaches to the Ed.D. and Graduate Education* (w/ Anthony Normore) and has published in numerous journals including *Journal of Educational Administration, Journal of School Leadership, and Journal of Research on Leadership and Education*. She is an associate editor of the *Journal of School Leadership*, book reviews editor of the *Journal of Educational Administration*, and president of Leadership for Social Justice AERA/SIG.

She is cofounder of Women's Work Foundation, a non-profit organization that provides support and works with organizations in underserved communities to enhance the lives of women and girls.

Lisa A. W. Kensler is an assistant professor of educational leadership in the College of Education's Educational Foundations, Leadership, and Technology department at Auburn University. Her original training as an ecologist continues to shape her research interests. She uses both quantitative and qualitative methods to explore the ecology of leadership and learning, or the characteristics of schools that facilitate individual and organizational learning among students, teachers, and administrators. Dr. Kensler's most recent research is focused on green schools and the leadership and learning required to transform schools into more socially just, ecologically healthy, and economically viable communities that engage intentionally with the global sustainability movement. Her research and writing has appeared in the *Journal of School Leadership*, the *Journal of Research on Leadership Education*, the *International Journal of Urban Educational Leadership*, and in the *High School Journal*. She also has work published in two recent handbooks of educational leadership.

Muhammad Khalifa is a faculty member in K-12 educational administration at Michigan State University. He was previously an urban school teacher and administrator in Detroit, and has taught at a number of higher education institutions abroad. His research addresses culturally responsive school leadership practice, a topic on which he is currently writing a book. He has looked at successful school leadership in domestic and local environments, including urban and alternative schools, as well as locations in Middle Eastern and African countries. He has most recently worked closely with school leaders in Somaliland, East Africa. His current research examines urban school leadership and disparities in school suspension, and urban school closures. His research has been published in *The Urban Review, Educational Administration Quarterly, The Journal of Negro Education, Education and Urban Society,* and *The Journal of School Leadership*. He is coeditor (with Grant-Overton & Witherspoon Arnold) of the forthcoming *Handbook on Urban School Leadership*. His goal is help promote safe spaces in which urban youth can be comfortable to learn in public school.

Gerardo R. López is professor of political science at Loyola University-New Orleans. His research focuses on school-community relations, parental involvement, and migrant/immigrant education. His work has been published in *Educational Administration Quarterly, American Educational Research Journal, Harvard Educational Review, Journal of School Leadership,*

Journal of School Public Relations, and *International Journal of Qualitative Studies in Education,* among other scholarly outlets. His current book (with Maria Pabón López) focuses on the education of undocumented children.

Marina Nayar López is an incoming ninth-grade student at Isidore Newman School in New Orleans. She plays piano, and was the 2009 winner of the Young Hoosier State Piano Competition (Sonatina Category). She enjoys reading, math, and science, and wants to be a professor when she grows up.

Cora Lucía López is an incoming fifth-grade student at Isidore Newman School in New Orleans. She loves to write short stories, and enjoys reading and math. She enjoys building new things with her Lego's and wants to be President of the United States when she grows up.

Catherine Lugg is a professor of education in the Department of Theory, Policy and Administration, Graduate School of Education, at Rutgers, the State University of New Jersey. Her research interests include educational politics and history, and the influences of social movements and political ideology have on educational politics and policy. Her research has appeared in *Educational Policy, Educational Administration Quarterly,* the *Journal of School Leadership,* the *Journal of Educational Administration, School Leadership and Management,* the *Journal of Curriculum and Practice,* the *American Journal of Semiotics, Pennsylvania History,* and *Education and Urban Society.* She is also the author of two books, *For God & Country: Conservatism and American School Policy* (Peter Lang), and *Kitsch: From Education to Public Policy* (Falmer).

Katherine Cumings Mansfield holds a PhD in educational policy and planning from The University of Texas at Austin and is currently an assistant professor of educational leadership and policy at Virginia Commonwealth University in Richmond. Her interdisciplinary scholarship focuses on the history and politics of education and the relationship of gender, race, religion, and class on educational and vocational access and achievement. She is published in *Journal of Educational Administration, Journal of Research on Leadership Education,* and *Journal of School Leadership.* Katherine and David, her husband of 26 years, are coparenting two teenaged children.

Joanne M. Marshall is a former high school teacher and a current assistant professor in educational leadership and policy studies at Iowa State University. Her long-term research agenda is driven by the question of how people's internal values and beliefs relate to their public school roles, particularly in the areas of religion/spirituality, moral and ethical leadership, philanthropy, social justice pedagogy, and work-life balance. She holds an EdD from the Harvard Graduate School of Education and has published in *The Journal of School Leadership, Equity and Excellence in Education, The School Administrator*, and *Phi Delta Kappan*. She is the series lead editor of the Work-Life Balance book series from Information Age Publishing and welcomes new submissions.

Carlos R. McCray is an associate professor at Fordham University in the Graduate School of Education at the Lincoln Center in Manhattan, New York. His research interest includes multicultural education, urban education, and building-level leadership. His research has appeared in journals such as the *Journal of Negro Education, International Journal of Education Policy and Leadership,* and *the Journal of School Leadership*. He teaches courses dealing with educational leadership, urban education, and social justice to aspiring educational leaders. He recently coauthored a book titled, *Cultural Collision and Collusion: Reflections on Hip-Hop Culture, Values, and Schools*. McCray also served as the first program chair for the Leadership for Social Justice SIG.

Kathryn Bell McKenzie is an associate professor in the Department of Educational Administration and Human Resource Development and affiliated faculty in Women and Gender Studies at Texas A&M University in College Station. Dr. McKenzie received her PhD in educational administration from The University of Texas in Austin. Her research focuses on school improvement, instructional leadership, anti-racist education, and critical white studies. Prior to becoming a professor, Dr. McKenzie was a public educator. During her more than 20 years in public education, Dr. McKenzie was a classroom teacher, curriculum specialist, assistant principal, principal, and deputy director of the University of Texas/Austin Independent School District Leadership Academy. Maintaining her commitment to practice and practitioners, Dr. McKenzie works extensively in public schools that serve diverse student populations, working with teachers and leaders in elementary and secondary schools as well as district leaders and school boards. In addition to her work in schools, Dr. McKenzie has published numerous articles in major journals, along with book chapters, and books. Her most recent book is, *Using Equity Audits in the Classroom to Reach and Teach all Students*. Additionally, Dr. McKenzie is coeditor of the *International Journal of Qualitative Studies in Education* and associate editor for *Educational Administration Quarterly*.

Peter Miller is an assistant professor in the Department of Educational Leadership and Policy Analysis at the University of Wisconsin-Madison, where he teaches classes on leadership and school-community relations. He has worked in various roles within schools, community-based organizations, and universities and, as a result, has a particular interest in learning about how they work together to serve families.

Matthew Militello is an associate professor in the Leadership, Policy, and Adult and Higher Education Department at North Carolina State University. He held a similar position at the University of Massachusetts, Amherst where he was also the educational administration program coordinator. Militello was recently named a Research Fellow at the NSCU Friday Institute for educational Innovation. Prior to his academic career, Militello was a middle and high public school teacher, assistant principal, and principal in Michigan. He received his undergraduate degree and teaching certification from the University of Michigan and his MEd (with principal certification) and PhD from Michigan State University. His research focuses on developing principals' knowledge and skills in the areas of school law, school data, and collective leadership. Militello can be reached at matt_militello@ncsu.edu.

Dominic Militello is a ninth-grade student at Athens Drive High School in Wake County Public Schools. He is the oldest of four boys and takes amazing care of all his brothers, especially his 1-year-old brother Oscar. Dominic is a car aficionado and is addicted to the to TV show *Top Gear*, British version only. Dominic can be reached at dominicmilitello @me.com.

Elizabeth T. Murakami is an associate professor and doctoral program director in the Department of Educational Leadership and Policy Studies at University of Texas at San Antonio. Dr. Murakami is a South American native who received her MA in curriculum and teaching, and her PhD in educational administration with specialization in international development from Michigan State University. She is an actively involved researcher focused on successful leadership and social justice issues for Latin@ populations, and urban and international issues in educational leadership. Her commitment to students and pedagogical involvement as a faculty in the University of Texas at San Antonio as a premier Hispanic Serving Institution have generated research published in prestigious journals such as *Academe, Journal of Studies in Higher Education;* and the *International Journal of Qualitative Studies in Education.* She is also actively involved in educational organizations such as AERA and UCEA, where she joins scholars in more than 14 countries in a project researching International Successful School Principals (ISSPP). Dr. Murakami's single and collaborative research in P-20 urban and international schools has been published in journals including the *Journal of School Leadership, Educational Management Administration and Leadership (EMAL)*, and the *Journal of School Administration*. Her latest coedited book focuses on a social justice agenda for P-20 professionals and is entitled *Educational Leaders Encouraging the Intellectual and Professional Capacity of Others: A Social Justice Agenda*.

Anthony H. Normore holds a PhD from OISE/University of Toronto. He is currently a professor and department chair of educational leadership in the Graduate School of Education at California Lutheran University located in southern California. Dr. Normore's research focuses on leadership development, preparation, and socialization of urban school leaders in the context of ethics and social justice. His most recent books include *Education-Based Incarceration and Recidivism: The Ultimate Social Justice Crime Fighting Tool* (2012, coedited with B. D. Fitch, Information Age Publishing); *Leadership in Education, Corrections, and Law Enforcement: A Commitment to Ethics, Equity, and Excellence* (2011, coedited with B. D. Fitch, Emerald Group Publishing); and *Global Perspectives on Educational Leadership Reform: The Development and Preparation of Leaders of Learning and Learners of Leadership* (2010, Emerald Group Publishing). His research has appeared in *Journal of School Leadership, Journal of Educational Administration, Values and Ethics in Educational Administration, Leadership and Organizational Development Journal, Canadian Journal of Education Administration and Policy, International Journal of Urban Educational Leadership, Educational Policy*, and *Journal of Research on Leadership Education*.

Rosemary Papa currently serves as The Del and Jewel Lewis Endowed Chair in Learning Centered Leadership and professor of educational leadership in the College of Education at Northern Arizona University—a position she has held since 2007. She has been an active member of NCPEA since her first summer conference Chadron Nebraska in 1987. In 1991-92, she served as the first female president of (NCPEA) and was the 2003 recipient of the NCPEA Living Legend Award. As well, she was honored to give the Walter Cocking lecture both in 1999 and in 2011. She currently serves as the NCPEA Publication Committee Chair and in 2000 she founded and serves as editor of the *eJEP: Journal of Education Policy*, one of the first open access, free, blind-peer reviewed journals in the world. In 2004, she was the recipient of the Outstanding Teacher Award from the College of Education at California State University, Sacramento. Her record of publications includes 10 books, numerous book chapters, monographs and more than 80 referred journal articles. She has served as a principal and chief school administrator for two districts in Nebraska, California State University system level assistant vice chancellor for academic affairs, vice president for Sylvan Learning, Inc., faculty director of a university-based Center for Teaching and Learning in California and founded two joint doctoral programs in educational leadership with University of California universities. She has worked internationally in China, Korea, and West Africa bringing adult learning practices and multimedia technology training to their university classrooms. She is a noted educator with expertise in leadership characteristics known as *accoutrements*, mentoring, adult learning and multi-media technology. Her 2011 book with coauthor Fenwick English is titled *"Turnaround Principals for Underperforming Schools."*

Latish Reed is an assistant professor of administrative leadership at the University of Wisconsin-Milwaukee. Her research interests include urban school leadership; the historical and contemporary context of Black principals; and social justice in administration and teaching practices.

Stacey A. Rutledge is an associate professor of educational leadership and policy in the Department of Educational Leadership and Policy Studies at Florida State University. Her research explores how policies aimed at improving teaching and learning, such as test-based accountability and teacher quality, shape the work of district and school administrators, teachers, and, ultimately, students' learning opportunities. She is also currently a project investigator for the National Center for Scaling Up Effective Schools.

Martin Scanlan is an assistant professor in educational leadership and policy analysis at Marquette University. He was a teacher and administrator for over a decade in urban elementary and middle schools. Dr. Scanlan's teaching and scholarship focuses on educational leadership and organizational learning, particularly with regards to promoting educational opportunities for traditionally marginalized students. He has published in the *Journal of School Leadership*, the *International Journal for Leadership in Education*, and *Education and Urban Society*.

Linda Skrla is a professor of educational administration at Texas A&M University. Prior to joining the Texas A&M faculty in 1997, Skrla worked as a middle school and high school teacher and as a campus and district administrator in public schools. Her research focuses on educational equity issues in school leadership, including accountability policy, high success school districts, and women superintendents. Skrla is vice president of Division A of the American Educational Research Association (AERA) and editor of *Educational Administration Quarterly*. She has published extensively in academic journals and has coauthored or coedited six books, the most recent of which is *Using Equity Audits in the Classroom to Reach and Teach All Students* (Corwin Press, 2011).

George Theoharis grew up in Wisconsin as part of an activist family committed to working to create a more just world. Currently, he lives in Fayetteville, NY and has two adorable children: Ella and Sam. He takes pride in being a dad—volunteering at his kids' elementary school, cooking delicious dinners, doing homework, putting up glow-in-the-dark stars, playing Wii, coaching soccer, organizing playdates, and so on. He entered the professoriate as half of dual-career faculty couple—a couple that is now separated but still coparents, spends time as a family 3 nights a week, and works together professionally in the same department. He is an associate professor in educational leadership and inclusive elementary education and the director of field relations at Syracuse University. He has extensive field experience in public education as a principal and as a teacher. His interests and research focuses on issues of equity, justice, inclusion, leadership, the principalship, and school reform. His book titled "The School Leaders Our Children Deserve" about school leadership, social justice, and school reform. He runs a summer leadership institute for school administrators focusing on issues of equity and inclusion as well as a school reform project called Schools of Promise. He can be reached at gtheohar@syr.edu

Autumn Tooms is a professor and director of The Center For Educational Leadership at the University of Tennessee. She received her doctorate from Arizona Sate University. Prior to joining academe, Autumn served as a biology/chemistry teacher and school administrator at the elementary, middle, and high school level in Phoenix, Arizona. Her research has centered on the politics of school leadership and school reform with an area of emphasis on the principalship. Autumn's primary area of interest is centered on building bridges between schools, those who lead schools, and those who prepare aspiring leaders. In addition to her books, Autumn's work can be found in journals such as *Educational Administration Quarterly, Kappan, Educational Leadership, The Journal of Cases in Educational Leadership, Education Policy, School Leadership and Management,* and *The Journal of School Leadership.*

Douglas Wieczorek is a doctoral candidate in teaching and curriculum at Syracuse University, with interests in educational leadership, teacher education, and education policy. He has taught undergraduate courses in learning theory and inclusive elementary social studies methods. He is a former secondary social studies teacher and school administrator, and has experience in private and public school settings. Doug lives in Syracuse,

NY, with his wife, Kathryn; daughters Mary (age 10), Ellen (age 5) and Sarah (age 5). When Doug is not working on his research, writing, and teaching, he likes to watch basketball, hike and fish with his girls, golf, grow a vegetable garden, and expand the ever-growing landscaping around the exterior of his house.

Michelle D. Young is a professor of educational leadership and policy at the University of Virginia and serves at the executive director of the University Council for Educational Administration. Dr. Young is nationally recognized for her work on the preparation, practice, and evaluation of educational leaders and education policies that facilitate equitable and quality experiences for all students and adults who learn and work in schools. In her scholarship, Dr. Young makes use of multiple theoretical frameworks in an effort to reframe traditional understandings of educational leadership policy and practice and the contexts in which they operate. Dr. Young is the recipient of the William J. Davis award for the most outstanding article published in a volume of the *Educational Administration Quarterly*. Her work has also been published in the *Review of Educational Research*, the *Educational Researcher*, the *American Educational Research Journal*, the *Journal of School Leadership*, the *International Journal of Qualitative Studies in Education*, and *Leadership and Policy in Schools*, among other publications.

CPSIA information can be obtained at www.ICGtesting.com
Printed in the USA
LVOW070915101012

302268LV00003B/98/P